Enterprise, Deprivation and Social Exclusion

Routledge Studies in Entrepreneurship

EDITED BY JAY MITRA (ESSEX UNIVERSITY, UK) AND
ZOLTAN ACS (GEORGE MASON UNIVERSITY, USA)

Enterprise, Deprivation and Social Exclusion

The Role of Small Business in Addressing Social and Economic Inequalities

Edited by Alan Southern

Routledge
Taylor & Francis Group
New York   London

First published 2011
by Routledge
711 Third Avenue, New York, NY 10017

Simultaneously published in the UK
by Routledge
2 Park Square, Milton Park, Abingdon, Oxon OX14 4RN

Routledge is an imprint of the Taylor & Francis Group, an informa business

Typeset in Sabon by IBT Global.
Printed and bound in the United States of America on acid-free paper by IBT Global.

Library of Congress Cataloging-in-Publication Data

Enterprise, deprivation and social exclusion : the role of small business in addressing social and economic inequalities / edited by Alan Southern.
    p. cm.—(Routledge studies in entrepreneurship ; 2)
    Includes bibliographical references and index.
 1. Small business—Social aspects. 2. Entrepreneurship—Social aspects.
 3. Discrimination—Economic aspects. 4. Social integration. 5. Marginality, Social. I. Southern, Alan, 1959–
    HD2341.E584 2011
    658.4'08—dc22
    2010044885

ISBN13: 978-0-415-45815-3 (hbk)
ISBN13: 978-0-203-81777-3 (ebk)

Contents

1 Introduction

Enterprise and Deprivation

Alan Southern

INTRODUCTION AND AIMS OF THE BOOK

The main proposition of this book is that enterprise and deprivation have a clear propinquity. At first glance this may seem counterintuitive, particularly as the former is considered to be positive, aspirational and life changing; the latter meanwhile is spoken of in a negative sense and associated with decline, individual despair and collective failure though of course is also life changing. There has been an increasing tendency to situate both enterprise and deprivation in the same sentence, as references have been made to anti-poverty strategies, particularly in the developing world through 'bottom of the pyramid' type initiatives for example (see Prahalad 2005). Latterly however, enterprise has been explicitly advocated as a means to address inner-urban decline in the developed world. One of the main challenges for this book is to recognise how and why this is happening now and to reveal greater understanding of the conceptual basis to this juxtaposition of enterprise and deprivation.

The ideas presented in this collection come from a variety of experiences and academic disciplines. One particular theme drawn from the book is the limitation of enterprise, this concept of hope and ambition, and particularly how enterprise and entrepreneurship might address social and economic exclusion. Here is a critique of how we understand the role of enterprise in turning around the conditions in some of our societies' worst affected communities. We see in a number of chapters that problems of deprivation have structural roots, and the questioning by authors of whether enterprise policy can address these problems, or whether it might even exacerbate them, is shown to be perfectly valid.

In this respect the book offers the reader an opportunity, through the combination of chapters, to examine an empirical base and to discuss the recent push for enterprise as a panacea for deprivation in the developed world. This push stems directly from the positive notions attached to enterprise rather than any clear theoretical or empirical framework. It simply is not easy in academia to write about enterprise without buying into a generic discourse concerning its progressive qualities. Here, authors have tried to move away from the dominant, and often neo-liberal, language associated with enterprise and have sought to bring into the debate a number of inter-related factors often concerning structures of class, race and gender. Thus some of the more opaque questions surrounding enterprise in communities of deprivation are faced here.

We ask, for example, is it feasible that some configurations of enterprise lock communities into certain types of deprivation? Alternatively, are some forms of enterprise locked into certain types of deprivation? Equally as pertinent is to ask whether there is a plausible argument in the suggestion that enterprise reinforces forms of structural inequity. We need to pose questions that help explain why particular forms of enterprise can be found in deprived neighbourhoods and why we tend to associate low value enterprise and often social enterprise with a particular place. The contributions made here should help us to comprehend why, on the one hand, enterprise is considered to be a feature of a particular group (see for example the work of the Global Entrepreneurship Monitor at www.gemconsortium.org), while on the other, deprivation can be regarded as characteristic of some alternative group, thereby creating difference based on deserving entrepreneurial attributes, in contrast to undeserving dependency traits.

To return to the main premise of the book, concerning the association between enterprise and deprivation, we find geography and metaphor shaping the analysis in the book. The reader will see authors investigating whether enterprise and deprivation are epidemic or endemic as cause and effect is examined. And to test the proposition of propinquity, not only is the limit of enterprise tested through a wider evidence base than previously available but also considered is the link between enterprise and inequity, for example through associations of enterprise with race and gender. We look critically at social enterprise and examine enterprise through a different political lens, through a consideration of worklessness and hidden systems of enterprise. To achieve these aims, some authors start from the point of enterprise while others start from the point of deprivation.

In the next part of the chapter a general framework is set out from which to consider the work of the authors. This begins by looking critically at the notion of renewal (the regeneration of deprived communities) being led through a market-based approach. Some suggestions are then made for a more systemic concept from which to analyse the juxtaposition of enterprise and deprivation before the structure of the book is outlined.

SUPPORTING ENTERPRISE, ADDRESSING DEPRIVATION

In the UK we can trace contemporary efforts to address deprivation through support for enterprise back to the late 1990s and the election of a new Labour administration. Firmly placing enterprise as a main response to poverty and deprivation, the Policy Action Team 3, part of the Social Exclusion Unit, pushed forward the view that more successful business start-ups in poor neighbourhoods should be encouraged as the way to regenerate communities. The ideas outlined, relatively simple in essence concerning improved business advice and better access to finance, could be traced in some form to the developments that had taken place in the US.

Central to this was Michael Porter's view (1995a, 1995b) that deprived communities should aspire to affluence by becoming more competitive. This struck an intuitive cord among UK policy makers on the wave of an 'everything new' political agenda forged from a 'third way' ideology (see Giddens 1999 but also Williams and Windebank 2003). The shape of the Boston-inspired Inner City 100 initiative influenced policy in the UK and specifically in England through the City Growth Strategy. A few years later this was made explicit in the 2003 Local Government Act, with the Local Enterprise Growth Initiative (LEGI) and through the formal introduction of Business Improvement Districts. Even as Porter was making reference to neighbourhoods as a homogenous entity, his concepts were received with interest in the UK despite what appeared to be difficulties in making these ideas operational.

The perception of problem, cause and solution was perfectly clear for Porter. His critique of previous intervention strategies, those that sought to help depleted communities through social investment, put forward an alternative based on a totemic market-led axiom. The logic behind this has been to establish a means by which the paternalistic focus on a redistribution of wealth can be displaced 'through private, for-profit initiatives and investments based on economic self-interest and genuine competitive advantage instead of artificial inducements, government mandates, or charity' (Porter 1995b: 304).

Here, without ambiguity, was the way to move from subsidies, inflated levels of income benefit and interventions aimed at stimulating economic development, social housing and physical regeneration. Porter made the case for

> an economic model [that] must begin with the premise that inner city businesses should be profitable and positioned to compete on a regional, national and even international scale. These businesses should be capable not only of serving the local community but also of exporting goods and services to the surrounding economy. The cornerstone of such a model is to identify and exploit the competitive advantages of inner cities that will translate into truly profitable businesses. (Porter 1995a: 56)

So instead of the dependency culture and subsequent self-pity that is often implicated in deprived communities, the way forward through this market-led approach is to populate the neighbourhood with enterprises that are competitive.

Those with a primary source of research focused on small business and entrepreneurial behaviour had previously attempted to identify causes behind start-up and sustainability in the context of location. For example, Storey (1994) cited population characteristics, unemployment, wealth, education and occupation, level of existing enterprise, housing and local government as impacting on geographical differences in new business start-up. More recently Fritsch and Muller (2004) suggested that spatial variance in start-up activity was related to the quality of start-up, indicating how the role of human capital is important. This is an important point; far from improving places the suggestion here is that more enterprise of the wrong kind can actually undermine local economic performance. Work of this nature, however, restricts our observation of the dynamics of localities and is what Gibson-Graham would refer to as the dominance of a 'centred vision of economic totalities' (1996: 185). In a similar vein, Leyshon and Lee (2003) point to the emphasis on 'an a-social economy controlled entirely by unfettered market exchanges' (2003: 8). We should not assume, then, that Porter's work was left without challenge.

It is relevant to question why the focus on poverty became marginal as Porter's ideas took hold. Townsend (1970), particularly with his idea of nation-based relational poverty, helps us to understand the persistence of poverty in the context of the push to support enterprise. His concepts around stratification, for example in relation to status and access to resources, initiated in the UK a debate on the relative position of poverty. Communities began to be compared within high income nations and the rank position of any particular neighbourhood reflected the relative deprivation and therefore plight of individuals and families. While this is also a contested debate, Townsend reminds us that social structures are important in understanding poverty, even though tendencies can exist that place the source of deprivation on to communities themselves. The focus has shifted away from poverty, and we have become more conditioned to use a refined language and to talk of social exclusion and inclusion.

While Levitas (2006) shows how the multi-dimensional character of social exclusion makes it difficult to assess its overall scale, Blackburn and Ram (2006) noted that UK policy makers seized the enterprise agenda in a drive to overcome social exclusion. They suggested that the competitiveness agenda, a subtle reference to Porter, and the social inclusion agenda were potentially contradictory, noting that small businesses are themselves part of a dominant system that has produced deprivation. Thus, social exclusion, inclusion and the drive for enterprise as a means of addressing such ills coincided with the pushing to one side of poverty, at least in the sense of the latter being a useable contemporary term.

Others, including some of the authors in this book, sought to demonstrate how enterprise and deprivation brought together a complex set of dynamics and wide range of relationships beyond those Porter seemed to be concerned with. Those such as Fainstein and Gray (1995) suggested Porter's initial position was incorrect, arguing how his views were limited in respect of the advances made through some forms of regeneration. To add to this Sawicki and Moody (1995) noted how Porter had transported his theories on international trade into the arena of the inner city without confirmative evidence, while Blakely and Small (1995) were equally as critical arguing that Porter had failed to grasp the complexity of inner-urban decline. A little later Bates (1997) was to add that the entrenched attitudes held by those such as Porter simply reinforced views on deprivation.

Looking specifically at the operation of finance institutions in US neighbourhoods, White Haag (2002) noted how lenders would literally 'draw a red line around certain geographic areas and then decline to make loans in those areas on the basis of the racial composition, age of housing stock, or other factors, regardless of the creditworthiness of individual loan applicants' (ibid.: 252).[1] While this is reminiscent of the work of Rex and Moore (1969) who explained the use of redlining in the UK context in the mid 1960s, the Bank of England (2000) were quick to dismiss this and argued that businesses in the most deprived locations access finance in the same way as those in affluent places. This is reflective of how the debate was taking shape well before the Labour Government came to power in the UK in the late 1990s, when they aligned their policy position with those of Porter.

Clearly Porter's work has become influential to policy. His approach is unambiguous in the support of enterprise. However, his views are contested, and critics point to the simplistic manner of his concepts and lack of empirical work to verify the turn of ideas into policy. Put plainly, supporting enterprise in the manner indicated by Porter has not necessarily proven to be the means to address deprivation. This debate has increased in quantity and quality thereon in. The following is an introduction to the framework in which enterprise is promoted and deprivation exists. Alongside is the idea of cumulative causation to provide a different perspective for looking at enterprise and deprivation. The aim is to take the debate beyond what can often appear to be a polemic view of market-led renewal or politically led regeneration.

THE VICIOUS CIRCLE AND INSTITUTIONAL FIX

The value from the work of those such as Gunnar Myrdal, Nicholas Kaldor and Karl Polanyi is not that they provide an answer to contemporary matters but that their ideas are transferable across time and allow current issues to be considered in alternative ways. For example, we could use the work of Myrdal (1944) to argue that deprivation is an outcome of the principle of cumulation. Equally, Polanyi (2001) would profess that the anxiety created by a market-inspired free-for-all would be counterproductive to an inclusive society. In this sense market dysfunction in deprived communities might be part of the cumulative effect that at some point would require a type of institutional intervention.

Kaldor's notion of cumulative causation can be linked to the period of Fordism and, to an extent, latterly took a form of resistance to the argument for monetarism that emerged in the 1970s. Myrdal's concept of cumulative causation, or the vicious circle, was broader than economic. His emphasis was placed on the dynamic social causation of a wide range of influences, a "conception of a great number of interdependent factors, mutually cumulative in their effects', thereby rejecting the idea that an outcome is related to a single cause (Myrdal 1944: 1069). If we are to accept the notion of a vicious circle of deprivation coupled to a low level of enterprise activity, we need to ask what it is that happens to initiate the cumulative process and to what extent the process becomes systemic.

Kaldor's work inspired Argyrous (1996) to speculate on how we might identify the structures and processes that facilitate cumulative causation. From this emerges the question of history and path dependency. Those places, those communities associated with deprivation, not only experience this decline in real terms but there is also an image created that itself becomes a factor in the cumulative process. Thus rankings of deprivation and estimates about levels of enterprise that feed into the imagination about places become locked into a cycle. By contrast the cumulative processes in the more affluent places work in a similar but opposite manner, with growth occurring that leads to a virtuous cycle.

Skott and Auerbach (1995) noted three important characteristics of uneven development that we might adapt in the context of the local economy. First, there are aspects of path dependency and instability and some form of feedback mechanism that influences the future trajectory of the local economy. Second, local economic instability is an outcome of the interaction of economic and non-economic factors that, in turn, are likely to provoke institutional intervention, which we might see as social, economic and physical regeneration. Third, as local economies come under global pressures, it becomes impossible to fully assess what external factors are likely to impact and how. More pertinently it is implausible to know what the limits of those externals factors might be. The indirect effect from the sub-prime housing market in the US on the local economy on a town in northern England, for example, is an illustration of this.

The danger of such an analysis becoming deterministic is obvious. This is particularly so when considering enterprise and deprivation through the economic lens initiated by Kaldor (1934, 1972). Rosenthal and Ross (2010) would argue that entrepreneurs take violent crime into account when bidding for locations within an urban area. Likewise, the Bank of England (2000) claimed that safety and security issues and spatial variance were more important influences in determining access to finance than any notion of contemporary redlining. Introducing the idea that something systemic is at play when we consider the propinquity of enterprise and deprivation is helpful. We might try and explain how the variables that we use to measure enterprise, specifically business start-up, and those variables we use to rank deprivation are systemically woven. The interaction, for example, of levels of education, access to finance, levels of crime and access to basic services such as health care may act to produce cumulative causation.

Thus we can attempt to use Myrdal's broader concept of cumulative causation in trying to understand the dynamics of enterprise and deprivation. This forces us to contemplate two things. First is to consider the individual components of a system that would lead to the levels of deprivation and enterprise experienced. The effects of the interaction of such components would be systemic in their impact and not equilibrium generating (O'Hara 2008). This is an important point because it takes us away from what can appear to be a polemic, idealised and unobtainable argument for or against the market, or for or against intervention. Second, we would need to incorporate ideas and arguments about the importance of political intervention simply because we recognise this is a significant part of the local system, whether ideologically one agrees with it or not. This leads us to review institutional structures and frameworks and provides a platform to consider Polanyi's perspective on the role of institutions. In a parody of Myrdal's analysis of race discrimination the systemic character of cause as everything being cause to everything else can help us to reflect on the propinquity of enterprise and deprivation (Myrdal 1944).

Polanyi's concepts can be used to problematize the notion of unfettered market decisions that lead to levels of enterprise and deprivation. As shown by authors in this book, these decisions may in some locations enable enterprise while at the same time locking in deprivation. Polanyi would reject the notion of intervention leading to a lack of market activity and therefore to decline. In fact, he felt that enterprise had to be protected from the unrestricted working of the market mechanism, something that on occasion we would find articulated by small business pressure groups, and that it was a fallacy to suggest socio-economic ills were caused by our lapse from economic liberalism (Polanyi 2001).

Polanyi's view was that the market would be a function of social order and thus actually enabled by political institutions. As he outlines:

A self-regulating market demands nothing less than the institutional separation of society into an economic and a political sphere. Such a dichotomy is, in effect, merely the restatement, from the point of view of society as a whole, of the existence of a self-regulating market. It might be argued that the separateness of the two spheres obtains in every type of society at all times. Such an inference, however, would be based on a fallacy. True, no society can exist without a system of some kind, which ensures order in the production, and distribution of goods. But that does not imply the existence of separate economic institutions; normally, the economic order is merely a function of the social order. Neither under tribal nor under feudal nor under mercantile conditions was there, as we saw, a separate economic system in society. Nineteenth-century society, in which economic activity was isolated and imputed to a distinctive economic motive, was a singular departure. (Polanyi 2001: 74).

There is, he suggests, a double movement. One is concerned with enabling the market that has largely been based on the principles of laissez faire and free trade. The other is concerned with social protection forming the basis of legislation, restriction of practice and other instruments of intervention brought forward by political institutions, such as local and central government.

There are a number of ways in which we can speculate how this institutional framework operates and is shaped today. We can identify how enterprise and entrepreneurship policy is seen as a means of social protection, for example as a vehicle for social improvement as suggested by the UK Social Exclusion Unit (Office of the Deputy Prime Minister 2004). We might suggest how encouragement for self-employment as a response to unemployment for disadvantaged groups can be seen in this way (see Abrahamson 2005, Glennerster et al. 1999, HM Treasury 2005, Social Investment Task Force 2003). Further evidence might be the focus on social enterprise and community not-for-profit initiatives that, it is argued, can better succeed in places requiring social and economic intervention (see for example Arum and Muller 2004, Servon 1999). We might also see the informal, hidden economy in this light.

Many of these aspects are considered by authors in this book. Just as the notion of cumulative causation allows us to reflect on the evidence presented here and to evaluate whether communities are indeed locked into a vicious cycle, the work of Polanyi (2001) helps us to consider the institutional fix for local neighbourhoods and communities. Not only does Polanyi develop a sophisticated line of reasoning to demonstrate that forms of regulation are required to moderate the excesses of the market, he shows that they actually support the longevity of certain economic relations. It is within this general systemic conceptual framework, of many inter-related factors of causation, including the mechanisms of the institutional framework, that the chapters of this book are presented.

THE STRUCTURE OF THE BOOK

The contributions to this book come from academics in the UK and North America who have worked for many years on issues presented here. From the UK there are examples that examine enterprise and deprivation in the north of England, from the West Midlands and from Scotland. These are complemented by research drawn from a US and Canadian experience, using panel data and individual case studies. The result is a book that sets out both quantitative and qualitative work in rich, developed nations to examine enterprise and deprivation providing both conceptual and empirical argument.

Most of the contributions here do not reflect one of the most turbulent times in recent history, that of the global financial crisis which unravelled during 2008. This crisis has been very relevant to localities, bringing home the risks of a globalised economy. However, in some ways they are also less important to deprived places in the sense that such communities are not struggling simply because of the recent financial crisis. While it may well add further context, the topics of respective authors here do not need to centre on this recent episode as it would simply detract from their focus on more entrenched deprivation and the role of enterprise.

The book opens up with two chapters that provide a quantitative focus on levels of enterprise in deprived communities. In the first of these, a serious question is posed about the judgement behind UK policy linking enterprise to disadvantage and deprivation. Frankish, Roberts and Storey show in chapter 2 that we should not expect to find any difference in owner (of enterprise) address and home address between deprived and affluent areas; and that owners of enterprises in deprived areas are more likely to be living in more prosperous areas. This helps them to argue that policy fails to recognise the distinction between business and owner and that the focus on personal prosperity is the way forward, thereby, initially at least, decoupling the link between enterprise and community. This, they argue, is because of the flawed logic that associates enterprise and deprivation: there is an assumption that enterprise rates are low in deprived areas; these low rates are therefore a cause of deprivation; therefore enterprise can be a route out of deprivation and publicly funded programmes are needed to support this.

In chapter 3, Bates and Robb suggest that while location can have a positive impact on enterprise there is little evidence to demonstrate that depleted neighbourhoods offer attractive opportunities for new enterprise. Using data drawn from the US Bureau of Census Characteristics of Business Owners database the authors provide an explicit challenge to Porter's thesis on the inner city, which they regard as an instrumentalist response to the urban poor. They argue that policy reflects the hegemony of the free market and that this tends to ignore what level and type of demand exists in deprived areas, for new business starting up. Bates and Robb enquire as to whether depleted communities have passed the point of no return. Although not explicit in the work of Frankish, Roberts and Storey, there is some consistency here in questioning whether processes of disinvestment experienced in poor communities have reduced the capacity to sustain local enterprise. Both chapters indicate the interlaced variables at play when the aim is to stimulate enterprise in deprived locations and in so doing lay the basis for the chapters that follow.

The next two chapters look specifically at race and enterprise. Jones and Ram develop a case study of ethnic minority businesses (EMBs) in

Birmingham, UK, while Dawkins provides a quantitative examination of the Black-white gap in self-employment in the US. For Jones and Ram (chapter 4), EMB tend to be situated in precarious market niches and they pose the question of why we should expect to see an entrepreneurial revolution in society's most deprived communities. EMB actually appear to be undercapitalised and labour intensive and struggle to survive in hostile, depleted neighbourhoods. Alongside this Dawkins is able to draw out the residential location characteristics that help explain the gap in self-employment between Black and white people. Dawkins, in chapter 5, points to mortgage market discrimination as a barrier to accessing finance for start-up, while Jones and Ram argue that self-employment should not necessarily be seen as an indicator of upward mobility with many EMB entrepreneurs victims of social exclusion. Both chapters therefore reinforce the matter of race and, to some extent, consider in different ways segregation that itself is informed by complex structures of race and class.

Rubin uses a case based in California in chapter 6 to argue how the idea that we see depleted communities as an emerging domestic market is problematic. Her Weberian analysis draws on the diversity that exists within and between communities and shows how, despite the availability of capital and access to capital, there is still a gap in accessing resources precisely because of constraints (to access) between ethnic groups. Her work looks at how pension funds deliver equity into enterprises operating in deprived communities, and she notes that it is not the quality of investment opportunity that leads to disparity in take-up but the operation of structures such as race. Rubin concludes with an important point, suggesting there may be an inclination to see some groups as more deserving of (access to) capital and others less deserving. Overall she notes how we see depleted communities in too generalised a manner.

Dayson then follows in chapter 7 with a consideration of community development finance in the UK. Looking specifically at the Community Development Finance Institutions (CDFIs), an idea imported to the UK from the US, Dayson draws contrasts and parallels with the provision of micro-finance in developing countries. He notes that CDFIs have been left sitting across the divide between social policy and economic development agendas and argues that the former UK Government's ideological commitment to community development finance in the context of social and economic policy can be questioned. He concludes by questioning the stance taken by the UK Government on community development finance and the provision of micro-credit.

The focus of the book then takes a slight divergence as chapters on rural enterprise, worklessness and the informal economy are presented. In their work on market and non-market activities in micro-enterprise households in rural north east England, Baines, Wheelock and Oughton (chapter 8) look at three characteristics of working life in rural micro-businesses: work within households and wider family, the work and family balance and the participation of non-family members in the enterprise. This chapter provides a feel for the unrelenting character of work and life in rural micro-enterprises, which the authors suggest rely on traditional practices. They find informal practical support from a spouse is often crucial but not necessarily an input of any specialist skills. Similar to points made earlier by Jones and Ram, the authors note that this is a gendered practice and often is a substitute for paying an additional employee. They show the participation of teenage family members, sometimes with remuneration and perhaps working alongside casual labour. There are also intergenerational exchanges, particularly involving owners' parents, that they argue is an extension to the boundaries of the household.

In chapter 9, Pemberton provides a review of UK policy and practice promoting enterprise as a tool for tackling worklessness. Worklessness, as he points out, is a key aspect of social exclusion, and Pemberton demonstrates how UK policy over the last decade has explicitly linked enterprise with social exclusion and low enterprise rates with high levels of worklessness. He argues that it is the quality of opportunity that is important and that this means appropriate enterprise interventions for the specific human capital of different places, echoing points made earlier by Frankish et al. and Bates and Robb.

Williams follows (chapter 10) by looking at the extent of a hidden enterprise culture made up of those engaging in the informal economy; that is paid exchanges that are unregistered by the state. He sets out to show how the informal economy is a major part of all economic activity and is made up of entrepreneurs and self-employed, not just low income workers. The 'wholesome ideal-type depiction' of the entrepreneur, he argues, that has prevailed in the entrepreneurship literature is now under challenge. Williams is keen to argue against the marginality theses of the informal economy and makes a strong case to demonstrate that the informal economy is not the preserve of deprived areas. In fact consumption of informal work is more prevalent in affluent areas, partly for reasons that the work is more highly remunerated.

Lionais brings a Canadian experience to the discussion and looks closely in chapter 11 at uneven development and deprivation, asking why enterprises would set up in depleted communities. The author argues that traditional location theory offers little explanatory value, other than through the notion of cost or maybe quality of local networks, and talks of placed based enterprise to demonstrate how economic exclusion over time means the community becomes less capable of developing its own capacity for growth. He shows how community embeddedness and low costs actually go hand in hand and may even be an important feature of the local depleted environment. Lionais is of the view that depleted communities lack the institutional infrastructure to support growth. In anticipation of the debate that follows he notes how social enterprise is expected to meet social needs and compensate for market failure and remain sustainable. It is little wonder, he suggests, that most fail. Lionais concludes his chapter by arguing how the link between enterprise as a means to address deprivation is weak, not least as most enterprise is simply personally motivated.

The two chapters that follow look specifically at social enterprise in the UK. In chapter 12, Howorth, Parkinson and Macdonald provide additional insights into how we understand the entrepreneurship paradigm in a highly socialised environment, asking how far this prevails at grassroots levels of social enterprise. They show how the language of business is held up as the way forward for social enterprise which in turn is regarded as a panacea to the failure of market and other social ills, claiming this is an instrumentalist perspective that disarms radical and ideological approaches that are fundamental to the third sector. They conclude by suggesting how a narrow use of the terms enterprise and entrepreneurship in respect of social enterprise can weaken the potential of the sector to bring about change through community initiatives.

The work of Whittam and Birch complements the previous chapter. Chapter 13 is a theoretical critique on social enterprise and social entrepreneurialism and provides a focus on social enterprise policy in Scotland. In contrast to Frankish, Roberts, and Storey, the authors argue that the focus on the individual comes at the expense of the collective, that is the community, and that the current predominance of social enterprise is because it is seen as a vehicle to develop within depleted communities, the social economy. Their conclusion is that this is part of the desire to extend market-led activities to address aspects of poverty that previously were seen to be, in part, the responsibility of the state.

The following chapter by Gordon Nembhard (chapter 14) provides a comparative review of two approaches to community economic development and poverty alleviation in marginalised communities in the US. These are member ownership cooperatives and micro-enterprise. The author is able to highlight the multiple advantages of cooperative enterprise and ownership for low income people and communities, some of which are shared with the more traditional micro-enterprise and micro-lending initiatives. She argues that there are various similarities between the US micro-enterprise and cooperative development models and that there are transferable lessons for micro-enterprise from the cooperative sector, particularly in terms of collaboration. The chapter concludes that, while micro-enterprise and cooperatives share many qualities, the collective and peer-to-peer aspects of cooperative enterprise could strengthen the micro-enterprise offering.

The penultimate chapter (chapter 15) is left to North. Here the normative discourse of enterprise and being entrepreneurial is challenged and what is presented is a theoretically led debate on seizing 'enterprise' as a political initiative to address deprivation. North uses examples in Argentina and from the UK of political activism and questions whether the experience of those involved is a form of entrepreneurial empowerment. This self-reflective piece by North provides a passionate argument for recognising the entrepreneurial behaviour of political activism and whether the debate around profit is something that the Left can take hold of. He argues for reclaiming the concept of enterprise, for the reconciliation of the Left with markets, as well as values like production for need rather than for profit, and for a greater role for planning. North's contribution here provides an essential prompt for the reader to remember that enterprise can take many forms and that critique is more powerful when alternatives are provoked.

As always with a book of this type, the interchangeable character of language is both welcome and distracting. We have authors from a wide range of backgrounds that view terms such as enterprise, entrepreneurship, small business, depletion, deprivation, renewal and regeneration in different ways. Rather than expect all to conform to a rigid editing of use of terminology, their use more generally has allowed the differences of authors to be managed in a more creative way that encourages ideas about the propinquity of enterprise and deprivation. It is hoped that the reader sees these terms in an interchangeable way also.

The tendency to situate enterprise and deprivation as cause and effect, as one being the panacea for the other, as an answer for all, is clearly misguided. The systemic nature of their proximity and the interwoven nature of the many variables we use to examine them result in a complexity that requires further attention. This attention is necessary so as to enable more investigation of their individual and collective character. The chapters in this book should allow for this and provoke further response in the academic tradition.

NOTES

1. For a very relevant discussion on community investment in US neighbourhoods reflecting conditions at this time see not only White-Haag (2002) but also the interchange between Drew Dahl, Douglas D. Evanoff and Michael F. Spivey (2002) and Maureen Kilkenny (2002). Look also at the work of Bates (2000) and Bhatt and Tang (2001) and then, of course, see the relevant authors in this book as a complement.

BIBLIOGRAPHY

Abrahamson, P. (2005) 'Coping with urban poverty: changing citizens in Europe?, International Journal of Urban and Regional Research, 29(3): 608–21.
Argyous, G. (1996) 'Cumulative causation and industrial evolution: Kaldor's four stages of industrialization as an evolutionary model', Journal of Economic Issues, 30(1): 97–119.
Arum, R. and Muller, W. (2004) The Re-emergence of Self-Employment: A comparative study of self-employment dynamics and social inequality, Oxford: Princeton University Press.
Bank of England (2000) Finance for Small Businesses in Deprived Communities, November 2000, London: Domestic Finance Division.
Bates, T. (1997) 'Michael Porter's conservative urban agenda will not revitalize America's inner cities: what will?', Economic Development Quarterly, 11(1): 39–44.

————(2000) 'Financing the development of urban minority communities: lessons of history', Economic Development Quarterly, 14(3): 227–41.

Bhatt, N. and Tang, S.-Y. (2001) 'Making microcredit work in the United States: social, financial and administrative dimensions', Economic Development Quarterly, 15(3): 229–41.

Blackburn, R. and Ram, M. (2006) 'Fix or fixation? The contributions and limitations of entrepreneurship and small firms to combating social exclusion', Entrepreneurship and Regional Development, 18(1): 73–89.

Blakely, E. J. and Small, L. (1995) 'Michael Porter: new gilder of ghettos', Review of Black Political Economy, 24(2/3): 161–82.

Dahl, D., Evanoff, D. D. and Spivey, M. F. (2002) 'Community Reinvestment Act enforcement and changes in targeted lending', International Regional Science Review, 25(3): 307–22.

Fainstein, S. and Gray, M. (1995) 'Economic development strategies for the inner city: the need for governmental intervention', Review of Black Political Economy, 24(2/3): 29–38.

Fritsch, M. and Mueller, P. (2004) 'Effects of new business formation on regional development over time', Regional Studies, 38(8): 961–75.

Gibson-Graham, J. K. (1996) The End of Capitalism (as We Knew It), Oxford: Blackwell.

Giddens, A. (1999) The Third Way: The renewal of social democracy, Malden, MA: Polity Press.

Glennerster, H., Lupton, R., Noden, P. and Power, A. (1999) 'Poverty, social exclusion and neighbourhood: studying the area bases of social exclusion', CASE paper 22, Centre for Analysis of Social Exclusion: London School of Economics.

HM Treasury (2005) Enterprise and economic opportunity in deprived areas: a consultation on proposals for a Local Enterprise Growth Initiative, March, London: The Stationery Office.

Kaldor, N. (1934) 'A classificatory note on the determinateness of equilibrium', The Review of Economic Studies, 1(2): 122–36.

————(1972) 'The irrelevance of equilibrium economics', Economic Journal, 82: 1237–55.

Kilkenny, M. (2002) 'Community credit', International Regional Science Review, 25(3): 247–51.

Levitas, R. (2006) 'The concept and measurement of social exclusion', in C. Pantazis, D. Gordon and R. Levitas (eds) Poverty and Social Exclusion in Britain, Bristol: The Policy Press.

Leyshon, A. and Lee, R. (2003) 'Introduction: alternative economic geographies', in A. Leyshon, R. Lee and C.C. Williams (eds) Alternative Economic Spaces, London: Sage.

Myrdal, G. (1944) An American Dilemma, New York: Harper & Brothers.

Office of the Deputy Prime Minister (2004) Jobs and Enterprise in Deprived Areas, Social Exclusion Unit Report, London: Office of the Deputy Prime Minister.

O'Hara, P. (2008) 'Principle of circular and cumulative causation: fusing Myrdalian and Kaldorian growth and development dynamics', Journal of Economic Issues, XLII(2): 375–87.

Polanyi, K. (2001) The Great Transformation: The political and economic origins of our time, 2nd Edition, Boston: Beacon Press.

Porter, M. E. (1995a) 'The competitive advantage of the inner city', Harvard Business Review, May–June: 55–71.

————(1995b) 'An economic strategy for America's inner cities: Addressing the controversy', Review of Black Political Economy, 24(2/3): 303–34.

Prahalad, C. K. (2005) The Fortune at the Bottom of the Pyramid: Eradicating poverty through profits, Upper Saddle River, NJ: Wharton School of Publishing.

Rex, J. and Moore, R. (1969) Race, Community and Conflict: A study of Sparkbrook, London: Oxford University Press.

Rosenthal, S. S. and Ross, A. (2010) 'Violent crime, entrepreneurship and cities', Journal of Urban Economics, 67: 135–49.

Sawicki, D. S. and Moody, M. (1995) 'Deja-vu all over again: Porter's model of inner-city development', Review of Black Political Economy; 24(2/3): 75–94.

Servon, L. J. (1999) Bootstrap Capital: Micro-enterprises and the American poor, Washington, DC: Brooking Institute Press.

Skott, P. and Auerbach, P. (1995) 'Cumulative causation and the 'new' theories of economic growth', Journal of Post Keynesian Economics, 17(3): 381–402.

Social Investment Task Force (2003) 'Enterprising communities: wealth beyond welfare', paper presented at the Community Development Finance Association conference, Cardiff, July.

Storey, D. J. (1994) Understanding the Small Business Sector, London: Routledge.

Townsend, P. (1970) The Concept of Poverty, London: Heinemann.

White Haag, S. (2002) 'Community reinvestment: a review of urban outcomes and challenges', International Regional Science Review, 25(3): 252–75.

Williams, C. C. and Windebank, J. (2003) Poverty and the Third Way, London and New York: Routledge.

2 Enterprise
A Route out of Disadvantage and Deprivation?

Julian Frankish, Richard Roberts and David Storey

INTRODUCTION

> Enterprise can be a route out of disadvantage and deprivation but we need a better understanding of what works. (Small Business Service [SBS] 2004: 59).

> The government will promote enterprise in more deprived areas and among the disadvantaged groups that are heavily represented there, to help raise enterprise levels in the UK as a whole . . . Our understanding of success around enterprise in deprived areas is best informed by the self-employment rate. (Department of Business Enterprise and Regulatory Reform [BERR] 2008: 88).

> Since 2006 around £150 million has been committed to implement proposals from England's most deprived local authorities to support enterprise initiatives. A further £280 million will be committed between 2008 and 2011. (BERR 2008: 89).

> The recent expectations of the role of small firms and entrepreneurship in combating social exclusion are over optimistic. (Blackburn and Ram 2006: 73).

The former UK Government had a well established commitment to encouraging enterprise in geographical areas that are identified as being deprived, as the first three of the above quotations demonstrate. Public policy has explicitly linked enterprise and deprivation over the past decade, based on a view that enterprise is a vital component in meeting economic and social policy objectives. However, recent analyses have been less positive about the role of enterprise in these areas, as illustrated by the final quotation from Blackburn and Ram (2006). Despite the commitment of substantial public funds, the logic of policy involvement on this topic has, to our knowledge, never been explicitly identified. This chapter seeks to provide a reasoned case for tax-payer funding, based upon a careful reading of government statements. A key element of that reasoned case is the identification of appropriate measures of policy impact. The chapter proposes, and then constructs, a new measure that could be used for this purpose.

The challenge was to convert the statement *'Enterprise can be a route out of disadvantage and deprivation'* into a measure by which policy effectiveness can be assessed. One metric could be the extent to which the business survives or grows in terms of either sales or employment. Another might examine the changing economic profile of the area of interest. We opted for an approach that focuses on the individual owner-manager and, more specifically, the extent to which business ownership results in owners becoming more prosperous as a result of engaging in enterprise. The key contribution of this chapter is, therefore, to develop a test for the prevalence of exit from deprivation that uses change in owner addresses over time. This approach assumes that improved accommodation is high on the list of priorities for individuals who find that their material circumstances have improved.

To analyse enterprise as a potential exit route, we focused on businesses in four local authorities of contrasting location and prosperity, using three datasets drawn from the customer records of Barclays Bank. The first is a cross section of the business stock in the selected study areas at March 2008. The second is a time series that looks at changes in firms present in the four areas in March 2003 over the following five years. The final dataset replicates the structure of the time series data using a sample of non-business owners drawn from Barclays' personal customer base. The analysis generated three key results that, overall, cast some doubt on whether enterprise, in terms of business ownership, is an effective 'exit route' by which individuals can improve themselves by moving house into a more prosperous neighbourhood.

The chapter provides first a brief overview of the rationale for UK public policy in the areas of enterprise and deprivation before setting out four hypotheses that formed the focus for the study. The cross section and time series datasets used to examine the link between enterprise and deprivation are then presented in more detail, followed by an analysis of the four hypotheses. Finally, the conclusion summarises the key results from the chapter and what they suggest for both future research and public policy.

ENTERPRISE AND DEPRIVATION: THE RATIONALE FOR UK PUBLIC POLICY

A reading of UK Government literature suggests there are five logical steps implicitly linking the contribution of enterprise to the addressing of disadvantage in local areas, each of which is 'evidence-based'. These 'evidence-based' steps are:

1. Enterprise rates are low in deprived areas;
2. low enterprise rates are one of the causes of poverty;
3. promoting enterprise is a key route out of disadvantage and deprivation;
4. the promotion of enterprise requires a range of public funded pro-grammes to support 'conventional businesses, social enterprises and community businesses';
5. the effectiveness of policy is reflected in increased business formation and self-employment rates.

In this section, the evidence in support of each step is set out. Some of the 'evidence base' for these steps we show to be more ambiguous than is implied in public policy documents.

STEP 1: ENTERPRISE RATES ARE LOW IN DEPRIVED AREAS

The clear inference from the following two statements is that disadvantaged areas are characterised by low levels of enterprise and that, as a result, policy should seek to raise enterprise rates.

SBS states:

> There is a clear trend for registration rates to fall as the level of deprivation increases. **Excluding London**, the 20 per cent most deprived local authority districts in England had 27 start-ups per 10,000 residents, compared to 51 in the least deprived districts . . . there is a clear statistical relationship between deprivation and levels of enterprise activity.[1] (SBS 2004: 56)

BERR repeats the arguments using different data:

> As Chart 2 shows, there is a strong correlation between localised deprivation and levels of enterprise; the higher the level of deprivation, the lower the level of business start-up. Overall, the start-up rate in the 20 most deprived local authority areas is only half (51 per cent) of the rate in the 20 most prosperous areas. (BERR 2008: 90–91)

However, the evidence for both statements is more ambiguous because it is based on two important, but possibly overlooked, caveats. The first is that the data sources for both statements are VAT registrations. Since registration is compulsory only for enterprises with annual sales of £67,000 or more (the threshold at 2008/09), many small businesses will be omitted from this dataset. Furthermore, if enterprises in deprived areas have lower annual sales than those in prosperous areas, then using the VAT data may magnify differences between the two groups.

Second, both SBS (2004) and BERR (2008) specifically exclude data on the London boroughs. London has relatively high rates of business formation and ownership compared with other regions of the UK. Therefore,

Table 2.1 Univariate Regressions for Enterprise and Deprivation Results

	Without London		With London	
	b coefficient	*R²*	*b coefficient*	*R²*
VAT registrations	.074	.534	.050	.089
Barclays start-ups	.058	.065	−.004	−.003
Self-employment rate	.014	.294	.012	.227

the effect of including them 'muddies the water' a little in terms of a clear association between deprivation and enterprise.

Figure 2.1 sets out three scatter charts plotting the 2007 deprivation rank of all local authorities in England against VAT registrations, a Barclays measure of start-up activity and the rate of self-employment.[2] On each chart, fit lines are shown for the whole country (solid) and the non-London areas (broken). The findings are summarised in Table 2.1.

In all three cases the introduction of the London boroughs lowers the correlation between deprivation and enterprise as reflected in the R^2 statistic. It also shows the *b* coefficient is insignificantly different from zero, where the Barclays measure of start-ups is used.

On balance, the evidence that 'enterprise rates are low in areas of deprivation' is less clearly the case when London is included in any assessment. It may also be less clearly supported when all enterprises are included in the calculation than when only the larger firms are included.

STEP 2: LOW ENTERPRISE RATES ARE A CAUSE OF POVERTY

Policies to address deprivation imply that a key element in the prosperity of certain geographical areas is that prosperous areas contain more individuals likely to create and grow enterprises than is the case in deprived areas. A number of reasons have been put forward to explain these differences. One relates to differences in access to financial resources. So, in deprived areas, individuals are more likely to have lower personal wealth and are less likely to hold assets that could be offered as collateral for loans or invested directly in businesses. A second reason is that the buoyancy of local markets is less in areas of deprivation, resulting in more limited sales opportunities. Third, such areas contain a disproportionate number of people who are either unemployed or living on incapacity benefits. In this sense, the human capital of individuals in areas of disadvantage may be lower than those in the more prosperous areas.

Where the evidence is less clear is in relationship to immigrant and ethnic minority groups, 70 per cent of whom live in deprived areas. BERR (2008) recognises this by acknowledging that self-employment rates for some ethnic minorities are below, but others above, those for the majority population.

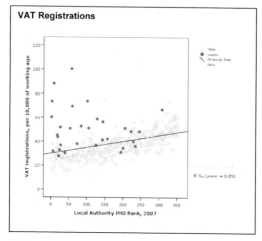

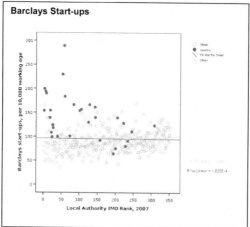

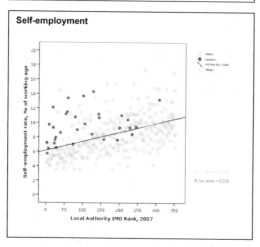

Figure 2.1   Measures of enterprise by deprivation rank.

However, whether there is supportive evidence that low enterprise rates are a *cause* of poverty is more open to question. As noted in Step 1, some selective choice of data enables an association to be made between poverty and enterprise rates, but correlation is not causation. The former can be plausibly explained by low income individuals lacking either the resources or the market opportunity to develop a business, with poverty the cause of low enterprise rather than the result.

It is then, in principle, an empirical question as to the direction of causation. The evidence on the closely linked topic of the relationship between enterprise and unemployment has been the subject of an extensive literature reviewed in Thurik et al. (2008). They conclude, 'The relationships between self-employment and unemployment are fraught with complexity and ambiguity for scholars and policy makers' (Thurik et al. 2008: 683).

Overall they conclude there is evidence that increases in unemployment cause increases in self-employment but also that increases in self-employment cause a lowering of unemployment. Similar work has not yet been undertaken in the UK to examine the link between poverty and enterprise but the Thurik et al. (2008) results suggest, at a minimum, that any link is 'more complex and ambiguous' than is implied in recent UK Government documents.

STEP 3: PROMOTING ENTERPRISE IS A KEY ROUTE OUT OF DISADVANTAGE AND DEPRIVATION

Here the logic appears to be that individuals who are either unemployed or suffering disadvantage in some other way can improve their personal position, and perhaps also the position of others, by becoming a business owner. It also implies that publicly funded programmes are able to enhance enterprise rates. This step in the logic of public policy is particularly significant for this study.

The evidence on this appears mixed on all three grounds. The first is whether there is evidence that policies to encourage entry into business ownership or self-employment amongst disadvantaged groups are effective. For example, Mueller et al. (2008) show that the employment impact of new firm formation is significantly positive in the existing high enterprise counties of Great Britain, whereas for the low enterprise counties it has a negative effect. In short, it appears possible to have 'the wrong type of entrepreneurship'. Case study evidence of this was provided by MacDonald and Coffield (1991), who documented stories of individuals who felt pressurised into starting an enterprise, even though they recognised that they lacked the necessary skills, ending up in a considerably worse position than beforehand. Deprived areas with relatively low proportions of individuals possessing sufficient human capital to start and run a business may therefore gain limited benefit from the encouragement of more enterprise.

A second issue is that the businesses started by such groups tend to be in the 'easy to enter' sectors. For example, during the 1980s more than one in five new firms in 'deprived' Teesside were in these fiercely competitive sectors. This compared with just 4 per cent in prosperous Buckinghamshire (Greene et al. 2004). The effect of having a high proportion of entrants into 'easy' sectors is that this increases the likelihood of displacing other local firms, without making a significant additional contribution to employment or productivity in the locality.

The final area of uncertainty relates to the extent to which public policy is able to raise new firm formation rates. Policy in this area is littered with spectacular failures, probably the clearest example of which was the Scottish Business Birth Rate policy (Fraser of Allander Institute 2001).

The evidence that it is possible or even desirable to seek to promote enterprise 'as a key route out of disadvantage and deprivation' is therefore also more mixed than is implied in public documents.

STEP 4: THE PROMOTION OF ENTERPRISE REQUIRES A RANGE OF PUBLICLY FUNDED PROGRAMMES TO SUPPORT 'CONVENTIONAL BUSINESSES, SOCIAL ENTERPRISES AND COMMUNITY BUSINESSES'

As noted earlier, BERR (2008) reported that £280 million will be committed between 2008 and 2011 to support enterprise initiatives in England's most deprived local authorities. These include funding for the Prince's Trust, the establishment of a risk capital fund for social enterprises and developing the community development finance sector.

BERR (2008) appears to adopt a rather sanguine view of the impact of such programmes. For example, the Prince's Trust is referred to as having 'a proven track record of helping young people realise their potential', possessing strong and established links with disadvantaged communities. This view contrasts with that provided by the review by Greene (2009), who concludes that, whilst case study and self-report methodologies point to the Trust being effective, more sophisticated statistical approaches fail to reach similarly supportive conclusions.

STEP 5: THE EFFECTIVENESS OF POLICY IS REFLECTED IN INCREASED BUSINESS FORMATION AND SELF-EMPLOYMENT RATES

The final step is to decide on the metrics for judging policy impact. These might include the extent to which business ownership rates, new firm formation or self-employment rates increase as a result of policy initiatives.

The UK Government has either used or proposed several metrics to judge policy impact. For example, in its chapter 'Encouraging More Enterprise in Disadvantaged Communities and Disadvantaged Groups', the SBS (2004) identified three measures. One of these was a reduction in '[t]he gap between the number of people in the most and least deprived areas starting up in business' (SBS 2004: 37).

Although this measure is not referred to in BERR (2008), the document points to policy success being reflected in self-employment rates in the 15 per cent most deprived wards in England increasing between 2004 and 2007. It also says 'the gap in self-employment levels between deprived areas and all other areas has increased slightly over the last 18 months but is still 4.2 percentage points smaller than it was in 2004'.[3]

The different metrics perhaps imply a shift in government thinking over time. The 2004 strategy seemed to imply the purpose of policy was to raise formation rates and self-employment rates as a whole. In the 2008 document, it had shifted towards reducing the difference in self-employment rates between the prosperous and deprived areas. However, neither document has a metric focused upon whether these businesses are created by individuals that were formerly unemployed or inactive, even though this is the focus of much of the £280 million expenditure on programmes referred to by BERR (2008).

Perhaps even more importantly, from the perspective of this chapter, there is no recognition that businesses located in deprived areas may be owned by individuals that do not live in that area. Hence it is possible for business formation rates to rise in deprived areas as a result of these being created by individuals living in prosperous areas. For such individuals, enterprise cannot, by definition, be an exit route from deprivation.

In summary, what is needed is a measure that more accurately captures the notion of 'enterprise as an exit route out of deprivation'. In the absence of a direct measure of owner wealth, we judged the most appropriate measure to be change in residential location. The key assumption is that moving home will have a high priority for individuals whose financial circumstances have seen significant improvement. Therefore, our exit test metric is concerned with comparing the movement patterns of owners in deprived and non-deprived areas.

DERIVING HYPOTHESES

To begin to address the link between enterprise and deprivation, a basic question was posed: what is the relationship between where a business is based and where its owner lives? The aim in asking this was to see if this relationship has different characteristics in areas of differing deprivation, adjusting for variations in the local stock of businesses. In terms of the cross-sectional analysis, two related hypotheses were considered:

> **H1:** Deprived areas are no more likely than other areas to have owners and their businesses at the same address.

> **H2:** Deprived areas are no more likely than other areas to have owners who live in a more prosperous area than the location of their business.

The question of 'enterprise as exit' was then addressed explicitly. As outlined above, the basic assumption was that, if enterprise does act as a route

Table 2.2 Selected Local Authority Areas Overview

Region	Durham City	Easington	Hackney	Kingston upon Thames
	North East	North East	London	London
Deprivation rank[a] of 353 authorities	180	7	2	245
Population, 2006 16 and over	78,500	75,700	162,200	127,800
% of working age				
Economically active	80.8	72.7	71.7	77.8
Employed	78.2	68.4	63.6	76.3
Self-employed	4.0	5.4	8.1	10.6
% of economically active				
Unemployed	3.3	5.8	11.3	2.0
Full-time income employees, median	21,100	19,800	27,800	32,900
Business start-ups *per 10,000 16+*				
VAT (04–06)	21	15	60	48
Barclays (05–06)	63	50	154	111

[a] Based on local authority average scores from the 2007 Index of Multiple Deprivation.

out of deprivation, it could be expected that owners living in deprived areas were both more likely to move out of those areas over time and more likely to move to less deprived areas than is the case for owners living in non-deprived areas. The final two hypotheses were therefore:

> H3: Individuals living and owning a business in a deprived area are no more likely to move to a less deprived area than other owners.

> H4: Business owners living and owning a business in a deprived area are no more likely to move to a less deprived area than other individuals living in the same area.

To examine these hypotheses, enterprise and deprivation were examined in contrasting UK study areas.

SELECTED STUDY AREAS

Four local authorities were identified, reflecting both contrasting locations in England and markedly differing levels of deprivation. Given the findings of Figure 2.1, it is clear that the links between deprivation and enterprise are very different in London, compared with elsewhere in England. London and the north east of England were therefore selected as our two regions on the grounds that differences in levels of enterprise were more extreme than between any other pair of regions. Within each region (London and the north east), a pair of prosperous and deprived local authorities was selected. The resulting areas were Durham City[4] and Easington in the north east, together with Hackney and Kingston upon Thames in London. Table 2.2 provides an overview of the key economic characteristics of these four areas.

In terms of deprivation, Hackney is the second, and Easington the seventh, most deprived local authority in England. However, their levels of enterprise activity are radically different, with Hackney having a self-employment rate 150 per cent that of Easington and between three and four times the rate of new business formation.

Both Durham City and Kingston upon Thames are considerably more prosperous. The former is selected as our north east comparator to Easington as it is the least deprived area in the region. Similarly, Kingston upon Thames has the second-best deprivation rank among the 32 London boroughs and is among the least deprived one-third of local authorities in England.

Table 2.2 also shows two other important differences between our selected study areas. First, median income for employees is considerably higher in London, even in deprived Hackney, than for the two areas in the north east. Second, the key economic factor associated with deprivation is the percentage of the population of working age that is economically active—being above 75 per cent in Durham City and Kingston upon Thames and in the low seventies in both Easington and Hackney.

Table 2.3 Cross section dataset, March 2008 Overview, unweighted

	All Selected Areas	Durham City	Easington	Hackney	Kingston upon Thames
Businesses	6,343	732	649	3,135	1,827
Owners	7,444	931	834	3,425	2,254
per firm	*1.48*	*1.62*	*1.48*	*1.48*	*1.62*
Sector					
Manufacturing	7.8	12.4	13.3	6.3	6.4
Construction	9.4	16.3	16.3	6.2	9.7
Distribution	25.1	26.4	36.2	23.9	22.6
Services	57.7	44.9	34.2	63.5	61.3
Turnover					
<£50k	51.9	53.7	59.2	51.2	49.8
£50–250k	27.0	25.4	24.3	26.6	29.3
£250k+	21.1	20.9	16.5	22.2	20.9

DATA AND DATASETS

All data used in this study were drawn from the customer records of Barclays Bank. Barclays is the main bank for 20 per cent of mainstream businesses in England and Wales. Their active customer base is in excess of 500,000 firms, providing a large population from which to draw the data used in the study.

Bank data have considerable advantages over other sources traditionally used in research—official or other private survey data. First, bank data are collected by commercial institutions with a strong incentive to ensure accuracy. Second, the majority of the data is captured automatically as part of the banking relationship, rather than requiring self-reported information. Third, the data are regularly updated, usually at least monthly, often due to regulatory reporting requirements.

As outlined earlier, two datasets were used on businesses and their owners in our selected areas together with an additional dataset on non-business owning individuals to test the hypotheses.

Table 2.4   Time Series Dataset, March 2003 Overview

	All Selected Areas	Durham City	Easington	Hackney	Kingston upon Thames
Businesses	3,846	558	488	1,628	1,172
% of all firms	*68*	*84*	*88*	*59*	*71*
Local owners	4,105	672	610	1,544	1,279
Sector *% of firms*					
Manufacturing	8	11	16	6	7
Construction	9	13	15	6	9
Distribution	27	28	38	26	22
Services	56	47	32	62	62
Turnover *% of firms*					
<£50k	58	59	59	58	56
£50–250k	27	26	27	27	28
£250k+	15	15	14	15	16
Surviving firms[a]	1,898	273	259	818	548
% of 2003	*49*	*49*	*53*	*50*	*47*
Remaining owners[b]	1,958	323	337	700	598
% of 2003	*48*	*48*	*55*	*45*	*47*

[a] Firms remaining on Barclays system and active (turnover greater than zero) at March 2008.
[b] Remaining local owners of surviving firms.

The first was a cross-sectional dataset used to test *H1* and *H2*. This consisted of active Barclays business customers at the end of March 2008. This provides a sample base of 6,343 firms and 7,444 owners.[5] For the purposes of the study, the most important aspect of this dataset was that it contained the postcodes of both the trading address of the firm and the residential address of the owner. This allowed us to examine the relationship between business and owner location. Summary information for the cross-sectional dataset is shown in Table 2.3.[6]

A number of contrasts appear in Table 2.3. First, the more prosperous areas have more business owners per firm than the deprived areas. Second, there are statistically significant differences in the business sector profiles of the two regions. The north east areas have a greater proportion of firms in manufacturing and construction, with correspondingly fewer in services than those in London. Finally, in Easington, the proportion of the largest firms[7] in the business stock is significantly lower than in any of the other three areas. Also of note is the fact that Hackney has a higher proportion of large firms than any of the other three study areas.

The data in Table 2.3 support the point made earlier about the contrast in the association between enterprise and deprivation in London and other regions. It certainly suggests that the relationship of enterprise and wider business activity with deprivation is very different in Easington to that found in Hackney.

The second dataset was a time series and is used to test *H3* and *H4*. As set out earlier, the chosen measure of the effectiveness of enterprise as a means of exiting deprivation was to look at changes in the residential addresses of business owners. Therefore, for this dataset firms of interest were restricted to those where at least one of the owners was also resident in the same local authority. The base date for the dataset was March 2003. At that point there were 3,846 active firms meeting the owner restriction, with 4,105 owners. Data were then obtained on the position of these firms and their owners, where available, five years later in March 2008.[8] Table 2.4 sets out a summary of this dataset.

The overview in Table 2.4 shows the same comparative structure of the local area business stocks at March 2003 that was noted for Table 2.3, with a high share of both service sector and larger firms in London. It is also interesting to note that Hackney differs from the other three areas in averaging more than one locally owned firm for each locally based business owner.

Just under 50 per cent of the initial sample base of firms remained with Barclays and were active after five years, with a similar proportion of owners also remaining. For three of the study areas the proportions of surviving firms and owners were broadly in line. Again, Hackney is an exception to this, experiencing a greater attrition of local owners than firms.

The final dataset moved away from businesses and their owners to a sample of non-business owning individuals. This was designed to permit comparison of the movement experiences of business owners with the wider population. The dataset consists of 9,694 individuals resident in our

Table 2.5   Analysis, Cross Section March 2008

weighted unweighted	All Selected Areas	Durham City	Easington	Hackney	Kingston upon Thames
Measure I	57	66	68	51	61
(home-based)	58	67	71	50	62
Owners resident in same local authority[a]	6	9	13	3	3
Firms where owners live in: *% of all firms*					
more deprived	10	15	6	10	10
	10	15	6	10	10
more prosperous	29	13	22	36	25
	28	12	19	35	24
Measure II	+19	-3	+15	+27	+15
(net balance)	+18	-3	+13	+25	+14
by turnover					
<£50k	+10	-3	+8	+16	+5
£50–250k	+17	-6	+10	+26	+13
£250k+	+42	+3	+40	+52	+41
Measure III	+7	-2	+5	+10	+4
(mean score)	+7	-2	+5	+10	+4
by turnover					
<£50k	+3	-3	+2	+6	+2
£50–250k	+6	-2	+5	+10	+4
£250k+	+15	0	+16	+20	+12

[a] Not home-based.

study areas at March 2003, aged between 18 and 74 and identified as not associated with any Barclays business customer at that point.[9] The residential address of these individuals was then noted and compared with that recorded for them five years later in March 2008,[10] to ensure comparability with our business time series dataset.

TESTING THE HYPOTHESES

Cross Section, H1 and H2

The first part of the analysis looks at *H1* and *H2*, both concerned with the static relationship between business and owner. This was examined as at March 2008.

H1: Deprived areas are no more likely than other areas to have owners and their businesses at the same address.

To test *H1*, the proportion of firms that have the same postcode for their trading address as their owner has for their residential address[11] (Measure I) was examined. Businesses located at their owner's residence have been described as 'home-based' (Mason et al. 2008). A proportion of them will be engaged in 'home working', with the business activity primarily occurring at that location. For the remainder the address acts as the administrative centre of the business while the majority of the firm's activity takes place elsewhere.

Table 2.5 sets out the weighted (and unweighted) results for Measure I. The results show that the majority of businesses across our four study areas (57 per cent) were home-based on the definition set out above.[12] Turning to our four study areas, there are marked differences in the incidence of home-based businesses, with one area standing out from the others. The exceptional area is Hackney, where only 51 per cent of businesses operate from the same address as their owner. The other three areas all have home-based business rates of more than 60 per cent, although Kingston upon Thames, at 61 per cent, is noticeably lower than either Durham City (66 per cent) or Easington (68 per cent).

The fact that the two London local authorities have lower proportions of home-based businesses suggests that the capital, and possibly other large urban areas, offers greater effective choice about business location. In the case of Hackney the figures may also be affected by the proximity of the area to both 'the City' and the wider business district of central London, making it attractive to business owners from outside of the borough, particularly for those looking to supply business services.

Taking the London pair, the proportion of home-based businesses is significantly lower in Hackney than Kingston upon Thames, pointing to the rejection of *H1*. Set against this, the opposite relationship is evident in the north east, with our prosperous area having fewer home-based firms. Taken together, the results suggested that it is not possible to reject *H1*. However, this conclusion should be balanced by the caveat that more areas in London should ideally be studied in order to judge whether Hackney is representative of other deprived areas in the Capital.

H2: Deprived areas are no more likely than other areas to have owners who live in a more prosperous area than the location of their business.

H1 examined only home-based businesses. In contrast, testing H2 required analysis of those firms where there is a separation between the domestic residence of the owner and the business premises.[13] The purpose was to determine the extent to which business owners have their domestic property in a more, or a less, prosperous area than their business. To conduct the test, two new measures were introduced. The first was a net balance measure that reflects the net proportion of owners living in more prosperous locations than their business relative to all the firms in our data-set (Measure II). This was accompanied by a mean score measure (Measure III) for those firms that are not home-based. This is the mean difference in the deprivation rank between the address of the firm and that of its owner, thereby taking account of not only the direction—more or less deprived—but also the magnitude of difference.[14]

Before considering what these measures told us about the relationship between business and owner, it was interesting to note what the dataset reveals about the 'localism' of the business stocks in our study areas. If the home-based firms identified as Measure I in Table 2.5 are taken and the businesses where owners live in the same local authority (row 3 of Table 2.5) added to them, the differences between London and the north east become even starker. Durham City (75 per cent) and Easington (81 per cent) have much higher local business shares than either Hackney (54 per cent) or Kingston upon Thames (64 per cent). Again this is probably a feature of the more fluid business market in London.

Returning to *H2*, Table 2.5 sets out the key results from the dataset. For the dataset as a whole 29 per cent of owners live in more prosperous areas than the location of their business and 10 per cent in more deprived areas, a Measure II score of +19.[15] This score shows a clear link with firm size, increasing from +10 for the smallest to +17 in the medium range and finally +42 for our largest size category. The larger the business, the more likely it is that the owner lives in a more prosperous area than the location of the business.

The mean score (Measure III) for the aggregate dataset was +7; i.e. the residential address of owners of non-home-based firms was a mean seven ranking places (percentile points) further up the deprivation scale than that of their business. As with Measure II, a relationship with firm size is apparent, increasing from +3 (small) to +6 (medium) to +15 (large). This means that the owners of large firms are not only more likely to live in more prosperous areas, but those areas will typically be a more marked step up from the business location.

Looking at each of the study areas, Measure II shows the highest score for owners of businesses based in Hackney (+27). Easington and Kingston upon Thames had equal scores (both +15), while Durham City is notable as the only area where the score was negative (−3). Measure III scores show a similar pattern. Hackney (+10) has the greatest positive differential between business and owner locations. Durham City has another negative score (−2), while Easington and Kingston upon Thames sit midway between the other two areas.

In part, the results for Measures II and III may reflect the differing incidences of home-based businesses. That is, Hackney simply has more scope for business owners to reside in markedly different areas. However, it seems likely that there are two more important factors: the relative deprivation of each area, and the ease of access.

The relative deprivation factor would apply to both Hackney and Easington. As these areas are very deprived (second and seventh most deprived in England) there are, by definition, relatively few locations that are similarly or even more deprived. Therefore, it is in practice comparatively difficult for business owners to live in more deprived areas.

The ease of access explanation relates more to the Durham City result. Here, because Durham City is a local 'peak' of prosperity (the least deprived area in the north east) a business owner might have to live a considerable distance away, perhaps 50 miles or more, to live in a more consistently prosperous location, even though Durham City is not exceptionally prosperous in a national context. In contrast, the business owner in Kingston upon Thames may have to live only a few miles away, even though it is a more prosperous area than Durham City. This effect, together with the relative deprivation point, may also explain why Durham City is the only one of the four areas not to see a significant difference in owner location by size of firm.

In summary, *H2* hypothesised that owners of businesses located in deprived areas would be more likely to live in more prosperous areas than their business were located. The data shows that owners of Hackney businesses are clearly more likely to live in 'better' areas than is the case for the other study areas. At the other end of the scale, there is little difference for owners with businesses based in Durham City. Between these two, the deprived and non-deprived areas of Easington and Kingston upon Thames show similar profiles. This would suggest that *H2* cannot be rejected. However, following on from above, if the study areas are considered in terms of regional pairs, the dataset shows that owners in deprived areas are more likely to live in less deprived areas. This points to the rejection of *H2*.

A final factor clouding any judgement is the point made about the possible effects of relative deprivation. That is, living in an area towards either end of the deprivation index makes it more difficult to move, either up in an area of limited deprivation, or down (in an area of high deprivation). On balance, the data contained in the dataset point to the rejection of *H2* but again with the caveat that it would be useful to examine other areas in both regions to better gauge whether this is a representative result.

Time Series, H3 and H4

Next, the core question of this study was considered—does enterprise serve as an effective route out of deprivation? To analyse this, attention was shifted on to changes in the residential addresses of owners over a five year period.

> *H3: Individuals living and owning a business in a deprived area are no more likely to move to a less deprived area than other owners.*

Table 2.4 provides an overview of the dataset of business owners in the four locations in March 2003. Of the initial 4,105 owners, valid 2008 residential postcodes for 3,868 (94 per cent) were obtainable. As noted earlier, only one-half of the locally owned businesses remained active after five years. A similar proportion of the 2003 business owners remained owners in 2008.[16] Survival rates show noticeable variation across the study areas. The final row of the table shows that 55 per cent of owners remain in Easington, but only 45 per cent in Hackney. These differences probably reflect the relative volume of start-up activity in each area.[17]

The dataset allowed examination of any changes in residential postcodes of business owners between March 2003 and March 2008. To assist in this, modified versions of Measures II and III were used, this time comparing residential addresses rather than residential and business addresses. As before, there is a net balance (Measure IV) and a mean score (Measure V) and these are set out in Table 2.6.

Using data on business owners, the second row of Table 2.6 shows that, in aggregate, 72 per cent of owners did not change their home address over the five year period. By implication therefore 28 per cent of owners moved in that time; 16 per cent to a more prosperous area, 9 per cent to a more deprived area with the remainder moving to an area with the same deprivation score. These results are reflected in a Measure IV score of +7 and a Measure V score of +8.

There are important differences between the study areas. The two London areas experienced higher movement rates than the north east. Over the five years Hackney (31 per cent) and Kingston upon Thames (29 per cent) saw roughly eight percentage points more of their owner base move address than was the case for Durham City or Easington.[18] The relative directions of movement across the four areas are similar to those seen when comparing business and owner locations for *H2*. Owners initially living in Hackney were the most likely to have moved to a more prosperous area (Measure IV +16), those in Durham City the least (−6), with the other two areas in between these extremes. Measure V scores confirm not only that Hackney owners were the most likely to move to more prosperous areas, but that they also experienced the greatest degree of improvement, a mean increase of 19 percentiles.

The results in the top section of Table 2.6 are based upon all local business owners in 2003 whose residential addresses were available in 2008. However, as Table 2.4 showed, there is a major divide within this group as one-half of these individuals ceased to be business owners at some point during the five year period.

The middle and lower sections of Table 2.6 distinguish between current or continuing and former owners. It shows that 79 per cent of continuing business owners did not move house—and by implication only 21 per cent moved in the period. In contrast, for former owners the movement rate was 34 per cent. The second key result is that, for those who did move, the former

Table 2.6 Analysis, Time Series Position at March 2008

	All Selected Areas	Durham City	Easington	Hackney	Kingston upon Thames
All identified owners	3,868	632	588	1,445	1,203
Owner address % *of owners*					
unchanged	72	79	77	69	71
more deprived	9	12	9	6	11
more prosperous	16	6	11	22	15
same deprivation	3	3	3	2	3
Measure IV (net balance)	+7	-6	+2	+16	+4
Measure V (mean score)	+8	-10	+5	+19	+3
Current owners	1,949	322	334	698	595
Owner address % *of owners*					
unchanged	79	85	81	77	75
more deprived	7	8	6	6	9
more prosperous	11	3	9	15	12
same deprivation	3	4	3	2	3
Measure IV (net balance)	+4	−4	+3	+9	+3
Measure V (mean score)	+8	−7	+1	+17	+3
Former owners	1,919	310	254	747	608
Owner address % *of owners*					
unchanged	66	73	72	62	67
more deprived	11	16	12	6	13
more prosperous	20	9	13	29	18
same deprivation	3	2	4	3	2
Measure IV (net balance)	+9	−7	0	+23	+5
Measure V (mean score)	+9	−11	+5	+20	+3

Owners at March 2003 with valid residential postcode at March 2008.

Table 2.7　Non-Business Owners Dataset Position at March 2008

	All Selected Areas	Durham City	Easington	Hackney	Kingston upon Thames
Identified individuals	9,694	1,490	1,050	3,741	3,413
Owner address *% of owners*					
unchanged	78	84	82	73	79
more deprived	7	8	6	6	9
more prosperous	13	6	8	19	12
same deprivation	2	3	3	2	1
(net balance)	+6	-2	+1	+13	+3
Measure V (mean score)	+8	-6	+6	+15	+3

Non-business owning Barclays customers at March 2003, with valid residential postcode at March 2008.

business owners were much more likely to have moved to a more prosperous area (Measure IV +9 against +4) than those who remained business owners.[19]

The local area profiles for continuing and former owners closely resemble those for the aggregate profile. In both cases, owners of businesses based in Hackney in 2003 were more likely to move to more prosperous areas, while those in Durham City tended to move sideways or down. The only slight difference between the two groups was that continuing owners in Kingston upon Thames were more likely to have moved (25 per cent) than those in Hackney (23 per cent), while this ranking was reversed for former owners.

The differences highlighted between current and former business owners are intriguing. However, they do not intrude on consideration of *H3*. This proposes that there are no differences in the movement patterns of owners based in deprived and non-deprived areas. The dataset suggests that there are regional differences in the propensity for residential moves. Therefore, it is sensible to consider *H3* in terms of the regional pairings used above in the section Cross Section H1/H2. On this basis, it is clear that owners in deprived areas are more likely to move to more prosperous areas over time. This is the case whether they continue to operate the business or cease trading at some point. Therefore, the data indicates the rejection of H3, albeit with the same caution as previously regarding the extrapolation of these results to other areas.

H4: Business owners living and owning a business in a deprived area are no more likely to move to a less deprived area than other individuals living in the same area.

A clear criticism of the analysis of H3 is that it lacks context. Therefore, the movement rates (and direction) of business owners over time were examined and contrasted across different areas, as well as split between continuing and former owners. However, the results were not compared to the wider population, as this limitation is addressed in considering *H4*.

To put the movement patterns of business owners in context, the dataset of non-business owning individuals was used. A limitation of the dataset in its original form is that the age profiles of the individuals do not match those of our business owners. This is not surprising, as business owners tend, in general, to be relatively old compared to the wider population. This matters since the propensity to move varies with age. The sample for each area was therefore weighted to align it with the age profile of the local business owners.[20] It is these weighted results that are discussed and presented in Table 2.7.

Table 2.7 shows that 78 per cent of individuals were at the same address over the five year period, and that by implication 22 per cent had moved. This compares with 28 per cent of business owners in the same period.

The similarities between Tables 2.6 and 2.7 are striking. Table 2.7 shows that, on balance, non-business owners that moved did so to more prosperous areas (Measure IV +6). For business owners, in aggregate, in Table 2.6 the Measure IV score was +7. These similarities continue for each of the four areas. Individuals living in London were most likely to move. Those initially living in Hackney (Measure IV +13) were the most likely to move to a more prosperous area, with those in Durham City the least likely (Measure IV–2). These results mirror very closely the findings for business owners as a group, where the Measure IV scores for Hackney and Durham City are +16 and–6 respectively.

The metric that measures the degree of improvement (Measure V) also generates very similar results at +15 for Hackney (+19 for business owners) and–6 for Durham City (–10). Overall, these results imply strong similarity between the movement rates and patterns of business owners and other residents in the area.

H4 is concerned with the movement of business owners living in deprived areas compared with other individuals. For Easington and Hackney any differences between these groups appear modest judged by Measures IV and V. In both cases, the proportion of business owners moving to more prosperous areas was three percentage points higher than for other individuals. However, this differential was only statistically significant (at the 10 per cent level) for Hackney. Given this mixed result, it is not possible to reject *H4*.

A statistically significant gap between business owners and other individuals on this measure was also present in Kingston upon Thames. This result, taken together with that for Hackney, means that it is possible that any enhanced likelihood of moving to more prosperous areas among business owners relates to regional factors, rather than those associated with deprivation. As with *H1* to *H3* these ambiguous results suggest that including additional study areas would be useful.

CONCLUSIONS

In the introduction to this chapter, it was argued that UK policy makers have observed that deprived areas exhibit lower levels of enterprise than more prosperous areas. Considerable sums of public money have been expended on seeking to raise enterprise rates in deprived areas, as a result, on the grounds that enterprise constitutes an exit route from deprivation for those exhibiting such enterprise.

The findings opened up the key assumptions of policy in this area. Firstly, they showed that the evidence base for the statement that enterprise rates are lower in deprived, than in prosperous, areas, is highly data-dependent. Second, taking two deprived and two prosperous areas, the importance of distinguishing between the location of the business and the owner's residence was highlighted. A further important distinction is between English regions: deprivation in London is radically different from deprivation in north east England.

To test whether enterprise does constitute an exit route from deprivation for the business owner, we put forward the proposition that 'enterprise as exit' is best assessed by examining changes in the residential addresses of owners. The first finding was that the incidence of home-based businesses was the same across deprived and non-deprived areas, allowing for region specific effects. Second, it was found that owners with firms in deprived areas were more likely to live in a more prosperous area than owners of businesses in prosperous areas.

When considering whether enterprise offers a particularly propitious route out of deprivation for the owner, evidence appeared that owners of business in deprived areas who moved house over a five year period were likely to move to more, rather than less, prosperous areas. However this apparent support for enterprise being an exit route out of deprivation was more than offset by several other findings. The first was that, amongst the business owners who moved, it was those who closed their businesses that were most likely to move house to a prosperous area. Those who continued in business were more likely to stay in the same house. Second, business owners in deprived areas were no more or less likely than the population as a whole in that area to move house to a more prosperous location. This suggests that enterprise may not serve as an exceptional exit route out of deprivation.

There are of course a number of limitations to this work. The conclusions are based upon a limited number of study areas. In particular, there is a valid debate about whether, for example, Hackney is 'representative' of the enterprise experiences of a deprived area, both in general and within London. Nevertheless, this chapter has set out an approach to considering enterprise and deprivation that could be applied to other areas.

So, while this analysis does indicate some differences in the relationship of owners and their business in deprived areas (those engaged in enterprise at a given point in these areas appear to be more likely to move to more prosperous areas in subsequent years), this does not seem to reflect the superiority of enterprise as an exit route. Rather it reflects the wider characteristics of population dynamics in these areas.

NOTES

1. The bold type is ours and does not appear in SBS (2004).
2. Taken from the Annual Population Survey (Office for National Statistics).
3. Page 88.
4. Note this is Durham City District Council, and not County Durham as a whole.
5. Identified by Barclays as being the 'owner of . . . ', 'director of . . . ' or 'partner of . . . ' a given firm. A number of these individuals are owners of more than one firm in the sample.
6. The analysis presented on this dataset in the next section uses weighting. As will be seen in the next section, there are strong associations between certain firm characteristics and the location of business and owner. The weighting used—on business size and sector—makes some allowance for the effect of these on the results. Essentially the sample base in each area is adjusted to match the wider Barclays customer profile.
7. Defined as those with annual sales in excess of £250,000.
8. Fraser (2004) reports that, over a three year period, 2 per cent of SMEs (small- and medium-sized enterprises) actually switched banks. This implies that monitoring businesses and individuals through the records of an individual bank, whilst not perfect, is acceptably accurate.
9. They may have been the owners of a business that banked elsewhere.
10. Some may have become business owners in this period.
11. Where there is more than one owner, there has to be at least one common pair of postcodes.
12. Although not shown in the table, the incidence of home-based businesses varies significantly by the type of activity and the size of firm. Home-based businesses are particularly common in the construction sector (74 per cent), while accounting for only one-half of firms engaged in manufacturing and distribution. Unsurprisingly, the proportion of home-based businesses also falls substantially as firm size rises. When turnover is less than £50,000, 69 per cent of firms are home-based. This proportion falls to 57 per cent when turnover is between £50,000 and £250,000. It then halves to 30 per cent for the largest firms in our dataset. Within this aggregate pattern, the business sector differences noted above remain prominent. Even when firm turnover is more than £250,000, 39 per cent of construction businesses remain home-based, against only 25 per cent of those in distribution and 26 per cent in manufacturing.
13. Firms identified as home-based are excluded from this analysis, even if one or more owner does not reside at the same address.
14. Using the 2007 Index of Multiple Deprivation and the National Statistics Postcode Directory, each postcode can be ranked in terms of relative deprivation. For this chapter the ranking was from 1 (most deprived) to 100 (least deprived).
15. The remaining 4 per cent of business owners lived in areas of equal deprivation.
16. That is, owners of the same firms. It is possible that individuals associated with inactive/closed firms had started up other businesses.

17. Supplemented in the case of Hackney by a high inflow of 'external' start-ups.
18. This probably reflects higher movement rates for the wider London popula-
    tion. This is touched on when examining *H4.*
19. It should be acknowledged that these individuals may have moved while they
    were still business owners.
20. This was done on the basis of five age groups—under 35, 35–44, 45–54,
    55–64, 65 and over.

BIBLIOGRAPHY

BERR (2008) Enterprise: Unlocking the UK's talent, London: Department of Busi-
    ness Enterprise and Regulatory Reform.
Blackburn, R. and Ram, M. (2006) 'Fix or fixation? The contributions and limita-
    tions of entrepreneurship and small firms to combating social exclusion', Entre-
    preneurship and Regional Development, 18(1): 73–89.
Fraser, S. (2004) Finance for Small and Medium Sized Enterprises, Coventry: War-
    wick Business School.
Fraser of Allander Institute (2001) Promoting Business Start-Ups: a new strategic
    formula. Progress review, final report, Glasgow: University of Strathclyde.
Greene, F. J. (2009) 'Assessing the impact of policy interventions: the influence of
    evaluation methodology', Government & Policy: Environment and Planning C,
    27(2): 216–29.
Greene, F. J., Mole, K. M. and Storey, D. J. (2004) 'Does more mean worse? Three
    decades of enterprise policy in the Tees Valley', Urban Studies, 41(7): 1207–28.
MacDonald, R. and Coffield, F. (1991) Risky Business: Riders, fallers and plod-
    ders, London: Falmer Press.
Mason, C., Carter, S. and Tagg, S. (2008) 'Invisible businesses: the characteristics
    of home-based businesses in the United Kingdom', Working Paper, Hunter Cen-
    tre for Entrepreneurship, University of Strathclyde, Glasgow.
Mueller, P., van Stel, A. J. and Storey, D. J. (2008) 'The effects of new firm forma-
    tion on regional development over time: the case of Great Britain', Small Busi-
    ness Economics, 30(1): 59–71.
SBS (2004) A Government Action Plan for Small Business: Making the UK the best
    place in the world to start and grow a business—the evidence base, London:
    Department of Trade and Industry, HMSO.
Thurik, A. R., Carree, M. A., van Stel, A. J. and Audretsch, D. B. (2008) 'Does
    self-employment reduce unemployment?', Journal of Business Venturing, 23(6):
    673–86.

3 Blind Faith

Entrepreneurship and the Revitalisation of Inner-City Minority Communities

Timothy Bates and Alicia Robb[1]

INTRODUCTION

Typifying widespread sentiment about the need to reduce the dependence of low income Americans on public assistance, former New York City mayor Rudolph Giuliani offered this advice to the poor; 'If you can't get a job, start a small business, start a little candy store. Start a little newspaper stand. Start a lemonade stand' (Deparle 1998: 89).

Rather suddenly in the 1990s, micro-enterprise development programmes (MDPs) were widely heralded in the US as creating jobs in economically depressed areas, increasing incomes of low income business owners, and generating indirect benefits as diverse as increasing the community involvement of programme participants and raising their self-esteem. An influential study from the Aspen Institute reported that MDPs assisting low income persons (most of whom were minorities) developed new firms and stabilized existing ones, created jobs, and alleviated poverty (Edgcomb et al. 1996). MDPs targeting poor recipients of government transfer payments, furthermore, moved individuals from unemployment and welfare dependence to economic independence (Raheim and Alter 1995).

The implication for US social policy was clear: self-employment among the disadvantaged was a powerful tool for addressing a wide range of persistent social and economic problems. A short course in entrepreneurial fundamentals, perhaps supplemented by a small loan, it seemed, could transform low income people into self-sufficient business owners, potent agents for generating local economic development in depressed regions of the nation.

In a context of declining government responsibility for assisting low income families, coupled with sharp cuts in economic development aid targeted to poor communities, free-market strategies are increasingly embraced as solutions to economic and social problems in the US. Rather than addressing issues of structural disadvantage, government often encourages poor communities to embrace entrepreneurship as a solution to poverty and underemployment. Can expanded small business ownership serve as an effective strategy for bootstrapping individuals, families and communities out of poverty? This is essentially an empirical question.

A series of empirically grounded scholarly studies, spawned by the astounding growth of MDP programmes in the 1990s, has thoroughly condemned the first-generation studies on MDP virtues—particularly those forthcoming from the Aspen Institute—as advocacy. Extensive counter evidence was presented, suggesting limited MDP utility as a tool for triggering local economic development or even assisting truly disadvantaged micro entrepreneurs (Servon and Bates 1998, Taub 1998, Bhatt and Tang 2002, Jurik 2005). Criticizing early MDP evaluations for relying 'on indirect measures of success, a lack of adequate comparison groups of nonclients, and a lack of long-term followup', Jurik concluded that MDP proponents were guilty of reinforcing 'images that poor and low-income people are responsible for their failures' (2005: 18). Furthermore, they exhibited 'an almost blind faith in market-centered solutions in a context of growing economic insecurity' (2005: 217). In the realm of micro-enterprise policy discussion, hard evidence has struggled against assertion and advocacy; in public policy circles, assertion and advocacy appear to have the upper hand.

Often advocated, rarely understood, local economic development programmes utilizing small firm expansion as a tool to assist low income urban areas (and persons) frequently proceed based upon premises rooted in wishful thinking. Consider Mr. Giuliani's lemonade stand proposal. Empirically based scholarly literature on entrepreneurship stresses that skills, education and work experience are success prerequisites for aspiring entrepreneurs, be they poor or affluent (Bates 1997b, Fairlie and Robb 2008). Successful small firm formation, furthermore, often requires financial investment; working capital, inventory and equipment are common prerequisites for viable business operation. For owners possessing appropriate human- and financial -capital resources, a third prerequisite is identification and penetration of a market segment capable of generating adequate sales revenues to support the venture (Bates 1997a, Porter 1997). Hard work and initiative alone are rarely enough to create lasting firms. People choosing self employment and small-business ownership who lack skills and financial resources or fail to identify viable market niches generate high business failure and self-employment exit rates (Servon and Bates 1998). On balance, a lemonade stand is an improbable vehicle for helping to spark local revitalisation and entrepreneurial upward mobility.

The micro-enterprise programmes, although the most influential in arguing that the poor could alleviate their own poverty by embracing entrepreneurship, were only one element in a broader 1990s public policy offensive linking enhanced business development strategies to solving long-standing problems facing economically depressed regions of the US. Harvard University Business School Professor, Michael Porter, in 1995 proposed revitalisation of low income, inner-city, minority communities with a combination of enhanced private business development and reduced public expenditure; emphasis had to be shifted from transfer payments to assisting business development (Porter 1995). Government expenditure was acceptable in the context of alleviating poverty and revitalising the poor areas in the inner city as long as it was not used to feed people: it would feed private enterprise development instead.

EMPIRICAL EVALUATION OF PROFESSOR PORTER'S UNDERSERVED MARKET CONCEPT

The debate on the policy concept of low income people revitalising their communities by pursuing entrepreneurship has, to date, paid little attention to the 'third prerequisite' for success among aspiring entrepreneurs: identifying and penetrating a market segment capable of generating adequate sales revenues to support the new business venture. Actual participants in US micro-enterprise programmes have most often been minorities, particularly Blacks and Latinos, residing in low income urban areas. Quite aside from issues of owner skills and capitalization requirements for starting viable small businesses, the issue of identifying market opportunities is key: do these economically depressed communities offer attractive market niches that aspiring entrepreneurs can exploit?

Michael Porter has addressed this concern and his 'findings' have been hugely influential (Porter 1995, 1997). Low income, predominantly minority inner-city areas, according to Porter, were absolutely brimming with enormous opportunities, which were particularly accessible to firms catering to local 'underserved' consumer markets. Unlike the proponents of MDP, Porter was not specifically interested in helping the poor to become business owners. When he wrote about 'harnessing the power of market forces', he envisioned an unfettered entrepreneurship in which public policy would play no role in picking owners of firms. The idea, instead, was to make poor inner-city areas so attractive that entrepreneurs would naturally gravitate there, drawn by attractive investment opportunities. Indeed, part of Porter's task was to alert entrepreneurs to the numerous underserved market opportunities that were already present in these areas.

Yet Porter's message was immensely complementary to the policy implications highlighted by micro-enterprise development proponents. MDP advocates had demonstrated that their clients, the majority of whom were minorities (largely African American and Hispanic), could escape poverty and government assistance roles by becoming business owners. Most already resided in precisely those low income inner-city neighbourhoods Porter planned to revitalise. He then proceeded to point out the precise kinds of 'underserved' markets where new firm creation was needed: inner-city, neighbourhood-oriented retail and consumer-service businesses could tap these markets. Thus, attractive prospects for low income entrepreneurs were already abundant right in the neighbour-hoods where most of them currently resided. Porter had no empirical evi-dence capable of backing up these claims but, then, neither did the MDP proponents. Poor inner-city residents could benefit from the hypothetical advantages that both the MDP proponents and Professor Porter claimed to have demonstrated.

The balance of this chapter investigates Porter's controversial 'under-served markets' hypothesis—that low income, urban minority neighbour-hoods offer attractive opportunities to household-oriented businesses (1995). An alternative interpretation of the generally distressed economic state of urban minority communities is the notion that the 'market' is work-ing; profit-seeking firms are correctly gauging opportunities and choosing rationally to invest elsewhere. Doeringer makes this point, observing 'it is hard to think of changes in market institutions that might improve the efficiency of inner-city businesses sufficiently to promote growth . . . From the perspective of inner-city economic development, the problem would seem to be less one of market failures than of well-functioning markets . . .' (1999: 512).

We tested Porter's underserved market hypothesis by constructing large representative samples of small businesses serving household clienteles in urban neighbourhoods; our data source is the US Bureau of the Census Characteristics of Business Owners (CBO) database. These uniquely pow-erful data describe urban firms along three target-market dimensions: (1) clientele served: household vs. non-household, (2) clientele served: minority vs. nonminority, (3) geographic scope of market served: local/neighbour-hood vs. city/county/national. Our analysis files of CBO data are struc-tured along geographic-scope-of-market and target-clientele dimensions, as described by the two-by-two matrix in Table 3.1.

Our primary task is to compare the viability of cell 1 and cell 3 small businesses. To accomplish this objective, the data are pooled across the above four cells, and appropriate statistical controls for geographic scope of market and minority/non-minority clientele are utilized. Our analysis pro-ceeds by comparing the traits and performance of firms serving minority clients predominantly to those selling their products largely to household clients who are non-minority whites. Controlling for firm/owner traits, we find that Porter's hypothesis of business opportunity rooted in substantial unmet local demand is untenable.

Table 3.1

	Neighborhood Clientele	*City/County/Regional or Broader Clientele*
Minority Clientele	Cell 1	Cell 2
Non-Minority Clientele	Cell 3	Cell 4

THE CONTROVERSY

Prior to Porter's 1995 and 1997 publications on urban revitalisation, inner-city markets were not seen as attractive sites for business creation or expansion. Influential scholarly works portrayed urban minority communities as declining areas plagued by a loss of economic base, disinvestment in housing stock and low rates of business formation (Fusfeld 1973, Schaffer 1973, Bates 1989). Because residents often have low and variable personal incomes, low rates of labour force participation and high unemployment rates, minority communities tend to have weak internal markets. This weakness, in turn, is reflected in the attenuated state of the local business community serving those markets (see, for example, Caplovitz 1967, Fusfeld and Bates 1984, Gittell and Thompson 1999).

Multi-dimensional disinvestment processes undermining the economic base of inner-city communities having predominantly minority populations included net outflows of capital, not only financial assets but housing and public infrastructure as well (Fusfeld 1973, Schaffer 1973). Housing abandonment was common; schools, roads, sewers and other infrastructures were often depreciating faster than replacement investment; banks were redlining. Business profits, on balance, flowed out, supporting little reinvestment (Schaffer 1973). Selective out-migration in many inner cities was reducing population overall, while simultaneously raising the proportion of residents who were subsisting on poverty-level incomes or exhibiting weak attachment to the labour force. Low household incomes were exacerbated by weak internal income flows and a resultant low regional multiplier (Oakland et al. 1971). The portrait emerging from these studies indicated that these sites were decidedly not attractive to entrepreneurs seeking underserved market niches.

Previous research utilizing the CBO small firm database explored the attractiveness of urban minority communities as sites for operating small businesses. Findings indicated that these areas were high risk sites. Analysis of small business viability in very large metropolitan areas indicated that white-owned firms operating outside minority communities were, on average, larger and less likely to go out of business than firms operating inside minority communities (Bates 1989). Black-owned firms as well did better, on average, by locating in non-minority—as opposed to minority—communities. Further analysis indicated that selling to a predominantly minority clientele, after controlling for firm and owner traits, was positively associated with firm closure and discontinuance of operations (Bates 1997b). These findings were broadly consistent with the dominant literature depicting urban minority areas as regions experiencing net disinvestment (Fusfeld 1973).

Michael Porter launched a new trajectory in urban research, taking the position that disinvestment had gone too far: inner-city, predominantly minority communities by the 1990s had become promising sites for business creation and expansion (1995). Despite their low average incomes, 'the consumer market of inner-city residents represents the most immediate opportunity for inner-city-based entrepreneurs . . . ' (Porter 1997: 14). These opportunities had been overlooked in part because of the 'many misperceptions and biases about inner cities and their opportunities—what economists call information imperfections' (Porter 1997: 17). Inner-city markets are poorly served, according to Porter, resulting in substantial unmet local demand, particularly in retailing and consumer services (1995). Despite low average resident incomes, high population density translates into 'an immense market with substantial purchasing power' (p. 58). Making this opportunity even more attractive to potential business entrants is the fact that 'there tend to be few competitors serving it' (Porter 1997: 14).

When Professor Porter boldly asserted that 'the economic potential of inner cities has been largely untapped', he cited none of the applicable literature summarized above. Regarding the magnitude of this untapped potential, reasons why it had remained untapped and the best methods for tapping it, Porter initially offered only broad generalizations and anecdotal evidence. An avalanche of scholarly criticism was quickly forthcoming. Porter 'has greatly underestimated the obstacles to revitalisation of inner-city economies' (Blakely and Small 1997: 181). 'Porter can validly be criticized for producing a superficial analysis of urban problems that relies upon overgeneralizations for evidence' (Bates 1997a: 39). These representative statements were certainly not the harshest of the criticisms levelled at Porter (see, for example, various readings in Boston and Ross 1997).

On the specific issue of business opportunity stemming from substantial unmet local demand, Porter's follow-up evidence to date consists of data measuring household purchasing power in selected cities. Launched by Michael Porter, the Initiative for a Competitive Inner City (ICIC) undertook the task of measuring this unmet demand. Resulting studies were often long on rhetoric, offering weak empirical analyses built upon methodologies that were not transparent. 'Communities with enormous buying power are going unserved,' unmet demand 'reaches 60 per cent' in some inner-city markets; retail firms have 'overlooked the promise of the inner-city market' (ICIC and the Boston Consulting Group 1998).

It is not worthwhile to review various ICIC reports in detail. They are often marred by journalistic tone, weak evidence and unsupportable conclusions but, in their defence, they were never designed to win over the academic sceptics (see, for example, PriceWaterhouseCoopers 1998). All parties agree that the ICIC studies lacked comprehensive information on the characteristics of businesses currently serving household clienteles in America's urban minority neighbourhoods. In fact, they did not contain any measures of business viability or of the capacity of firms to serve urban households. Porter acknowledges that 'this remains an important priority for future research' (1997: 25).

Porter's underserved market hypothesis has, in fact, been indirectly addressed by scholars tracking the large-scale expansion of Korean immigrant-owned firms in urban African American neighbourhoods. Yoon (1997), for example, claimed that absence of competition attracted Korean merchants to Black communities in Chicago: they were simply 'filling a vacuum . . . ' (p. 34). In this vein, Light and Bonacich (1988) observed that Korean small businesses in Black Los Angeles neighbourhoods 'were akin to the middlemen of colonial regions . . . ' (p. 393).

The conventional wisdom on the attractiveness of investing in inner-city minority communities evolved in a time period (1960s–1980s) of rapid net out-migration of population and large-scale disinvestments by established enterprises. These same areas often stabilized in the 1990s (Hill and Brennan 2005). Substantial progress—population stabilization, even slight poverty reduction—was apparent between 1990 and 2000 in many census tracts where concentrated poverty had been pronounced in 2000 (Berube and Frey 2005). The fact that these areas might have been poor prospects for small business creation in the 1970s and early 1980s (Bates 1989) does not logically indicate that below-average returns awaited new firms venturing into these same areas in the 1990s (Bates 2006). The very disinvestment process documented by scholars like Schaffer (1973) may have reduced the capacity of local businesses to the point where the previously harsh small business operating environment was erased. The logic of Porter's underserved market position indeed suggests that the earlier period of disinvestment was overdone.

One study actually addressed the Porter hypothesis, utilizing data and methodology that are capable of supporting empirical results. Alwitt and Donley (1997) analyzed numbers and types of retail establishments in 53 City of Chicago neighbourhoods, using individual zip codes as their 'neighbourhood' proxy. Comparing the retail presence in Chicago's poorest zip codes to the rest of the city, they calculated the number of retail outlets per million dollars in household purchasing power. They found a city-wide ratio of 0.413 retail outlets per million dollars in purchasing power, with retail presence thus measured not differing significantly in the poor zip code areas versus the rest of the city. No evidence that poor inner-city neighbourhoods with 'enormous buying power are going unserved' (ICIC and the Boston Consulting Group 1998) was forthcoming.

The case for expecting a riskier operating environment for small businesses serving consumer markets in inner-city neighbourhoods logically rests in part on the same basis as Porter's hypothesis: information asymmetries, misperceptions and the like. These certainly do exist. Constrained credit availability, even redlining, does appear to afflict many urban minority communities (Immergluck 2004). Relatively higher levels of financial market development tend to produce higher levels of economic performance (and vice versa) in impacted areas (Guiso et al. 2004). We expect that constrained credit availability indeed reduces small business viability in inner-city minority communities, other factors constant. A high degree of information asymmetry appears to typify these areas, causing credit rationing and constituting failure of the credit market to function efficiently (Craig et al.2007). Stiglitz and Weiss (1981) argue that the lack of perfect information on borrowers/credit markets causes 'adverse' effect problems, which tend to harm borrowers located in urban minority communities. This is a consequence of different borrowers having different probabilities of repaying their loans. Since the expected return to the bank on a loan obviously depends on the probability of repayment, the bank seeks to identify borrowers who are more likely to repay. Yet, it is difficult to identify such borrowers. Often the bank will use various screening devices to do so. Inner-city location is a possible screening device; firms with this trait may be assigned to a high risk category by the bank. As a high risk, the loan applicant may be rejected outright or offered harsh loan terms such as a high rate of interest. However, borrowers who are willing to pay higher interest rates may be worse risks. As the interest rate rises, the average riskiness of the resultant borrowers thus increases and this may actually result in a lowering of the bank's expected profits from lending.

Under conditions of adverse selection, the demand for credit may exceed the supply in equilibrium. The presence of an excess demand for loans may cause unsatisfied borrowers to offer to pay higher interest rates to the bank but the bank will not lend to them because these borrowers may be a worse risk than the average current borrower. Hence, competitive forces will not cause the supply of loans to equal demand, and credit is rationed. Stiglitz and Weiss (1981) argue that when borrowers are distinguishable in terms of some trait (race) positively linked to higher default risk, the lender may choose to deny credit to the entire group. This is the classic Stiglitz-Weiss redlining argument.

The decisions of insurance companies providing casualty insurance to firms located in inner-city minority communities exactly parallel those of commercial banks as far as information asymmetries are concerned. As in small business lending, the empirical evidence points towards a reality of constrained access to casualty insurance for firms located in such urban areas (Squires 2003).

We address the Porter hypothesis in the next section, utilizing CBO data describing young firms—those formed in the 1986–92 period—and tracking their survival through the fall of 1996. The 5,000 plus young firms examined below were in operation in 1992 and all relied upon households (as opposed to business and government) as a major source of sales revenues. Further, our analysis includes only those firms located within metropolitan areas in the US. Our primary measure of young firm viability is survival—those still operating in late 1996 are the survivors; those closing down or discontinuing operations are viewed as less viable. Robustness of our firm survival analysis is investigated utilizing an alternative measure of firm viability: profitability.

Controlling statistically for firm and owner traits, we interpret a finding of minority-clientele-oriented firms surviving at higher rates than firms
serving non-minority clients as supporting Porter's hypothesis. We identify 'minority-clientele-oriented' firms as those operating in urban minority
neighbourhoods *and* serving a client base comprised of 50 per cent or more
minority customers. The survival record of minority-clientele-oriented
firms is contrasted with that of young small businesses operating in non-
minority neighbourhoods and serving a clientele made up of 50 per cent or
more non-minority customers.[2]

ANALYSIS OF SURVIVAL PATTERNS AMONG
YOUNG FIRMS OPERATING IN URBAN AREAS

Our analysis utilizes CBO data describing only those urban firms that
sold products to household clients. Well over half of all urban firms did
not identify households as a major client group in their CBO survey
responses; most of these reported that their targeted market consisted
of selling products to other private firms: all such firms were dropped.
The small firm data were further constrained to include only those
firms with owners actively involved in running the business in 1992.
Attempting to weed out 'casual' businesses, we excluded those reporting annual sales revenues under $5,000 in 1992, a step that reduced the
sample size substantially. Remaining young, urban, household-oriented
firms were tracked through 1996, and those shutting down/halting
operations were labelled 'discontinued'; firms still operating in 1996
with either the 1992 owner of record or a new owner were 'active', and
the first objective of our econometric analysis is to delineate the active
from the discontinued ventures.

The CBO data offer unique advantages to urban researchers in the sense
of providing very large, representative samples of young urban small businesses, each of which is described in rich detail. To delineate those active in
1996 from those that discontinued during the 1992–96 period, we utilize
firm and owner traits as explanatory variables.

A large, growing body of literature reviewed briefly at the beginning
of this chapter predicts increased survival odds for well capitalized small
firms that are run by owners having the human capital (expertise, experience) appropriate for operating a viable venture. Owner human capital is
described in the CBO data by multiple qualitative and quantitative measures of education and experience. Two types of work experience strongly
predict improved firm survival prospects. First, prior work experience in
a business whose products were similar to those provided by the owner's
current venture is important (Bruderl et al. 1992, Fairlie and Robb 2008).
Second, prior experience working in a family-owned business increases the

likelihood of young firm success and survival (Fairlie and Robb 2008). Furthermore, previous findings indicate that highly educated owners are more likely than poorly educated ones to operate firms that remain active (Bates 1990). Quantity of owner effort, furthermore, shapes business outcomes: part-time businesses exhibit higher discontinuance rates than full-time operations (Bates 1997b).

The dynamics of small firm survival depend upon a variety of factors beyond owner human capital, hours of work and financial investment in the firm. Very young firms are much more volatile and failure-prone than ventures that have built up customer goodwill and an established client base (Jovanovic 1982, Bates 1990). A possible short-cut to successful firm creation entails entering business by purchasing an ongoing firm that already has an established customer base.

All of these explanations are really hypotheses used in this study to explain closure patterns among young household-oriented firms doing business in metropolitan America. Once these firm and owner traits are controlled for statistically, owner demographic traits—race and gender— are expected to have little impact upon firm closure patterns. We undertake our analysis of isolating possible impacts of a firm's strategic choice of target market by first controlling for impacts of the applicable characteristics discussed above.

Small businesses choosing to sell products to an urban, predominantly minority household clientele has been variously described above as (1) a brilliant strategy (Porter), (2) as fraught with uncertainty due to powerful information asymmetries and various inner-city market characteristics. Finally, Borjas and Bronars (1989) further complicate matters by suggesting that minority entrepreneurs are often forced to self-select into this market segment because consumer discrimination limits the range of minority ventures that white non-minority households are willing to patronize. In light of these diverse hypotheses, we proceed to our empirical analysis of firm survival and discontinuance with no *a priori* expectations about target-market viability.

Table 3.2 summarizes the traits of three groups of young urban firms that were actively selling their products to urban clients in 1992. Statistics describing the entire sample of young urban household-oriented firms (column 1) are presented to provide a reference point, a basis for comparison for the subgroups of interest: (1) firms serving minority clients that are located in minority neighbourhoods (column 2) and (2) firms in non-minority neighbourhoods that are serving non-minority clients (column 3). Differences in outcomes are striking: 29.0 per cent of the former and 21.2 per cent of the latter had shut down business operations by late 1996. Firms in minority neighbourhoods serving minority clients were 36.7 per cent more likely to discontinue operations, relative to firms in non-minority neighbourhoods catering to a non-minority client base [(29.0—21.2)/21.2 = 36.7 per cent] (see Table 3.2).

Table 3.2   Firm and Owner Traits: Young Small Businesses Located in
Metropolitan Areas (includes firms selling products to households only)

	All Urban Small Businesses Serving Households	Firms Serving Neighborhood Clienteles Only	
		Minority Clientele Only	Non-minority White Clientele Only
A. Owner Characteristics			
1. Demographic Traits:			
% minority	14.6%	57.6%	15.1%
% male	67.0%	64.2%	64.3%
% immigrant	14.1%	42.3%	17.4%
2. Human-Capital Traits:			
% high school or less	29.1%	37.3%	36.1%
% college, 1–3 years	32.6%	25.1%	33.7%
% college graduate	38.4%	37.6%	30.1%
% with experience working in this line of business	54.5%	42.3%	52.1%
% with experience working in a family firm	19.0%	14.0%	20.2%
Hours worked in the firm in 1992 (mean)	1,868 hrs.	1,732 hrs.	1,735 hrs.
B. Firm Characteristics			
Total sales revenues in 1992 (mean)	$117,681	$76,276	$124,199
% discontinued operations by late 1996	23.2%	29.0%	21.2%
Startup capitalization (mean)	$28,922	$30,302	$45,259
% with paid employees	25.5%	23.8%	33.0%
% started in 1991, 1992	49.7%	66.1%	52.3%
% serving neighborhood market	23.5%	100%	100%
% serving minority clientele	13.9%	100%	0

Perhaps underlying their greater tendency to close down, the minor-ity-neighbourhood-oriented ventures, on average, were much smaller in terms of sales revenues and began operations with less owner invest-ment of financial capital than their non-minority-oriented counterparts.

Annual sales averaged $76,276 for the former and $124,199 for the latter, while corresponding amounts of start-up capital were $30,302 and $45,259, respectively (Table 3.2). Even more striking was the pattern of owner demographics across these market segments: 57.6 per cent of the minority-neighbourhood subgroup of firms were owned by minorities, while 84.9 per cent of the firm owners in the non-minority neighbourhoods were white (Table 3.2). In terms of the demographics of urban firms serving household clients, the predominant pattern is minority firms in minority neighbourhoods and non-minority-owned firms in non-minority communities.

Summary statistics alone do not demonstrate that the minority-community-oriented firms are more prone to go out of business *because of* their decision to target a minority household clientele. Relative to their non-minority-oriented counterparts, they are younger, thinly capitalized small businesses and their owners are less likely to possess the kinds of operational experience that are associated with heightened survival prospects (Table 3.2). To isolate possible negative consequences of targeting a minority clientele, we proceed by controlling econometrically for differences in firm and owner traits. This is undertaken in Table 3.3's logistic regression exercise: firms active in late 1996 are assigned a dependent value of one; discontinued firms are zeros.

This logit exercise delineates firms discontinuing operations in the 1992–96 period from those still active at the end of 1996. Our CBO sample of 4,980 small firms includes all firms that meet the selection criteria of being young, urban, active in 1992 and household-oriented regarding targeted clients. The underlying CBO data (and regression results) are weighted to be nationally representative of small firms meeting these selection criteria. By late 1996, 23.2 percent of these urban businesses had discontinued and closed down.

The geographic scope of market served by the individual CBO small businesses has been defined and segmented by the 'neighbourhood market' explanatory variable, subdividing firms into (1) those catering to a specific neighbourhood market versus (2) those serving city-, county-, region- or nation-wide clients. This variable was defined using owner responses to the CBO survey instrument (see the detailed variable definitions in the Appendix A: The CBO Database). Similarly, the 'minority market' variable separates the firms into subgroups of those selling to household clients who are either (1) predominantly minority or (2) predominantly non-minority. These two binary variables were then interacted to create the 'minority neighbourhood' explanatory variable.

Findings of Table 3.3's logistic regression exercise include a highly negative (–.692), statistically significant minority neighbourhood variable coefficient, unambiguously indicating that targeting this niche is strongly linked to heightened firm closure prospects, other things equal. This finding stands

Table 3.3   Logistic Regression Analysis—Among Firms Operating in 1992, Delineating Small Businesses Still Active at the End of 1996 from Closures (includes firms selling products to households only)

Explantory Variables	Regression Coefficient	Coefficient Standard Error
Constant	−2.841*	.534
Education:		
College: 1–3 years	−.073	.082
College graduate	.219*	.099
Graduate school	.892*	.139
Prior work experience in a similar business	.223*	.073
Prior work experience in a family member's business	.275*	.094
Owner age in years	.172*	.024
Owner age squared	−.002*	.00027
Financial capital at startup ($000)	.001*	.0007
Firm started de novo	−.214*	.105
Year entered, 1990, 1991 or 1992	−.471*	.074
Owner labor input in hours (00)	−.002	.004
Minority-owned firm	−.003	.132
Immigrant-owned firm	.681*	.139
Female-owned firm	−.270*	.074
Employer firm	.786*	.109
Minority market orientation	−.031	.142
Geographic scope of market: neighborhood	.237*	.100
Minority market*neighborhood interaction	−.692*	.223
N	4,980	
−2 Log L	4,904.6	
Chi square	486.9	

* Statistically significant at the .05 significance level.

in contradiction to Porter's hypothesis of attractive opportunities rooted in underserved markets.

Heightened likelihood of closure is not positively associated with a neighbourhood orientation per se; indeed, the neighbourhood-market coefficient was positive and statistically significant (Table 3.3). Small firm closure, furthermore, was not associated with the minority-market coefficient (which was small and insignificant statistically). It was only the interaction of these two factors (minority and neighbourhood) that powerfully predicted small firm discontinuance of business operations. This finding, coupled with the insignificance of the minority-market trait per se, causes us to reject the hypothesis that small businesses can achieve viability most readily by targeting household clients in underserved inner-city minority communities. Logistic regression findings indicate that firm survival chances are not enhanced by pursuing this strategy.

The factors that predict firm survival through 1996 largely mirror those highlighted by previous studies of small business discontinuance patterns (Table 3.3). The college-graduate owner, the entrepreneur with prior experience in a similar line of business or a family member's business: these are the owners whose firms are most likely to be active at the end of 1996. The very youngest firms, the poorly capitalized ventures, the smaller firms lacking paid employees, in contrast, are the ones most prone to discontinue operations. Capitalization and employees, although statistically significant factors in the Table 3.3 logit exercise, are actually correlated; dropping either variable causes the statistical significance of the other to rise.

Minority owners, although strongly attached to the neighbourhood minority-market niche, were neither more nor less likely to experience firm closure than non-minority owners, controlling for firm and owner traits. The firms of immigrant owners, in contrast, were in fact more likely to remain in operation, other things equal.

Several tests of robustness of our Table 3.3 logistic regression analysis findings reinforce our rejection of Porter's underserved market hypothesis. First, we dropped neighbourhood-oriented firms and re-estimated Table 3.3's logit exercise solely for firms serving broader city, regional or national markets (the household clientele prerequisite was retained). We found that 10.7 per cent of the firms serving these broader geographically defined markets reported that their clients were predominantly minorities. The minority orientation, once again, was found, in the logit model context, to be a small, statistically insignificant factor having no explanatory power for delineating firms still active in late 1996 from the closures.

Finally, we compared the profitability of the minority-clientele-oriented neighbourhood firms to their non-minority counterparts (as defined in Table 3.2, columns 2 and 3). Our measure—taxable income as reported on the 1992 federal income-tax return—was crude conceptually and was recorded in the CBO data only in broad interval form (zero to $10,000, for example). Further, item non-response was high, reflecting the common aversion of small business owners to report profits on survey questionnaire forms. Abstracting from these issues, an underlying pattern of lower profitability typified the firms serving the minority-neighbourhood market niche. Greater viability, whether measured by closure or profit differentials, characterized the small businesses operating in the non-minority neighbourhood markets.

CONCLUDING REMARKS

We have analyzed survival patterns of new and recently formed small businesses that were located in the nation's metropolitan areas, paying particular attention to the longevity of those choosing to target local household clients in minority communities. Our analysis of very large, representative samples of firms active in 1992 revealed that neighbourhood businesses catering to a neighbourhood minority clientele were over 36 per cent more likely than their counterparts selling predominantly to non-minority clients to close down and discontinue operations by year end 1996. Controlling statistically for firm and owner traits—owner human capital and demographics, firm capitalization and other characteristics—the minority neighbourhood niche was shown to be strongly related to small business closure and discontinuance of operations.

Our empirical findings do not support Michael Porter's controversial claim that urban minority neighbourhoods offer attractive opportunities to household-oriented businesses, such as retail and consumer-service firms. The underserved market that Dr. Porter and the ICIC claim to have discovered in the inner cities of this nation was not discernible. Our further analysis of metro-area firms serving household regional and national clienteles revealed that slightly over 10 per cent of them derived most of their sales revenues from minority clients. Yet these businesses, which might or might not have been located in minority neighbourhoods, did neither better nor worse than firms that sold predominantly to non-minority clients. Whether neighbourhood or city-wide in orientation regarding geographic scope of their targeted market, new and recently formed urban small businesses derived no advantage, regarding survival or longevity, from serving a clientele consisting of urban minority customers predominantly.

Our findings certainly do not rule out the possibility that some type of firm, such as a big-box Wal-Mart venture, might find a receptive environment in an inner-city minority community. Nor do we claim that individual small firm ventures are doomed to marginality if they choose to do business in urban minority neighbourhoods. We have not examined survival patterns of small firms that serve client segments—other business customers, government clients and the like—outside of the household market sector. Our analysis has simply shown that the likelihood of surviving the rigours of the early stages of small business operation are lower in the minority neighbourhood niche, relative to other market segments in urban America.

The presumed advantages that are implied in Michael Porter's underserved market hypothesis motivated us to undertake our analysis of small firm survival patterns. We did so by narrowly focusing upon the small firm subset that would potentially gain most if the inner-city minority household niche did offer rich opportunities to retail and consumer-service firms in the form of abundant purchasing power and little competition. On balance, the evidence considered here suggests to us that Porter's hypothesis of underserved markets is without merit.

APPENDIX A

Variable Definitions, Table 3.3 Logistic Regression

Regression analysis dependent variable—active (or survive): Firm stayed in business over the period 1992–96, irrespective of presence or absence of ownership changes, then active = 1; otherwise, active = 0.

Female-owned firm: Firm owner is female, then female-owned firm = 1; otherwise, female-owned firm = 0.

Minority-owned firm: Firm owner is Hispanic, Black, Asian, or Native American. In multi-owner firms, the minority-owned share is 51 per cent or higher, then minority-owned firm = 1; otherwise, minority-owned firm = 0.

Immigrant-owned firm: Firm owner is an immigrant (not born in the US), then immigrant-owned firm = 1; otherwise, immigrant-owned firm = 0.

Owner age in years: self-explanatory.

Owner age squared: self explanatory.

High school (excluded variable): Education level of owner, has high school degree only or less, then high school = 1; otherwise, high school = 0.

College, 1–3 years: Education level of owner, has some college, then college 1–3 years = 1; otherwise, college 1–3 years = 0.

College graduate: Education level of owner, has a college (bachelor's) degree, then college graduate = 1; otherwise, college graduate = 0.

Graduate school: Education level of owner, has some post-graduate education (master's, Ph.D., etc.), then graduate school = 1; otherwise, graduate school = 0.

Prior work experience in a similar business: Previously worked in a business similar to the one now owned, then this variable = 1; otherwise, this variable = 0.

Prior work experience in a family member's business: Has worked in the past for a parent or relative who owned a business, then this variable = 1; otherwise, this variable = 0.

Firm started de novo: Founded the business (compared with bought, inherited, received as a gift), then this variable = 1; otherwise, this variable = 0.

Owner labour input in hours: total hours worked in a year, 1992.

Year entered, 1990, 1991, or 1992: Firm age is 0–2 years in 1992 (firm started 1990–92), then this variable = 1; otherwise, this variable = 0.

Financial capital at start-up—dollar amount of financial capital used at start up to launch the business.

Employer firm : Firm has at least one employee, then employer firm = 1; otherwise, employer firm = 0.

Minority market orientation: Firm serves a minority market (clientele) 50 per cent+ of clients are minorities; then this variable = 1; otherwise, this variable = 0.

Geographic scope of market—neighbourhood: Firm serves a local market, a neighbourhood clientele and not a city-wide, county-wide, regional or broader market, then this variable = 1; otherwise, this variable = 0.

Minority market*neighbourhood interaction: Firm serves a local market that is predominantly minority, then minority market*neighbourhood interaction = 1; otherwise, minority market*neighbourhood interaction = 0.

APPENDIX B

The CBO Database:

The 1992 Characteristics of Business Owners (CBO) Survey is the third survey of its kind conducted by the Bureau of the Census (the first two were conducted for 1982 and 1987; it was unfunded for 1997). Three surveys were conducted each time: a sole proprietor survey, an owner survey for each owner in partnerships and S corporations,[3] and a firm survey for each partnership and S corporation (C corporations were excluded). Responses from these three surveys were aggregated to create the CBO database. Selected additional information was drawn from administrative records. The resulting owner data file contains 116,589 records while the firm survey has 78,147 records; the differential reflects multiple owners of the same firm responding to the survey. More than 40,000 employer businesses are on this file. Women and minorities were over-sampled to allow researchers to more reliably study these businesses and business owners. The CBO sample includes businesses with more than $500 in receipts, but we imposed a $5,000 minimum cut-off for purposes of this study.

Many individuals that did respond did not fill out the survey in its entirety. Thus, item non-response varied and was high for selected items like firm profitability. The addition of each additional variable into the econometric model specifications resulted in the exclusion of additional businesses. For this reason, only the variables that were deemed absolutely necessary for the regression analysis were included.

NOTES

1. The research in this chapter was conducted while one of the authors was a Special Sworn Status researcher of the US Census Bureau at the Center for Economic Studies. Research results and conclusions expressed are those of the authors and do not necessarily reflect the views of the Census Bureau. This chapter has been screened to ensure that no confidential data are revealed. The data can be obtained at a Census Research Data Center or at the Center for Economic Studies (CES) only after approval by the CES and IRS. See http://www.ces.census.gov/ for details on the application and approval process.
2. The nature of the Census Bureau questionnaire utilized to create the CBO database rules out the possibility of a respondent identifying its customer base as precisely 50 per cent minority and 50 per cent non-minority. In fact,

respondents tend to report that clients are either overwhelmingly minority or largely non-minority; few responses fall in mid ranges.
3. Up to 10 owners.

BIBLIOGRAPHY

Alwitt, L. and Donley, T. (1997) 'Retail stores in poor urban neighbourhoods', The Journal of Consumer Affairs, 31(1): 139–64.

Bates, T. (1989) 'Small business viability in the urban ghetto', Journal of Regional Science, 29(4): 625–43.

——(1990). 'Entrepreneur human capital inputs and small business longevity', Review of Economics and Statistics, 72(4): 551–59.

——(1997a) 'Michael Porter's conservative urban agenda will not revitalize America's inner cities: what will?', Economic Development Quarterly 11(1): 39–44.

——(1997b), Race, Self-Employment and Upward Mobility, Baltimore: Johns Hopkins University Press.

——(2006) 'The urban development potential of Black-owned businesses', Journal of the American Planning Association, 72(2): 227–37.

Berube, A. and Frey, D. (2005) 'A decade of mixed blessings: urban and suburban poverty in census 2000', in A. Berube, B. Katz and R. Lang (eds) Redefining Urban and Suburban America: Volume II, Washington, DC: Brookings Institution Press.

Bhatt, N. and Tang, S. (2002) 'Determinants of repayment in microcredit: evidence from programs in the United States', International Journal of Urban and Regional Research, 26(2): 360–76.

Blakely, E. and Small, L. (1997) 'Michael Porter: new gilder of ghettos', in T. Boston and C. Ross (eds) The Inner City, New Brunswick, NJ: Transaction.

Borjas, G. and Bronars, S. (1989) 'Consumer discrimination and self-employment', Journal of Political Economy, 97(3): 581–605.

Boston, T. and Ross, C. (eds) (1997) The Inner City, New Brunswick, NJ: Transaction.

Bruderl, J., Preisendorfer, P. and Ziegler, R. (1992) 'Survival chances of newly founded organizations', American Sociological Review, 57(2): 227–42.

Caplovitz, D. (1967) The Poor Pay More, New York: Free Press.

Craig, B., Jackson, W. and Thompson, J. (2007) 'Small firm credit market discrimination, Small Business Administration guaranteed lending, and local market economic performance', Annals of the American Academy of Political and Social Science, 613: 73–94.

Deparle, J. (1998) 'What welfare-to-work really means', The New York Times Magazine, 20(December): 89–90.

Doeringer, P. (1999) 'Comment on Ross and Thompson', in R. Ferguson and W. Dickens (eds) Urban Problems and Community Development, Washington, DC: Brookings Institution Press.

Edgcomb, E., Klein, J. and Clark, P. (1996). The Practice of Microenterprise in the US, Washington, DC: Aspen Institute.

Fairlie, R. and Robb, A. (2008) Race and Entrepreneurial Success: Black-, Asian- and white-owned businesses in the United States, Cambridge, MA: MIT Press.

Fusfeld, D. (1973) The Basic Economics of the Urban Racial Crisis, New York: Holt, Rinehart and Winston.

Fusfeld, D. and Bates, T. (1984) Political Economy of the Urban Ghetto, Carbondale: Southern Illinois University Press.

Gittell, R. and Thompson, J. P. (1999) 'Inner-city business development and entrepreneurship: new directions for policy and research', in R. Ferguson and W.T. Dickens (eds) Urban Problems and Community Development, Washington, DC: Brookings Institution Press.

Guiso, L., Sapienza, P. and Zingales, L. (2004). 'Does local financial development matter?', Quarterly Journal of Economics, 119(4): 929–69.

Hill, E. and Brennan, J. (2005) 'America's central cities and the location of work: can cities compete with their suburbs?', Journal of the American Planning Association, 71(4): 411–32.

Immergluck, D. (2004) Credit in the Community, Armonk, NY: M.E. Sharpe.

ICIC and the Boston Consulting Group (1998) 'The business case for pursuing retail opportunities in the inner city,' Working Paper, Initiative for a Competitive Inner City (ICIC), June.

Jovanovic, B. (1982) 'Selection and the evolution of industry', Econometrica, 50(2): 649–70.

Jurik, N. (2005) Bootstrap Dreams: US microenterprise development in an era of welfare reform, Ithaca, NY: Cornell University Press.

Light, I. and Bonacich, E. (1988) Immigrant Entrepreneurs: Koreans in Los Angeles, 1965–1982, Berkeley: University of California Press.

Oakland, W., Sparrow, F. and Stettler, H. L. (1971) 'Ghetto multipliers: a case study in Hough', Journal of Regional Science, 11(3): 337–45.

Porter, M. (1995) 'The competitive advantage of the inner city', Harvard Business Review, 73(3): 55–71.

——— (1997) 'New strategies for inner-city economic development', Economic Development Quarterly, 11(1): 11–27.

PriceWaterhouseCoopers (1998) The Inner-City Shopper: A strategic perspective, Boston: ICIC.

Raheim, S. and Alter, C. (1995) Self-Employment Investment Demonstration: Final evaluation report, Washington, D.C.: Corporation for Enterprise Development.

Schaffer, R. (1973) Income Flows in Urban Poverty Areas, Lexington, MA: Lexington Books.

Servon, L. and Bates, T. (1998) 'Microenterprise as an exit route from poverty', Journal of Urban Affairs, 20(4): 419–41.

Squires, G. (2003) 'Racial profiling, insurance style: insurance redlining and the uneven development of metropolitan areas', Journal of Urban Affairs, 25(4): 319–410.

Stiglitz, J. and Weiss, A. (1981) 'Credit rationing in markets with imperfect information', American Economic Review, 71(3): 393–410.

Taub, R. (1998) 'Making the adoption across cultures and societies: a report on an attempt to clone the Grameen Bank in southern Arkansas', Journal of Developmental Entrepreneurship, 3(1): 53–69.

Yoon, I.-J. (1997) On My Own, Chicago: University of Chicago Press.

4 Ethnic Entrepreneurs and Urban Regeneration

Trevor Jones and Monder Ram

INTRODUCTION

Ever since Lord Scarman's report on the Brixton disorders of 1981, with its focus on entrepreneurship as a means of addressing racialised disadvantage and alienation, official support for ethnic minority business (EMB) has been a feature of the British policy agenda. Though commitment has waxed and waned, the state-sponsored EMB support system has become an established and ever-expanding presence, with the former government's aim of promoting 'enterprise for all' representing a further thrust in this direction (Blackburn and Ram 2006). In parallel to, and historically pre-dating, this question of how the state might contribute to EMB development, attention has also been paid to how far EMB itself might contribute to the development of the local economies in which it is embedded. Prompted by a widespread 1970s perception of an inner-cities crisis, social commentators like Forrester (1978) were struck by the meteoric rise of South Asian shops and services swimming heroically against the flood tide of urban decay. From this it has been inferred that entrepreneurial 'new blood' might offer more to urban regeneration than the conventional bureaucratic planning approaches (Werbner 1990), and the economic renewal effect of ethnic enterprise is also a prominent theme in Sassen's (1996) influential work on urban restructuring. More recently it has even been suggested that, with its advantageous transnational trading and investment connections, EMB actually occupies pole position in local economies striving to cope with the new challenges of globalisation (McEwan et al. 2005). Moreover, in a new world of inter-city competitiveness and urban re-branding, the 'exotic' products of EMB also offer a colourful exciting multi-cultural trump card for places dealt an otherwise poor hand by economic history and the forces of capitalist restructuring (Webster 2001).

Much as we ourselves are enthused by such idealism, as researchers who have spent the past two decades damping down fevers of over-excitement about EMB, we feel bound to inject a note of realism. Such bullish accounts of dynamism ignore a lengthy catalogue of evidence that many, if not most, ethnic minority small business owners are stuck in impossibly competitive and precarious market niches, are acutely undercapitalised and labour-intensive, work long hours supported by family and co-ethnic workers and struggle to survive in hostile inner-city environments (see Barrett et al. 1996, Macarenhas-Keyes 2006, Ram and Jones 2008 for a review of this evidence). Given that much EMB is thus preoccupied with the struggle simply to stay alive, often aggravated by all manner of discriminatory barriers, we wonder how it can be expected to breathe life into other areas. In this chapter, we shall argue that, if not handled carefully, the promotion of ethnic minority entrepreneurs as agents of renaissance might degenerate into little more than development on the cheap, with the true costs off-loaded on to the shoulders of those least able to bear them. In the spirit of constructive criticism, we shall suggest ways in which this might be avoided.

SWIMMING AGAINST THE TIDE

When contemplating the rise of ethnic entrepreneurialism in countries like Britain, the word 'counterintuitive' immediately springs to mind. That some of society's most disadvantaged socially excluded groups located in its most deprived urban environments should be at the cutting edge of the entrepreneurial revolution appears as a quite stunning reversal of every known law of economics, sociology and even gravity itself. Among scholars in the field, the most widely touted explanation of this glaring paradox hinges upon the unusually dense *social capital* networks characteristic of close-knit, immigrant-origin communities, an informal source of a rich array of business resources, supporting notably high self-employment rates among South Asians and Chinese (see Ram and Jones 2008 for a summary of this literature). In parallel with this, Werbner (1990) makes the illuminating point that, as outsiders, new immigrants like the Asians of the 1960s bring a completely fresh eye to the possibilities of ostensibly hopeless locations. Perceived by native business owners as irredeemably worn out and commercially unviable, they are seen as places of opportunity by the newcomers. In a similar vein, Blackburn and Ram (2006: 77) recognise that 'situations of adversity can provide opportunities to respond in an entrepreneurial fashion', though they would caution that this is often an uphill battle. Continuing the theme, Porter (1995) presents the inner city as actually offering competitive advantages to private entrepreneurs, especially in terms of lower costs. Abandoned by its previous incumbents, the inner city might almost be seen as a slate wiped clean on which a new generation can write their own, fresh version of history.

At this point, the sceptic would have to question whether enterprise in depressed urban black-spots is genuinely a matter of hyper-alert lateral thinkers spotting gold nuggets among the dross or a rather desperate survival strategy for those so lacking in resources as to have no alternative job or career options. Recent trends for an increasingly educationally qualified rising generation to seek social mobility through professional careers are certainly consistent with the latter view that high self-employment rates were previously a reflection of ethnic minority labour market exclusion (McEvoy and Hafeez

2006). Now that ethnic minority youth enjoys a real career choice, it seems that entrepreneurship is no longer necessary as a fall-back option. Whichever side of this fence we come down on, however, there is no denying the *fact* of ethnic business expansion in problematic urban areas. In particular, it would be no exaggeration to say that the achievements of Asian business have often defied credibility. This is underlined by Tripathi (2003), who talks of the 'collective amnesia' descending on Leicester on the 30th anniversary of the arrival of Ugandan Asian refugees in the city, an event attended at the time by near panic on the part of local government, media and public alike. All this is now forgotten in the light of the estimated 30,000 jobs subsequently created by an extraordinary proliferation and expansion of Ugandan Asian firms. This is a significant contribution to the total jobs in the local labour market. Indeed, this job-creating capacity is one of the most noteworthy features of the Asian enterprise economy (Soni et al. 1987). In one very telling recent case, it was found that a tiny (but representative) sample of 20 Asian catering and clothing firms in the West Midlands accounted for 180 jobs (Jones et al. 2006). Official figures rarely pick up the extent of co-ethnic employment in such firms; there is no reason to assume the experience of such firms is untypical. It goes almost without saying that the bulk of these are located where they are most urgently needed in deprived areas of high unemployment and social exclusion.

Even so, there are numerous question marks hovering over this ostensibly benign tendency. Apart from any other consideration, there are problems with basic data. Such information as we have about EMB employment is fragmented and localised, with no basis for drawing systematic national level conclusions about its contribution. Care needs to be taken to avoid exaggerating, since all research evidence suggests that Asian firms in small retailing rarely employ anyone outside the extended family, and since shop-keeping is still one of the leading sectors for Asian self-employment, this drags down the number of jobs created for non-family members. Where technical and scale considerations require hiring beyond the family, as in lines like restaurant catering and the rag trade, most workers are recruited from within the co-ethnic community, which raises questions about exactly what kind of economic contribution we expect from EMB. If, like Scarman, we see it mainly as a means of inclusion for those otherwise excluded from the labour market, then this process of co-ethnic recruitment does unarguably act to mop up a portion of the surplus labour floating around in heavily unemployed populations such as the Pakistani and Bangladeshi communities. The value of such opportunities for people lacking qualifications and skills and exposed to discrimination cannot be overstated.

As we shall see in the following section, it is possible to envisage wider regenerative potential for EMB on a far grander stage beyond the parochial confines of community and neighbourhood. Yet even at the most modest social and spatial scales, there are doubts about 'whether business ownership can contribute significantly to overcoming the structural conditions that contribute to social exclusion' (Blackburn and Ram 2006: 77). For these authors, the problem is not simply one of employment itself but of multiple disadvantage, in which housing, transport, education and other infrastructural conditions also need to be addressed simultaneously. Even more fundamentally, they see a potential contradiction between ends and means, since the notion of social inclusiveness appears, at first sight, to be the very antithesis of competitive entrepreneurship. According to Boddy and Parkinson (2004: 5), 'the relationships between competitiveness, cohesion and exclusion are not . . . clear' and there is a distinct possibility that 'the impacts of competitive success on the structure of the labour market . . . [might] . . . lead to increased social exclusion'.

Aside from this there are further questions about the quality of EMB jobs. Many of the problems here are those of small firms as a whole, and as Mascarenhas-Keyes (2006) shows, EMBs tend to be smaller than the UK norm. As is well documented, workers in small firms can expect inferior wages and conditions, with an absence of the kind of facilities and personal welfare provision usually taken for granted in larger organisations (Waters 2001, Marlow 2005). In ethnic minority firms, so many of which are cash-strapped and struggling at the margins, such problems tend to be aggravated. As recent studies of the labour process in Asian firms has confirmed, pitifully low wages and long unsocial hours are underpinned by patriarchal practices ensuring that employees become complicit in their own exploitation (Ram et al. 2007). Even more problematically, these studies also find a significant minority of workers to be illegal immigrants or paid below the statutory National Minimum Wage (NMW) (Jones et al. 2004, 2006, Ram et al. 2007).

Serious though these breaches may be, we would strongly urge against unqualified judgementalism, since cutting legal corners is a last resort survival strategy for firms in ferociously competitive markets where they earn a pittance, and there are even cases of entrepreneurs earning so little as to be eligible for family income supplement (Jones et al. 2006). Not only are such entrepreneurs receiving no return on capital investment or management but they are failing even to earn a due wage for their labour. Far from contributing to the elimination of social exclusion, many entrepreneurs themselves are actually victims of that condition.

Equally to the point, such derisory returns are the reward for producing a range of valued contributions like restaurant meals and garments at unfeasibly cheap prices. The unpleasant truth is that this system would be entirely unsustainable if obliged to operate transparently in conformity to regulations. In effect, the state tolerates these informal rule-bending enterprises, since to eliminate them would be to kill off a host of jobs and services, the latter a vital and taken-for-granted lynch pin of the urban social scene (Jones et al. 2006). In the case of Asian-owned clothing manufacture, for example, the main benefits are reaped by large retailers and their customers while the costs and risks are borne by those who toil in the legal twilight to supply goods at sub-market prices. In the case of restaurants, the dining out experience of mainly middle class white customers is widely subsidised by the sub-standard returns of marginal entrepreneurs themselves kept afloat by the presence of underpaid invisible workers (Jones et al. 2006). On this question, Light (2007: 3) reminds us of Max Weber's term 'pariah capitalism' to describe the ascribed role of immigrant entrepreneurs, one of performing economic functions absolutely necessary to the host population but frowned upon as socially inferior and often morally and legally dubious. In effect, they are stigmatised and being made scapegoat for carrying out tasks deemed to be beneath the dignity of mainstream citizens. As will become increasingly apparent, such unacknowledged double standards pervade the entire question of the EMB contribution to the urban economy even to this day.

GLOBALISATION AND TRANSNATIONALISM

As well as arguably revitalising problematic inner-city communities, other, more expansive possibilities for EMB are also envisioned. Recently there have been moves to reposition EMB as a potential leading player within an ever more globalised urban matrix. Notable here are McEwan et al. (2005), with their vision of Birmingham as a local economy, where ethnic entrepreneurs can now draw on their extensive transnational networks to achieve an 'an economic presence that is . . . increasingly significant'. This vision chimes with a growing current literature on the potency of transnational entrepreneurs, a theme encapsulated in Light's claim (2007: 11) that they 'enjoy linguistic and social capital advantages that out fit them advantageously for international commerce and entrepreneurship'. Far from occupying the marginal status of 'ethnic entrepreneurial sweatshops' (McEwan et al. 2005: 920), EMB is now seen as enjoying unique advantages in spearheading the city's bid to compete economically in an age of increasing globalisation. Such is the magnitude of this role reversal that we might paraphrase the famous J. F. Kennedy exhortation, 'Ask not what Birmingham can do for EMB but what EMB can do for Birmingham'. Examples are cited of large, dynamic Chinese and Indian companies in such lines as 'exotic' food manufacture. Highly significant wealth and job creators, these enterprises derive major strength from investment and trading links throughout the co-ethnic diaspora, in effect a social capital network on a vastly enlarged geographical scale. Cited as a further and significantly more technologically advanced example of beneficent transnationalism is a local Chamber of Commerce initiative to recruit IT specialists from India, an exercise which 'has the potential to position Birmingham within global IT networks' (McEwan et al. 2005: 918–19). Given that the Far East and India are now mooted as the future prime movers of the world economy, it is tempting to contemplate the commercial benefits to be showered on cities like Birmingham through their direct stake via ethnic and family links.

As is almost always the case, sober reflection and painstaking evidence reveal a somewhat less inspirational reality. To their credit, McEwan et al.

(2005) are scrupulous in acknowledging that their case study firms may be substantially unrepresentative of the rank and file of EMB. Indeed they are almost certainly companies blessed with exceptionally rich resources derived more from class position than ethnic membership. Be they transnational or parochial, the effectiveness of social capital networks is critically influenced by class (Li et al. 2003), with membership of, for example, an old school tie network likely to yield immeasurably greater economic resources than membership of a working class family in Birmingham Sparkbrook. Bearing this out, a recent survey of the quintessentially transnational Somali business community in Leicester shows that it is members of a minority of richer families who perform best, with the vast mass simply replicating the marginal existence classically typical of EMB as a whole (Ram et al. 2008). While many Somali businesses certainly do have extensive financial and supply links throughout their diaspora, these are not generally sufficient to raise them above the low level EMB business trap. Geographical extensiveness is outweighed by the limitations of class resources in this instance.

In its polarisation between a thin upper layer of fast-track over-achievers and a mass of strugglers, EMB is no more than a microcosm of the structure of business as a whole. Since the historical tendency of capital to concentrate itself into fewer and fewer hands has been public knowledge ever since Marx and others identified it 150 years ago, this should come as no surprise. Yet, as an inconvenient truth incompatible with the utopian tendencies in this field, it is rarely acknowledged anywhere in the enterprise literature, still less in that branch of it specialising in EMB. Elsewhere we have argued that it is this very historical myopia that results in the unrealistic, exceptionalist and constantly repeated exaggerations of the potential of ethnic entrepreneurs. While this may be controversial, what is unarguable is that, wherever it is found and whatever the ethnic identity of its owners, EMB is invariably characterised by a small elite of high profit, fast growth ventures (Ram and Jones 2008), whose orientation is towards mainstream rather than co-ethnic markets and whose success is derived from *class* resources rather than *ethnic* resources. By class resources (Light 1972) we mean ready access to financial capital and the possession of human capital in the form of educational qualifications, experience and other recognised credentials.

In the case of financial capital, the demands of growth and scale are usually too great to be met via the classic ethnic minority reliance on family and community, even when these personal networks are transnational. Consequently, top-end EMB companies tend to be increasingly locked into formal credit markets, with high street banks supplying a major proportion of their investments (Ram et al. 2003). Similarly with human capital, managerial and skilled worker posts can no longer be filled by family members and face-to-face recruitment within the community. Somewhat against the grain of the EMB literature, we would have to conclude that these high profile ethnic ventures are to a great extent defined by their lack of exceptionalism, their broad similarity to the general run of successful expanding enterprises.

Chiming with this are recent studies of the ethnic business support system, in which many young Asian business owners express their resentment at being officially pigeon-holed into an ethnic category (Ram et al. 2008). They would wish simply to be recognised as entrepreneurs. In a sense their very success derives from their ability to transcend their ethnic identity, in itself an invaluable resource base for new micro-business but a serious brake on major expansion and diversification, with its urgent demand for heavy financial injections.

What are the implications of all this for development and regeneration? Just as with any other fast growth organisations, these elite EMB enterprises will make, by definition, a substantial contribution to their local economy, be it Birmingham, Leicester or wherever. Given their larger than average scale, they can hardly fail to be important employment creators, providing jobs beyond the confines of their own communities. Given also that such firms tend to be located in advanced sectors such as financial services and IT (Deakins et al. 1997, Ram et al. 2003), they will do much towards raising the quality of available work, in many cases replacing dead end jobs with careers for the qualified and ambitious. Here we welcome a growing penetration of these advanced knowledge-based sectors by EMB (Deakins et al. 1997), including not only South Asians (as might be expected) but also Africans, African-Caribbeans and Chinese. As well as high tech firms, there are also promising new ventures in such cultural industries as fashion design and leisure (Deakins et al. 1997). Alongside jobs growth, the benefits to local economies must also include enhanced income, spending power and productivity (Boddy and Parkinson 2004). Where, as with McEwan et al.'s cases (2005), there are also strong transnational links, the prospects for exporting and for inward investment are also bright.

Insofar as these contributions can be enhanced by policy intervention, this could perhaps take the form of supporting ambitious but resource-poor young entrepreneurs on to the growth ladder, though in the light of Ram et al.'s (2008) evidence, support needs to be channelled through business networks based on some kind of common interest other than ethnicity. There is also a case for strengthening such networks among established fast-trackers, with Cooke (2004) laying strong emphasis on the value of knowledge exchange. Furthermore, recent findings about problematic EMB relationships with the banking system point to a need for greater intervention by support agencies on behalf of growing firms unable to access adequate finance for expansion (Ram et al. 2003), as funding blockages can often threaten what would be an invaluable contribution to local economic development. Whatever the means, at least the broad ends are clear in the case of this top end of the EMB hierarchy, where for once the slogan 'more of the same' actually does ring true. While the unselective target-obsessed promotion of sheer quantity of enterprise is often a flawed strategy, leading to excessive numbers of firms and market saturation (Jones et al. 1989), in this instance the emphasis is strictly on the quest for excellence. At the risk of sounding repetitive, the message has nonetheless to be qualified by the reminder that these enterprises are unrepresentative of rank and file EMB. Since the key resources of financial and human capital are almost by definition stringently rationed, the great bulk of EMB is undercapitalised and is consequently motivated by survival rather than profit maximisation and growth. This is not to suggest that such enterprises do not have a contribution to make but rather to call for a careful reappraisal of their role. As things stand, they already do play a valuable if unheralded part in the life of their localities but, unlike the fast-trackers, this ought to be evaluated in social rather than economic terms. Not only do they offer paid work to those otherwise excluded from the labour market but they also provide shops and services in some of the nation's most underserviced places for some of the poorest, most immobile residents.

Such provision is entirely consistent with the objective of addressing social exclusion, since it is the unemployed, the working poor, the elderly and other vulnerable people who bulk large among the beneficiaries. As well as ethnic minority members themselves, EMB also serves the socially excluded among the majority population, not only in the inner city but also in such areas as all-white council estates. Here we make no apology for reiterating that most of these providers are very poorly reimbursed for their pains. Once again, the theme is of under-remunerated owners and workers, of cutting every available corner to reduce costs and of a distinctly low tech reliance on labour intensiveness, sustained by arduous long and unsocial hours of work (Jones et al. 1994). Since the market value of this contribution falls so calamitously short of its true social value, thought might be given to how this imbalance might be rectified by some kind of policy intervention. While we might feel it to be morally repugnant that essential service provision must be done on the cheap at the expense of the providers, we might also consider how much the quality of such provision could be improved by proper funding.

EMB, MULTI-CULTURALISM AND URBAN COMPETITIVENESS

Reflecting the onset of post-industrialism, a new agenda of inter-urban competitiveness has come to the fore over the past two decades or so (Harvey 1987). Increasing inter-urban competition has brought the question of competitive advantage to the forefront, not least at the policy level, with the publication of numerous UK government White Papers from the 1990s onwards (see contributors to Begg 2002). Previously, of course, spatial analysts had tended to prioritise the regional dimension but now attention has re-focused on an urban entrepreneurial struggle, in which cities are seen as vying for their due share of inward investment and consumer spending through tourism and visiting shoppers. Strictly speaking of course, it is businesses not cities per se who are engaged in competition, and the issue is one of sharp inequalities in the quality of local urban business environments.

The historical context for all this is post 1960s deindustrialisation, with its destruction of the competitive base of formerly prosperous local economies built on traditional manufacturing and goods handling activities. In response, public policy has sought to restore competitiveness by modernising local economies, a process sometimes involving a virtual re-invention of the entire persona of a city. Such 'place promotion', in effect a cosmetic image makeover, is seen as essential in raising the profile of a city and the attractiveness in which it is regarded by the outside world of potential investors and spenders. For most cities, this requires little more than light cosmetics. As we shall see, however, for others far more drastic measures would be required.

Turning to the part to be played by EMB, we have already given due prominence to a growing EMB presence in leading-edge sectors of the New Economy. For Begg (1999), the nurturing of high value-added, knowledge-based activities based on the most advanced technologies is one of the most obvious ways of enriching the local economy. This point is even more sharply underlined by Cooke (2004: 153), for whom '[s]trongly competitive areas . . . have high densities of innovative firms' (see also Simmie 2002). Here the top-end ethnic business owners are a growing element in a local pool of entrepreneurial talent, whose human capital endowments enable them to punch above their weight in competitive markets. Where this is further underpinned by the kind of transnational connectedness discussed in the previous section, the city's competitive position becomes vitally enhanced at the global level itself.

Beyond this, however, the very presence of ethnic minorities and their businesses is now seen as a trump card for cities intent on re-branding themselves with a new twenty-first century logo and using this as a selling point. Musing on the visionary possibilities for a New Age Manchester, Halfpenny et al. (2004) wax lyrical about a city 'vibrant and alive . . . its public spaces thronged with affluent consumers and tourists from far and wide'. As signifiers of the colourful and exotic, ethnic minorities are assured of a lead position in this consumerist Nirvana. Not to beat about the neo-liberal bush, Foord and Ginsburg (2004: 289) bluntly remind us that nothing is now immune from commodification and that '[c]ultural difference and diversity . . . can be marketed'. While we may instinctively flinch at the thought of the great heritages of Africa, the Indian sub-continent and the Far East being reduced to the level of extra-strong lager and pork scratchings, in a post-Lyotardian world where virtuality and reality are no longer distinct (Castells 2000), this logic makes some kind of perverted sense. At the level of urban boosterism, where 'quality of life' is a prime selling point 'multi-culturalism' is one of a number of zeitgeist plus points to be ticked off along with 'environmental friendliness', 'landmark architecture' and 'historical interest'. There is something compellingly contemporary about the notion of a multi-cultural city, with its narrative of colourful cosmopolitan diversity, home to all the children of the earth, old fashioned monochrome racist parochialism banished to the over-flowing landfill site of History. What more powerful statement of intent could there be?

Though it is impossible to resist the urge to satirise some of the more egregiously pretentious extremes of post-modernism, it must nevertheless be conceded that urbanism is no longer secured by tangible nuts-and-bolts. It is hard to disagree with writers like Mullins (1991), who argue that 'the consumption of pleasure' has replaced the production of necessary goods and services as the city's chief *raison d'être*. Very much in the spirit of this is the widespread drive on the part of deindustrialised communities, like Gateshead and Liverpool, to re-invent themselves as centres of cultural tourism. Moreover, tourism is indeed a stage almost tailor-made for ethnic minority entrepreneurs to play a leading part. Here it must be assumed that the most immediate role will be performed by ethnic gastronomy. Simply at the sensory level, the conspicuous visibility and aromatic appeal of 'exotic' eating houses and the atmosphere thereby created are the purest possible distillation of the multi-cultural message. At a more practical level, ethnic restaurants can act both as a magnet in their own right and as an additional bonus for visitors drawn to the city by its other attractions. In the next section, we illustrate by reference to our previous work on South Asian curry houses in Birmingham (Ram et al. 2002, Jones et al. 2006), stressing not only their potential contribution to the city's regeneration but also the costs to the participants themselves.

THE BIRMINGHAM CASE STUDY

For the past decade or more, Birmingham has been busily re-inventing itself by erasing various elements of its past persona as the living embodiment of dreary regimented Fordism and making a bid for a new post-industrial identity along the lines described in the previous section. As Webster (2001) reminds us, this requires more than usually invasive surgery, given the nature of the city's entrenched image as a profoundly dull and materialistic hive of industry, devoted to (now almost vanished) automotive manufacture and metal bashing, blighted by post-war Stalinist architecture and choked by motor traffic. Alongside major re-building, conservation and heritage projects (Iafrati 2000, Webster 2001), the city has also sought to radically modernise and upgrade its shopping and leisure facilities. If more recent accounts are to be believed, this makeover is already bearing early fruit.

Although the only ethnic restaurant cited here under the rubric of 'spectacular food' is a Malay-Thai-Chinese emporium, residents of the city will be aware that by far the most numerous of the local ethnic cuisines is that of the Indian sub-continent. As well as a strong presence in the city centre and a widespread diffusion throughout the suburbs, the most distinctive feature of Birmingham's curry house geography is the so-called 'Balti Quarter', a tight inner-city swarm of restaurants numbering over 60 when last enumerated (Ram et al. 2000). Renowned far beyond the bounds of the city, the Balti Quarter is virtually a national institution on a par with East London's Brick

Lane (Rhodes and Nabi 1992). In some senses it is ahead even of Brick Lane in the self-promotion game, since the Balti cuisine—a distinctive variation on the standard curry themes—is its own invention, a 'brand' which attracts custom in its own right from as far away as Northern England and North Wales (Jones et al. 2004). For any city intent on a tourist and leisure future, such an iconic dining out locality conveniently situated for many of its other main attractions can only be a prize asset and must figure prominently in any local development strategy. A world class attraction in its own right, it also has an obvious hospitality function servicing the footsore hordes drawn by other attractions. Neither should it be forgotten that such a prize asset also has a further role in servicing the new professionalization and gentrification resulting from the promotion of the city as a location for high tech innovatory industrial development.

Seductive though all this may be in the context of a city quite understandably striving to convert the sow's ear of the past into the silk purse of a Brave New World, it is nevertheless history from above, a narrative which wordlessly implies that all participants alike will share in the glory and will be showered with rewards. Experience suggests that in the real world the most enviable benefits will be reaped by the usual network of financiers, property developers, architects, urban professionals, careerist local politicians and not least 'consultants'. History from below, notably from the viewpoint of Weber's pariahs, is entirely another matter. As Sassen (1996) insists, urban restructuring is a characteristically polarised process, in which a burgeoning top layer can flourish only with the support of a menial, underpaid lower layer of service workers. The so-called 'hospitality industry' of which the Balti Quarter is part, is particularly notorious here. Inherently low tech and labour-intensive and operating extensively on the basis of casualized, non-unionized and often part time labour, it is one of the leading repositories of the working poor in post-industrial society (Ram et al. 2000). Not coincidentally, given their lack of alternatives, their low expectations and their occupational stereotyping, immigrants and racialised minorities are heavily over-represented in this sector.

In the case of our own interviewees, not even the *ownership* of a catering business can absolve them from this structural disadvantage. Such is the excessive number of outlets in the hyper-competitive Asian restaurant trade that even a rapidly growing market is unable to provide a viable living for all. Here it is important to note that, as controllers of an esoteric cuisine, Asian restaurateurs do enjoy a certain creative leeway and the ability to compete on the basis of the 'unique selling point' (see Oliveira 2007 on ethnic entrepreneurial strategic choices). Unhappily, this ability to create a distinctive cuisine and ambience is mostly restricted to the well-capitalised minority of firms (Jones et al. 2006). Most of the rest are reduced to a self-destructive strategy of frantic price competition, driving down their returns to sub-economic levels. Consequently, for all the Balti Quarter's qualities as a promotional flagship, in the material world many of its restaurateurs are fighting a daily battle for survival. Often, low returns do not even compensate the proprietor for his labour, far less his capital and management inputs. Presumably the opportunity to star in the great drama of Birmingham's renaissance is sufficient reward in itself.

Inevitably, of course, the sub-normal returns and personal sacrifices of the owners must be passed on to the employees. From the testimony of our Asian worker respondents, interviewed in 2003, weekly hours worked are rarely less than 50, for which chefs are paid in the range £200–£300 and waiters £150 to £200 (Jones et al. 2006). Such bald figures do not tell the whole story, since the underpaid drudgery of working life is softened by a paternalistic labour process in which the absence of hierarchical authoritarian control enables individual workers to negotiate all manner of concessions and exert a certain degree of discretion over their work routines (Ram et al. 2007). In the final analysis, however, the bonds of ethnic solidarity between boss and workers cannot completely override the inherent conflict of interest and 'in the worst case, this results in the exploitation of co-ethnic employees, who are obliged to work . . . under bad working conditions, hard work, low salary' (den Butter et al. 2007: 56). The most extreme casualties here are the kitchen porters, often undocumented immigrants, whose weekly pay can be as low as £2 per hour, a lavish improvement on their previous earnings in Bangladesh but painfully depressed by the British standards by which they should be judged. Presumably, however, even non-compliance with immigration regulations and the National Minimum Wage has to be overlooked in the interests of the greater urban good.

In large measure, this case study captures many of the questions which ought to be central to any consideration of the role of EMB in urban regeneration. We are reminded of the essential marginality of EMB entrepreneurs, a marginality stemming not simply from their racialised status but also from their lack of class resources and consequent reliance on limited social capital networks. In an unmediated free market, their unenviable role in urban regeneration is that of as invisible providers to those with greater access to resources. Enterprise policy needs to be aware of this and to take measures to properly compensate EMB for its true contribution.

CONCLUSIONS

The preoccupation of encouraging 'enterprise for all' appears to be an integral feature of the small firm policy agenda until recently. Much attention has been accorded to developing initiatives that will encourage entrepreneurship in 'disadvantaged' areas. There has been a flurry of activity in recent years, prompting one recent review of business support and ethnic minority entrepreneurship to conclude, 'The restructuring of the business support system . . . appears to be associated with a new commitment to the inclusion of all groups of entrepreneurs, including those from ethnic minorities' (Deakins et al. 2003: 856). This has been complemented by considerable growth in the ethnic minority based community organisations; one estimate suggests that there are 5,500 such bodies in England and Wales (cited in Blackburn et al. 2005).

However, the evidence that we have presented casts considerable doubt upon the efficacy of such initiatives. The anatomy of EMB is such that the profound structural constraints that it operates under means that is ill-equipped to occupy the role of 'racialised saviours of the inner city' (Keith 1995: 359). Despite the rhetoric of enterprise that often accompanies such discourses of regeneration and disadvantage, the plethora of schemes that we have witnessed in recent years, at best, might fulfil certain 'social' objectives, rather than the grand claims relating to job generation and business competitiveness (Storey 1994). Hence, the prescription of self-employment as a means of addressing disadvantage amongst ethnic minority communities has to be seriously questioned. As we have seen, it is undoubtedly the case that entrepreneurship has constituted a very important ladder of opportunity for some ethnic minority groups. However, the 'motor' for much of this self-employment is the intensive utilisation (or exploitation) of group-specific social capital, rather than support from public sector interventions. Furthermore, although some ethnic groups have much higher than average levels of self-employment, this should not be seen as an unqualified indicator of 'upward mobility'.

The argument here is not that these initiatives should necessarily be abandoned. Indeed, policy interest in this area is at least partly stimulated by the finding that ethnic minority business owners are often less inclined to utilise business support than the wider small business population (Ram and Smallbone 2002). Further, there is evidence, albeit limited, of benefits accruing to ethnic minorities participating in such schemes (Blackburn et al. 2005). Hence, rather then abandoning such policies, the main policy point is to recognise that their effectiveness is always socially mediated. Policy needs to be refined to ask for whom it might be effective and under what conditions. Such questions rarely get a look-in amidst the hegemonic discourse that often dominates debates on the promotion of entrepreneurship and urban regeneration.

BIBLIOGRAPHY

Barrett, G. A., Jones, T. P. and McEvoy, D. (1996) 'Ethnic minority business: theoretical discourse in Britain and North America', Urban Studies, 33(4–5): 783–809.

Begg, I. (1999) 'Cities and competitiveness', Urban Studies, 36(5/6): 798–809.

——(ed.) (2002) Urban Competitiveness: Policies for dynamic cities, Bristol: The Policy Press.

Blackburn, R. and Ram, M. (2006) 'Fix or fixation? The contributions and limitations of entrepreneurship and small firms to combating social exclusion', Entrepreneurship and Regional Development, 18: 73–89.

Blackburn, R., Bannon, K. and Odamtten, T. (2005) Reaching Businesses through Community-Based Organisations: Evidence from business advice beneficiaries, Kingston: Small Business Research Centre, Kingston University.

Boddy, M. and Parkinson, M. (2004) 'Introduction', in M. Boddy and M. Parkinson (eds) City Matters: Competitiveness, cohesion and urban governance, Bristol: The Policy Press.

Castells, M. (2000) End of Millennium Vol 111: The information age, economy, society and culture, Oxford: Blackwell.

Cooke, P. (2004) 'Competitiveness as cohesion: Social capital and the knowledge economy', in M. Boddy and M. Parkinson (eds) City Matters: Competitiveness, cohesion and urban governance, Bristol: The Policy Press.

Deakins, D., Majmudar, M. and Paddison, A. (1997) 'Developing success stories for ethnic minorities in business: evidence from Scotland', New Community, 25: 325–42.

Deakins, D., Ram., M. and Smallbone, D. (2003) 'Addressing the business support needs of ethnic minority firms in the United Kingdom', Government and Policy (Environment and Planning 'C'), 21: 843–59.

Foord, J. and Ginsburg, N. (2004) 'Whose hidden assets? Inter-city potential for social cohesion and economic competitiveness', in M. Boddy and M. Parkinson (eds) City Matters: Competitiveness, cohesion and urban governance, Bristol: The Policy Press.

Forrester, T. (1978) 'Asians in business', New Society, February: 420–21.

Halfpenny, P., Britton, N., Devine, F. and Mellor, R. (2004) 'The "good" suburb as an asset in enhancing a city's competitiveness', in M. Boddy and M. Parkinson (eds) City Matters: Competitiveness, cohesion and urban governance, Bristol: The Policy Press.

Harvey, D. (1987) 'Three myths in search of a reality in urban studies', Society and Space, 5(4): 53–65.

Iafrati, S. (2000) 'From labour to leisure: the changing role of canals in Birmingham', Journal of Regional and Local Studies, 20(1): 29–39.

Jones, T., Cater, J., De Silva, P. and McEvoy, D. (1989) Ethnic Business and Community Needs, Report to the Commission for Racial Equality, Liverpool, Liverpool Polytechnic.

Jones, T., McEvoy, D. and Barrett, G. (1994) 'Labour intensive practices in the ethnic minority firm', in J. Atkinson and D. Storey (eds) Employment, the Small Firm and the Labour Market, London: Routledge.

Jones, T., Ram, M and Abbas, T. (2004) 'Ethnic enterprise in an urban context: the case of the independent restaurant sector in Birmingham', in M. Boddy (ed.) Cities, Competitiveness and Cohesion, Bristol: Polity Press.

Jones, T., Ram, M. and Edwards, P. (2004) 'Illegal immigrants and the Asian underground economy in the West Midlands', International Journal of Economic Development, 6(1): 92–113.

———(2006) 'Shades of grey in the informal economy', International Journal of Sociology and Social Policy, 26: 357–73.

Keith, M. (1995) 'Ethnic entrepreneurs and street rebels', in S. Pile and N. Thrift (eds) Mapping the Subject: Geographies of cultural transformation, London: Routledge, 355–70.

Li, Y., Savage, M. and Pickles, A. (2003) 'Social capital and social exclusion in England and Wales (1972–1999)', British Journal of Sociology, 54(4): 497–526.

Light, I. (1972) Ethnic Enterprise in America, Berkeley: University of California Press.

———(2004) 'The ethnic ownership economy', in C. Stiles and C. Galbraith (eds) Ethnic Entrepreneurship: Structure and process, Oxford: Elsevier.

————(2007) 'Global entrepreneurship and transnationalism', in L. Dana (ed.) Handbook of Research on Ethnic Minority Entrepreneurship, Cheltenham, UK and Northampton, US: Edward Elgar.

Macarenhas-Keyes, S. (2006) 'Ethnic minority small and medium enterprises in England: diversity and challenges', paper presented at the 51st Conference of the International Council for Small Business, Melbourne, Australia, June.

Marlow, S. (2005) 'Introduction', in S. Marlow, D. Patton and M. Ram (eds) Managing Labour in Small Firms, Abingdon: Routledge.

McEvoy, D. and Hafeez, K. (2006) 'The changing face of ethnic minority entrepreneurship in Britain', paper presented at the 4th European Conference on Entrepreneurship Research, University of Regensburg, February.

McEwan, C., Pollard, J. and Henry, N. (2005) 'The "global" in the city economy: multi-cultural economic development in Birmingham', International Journal of Urban and Regional Research, 24: 916–33.

Mullins, P. (1991) 'Tourism urbanisation', International Journal of Urban and Regional Research, 15: 326–42.

Oliveira, C. R. (2007) 'Understanding the diversity of immigrant entrepreneurial strategies', in L.-P. Dana (ed.) Handbook of Research on Ethnic Minority Entrepreneurship, Cheltenham, UK and Northampton, US: Edward Elgar.

Porter, M. (1995) 'The competitive advantage of the inner city', Harvard Business Review, 73: 55–71.

Ram, M., Abbas, T., Sanghera, B. and Hillin, G. (2000) '"Currying favour with the locals": Balti-owners and business enclaves', International Journal of Entrepreneurial Behaviour and Research, 6(1): 41–55.

Ram, M., Edwards, P. and Jones, T. (2007) 'Staying underground: informal work, small firms and employment regulation in the United Kingdom', Work and Occupations, 34(3): 318–44.

Ram, M. and Jones, T. (2008) Ethnic Minorities in Business, 2nd Edition, Milton Keynes: Small Business Research Trust.

Ram, M. and Patton, D. (2003) A Strategy for the Support of Black and Minority Ethnic Businesses in Leicestershire, report prepared for Business Link Leicestershire.

Ram, M. and Smallbone, D. (2002) 'Ethnic minority business support in the era of the Small Business Service', Government and Policy (Environment and Planning 'C'), 20: 235–49.

Ram, M., Smallbone, D. and Deakins, D. (2002) The Finance and Business Support Needs of Ethnic Minority Firms in Britain, British Bankers Association Research Report.

Ram, M., Smallbone, D., Deakins, D. and Jones, T. (2003) 'Banking on "breakout": finance and the development of ethnic minority businesses', Journal of Ethnic and Migration Studies, 29(4):663–81.

Ram, M., Theodorakopoulos, N. and Jones, T. (2008) 'Forms of capital, mixed embeddedness and Somali enterprise', Work, Employment and Society, 22(3): 427–46.

Rhodes, C. and Nabi, N. (1992) 'Brick Lane: A village economy in the shadow of the city', in L. Budd and S. Whimster (eds) Global Finance and Urban Living, London: Routledge.

Sassen, S. (1996) Losing Control: Sovereignty in an age of globalization, New York: Columbia University Press.

Simmie, J. (2002) 'Knowledge spillovers and the reasons for the concentration of innovative SMEs', Urban Studies, 39(5): 885–902.

Soni, S., Tricker, M. and Ward, R. (1987) Ethnic Minority Business in Leicester, Birmingham: Aston University.

Storey, D. (1994). Understanding the Small Business Sector, London: Routledge.

Tripathi, S. (2003) 'Powers of transformation', Index on Censorship, 32: 125–31.

Waters, D. (2001) Health and Safety in Small Firms, London: PIE Peter Lang.

Webster, F. (2001) 'Re-inventing place: Birmingham as an information city?', City, 5(1): 27–46.

Werbner, P. (1990) 'Renewing an industrial past: British Pakistani entrepreneurship in Manchester', Migration, 8: 17–41.

5 Race, Space and the Dynamics of Self-Employment

Casey J. Dawkins

INTRODUCTION

Black males in the US are self-employed at a rate that is roughly one-third the rate of white self-employment, and this gap has remained roughly constant over the last century (Fairlie and Meyer 2000). This gap has been shown to result from both a lower rate of entry into self-employment among Blacks and a much higher rate of exit. In one recent study, Black males were shown to enter self-employment at a rate that was half that of whites and exit at a rate that was roughly twice the white exit rate (Fairlie 1999).

The dearth of African American entrepreneurs and weaker economic performance of African American-owned businesses has attracted the attention of policy makers. A variety of US policies, including minority business set-asides, Small Business Association (SBA) loan guarantee programmes and various state and federal welfare-to-work initiatives, have the goal of reducing the Black-white self-employment gap by increasing the incidence of self-employment among African Americans (Fairlie 2005). Given the persistent discrimination in wage sector employment, boosting the African-American self-employment rate has been cited as a potential strategy for reducing the Black-white gap in labour force participation (Glazer and Moynihan 1963). Since self-employed workers also report higher earnings than similarly employed wage workers, minority self-employment may also be an important vehicle for alleviating the racial gap in earnings and wealth accumulation. Finally, since Black business owners also hire large numbers of Black employees, Black self-employment promotion has been held to be an important ingredient of a successful local economic development initiative (Bates 2006).

It is important to understand the causes of the Black-white self-employment gap so that policies designed to promote minority self-employment can be more effectively targeted. Blacks' limited access to financial capital (Fairlie 1999, 2005), Blacks' limited intergenerational transfer of family-owned business capital and entrepreneurial expertise (Hout and Rosen 2000), Blacks' lower average education levels (Bates 1989), discrimination against Blacks in wage sector employment (Glazer and Moynihan 1963), and white consumers' reluctant to purchase products from Black-owned businesses (Borjas and Bronars 1989) have all been cited as causes of the

Black-white self-employment gap. Of these factors, Fairlie (1999, 2005) finds that Blacks' relatively lower wealth holdings explain the largest portion of the Black-white self-employment gap.

A relatively unexplored explanation for the Black-white self-employment gap is racial differences in residential location. As of 2000, the average white household resided in a neighbourhood that was 80.2 per cent white, and the average Black household resided in a neighbourhood that was 51.4 per cent Black (Lewis Mumford Center 2001). Although levels of segregation have declined over the last several decades, most Blacks and whites (approximately 65 per cent) would still have to move to eliminate current levels of segregation in most metropolitan areas (Glaeser and Vidgor 2001). Not only are Blacks and whites spatially isolated from one another but the observable characteristics of majority-Black and majority-white residential locations also differ. On average, Blacks reside in locations with lower than average rates of housing price appreciation (Kim 2000, Quercia et al. 2000), lower median family incomes (Logan 2002) and lower overall neighbourhood quality (Boehm and Ihlanfeldt 1991).

If residential location characteristics affect a nascent entrepreneur's decision to become an entrepreneur, and Blacks and whites initially reside in locations that exhibit different observable characteristics, then racial differences in residential location may contribute to racial gaps in entry into self-employment. Furthermore, residential segregation itself may perpetuate this gap if Black and white entrepreneurs face different local consumer markets and participate in different social networks.

To date, no study has directly examined how racial differences in residential location characteristics influence the dynamics of the Black-white self-employment gap. While several studies enter residential location characteristics into models of self-employment, most measure residential location characteristics at a highly aggregated geographic scale such as the surrounding metropolitan area. Furthermore, several important residential location characteristics, particularly access to local social networks, access to financial capital and local crime rates, are typically omitted from such analyses. Finally, and perhaps most importantly, existing studies tend to focus on residential segregation per se and not on racial differences in the characteristics of areas where Blacks and whites reside. It may be that residential segregation is simply a proxy for racial differences in access to local consumer markets, for example.

In this chapter, a unique geocoded version of the Panel Study of Income Dynamics (PSID) is employed to estimate probit regression models explaining the transition into, and out of, self-employment as a function of various covariates, including measures of residential location characteristics. This study improves upon earlier studies by examining the relative contribution of racial differences in various observed residential location characteristics towards the Black-white gap in self-employment entry and exit. This study is also one of the few to focus explicitly on the dynamics of self-employment, as opposed to cross-sectional differences in self-employment. A dynamic approach is useful in this case because it alleviates the problem of reverse causality between self-employment decisions and residential location decisions. As an additional test for endogeneity bias, I also examine models which control for individual-level and family-level heterogeneity.

The remainder of the chapter begins with a discussion of the empirical literature on the Black-white self-employment gap, emphasizing studies that have included controls for residential location characteristics. The data is then discussed, together with the econometric approach taken to decompose the relative contribution of racial differences in various residential location characteristics towards the Black-white gap in self-employment entry and exit. Next the results from several probit models and the decompositions are examined. The sensitivity of the results to possible endogeneity bias resulting from unobserved characteristics which influence both location choice and self-employment decisions is also examined. The results from these analyses suggest that racial differences in residential location influence the dynamics of the Black-white self-employment gap in important ways. The concluding section of the chapter explores these findings further and discusses policies which might serve to alleviate the Black-white self-employment gap.

THE BLACK-WHITE SELF-EMPLOYMENT GAP

Theoretical models of self-employment characterize the self-employment decision as a comparison between the expected returns from self-employment relative to wage employment. If the expected returns from self-employment, which may include both pecuniary and non-pecuniary benefits (Hamilton 2000), exceed those from wage employment, the worker chooses to 'be his/her own boss'. Models of this sort suggest that the self-employment decision is influenced by subjective tastes for self-employment, which are in turn influenced by demographic characteristics such as marital status, age and the number and age of children in the family. Demographic characteristics may also influence the relative risk aversion of householders. Householders who are older, married and support families with children are likely to be more risk averse and hence less likely to enter an employment state exhibiting more volatile returns (Kihlstrom and Laffont 1979). Entrepreneurial ability and managerial skills are also assumed to be positively associated with the decision to become a self-employed worker (Lucas 1978). Experience in a given wage sector occupation is generally assumed to negatively influence the decision to become self-employed, particularly if the skills gained through experience are assets specific to the worker's wage sector occupation (Lazear and Moore 1984). Finally, given that new business formation often requires a substantial initial capital investment, those with higher levels of wealth can more easily finance new business formation if credit market constraints are binding (Evans and Jovanovic 1989).

Of the empirical studies examining the determinants of self-employment, few emphasize the relative contribution of these factors towards the
Black-white gap in self-employment rates. Existing evidence suggests that
inter-racial differences in demographic characteristics explain only a small
portion of the total Black-white gap in self-employment (Fairlie and Meyer
1996, Fairlie 1999). Similarly, although the average education level of Blacks
has increased dramatically in the last several decades, this increase explains
a relatively small proportion of the overall change in self-employment rates
(Fairlie and Meyer 2000). Inter-racial differences in industry composition
also explain a small proportion of the Black-white self-employment gap
(Fairlie and Meyer 2000).

So what explains the persistence of the Black-white self employment
gap? Racial differences in entrepreneurial skills provide one possible explanation. While few studies include direct controls for entrepreneurial skills,
it is reasonable to assume that unobserved entrepreneurial and managerial skills will be transmitted from self-employed adults to their children,
particularly if children enter the family business. Hence, one should expect
to find strong intergenerational links in the probability of becoming and
remaining self-employed. This argument is supported by Fairlie (1999),
who finds that racial gaps in the probability of having a self-employed father
explain a large proportion of the Black-white gap in self-employment rates.

Among all factors, racial differences in wealth holdings have been shown
to be the most significant in explaining Black-white differences in self-
employment rates. As of 2000, the median net worth of Black households
was a meagre $6,166, compared to $67,000 for whites. Furthermore, during the last two decades, real net worth rose for whites and fell for Blacks
(Wolff 1998). The racial wealth gap may stall Black self-employment rates
by limiting access to financial capital if credit market constraints are binding. Furthermore, low wealth levels may place new Black business owners
at a higher risk of loan default, thereby accelerating business exit. Evidence
supports each of these arguments. Fairlie (1999) and Fairlie and Meyer
(1996) find that wealth explains a large portion of the Black-white gap in
the transition to self-employment, while Fairlie (1999) and Bates (1989)
find that wealth differences explain racial gaps in business failure rates.
Counter evidence is provided by Meyer (1990), who examines data from
the Survey of Income and Program Participation and finds that racial differences in net worth do not explain a large portion of the Black-white gap
in self-employment rates. Furthermore, Hurst and Lusardi (2004) find that
liquidity constraints may not be binding for most households.

The Role of Residential Location

As of 2000, approximately 65 per cent of Blacks would have to relocate
to eliminate Black-white segregation within the surrounding metropolitan
area, compared to 52 per cent of Hispanics and 42 per cent of Asians (Lewis
Mumford Center 2001). Given that Black households have traditionally

resided in areas that are closer to metropolitan central cities than the locations chosen by whites, the characteristics of majority-Black and majority-white residential locations also differ. On average, Blacks live in areas with lower median incomes, higher poverty rates, lower average educational attainment levels and lower concentrations of regional employment opportunities (Logan 2002, Dawkins et al. 2005). Blacks are also more likely than whites to report living in a poor-quality neighbourhood. The most important factors in explaining these racial differences in neighbourhood quality are differences in crime rates, amount of litter and trash, quality of surrounding buildings and number of abandoned buildings (Boehm and Ihlanfeldt 1991).

There are several ways in which the geographic segregation of Black and white households may influence incentives to enter and remain in self-employment. Perhaps the most well-developed theory linking segregation to racial gaps in self-employment is the 'protected market hypothesis' (Glazer and Moynihan 1963, Brimmer 1968, Light 1972, Aldrich et al. 1985). The absence of white-owned businesses within majority-Black areas possibly insulates infant Black-owned businesses from market competition. Racial discrimination against Black customers within white-owned businesses may reinforce loyalties among Blacks to local Black-owned businesses. Together, these factors may help to explain the finding that, while only 6.3 per cent of all businesses serve customer bases that are more than 90 per cent minority, more than 28 per cent of Black-owned businesses serve a customer base that is more than 90 per cent minority.[1] Evidence in support of this argument comes from Borjas and Bronars (1989), who find that minority self-employment increases with the minority proportion in the surrounding metropolitan area. Counter evidence is provided by Meyer (1990), who finds that Black businesses are relatively more common in industries where white customers patronize Black businesses.

Some evidence suggests that the market protection benefits of segregation may harm protected minority firms in the long run. Bates (1997) provides an estimate of the likely market effects of serving a primarily Black clientele. In regression models explaining entrepreneurship outcomes for Black-owned businesses, he finds that while serving a minority clientele does not have a statistically significant effect on firm survival, firms serving minority clienteles tend to be less profitable than other Black-owned firms. Similar findings are reported by Aldrich and Reiss (1976), who examine the impact of racial residential succession on processes of white business survival and find that the changing economic status of neighbourhoods and the profit status of a business are more important determinants of business survival than changes in racial composition per se.

Economic conditions within majority-Black areas may also temper the market protection offered by racial segregation. Given that median incomes within majority-Black neighbourhoods tend to be about 70 per cent that of white neighbourhoods (Logan 2002), local-serving Black-owned businesses often must cater services to a customer base exhibiting weaker purchasing power. Black et al. (2001) examine 1990 Public Use Micro Sample (PUMS) data from the US Census to find that the metropolitan-level purchasing of minority groups, not residential segregation per se, explains differences across metropolitan areas in rates of minority self-employment.

Many researchers have emphasized the important role that local social networks play in enhancing labour market outcomes (see Jencks and Mayer 1990 and Ellen and Turner 1997 for reviews). Local interactions between young nascent entrepreneurs and successful incumbent entrepreneurs may motivate youths to become business owners. Furthermore, local social interactions between new entrepreneurs and existing business owners may help to diffuse information regarding product development, business management, financing and business strategy. Racial segregation, to the extent that it brings nascent and new entrepreneurs in contact with successful existing business owners, may enhance the social networks required for productive entrepreneurial ventures. Of course, if racial segregation is highly correlated with economic segregation, racial segregation may exacerbate the social distance between nascent entrepreneurs and incumbent business owners. According to Wilson (1987), the outmigration of middle to upper income Blacks from traditional central city Black neighbourhoods during the 1980s and 1990s has robbed existing lower income residents of potentially beneficial social interactions. Although no study has yet quantified the net impacts of segregation on the social networks supporting entrepreneurship activity, Fischer and Massey (2000) present findings consistent with the hypothesis that high levels of racial segregation exacerbate the concentration of poverty, which serves to widen racial gaps in entrepreneurial activity.

Geographic segregation may also exacerbate racial differences in accumulated housing wealth. Evidence suggests that housing prices in majority-Black neighbourhoods appreciate at much slower rates than housing prices in majority-white neighbourhoods (Kim 2000, Quercia et al. 2000). Furthermore, Blacks tend to hold a much higher proportion of total wealth in home equity compared to financial assets (Oliver and Shapiro 1995). If home equity provides an important source of business financing, either by liquidating accumulated equity, or by leveraging equity for home equity financing, racial differences in home price appreciation rates may contribute to the racial gap in entrepreneurship. While several studies have examined the impact of non-housing wealth on racial gaps in self-employment, no studies have yet focused on the role of home equity.

Geographic segregation may also influence access to business capital if the banking institutions serving majority-white and majority-Black areas provide different levels of support to small businesses. Given the uneven distribution of bank locations, and given the importance of face-to-face contact in establishing business financing relationships, having a residential location in areas with high concentrations of small business lending may facilitate entry into self-employment. No studies to date have examined the influence of proximity to small business lending on racial gaps in self-employment.

DATA AND ECONOMETRIC APPROACH

The Panel Study of Income Dynamics (PSID) is a longitudinal study of individuals and their families that has been administered by the University of Michigan's Institute for Social Research (ISR) since 1968. The PSID includes detailed data on family demographics, income, wealth and labour market status and has been utilized extensively in the past for labour market and self-employment research. Using the 1980–97 waves of the PSID,[2] I propose to estimate the following probit regression model for separate samples of Black and white male workers aged 16–64 who are heads of family units during the 1980–97 time period and who reside in metropolitan statistical areas:

$$Pr(Y = 1 \mid X) = F(Xb) \tag{5.1}$$

where Y is a dependent variable coded '1', if a particular self-employment outcome is observed, and zero otherwise. Models explaining the transition into and the transition out of self-employment are examined. In addition to providing a dynamic perspective on the self-employment decision, an emphasis on transitions also reduces the likelihood of endogeneity bias, given that the variables in X are all measured in the year just prior to the self-employment transition in question.

As in previous studies (Borjas 1986, Fairlie 1999, Fischer and Massey 2000), entry into and out of entrepreneurship activity is defined as entry into or out of self-employment, relative to wage/salary work. As is common in the self-employment literature, transitions into self-employment from other work statuses and out of self-employment to other work statuses are removed from the sample. Separate regressions are estimated for Blacks and whites. Female workers are omitted from this analysis, because the definition of 'household head' employed by the PSID would inappropriately bias the female sample towards single female-headed households.

Independent variables include measures of the determinants of self-employment discussed in the previous section, plus additional measures of the characteristics of the individual's residential location at the time period immediately prior to the time in which the employment outcome is observed.[3] Individual- and household-level controls include age of the worker, current and prior marital status of the worker, number of children in the worker's family and age of the worker's youngest child. As suggested above, these variables capture tastes for self-employment and relative risk aversion. Also included are measures of educational attainment of the worker and his father and work experience and its quadratic. Several measures of wealth are included: interest income (income from interest, dividends, trust funds, rent and royalties), cash payments including insurance settlements and inheritances and home equity, measured as the difference between the household's estimated home value and the remaining principal owed on home mortgages. As in Fairlie (1999) and Hurst and Lusardi (2004), all wealth measures are entered directly and in quadratic form. All dollar values are expressed in 1997 adjusted values.

A dummy variable is used to indicate the worker's home ownership status. As Oswald (1996, 1997) suggests, home ownership may stall labour market adjustments given that the transaction costs of moving are much larger for home owners. If home owners find it more difficult than renters to move to a location that is optimal for starting a new business, then these transaction costs may reduce incentives to enter self-employment. The relevant empirical question is whether these transaction costs are outweighed by the home equity benefits of home ownership.

Residential location characteristics are obtained from several sources and matched to individual respondents using confidential PSID geocode match files.[4] All residential location characteristics for each individual are measured at the county level and are based on the most recently available data just prior to the date of employment transition. The county was chosen as the basis for measurement of geographic variables for several reasons. First, geographic characteristics data are more consistently available over time at the county level than at any other level of geography. Second, the county represents a compromise between two factors. First, smaller areas such as census tracts are more likely to capture the local geographic constraints facing residents who seek to start a business. On the other hand, larger areas are more likely to approximate the geographic extent of potential search areas for a new self-employment location. Counties fall within these two extremes. Metropolitan areas were deemed too large to accurately capture intra-area differences in the residential location characteristics facing nascent entrepreneurs. Furthermore, focusing only on metropolitan areas would preclude attempts to examine urban-rural differences in entrepreneurship dynamics. Given evidence suggesting that entrepreneurship may prove an important ingredient in rural economic development (Gladwin et al. 1989), rural cases were included in the analysis.

To determine if the county is poorly correlated with the actual location of one's self-employment location, the distribution of commute distances for those transitioning into self-employment in years for which the PSID provides accurate commuting data (prior to 1985) were examined. For those transitioning into self-employment during this period, the average distance travelled was 17.74 miles. At this distance travelled, census tracts would not accurately capture the actual geographic characteristics of self-employment location.

Based on the discussion above, several residential location character-istics in the model represented by equation (5.1) were included. Dummy variables denoting US Census region of residence and central county/sub-urban county/rural status are entered to capture regional heterogeneity and intra-metropolitan location. Population density is entered to capture poten-tial consumer density, while median family income and its quadratic are entered to capture local consumer purchasing power. The chosen measure of racial integration is the percentage of the worker's county that is from the 'other' racial group in the sample.[5] The county unemployment rate is entered to capture local economic distress. As suggested by Audretsch and Fritsch (1994) and Armington and Acs (2002), the hypothesized impact of local unemployment rates on new firm formation is ambiguous, because unemployed workers may find self-employment more attractive during an economic downturn.

As in the models estimated by Acs and Armington (2004), a measure of local human capital is included, measured as the share of adults with college degrees, as well as a measure of industry intensity, measured as the number of establishments per capita. The hypothesized sign of the measure of industry intensity is ambiguous. On the one hand, a higher number of local establishments may deter self-employment entry due to the competitive effects of local industry presence. On the other hand, a higher number of establishments may be associated with external urban-ization economies (Glaeser et al. 1992). Which of these effects dominates is an empirical question.

Three variables not examined in other studies of the geography of self-employment are included here. First is a measure of the total number of crimes per capita in the surrounding county. If crime rates are higher in majority-Black areas, racial differences in exposure to crime may affect racial differences in the perceived risk associated with business ownership relative to wage and salary work. Second is a measure of the percentage of workers residing in the surrounding county who earn self-employment income. This measure is designed to capture the knowledge spill-over effects associated with residing in an area with a large concentration of entrepreneurs. Local exposure to other self-employed workers may serve as both a source of information for potential 'nascent' entrepreneurs looking to start a business, as well as serving as a social support network among existing business owners seeking to share business strategy ideas. Finally, a measure of access to local small business financing is included, measured as the dollar value of local 504 Small Business Association (SBA) lending as a percentage of total deposits for banks within the surrounding county. In contrast to other programmes sponsored by the SBA, the 504 programme is designed to serve as a local economic development financing tool that is implemented directly by local Community Development Corporations (CDCs). Unlike other programmes, it has an explicit goal of promoting the 'expansion of minority business development'. As such, it may serve to reduce Black-white gaps in self-employment by promoting local access to business start-up capital. All location characteristics are derived from the USA Counties CD-ROM, with the exception of the SBA loan measure, which was acquired directly from the SBA through a Freedom of Information Act (FOIA) request.

DECOMPOSITION ANALYSIS

The primary purpose of this research is to estimate the contribution of observed differences in residential location characteristics towards the overall gap in self-employment transitions. This extends the approach taken by Fairlie (1999) to examine the contribution of racial differences in geographic variables towards the overall gap in self-employment transitions. Fairlie's (1999) method extends the traditional Blinder-Oaxaca (Blinder 1973, Oaxaca 1973) decomposition to the case of a non-linear model such as logit or probit. To determine the contribution of a given residential location characteristic towards the overall Black-white self-employment gap, first partition X in equation (5.1) into a vector of household characteristics (X_h) and a vector of residential location characteristics (X_l). Assume for simplicity that the Black sample size (N_B) is equal to the white sample size (N_W). Following Fairlie (1999, 2003) the contribution of X_h towards the overall racial gap can then be written as:

$$\frac{1}{N^B}\sum_{i=1}^{N^B} F(X^W_{hi}\beta_h + X^W_{li}\beta_l) - F(X^W_{hi}\beta_h + X^W_{li}\beta_l) \qquad (5.2)$$

Similarly, the contribution of X_l towards the overall racial gap can then be written as:

$$\frac{1}{N^B}\sum_{i=1}^{N^B} F(X^B_{hi}\beta_h + X^W_{li}\beta_l) - F(X^W_{hi}\beta_h + X^B_{li}\beta_l) \qquad (5.3)$$

The contribution of each vector of variables towards the overall gap is equal to the change in the average predicted probability associated with replacing the Black distribution with the white distribution of the vector of variables, holding the distribution of the other variables constant (Fairlie 2003: 4). This approach can also be used to determine the relative contribution of individual variables within X_l towards the overall Black-white gap in self-employment transitions.

To calculate equations (5.2) and (5.3), the method outlined in Fairlie (1999, 2003) is employed. Briefly stated, this procedure involves matching the minority sample with 1,000 randomly chosen white subsamples and calculating the average change in the predicted probability from replacing the Black distribution with the white distribution of X, while holding the distribution of the other variables constant. By relying on probit models to estimate β, the cumulative distribution function (CDF) used to calculate $F(-)$ in equation (5.2) and (5.3) is derived from the CDF of a standard normal distribution.

RESULTS

The results show raw transition rates and draw comparisons with Fairlie (1999). The Black-white gap in the transition to self-employment is estimated to be 1.39 per cent. The racial gap in the likelihood of transitioning out of self-employment is much larger. Blacks are 12.60 per cent more likely to transition out of self-employment than are whites. Stated differently, Blacks enter self-employment at a rate that is roughly 65 per cent that of whites and leave self-employment at a rate that is about 1.8 times that of whites. These estimates, displayed in Table 5.1, are largely comparable to those reported by Fairlie (1999).

Probit Regression Results: Transitions into Self-Employment

Table 5.2 displays the initial set of regression results. The estimates point to significant racial differences in the factors contributing to the self-employment entry decision. Household demographic characteristics, including marital status and number of children, are significant only in explaining Blacks' decision to move into self-employment. Age and its square are significant factors explaining self-employment transitions in the full sample, however. As predicted, years of experience deter self-employment entry for both Blacks and whites, at least over most of the range of the independent variable. The relative influence of experience is nearly twice as large for Blacks as for whites, while for Blacks, the father's education level is positively associated with self-employment entry. These findings are largely consistent with Fairlie (1999).

In contrast to Fairlie (1999), I find that liquidity constraints are binding for Blacks only, when one considers non-housing wealth alone. The coefficient on interest income for Blacks is large in magnitude. Based on the

Table 5.1

Descriptive Statistics for Self-Employment Transitions, Black + White Workers			
	White Workers	Black Workers	Black-White Gap
Transition into Self Employment	3.96%	2.58%	1.39%
N	17889	7371	25260
Transition out of Self Employment	15.88%	28.48%	-12.60%
N	3811	460	4271

Table 5.2

Probit Regressions for Transition into Self-Employment

Sample	Black Workers			White Workers			Black + White Workers		
Variable	Coef.	St. Error	Sig.	Coef.	St. Error	Sig.	Coef.	St. Error	Sig.
Personal and Household Characteristics									
Constant	-4.5741	0.9639	***	-1.0841	0.4741	**	-1.9915	0.4100	***
Black	--	--		--	--		-0.2778	0.0802	***
Currently Married	-0.2591	0.0979	***	-0.0758	0.0643		-0.1177	0.0528	**
Previously Married	0.0123	0.1165		-0.0010	0.0859		0.0106	0.0684	
Number of Children	0.0490	0.0263	*	0.0115	0.0177		0.0200	0.0145	
Age of Youngest Child	-0.0079	0.0082		-0.0033	0.0043		-0.0041	0.0038	
Age	0.0384	0.0244		0.0179	0.0137		0.0215	0.0118	*
Age Squared	-0.0004	0.0003		-0.0002	0.0002		-0.0002	0.0001	*
Interest Income ($1,000s)	0.2829	0.1160	**	0.0021	0.0047		0.0016	0.0047	
Interest Income Squared ($1,000s)	-0.0409	0.0221	*	0.0000	0.0000		0.0000	0.0000	
Cash Payments Received ($1,000s)	0.0320	0.0232		0.0025	0.0021		0.0024	0.0021	
Cash Payments Received Squared ($1,000s)	-0.0005	0.0005		0.0000	0.0000		0.0000	0.0000	
Homeowner	-0.0364	0.0973		-0.2468	0.0492	***	-0.1764	0.0425	***
Home Equity ($10,000s)	0.0358	0.0242		0.0293	0.0053	***	0.0267	0.0049	***
Home Equity Squared ($10,000s)	-0.0009	0.0013		-0.0003	0.0001	***	-0.0003	0.0001	***
Years of Experience	-0.0418	0.0090	***	-0.0227	0.0057	***	-0.0280	0.0047	***
Years of Experience Squared	0.0008	0.0002	***	0.0004	0.0002	**	0.0005	0.0001	***
High School Degree	-0.1293	0.0806		-0.0368	0.0518		-0.0700	0.0427	
Attended College	-0.0013	0.0975		0.0518	0.0591		0.0249	0.0496	
College Degree	-0.0247	0.1280		0.0520	0.0595		0.0200	0.0519	
Father Has High School Degree	-0.1497	0.1023		-0.0136	0.0441		-0.0222	0.0398	
Father Attended College	0.2872	0.1630	*	-0.0991	0.0677		-0.0548	0.0619	
Father Has College Degree	0.2107	0.1806		0.0856	0.0596		0.0966	0.0555	*
Residential Location Characteristics									
Midwest Region	0.0787	0.1667		0.0726	0.0589		0.0717	0.0545	
South Region	0.0087	0.1654		0.0251	0.0655		0.0247	0.0576	
West Region	-0.3211	0.2115		0.0795	0.0649		0.0223	0.0605	
Central County	0.0880	0.1862		-0.1126	0.0811		-0.0688	0.0729	
Rural County	-0.0498	0.1948		-0.0919	0.0829		-0.0650	0.0748	
Population Density	0.0000	0.0000		0.0000	0.0000		0.0000	0.0000	
% Other Race	0.0041	0.0032		0.0009	0.0021		0.0023	0.0013	*
Median Family Income	6.9E-05	0.0000	**	-2.5E-05	0.0000	*	2.7E-06	0.0000	
Median Family Income Squared	-8.3E-10	0.0000	**	1.4E-10	0.0000		-1.2E-10	0.0000	
Crime Per Capita	1.8807	1.5104		0.0400	0.7506		0.3339	0.6484	
Unemployment Rate (%)	-0.0054	0.0213		-0.0221	0.0105	**	-0.0140	0.0089	
Adults With College Degree (%)	0.0167	0.0090	*	0.0088	0.0044	**	0.0105	0.0039	***
Self-Employment Rate (%)	0.0564	0.0295	*	0.0113	0.0069		0.0211	0.0064	***
Establishments Per Capita	-16.6590	8.5705	*	-5.8664	3.7944		-7.3357	3.4088	**
SBA Lending Per $1M in Bank Deposits	0.0046	0.0157		0.0160	0.0067	**	0.0134	0.0060	**
Log-Likelihood	-836.1300			-2914.4270			-3784.7300		
Pseudo R-Square	0.3574			0.1854			0.1780		
Sample Size	7371			17889			25260		

*** p < .01; ** p < .05; * p < .10

estimated marginal effects (not reported for brevity), a $1,000 increase in interest income increases the Black transition probability by .0135, not considering the quadratic effect. For whites, the marginal effect is .00017 and not significant. Cash payments are not statistically significant for whites or Blacks.

Perhaps the most interesting finding is the large and highly significant influence of home ownership and home equity on white self-employment transition decisions. Being a home owner is associated with a .0215 reduction in the probability of transitioning into home ownership for whites. This finding is consistent with Oswald's (1996, 1997) hypothesis outlined earlier. Furthermore, a $10,000 increase in home equity is associated with an increase in the probability of employment entry of .0024, not considering the quadratic term. This would seem to indicate that whites, not Blacks, face liquidity constraints resulting from home-equity financing for business start-up purposes. Given that whites in the sample have nearly three times more accumulated home equity than Blacks, this explanation does not seem likely. A more likely explanation is that Blacks do not directly face liquidity constraints because they opt for other forms of financing over home-equity based financing. Low accumulated levels of home equity may discourage Blacks from liquidating assets or leveraging assets for business financing. Furthermore, mortgage market discrimination may further limit Blacks' access to home equity financing sources.

Regarding the influence of residential location characteristics, several factors are important. First note that in the Black and white subsamples, racial integration per se is less important than racial differences in observed characteristics. Among the significant residential location characteristics, the presence of additional establishments per capita strongly deters entry into self-employment for Blacks, which suggests that the effects of local business crowding and inter-firm competition outweigh external economies of urbanization for prospective Black entrepreneurs. The estimated sign of this coefficient is consistent with the findings of Acs and Armington (2004).

Measures of local economic activity are also associated with self-employment transition. Median family income is positively associated with the probability of self-employment for Blacks. Also, as in Black et al. (2001), the effect of median family income is non-linear. For whites, the quadratic term is not significant, suggesting that median family income has a negative influence on self-employment. This is possibly due to the fact that higher incomes are associated with not only higher local purchasing power but higher wages. If this interpretation is correct, the purchasing power effect dominates for Blacks, while the wage effect dominates for whites. This could possibly reflect inter-racial differences in industry composition of the self-employed. Finally, higher local unemployment rates deter entry into self-employment for whites but not for Blacks.

Local concentrations of highly educated adults and self-employed adults influence self-employment transitions. Both whites and Blacks are more likely to enter self-employment when a greater number of college-educated workers reside in the surrounding county. Black entry into self-employment is also positively associated with the concentration of local self-employed workers. The influence of local self-employment concentrations is likely to be due to one of two effects. First, if knowledge spill-overs are important, nascent entrepreneurs may benefit from interactions with other successful local business owners. A second hypothesis is that local concentrations of local self-employed workers may serve as a proxy for unobserved local amenities and other characteristics supportive of self-employment. Further research is required to separate these effects.

The local concentration of SBA lending is positively associated with self-employment entry for whites only. This finding is troubling, given that a primary purpose of the SBA 504 loan guarantee programme is to spur Black business development. Furthermore, when viewed in light of the importance of home equity lending for whites only, these findings suggest that Blacks face unique barriers to accessing financial capital that are not similarly faced by whites.

Table 5.3

Probit Regressions for Transition Out of Self-Employment

Sample	Black Workers			White Workers			Black + White Workers		
Variable	Coef.	St. Error	Sig.	Coef.	St. Error	Sig.	Coef.	St. Error	Sig.
Personal and Household Characteristics									
Constant	-0.5793	2.2537		0.5776	0.7334		0.3185	0.6683	
Black	--	--					0.2332	0.1353	*
Currently Married	0.0820	0.2388		-0.0140	0.1085		-0.0173	0.0967	
Previously Married	-0.1968	0.2908		0.1671	0.1349		0.0893	0.1197	
Number of Children	0.0261	0.0589		0.0008	0.0276		0.0053	0.0244	
Age of Youngest Child	0.0044	0.0154		-0.0023	0.0061		-0.0011	0.0056	
Age	-0.0343	0.0539		-0.0631	0.0204	***	-0.0595	0.0187	***
Age Squared	0.0000	0.0006		0.0007	0.0002	***	0.0006	0.0002	***
Interest Income ($1,000s)	0.1143	0.1208		-0.0032	0.0027		-0.0033	0.0027	
Interest Income Squared ($1,000s)	-0.0120	0.0121		0.0000	0.0000		0.0000	0.0000	
Cash Payments Received ($1,000s)	-0.1174	0.1726		0.0036	0.0033		0.0044	0.0037	
Cash Payments Received Squared ($1,000s)	0.0049	0.0112		0.0000	0.0000		0.0000	0.0000	
Homeowner	-0.3732	0.2002	*	-0.2466	0.0742	***	-0.2679	0.0678	***
Home Equity ($10,000s)	0.0173	0.0289		-0.0185	0.0068	***	-0.0150	0.0065	**
Home Equity Squared ($10,000s)	0.0000	0.0009		0.0001	0.0001		0.0001	0.0001	
Years of Experience	-0.0367	0.0244		-0.0469	0.0067	***	-0.0436	0.0062	***
Years of Experience Squared	0.0012	0.0007		0.0006	0.0001	***	0.0006	0.0001	***
High School Degree	0.0477	0.1812		0.0387	0.0797		0.0264	0.0706	
Attended College	-0.2362	0.2274		0.0515	0.0909		0.0179	0.0816	
College Degree	-0.2121	0.2769		0.0470	0.0883		0.0298	0.0804	
Father Has High School Degree	0.3980	0.2125	*	-0.0036	0.0659		0.0243	0.0620	
Father Attended College	-0.9784	0.4931	**	-0.0139	0.0920		-0.0461	0.0893	
Father Has College Degree	-0.4809	0.4075		-0.2859	0.0914	***	-0.3045	0.0876	***
Residential Location Characteristics									
Midwest Region	0.4854	0.4468		-0.1141	0.0881		-0.0655	0.0846	
South Region	0.5246	0.4165		-0.0853	0.0991		-0.0449	0.0922	
West Region	1.0643	0.4908	**	-0.0471	0.0976		-0.0323	0.0934	
Central County	-0.0364	0.3738		-0.0421	0.1301		0.0279	0.1197	
Rural County	1.0525	0.3991	***	0.1864	0.1276		0.2672	0.1185	**
Population Density	0.0000	0.0000		0.0000	0.0000		0.0000	0.0000	
% Other Race	0.0091	0.0075		0.0019	0.0030		0.0007	0.0023	
Median Family Income	0.0001	0.0001		0.0000	0.0000		0.0000	0.0000	*
Median Family Income Squared	0.0000	0.0000		0.0000	0.0000		0.0000	0.0000	*
Crime Per Capita	4.1540	3.8552		-1.1083	1.1428		-0.6511	1.0151	
Unemployment Rate (%)	-0.0320	0.0481		-0.0099	0.0158		-0.0072	0.0143	
Adults With College Degree (%)	0.0247	0.0190		-0.0098	0.0066		-0.0066	0.0060	
Self-Employment Rate (%)	-0.2369	0.0901	***	-0.0345	0.0095	***	-0.0352	0.0090	***
Establishments Per Capita	-25.4039	19.8707		0.7713	5.5842		-1.8388	5.2278	
SBA Lending Per $1M in Bank Deposits	0.0233	0.0372		0.0099	0.0093		0.0102	0.0089	
Log-Likelihood	-232.7454			-1517.0800			-1776.8810		
Pseudo R-Square	0.8291			0.3811			0.3921		
Sample Size	460			3811			4271		

*** p < .01; ** p < .05; * p < .10

Probit Regression Results: Transitions out of Self-Employment

The results presented in Table 5.3 explain the transition out of self-employment for those initially self-employed. The reader is cautioned to interpret the estimates from Table 5.3 with some care, given that the sample size of Black workers who were initially self-employed is quite low.

Fewer household characteristics are significant in explaining transitions out of self-employment. Older white workers with increased experience in their prior job are less likely to transition out of self-employment. Self-employed Blacks are less likely to exit self-employment if their fathers attended college, while having a father with a college degree deters self-employment exit among whites. Interestingly, having a father with only a high school degree actually promotes exit among Blacks.

Home ownership, which was associated with reduced probability of self-employment exit, is shown to deter self-employment exit for both whites and Blacks. One possible explanation for this finding is that those home owners who were not constrained by transaction costs of moving in their

search for a self-employment location may learn skills from the home ownership experience, such as bookkeeping, maintenance skills and general
facility management skills that are then transferred to business practices,
as suggested by Dietz and Haurin (2003). Higher levels of home equity
are also associated with a lower probability of self-employment exit for
whites but not for Blacks. This is probably due to the loan default protection offered by large equity holdings. Home equity also serves as leverage
for borrowing to finance business expansion. Apparently, these benefits do
not accrue to Black home owners.

The only residential location characteristic influencing the transition out
of self-employment is the concentration of self-employed workers in the
surrounding county. The effect of having self-employed workers nearby is
statistically significant for both Blacks and whites, but the magnitude of
the effect is much larger for Blacks. For Blacks, a percentage increase in the
number of self-employed workers reduces the probability of exiting self-
employment by .0761. For whites, the reduction in the probability of exit
from a percentage increase in self-employed workers is only .0075.

Decompositions of the Black-White Self-Employment Gap

The following examination begins with a discussion of decompositions
of the racial gap in the transition into self-employment, reported in Table
5.4. Using the approach outlined in the previous section, decompositions
are calculated using the coefficients from the Black sample, the white
sample and the pooled sample of Black and white households using the
technique outlined in Fairlie (2003). All decompositions are based on

Table 5.4

Decompositions of the Estimated Black-White Gap in Transitions Into Self-Employment

	Black Coefficients		White Coefficients		Full Sample Coefficients	
	Total Gap	% of B-W Gap	Total Gap	% of B-W Gap	Total Gap	% of B-W Gap
Estimated Black-White Transition Probability Gap	0.0139		0.0139		0.0139	
Contributions from Racial Differences in:						
Personal and Household Characteristics						
Household and Personal Characteristics	0.0014	10.27%	-0.0002	-1.56%	-0.0009	-6.59%
Home Equity + Homeownership	0.0025	17.76%	0.0009	6.56%	0.0022	15.71%
Location Characteristics						
Region of Residence	-0.0007	-5.20%	0.0009	6.34%	0.0003	2.52%
Central County / Suburban / Rural Status	-0.0007	-4.74%	0.0003	1.94%	0.0000	0.29%
Population Density	-0.0002	-1.58%	-0.0002	-1.41%	-0.0002	-1.10%
% Other Race	-0.0122	-88.37%	-0.0041	-29.77%	-0.0112	-81.19%
Median Family Income	-0.0008	-5.45%	-0.0033	-24.03%	-0.0023	-16.28%
Crime Rate	-0.0026	-18.48%	-0.0001	-0.43%	-0.0006	-4.15%
Unemployment Rate	0.0003	2.26%	0.0018	12.95%	0.0011	8.00%
% College Degree	-0.0022	-15.65%	-0.0001	-0.53%	-0.0005	-3.69%
Self-Employment Rate	0.0097	69.71%	0.0019	13.67%	0.0042	30.38%
Establishments Per Capita	0.0010	7.21%	0.0000	-0.23%	0.0001	0.54%
SBA Lending Rate	0.0001	0.54%	0.0003	2.32%	0.0003	2.26%
All Personal and Household Characteristics	0.0039	28.03%	0.0007	5.00%	0.0013	9.11%
All Location Characteristics	-0.0083	-59.75%	-0.0027	-19.18%	-0.0086	-62.42%
All Location Characteristics Excluding Racial Composition	0.0040	28.62%	0.0015	10.59%	0.0026	18.76%
All Included Variables	-0.0044	-31.72%	-0.0020	-14.18%	-0.0074	-53.31%

averages of 1,000 randomly selected matches between Black and white subsamples.

Including home equity and home ownership, household characteristics explain between 5 per cent and 28 per cent of the Black-white gap in the transition into self-employment, depending on the specification. Most of this relative contribution (between 7 per cent and 18 per cent) is driven by the effect of home equity and home ownership, however. This suggests that the Black-white gap in transitions into self-employment would be substantially reduced if Blacks owned homes at rates of whites and had home equity levels of whites.

Examining the effect of residential location characteristics, equating Black and white residential location characteristics actually serves to increase the Black-white self-employment gap by between 19 per cent and 63 per cent. This is somewhat misleading, however, because the direction of the gap reduction is highly variable from characteristic to characteristic. Furthermore, equating Black and white 'other' racial compositions results in an extremely large change in racial composition, given that whites reside in counties that are 9.68 per cent Black, while Blacks reside in counties that are 63.95 per cent white. Given that racial composition is not statistically significant in the estimated models, it is useful to examine the relative gap with this variable omitted. Removing racial composition, equating the remaining observed residential location characteristics for Blacks and whites results in a 28.62 per cent reduction in the self-employment transition gap when the Black coefficients are used, a 10.59 per cent reduction with the white coefficients, and a 18.76 per cent reduction with the full sample coefficients. In other words, if racial composition were held constant, but the observed non-racial residential location characteristics of Blacks and whites were equated, the Black-white gap in self-employment transitions would decline by between 11 per cent and 29 per cent, a large change compared to the influence of household characteristics.

Equalizing the racial gap in exposure to self-employed workers would have the largest impact on reducing the racial gap in self-employment entry. This variable alone explains 70 per cent of the Black-white gap in self-employment transitions when the Black coefficients are applied. When the white coefficients are applied, the percentage is still largest among all residential location characteristics at 14 per cent.

Table 5.5 displays the results of decompositions of the racial gap in the transition out of self-employment, using the same technique employed to decompose the entry gap. Home ownership and home equity explain a large portion of the gap in self-employment transitions when the white coefficients are applied. When the Black coefficients are applied, the per cent of the gap explained declines from 23 per cent to 4 per cent. This is due to the relatively larger impact of home ownership on exit probabilities for whites relative to Blacks.

Table 5.5

	Black Coefficients		White Coefficients		Full Sample Coefficients	
Decompositions of the Estimated Black-White Gap in Transitions Out of Self-Employment	Total Gap	% of B-W Gap	Total Gap	% of B-W Gap	Total Gap	% of B-W Gap
Estimated Black-White Transition Probability Gap	-0.1260		-0.1260		-0.1260	
Contributions from Racial Differences in:						
Personal and Household Characteristics						
Household and Personal Characteristics	-0.0309	24.48%	-0.0235	18.63%	-0.0224	17.78%
Home Equity + Homeownership	-0.0048	3.83%	-0.0296	23.45%	-0.0284	22.53%
Location Characteristics						
Region of Residence	0.0001	-0.08%	0.0026	-2.06%	0.0010	-0.78%
Central County / Suburban / Rural Status	0.0094	-7.46%	0.0098	-7.80%	0.0103	-8.19%
Population Density	0.0007	-0.52%	0.0029	-2.26%	0.0023	-1.82%
% Other Race	-0.0791	62.74%	-0.0276	21.92%	-0.0090	7.15%
Median Family Income	-0.0080	6.36%	0.0001	-0.06%	-0.0002	0.18%
Crime Rate	-0.0088	6.95%	0.0056	-4.45%	0.0032	-2.51%
Unemployment Rate	0.0033	-2.61%	0.0009	-0.69%	0.0007	-0.53%
% College Degree	0.0002	-0.12%	0.0030	-2.41%	0.0021	-1.64%
Self-Employment Rate	-0.0611	48.47%	-0.0187	14.88%	-0.0182	14.43%
Establishments Per Capita	-0.0021	1.68%	0.0002	-0.16%	-0.0004	0.32%
SBA Lending Rate	0.0023	-1.82%	0.0011	-0.87%	0.0011	-0.90%
All Personal and Household Characteristics	-0.0357	28.31%	-0.0530	42.08%	-0.0508	40.31%
All Location Characteristics	-0.1432	113.60%	-0.0202	16.03%	-0.0072	5.70%
All Location Characteristics Excluding Racial Composition	-0.0641	50.86%	0.0074	-5.89%	0.0018	-1.45%
All Included Variables	-0.1788	141.90%	-0.0732	58.12%	-0.0580	46.01%

Examining the combined influence of residential location character-istics other than racial composition, residential location characteristics explain a large portion of the Black-white gap in self-employment exit when the Black coefficients are applied. When this simulation is performed with the white coefficients and full sample models, the Black-white gap is actually increased slightly. This is somewhat illusory, however, because local self-employment concentration is the only significant residential location characteristic in the exit models. Examining this variable alone, exposure to self-employed workers has a large and significant impact on the exit gap. When the percentage of self-employed workers in the sur-rounding county is equated for Blacks and whites, the exit gap is reduced by between 14 per cent and 48 per cent, with the largest reductions occur-ring in the Black model.

The Endogeneity of Residential Location

Any researcher attempting to examine the influence of residential loca-tion on employment outcomes must grapple with a difficult problem: while residential location may influence employment outcomes, an indi-vidual's labour market status may also influence his or her choice of resi-dential location. This problem has been addressed in the past by focusing on a subsample of those for whom residential location can be considered exogenous (youths living with their parents, for example) or by jointly modelling the choice of residential location with the relevant employ-ment outcome.

In this study, measured are residential location characteristics for the location observed prior to self-employment transition and an assumption made that the residential location decision was not made on the basis of whether or not to start a business. If one assumes that unobserved individual characteristics do not jointly influence location decisions and self-employment decisions, this strategy is sufficient to ensure unbiased estimates of the coefficients in equation (5.1). To determine the sensitivity of the results presented above to possible endogeneity bias, the results are compared with fixed effects estimates of equation (5.1) which control for both individual- and family-level unobserved heterogeneity. Individual-level fixed effects control for unobserved time-invariant individual factors which may jointly affect location choice and self-employment outcomes. One problem with estimating such models, however, is that the number of observations per individual in the panel is quite small (approximately five observations per individual on average). With a small number of observations per individual, the well-known incidental parameters problem results (Lancaster 2000). As a second-best robustness check, models that control for family-level heterogeneity are also examined. In these models, group membership is defined by each worker's original 1968 PSID family. As such, the models examine intra-family differences, with families defined by all parents, siblings, and other household members living in the worker's original PSID household. If entrepreneurial and business management skills are transferred through intergenerational links, as suggested by Hout and Rosen (2000), controls for family-level heterogeneity would capture all unobserved family-level traits which influence one's business decisions, including decisions related to the location of one's business, and hence, the location of one's residence. Given the high correlation between individual-level covariates and the fixed effects, fixed effects models of this sort could only be estimated for the pooled model explaining transitions into employment. These results are reported in Table 5.6 below.

Comparing these results with those presented in the third column of Table 5.2, I find that controls for heterogeneity are associated with increases in the estimated coefficients for all residential location controls that are statistically significant in the original model displayed in Table 5.2. The coefficient on local self-employment concentrations, for example, increases from .0211 to .0314 in the model with family-level fixed effects to .0408 in the model with individual fixed effects. The only exception is 'per cent other race', which becomes negative and statistically insignificant in the model with family-level heterogeneity. While by no means a definitive test for endogeneity bias, these results suggest that if endogeneity influences the estimates of the impact of residential location as reported in Tables 5.2 and 5.3 and the decompositions reported in Tables 5.4 and 5.5, the impact of endogeneity is likely to bias the

Table 5.6

Fixed Effects Probit Regression for Transition Into Self-Employment, Black + White Workers

Variable	Individual Fixed Effects			Family Fixed Effects		
	Coef.	St. Error	Sig.	Coef.	St. Error	Sig.
Personal and Household Characteristics						
Black	-6.1244	13442.9918		-1.3211	0.7960	*
Currently Married	0.2542	0.2109		-0.1437	0.0841	*
Previously Married	0.3188	0.2380		0.0512	0.1085	
Number of Children	0.0939	0.0453	**	0.0200	0.0240	
Age of Youngest Child	-0.0047	0.0091		-0.0071	0.0057	
Age	0.0353	0.0393		0.0563	0.0189	***
Age Squared	-0.0002	0.0005		-0.0007	0.0002	***
Interest Income ($1,000s)	0.0202	0.0127		0.0092	0.0074	
Interest Income Squared ($1,000s)	-0.0001	0.0001		0.0000	0.0000	
Cash Payments Received ($1,000s)	0.0000	0.0046		0.0009	0.0032	
Cash Payments Received Squared ($1,000s)	0.0000	0.0000		0.0000	0.0000	
Homeowner	0.0423	0.1196		-0.2383	0.0661	***
Home Equity ($10,000s)	0.0038	0.0131		0.0313	0.0083	***
Home Equity Squared ($10,000s)	-0.0001	0.0002		-0.0003	0.0002	
Years of Experience	0.0238	0.0178		-0.0280	0.0087	***
Years of Experience Squared	-0.0004	0.0007		0.0008	0.0003	***
High School Degree	0.2049	0.2155		-0.0788	0.0716	
Attended College	0.1616	0.2913		-0.0922	0.0863	
College Degree	0.6052	0.3956		-0.0135	0.0989	
Father Has High School Degree	-1.8174	0.8919	**	-0.1080	0.0728	
Father Attended College	-1.8301	1.2069		-0.0866	0.1158	
Father Has College Degree	11.3855	7317.8893		-0.0659	0.1058	
Residential Location Characteristics						
Midwest Region	0.0870	0.4429		0.1286	0.1861	
South Region	-0.0391	0.4399		-0.0299	0.1818	
West Region	-0.1246	0.4486		-0.1110	0.1976	
Central County	0.3549	0.3013		-0.2284	0.1480	
Rural County	0.6638	0.3133	**	-0.1823	0.1567	
Population Density	7.8E-06	1.9E-05		0.0000	9.2E-06	
% Other Race	0.0086	0.0067		-0.0005	0.0031	
Median Family Income	1.3E-06	0.0000		-1.5E-05	2.4E-05	
Median Family Income Squared	-2.6E-10	0.0000		-4.5E-11	2.3E-10	
Crime Per Capita	-1.6530	2.9206		-0.3490	1.3478	
Unemployment Rate (%)	0.0149	0.0307		-0.0213	0.0175	
Adults With College Degree (%)	0.0320	0.0145	**	0.0173	0.0075	**
Self-Employment Rate (%)	0.0408	0.0246	*	0.0314	0.0124	**
Establishments Per Capita	-1.9020	12.4080		0.9266	6.1765	
SBA Lending Per $1M in Bank Deposits	0.0360	0.0164	**	0.0230	0.0100	**
Log-Likelihood	-1339.5080			-2353.2700		
Pseudo R-Square	0.8940			0.2285		
Sample Size	25260			25260		

*** p < .01; ** p < .05; * p < .10
Fixed effects estimates not reported for brevity.

coefficients downward. Therefore, these estimates should be interpreted as conservative estimates of the total influence of residential location on self-employment transitions.

CONCLUSION

This chapter examined the influence of racial differences in residential location characteristics on the Black-white gap in self-employment entry and exit. Estimated were probit models of self-employment entry and exit for subsamples of Black and white workers from the PSID. The coefficient estimates from these models towards a decomposition of the total contribution of racial differences in various covariates towards the Black-white gap in self-employment transitions were applied. Several findings emerge from this analysis. First, home ownership reduces the probability of transitioning into self-employment for whites but increases the probability of remaining self-employed conditional on transitioning into self-employment. Home equity, on the other hand, increases the probability of self-employment entry and reduces the probability of exit for whites only. These results suggest that while home ownership may discourage self-employment due to the higher transaction costs associated with relocation among home owners, the equity gained through home ownership provides an important financial cushion for those with enough accumulated equity. Racial differences in the impact of home ownership probably reflect the lower home equity position of Blacks relative to whites, and possibly discriminatory barriers in mortgage lending, given that whites in the sample have nearly three times more accumulated home equity than Blacks.

Residential location characteristics play an important role in shaping the incentives to enter and exit self-employment, and the relative influence of residential location characteristics on the dynamics of self employment is highly variable across racial groups. Among Blacks, access to higher income households, educated adults, higher local concentrations of self-employed workers and weaker competition from surrounding establishments is associated with increased entry into self-employment, while residence in a non-rural county, residence in non-Western regions and local concentrations of self-employed workers all reduce the probability of self-employment exit. Among whites, lower median family incomes, lower unemployment rates, local concentrations of more highly educated adults and local concentrations of SBA lending all catalyze entry into self-employment, while the local concentration of self-employed workers is the only factor reducing the probability of exit. Further research is needed to determine whether racial differences in SBA lending reflect discriminatory barriers, liquidity constraints or other factors. At a minimum, these results suggest that the SBA 504 programme's goals of expanding minority business development are yet to be fully realized.

Regarding the combined influence of residential location characteristics, racial differences in the observed characteristics of residential location, rather than residential segregation per se, play an important role in influencing self-employment entry and exit. If racial composition were held constant, but the observed non-racial residential location characteristics of Blacks and whites were equated, the Black-white gap in self-employment entry would decline by between 11 per cent and 29 per cent. The influence of residential location on racial gaps in self-employment exit occurs primarily through the influence of local concentrations of self-employed workers. When the percentage of self-employed workers in the surrounding county is equated for Blacks and whites, the exit gap is reduced by between 14 per cent and 48 per cent, with the largest reductions occurring in the Black model.

The percentage of workers within the surrounding county who are self-employed has the most consistent impact on self-employment transitions across all models examined. Residing in counties with more self-employed workers serves to both increase the probability that one transitions into self-employment and reduce the probability that one leaves self-employment conditional on entering. Furthermore, the marginal effects of local self-employment concentrations are largest for Blacks. These results suggest that either knowledge spill-overs influence the dynamics of self-employment entry or local unobserved residential characteristics attractive to existing self-employed workers support further entry into self-employment. If knowledge spill-overs are important, identifying such concentrations and providing access to other self-employed workers is also likely to prove to be a successful strategy for reducing the Black-white self-employment gap.

Appendix 5.1

Descriptive Statistics for Transitions Into Self-Employment, Black + White Workers

Sample:	Full Sample N=25260		White Workers N=17889		Black Workers N=7371	
	Mean	Std. Dev.	Mean	Std. Dev.	Mean	Std. Dev.
Dependent Variable						
Transition into Self Employment	0.0356	0.1853	0.0396	0.1951	0.0258	0.1585
Independent Variables						
Personal and Household Characteristics						
Currently Married	0.8027	0.3980	0.8349	0.3713	0.7245	0.4468
Previously Married	0.0829	0.2757	0.0709	0.2566	0.1121	0.3155
Number of Children	1.1905	1.2543	1.1269	1.1945	1.3447	1.3766
Age of Youngest Child	3.5857	4.8153	3.6104	4.8752	3.5260	4.6664
Age	36.2400	10.6062	36.6436	10.7341	35.2605	10.2238
Age Squared	1425.8227	854.8521	1457.9655	867.3561	1347.8140	818.5416
Interest Income ($1,000s)	0.9165	4.5927	1.2136	5.3656	0.1955	1.2966
Interest Income Squared ($1,000s)	21.9324	682.9106	30.2611	811.2401	1.7191	21.5694
Cash Payments Received ($1,000s)	0.7381	12.2025	0.9495	14.3971	0.2250	2.6192
Cash Payments Received Squared ($1,000s)	149.4392	11434.3496	208.1671	13586.3321	6.9099	215.5578
Homeowner	0.6086	0.4881	0.6715	0.4697	0.4560	0.4981
Home Equity ($10,000s)	3.5027	6.1244	4.3138	6.8015	1.5342	3.2861
Home Equity Squared ($10,000s)	49.7759	281.1452	64.8669	325.6862	13.1510	107.4995
Years of Experience	5.3175	6.4094	5.2006	6.3508	5.6012	6.5414
Years of Experience Squared	69.3548	187.1646	67.3762	182.2563	74.1568	198.5037
High School Degree	0.3778	0.4848	0.3637	0.4811	0.4119	0.4922
Attended College	0.1887	0.3913	0.1965	0.3974	0.1699	0.3755
College Degree	0.1998	0.3999	0.2502	0.4331	0.0776	0.2676
Father Has High School Degree	0.2354	0.4242	0.2730	0.4455	0.1439	0.3511
Father Attended College	0.0721	0.2586	0.0910	0.2876	0.0262	0.1597
Father Has College Degree	0.0837	0.2770	0.1084	0.3109	0.0239	0.1527
Residential Location Characteristics						
Midwest Region	0.2367	0.4250	0.2772	0.4476	0.1382	0.3452
South Region	0.4455	0.4970	0.3315	0.4708	0.7220	0.4480
West Region	0.1595	0.3662	0.1953	0.3965	0.0726	0.2595
Central County	0.7423	0.4374	0.7185	0.4497	0.8000	0.4000
Rural County	0.2070	0.4051	0.2324	0.4224	0.1452	0.3523
Population Density	1680.4999	4498.1654	1371.7314	4335.1862	2429.8635	4789.3046
% Other Race	25.5114	27.5754	9.6754	10.8125	63.9446	15.3729
Median Family Income	41468.1251	9506.4880	42388.9474	9684.7935	39233.3414	8661.8171
Median Family Income Squared	1.8E+09	8.8E+08	1.9E+09	9.1E+08	1.6E+09	7.6E+08
Crime Per Capita	0.0577	0.0328	0.0530	0.0316	0.0690	0.0328
Unemployment Rate (%)	6.4955	2.3504	6.3249	2.2428	6.9098	2.5463
Adults With College Degree (%)	18.4505	7.5524	18.4032	7.5724	18.5655	7.5030
Self-Employment Rate (%)	6.6579	3.1020	7.1214	3.4156	5.5329	1.8954
Establishments Per Capita	0.0225	0.0064	0.0227	0.0063	0.0221	0.0064
SBA Lending Per $1M in Bank Deposits	1.4420	2.4697	1.4686	2.4398	1.3774	2.5397

Appendix 5.2

Descriptive Statistics for Transitions Out of Self-Employment, Black + White Workers

Sample:	Full Sample		White Workers		Black Workers	
	N=4271		N=3811		N=460	
	Mean	Std. Dev.	Mean	Std. Dev.	Mean	Std. Dev.
Dependent Variable						
Transition into Self Employment	0.1723	0.3777	0.1588	0.3655	0.2848	0.4518
Independent Variables						
Personal and Household Characteristics						
Currently Married	0.8593	0.3478	0.8725	0.3336	0.7500	0.4335
Previously Married	0.0745	0.2625	0.0680	0.2517	0.1283	0.3347
Number of Children	1.1627	1.2061	1.1425	1.1769	1.3304	1.4156
Age of Youngest Child	4.2943	5.2914	4.2973	5.2836	4.2696	5.3620
Age	40.6282	10.6356	40.6216	10.7262	40.6826	11.7150
Age Squared	1768.0326	930.4171	1765.1375	919.3338	1792.0174	1018.3761
Interest Income ($1,000s)	4.3747	19.4951	4.8128	20.5648	0.7453	3.2220
Interest Income Squared ($1,000s)	399.1064	8902.3523	445.9625	9423.3187	10.9140	91.9382
Cash Payments Received ($1,000s)	2.1516	39.3408	2.3630	41.6078	0.3996	4.9361
Cash Payments Received Squared ($1,000s)	1551.9686	55854.3696	1736.3424	59127.1913	24.4715	483.2115
Homeowner	0.7588	0.4278	0.7817	0.4132	0.5696	0.4957
Home Equity ($10,000s)	7.3012	10.1830	7.8554	10.4896	2.7093	5.2572
Home Equity Squared ($10,000s)	156.9773	580.6004	171.7102	607.7424	34.9182	231.0173
Years of Experience	8.5921	9.1782	8.7034	9.1855	7.6705	9.0750
Years of Experience Squared	158.0445	350.9231	160.1003	355.9331	141.0126	306.0950
High School Degree	0.3217	0.4672	0.3227	0.4676	0.3130	0.4642
Attended College	0.1969	0.3977	0.2002	0.4002	0.1696	0.3757
College Degree	0.2952	0.4562	0.3188	0.4661	0.1000	0.3003
Father Has High School Degree	0.2222	0.4158	0.2341	0.4235	0.1239	0.3296
Father Attended College	0.0880	0.2834	0.0958	0.2943	0.0239	0.1529
Father Has College Degree	0.1276	0.3337	0.1370	0.3439	0.0500	0.2182
Residential Location Characteristics						
Midwest Region	0.2622	0.4399	0.2810	0.4496	0.1065	0.3088
South Region	0.3863	0.4870	0.3430	0.4748	0.7457	0.4360
West Region	0.1782	0.3827	0.1887	0.3913	0.0913	0.2884
Central County	0.6706	0.4701	0.6536	0.4759	0.8109	0.3920
Rural County	0.2749	0.4465	0.2955	0.4563	0.1043	0.3060
Population Density	1573.6732	5290.0005	1483.3804	5435.6343	2321.7286	3801.4255
% Other Race	15.6878	20.5731	9.8716	11.5980	63.8738	14.5970
Median Family Income	41527.7801	10531.8628	41610.1784	10672.4254	40845.1280	9268.1194
Median Family Income Squared	1.8E+09	1.0E+09	1.8E+09	1.0E+09	1.8E+09	8.7E+08
Crime Per Capita	0.0533	0.0346	0.0512	0.0343	0.0705	0.0331
Unemployment Rate (%)	6.1614	2.2801	6.1053	2.2304	6.6259	2.6133
Adults With College Degree (%)	18.5076	7.7989	18.3786	7.7484	19.5771	8.1357
Self-Employment Rate (%)	8.0593	4.8524	8.3485	5.0306	5.6629	1.5905
Establishments Per Capita	0.0234	0.0066	0.0235	0.0066	0.0222	0.0061
SBA Lending Per $1M in Bank Deposits	1.5684	3.0205	1.6115	3.1086	1.2108	2.1252

NOTES

1. 1992 US Economic Census, Characteristics of Business Owners, Table 30b, 'Percent of Minority Customers by Receipts Size of Firm: 1992', US Bureau of the Census.
2. This time period was chosen due to the fact that census tract geocodes prior to 1980 are less precise than those for 1980 and 1990. The year 1997 is chosen as the terminal period, because this is the final year in which consecutive year-to-year information for PSID respondents is available.
3. Descriptive statistics for all independent variables are shown in Appendix 5.1 and 5.2.
4. The data used in this analysis are derived from Sensitive Data Files of the Panel Study of Income Dynamics, obtained under special contractual arrangements designed to protect the anonymity of respondents. These data are not available from the authors. Persons interested in obtaining PSID Sensitive Data Files should contact the ISR through the internet at PSIDHelp@ isr.umich.edu.
5. The results are not sensitive to alternative approaches to measuring racial integration.

BIBLIOGRAPHY

Acs, Z. J. and Armington, C. (2004) 'The impact of geographic differences in human capital on service firm formation rates', Journal of Urban Economics, 56: 244–78.

Aldrich, H., Cater, J., Jones, T., McEvoy, D. and Velleman, P. (1985) 'Ethnic residential concentration and the protected market hypothesis', Social Forces, 63(4): 996–1009.

Aldrich, H. and Reiss Jr, A. J. (1976) 'Continuities in the study of ecological succession: changes in the race composition of neighbourhoods and their businesses', The American Journal of Sociology, 81(4): 846–66.

Armington, C. and Acs, Z. J. (2002) 'The determinants of regional variation in new firm formation', Regional Studies, 36: 33–45.

Audretsch, D. B. and Fritsch, M. (1994) 'The geography of firm births in Germany', Regional Studies, 28: 359–65.

Bates, T. (1989) 'The changing nature of minority business: a comparative analysis of Asian, non-minority, and Black-owned businesses', The Review of Black Political Economy, 18: 25–42.

——(1997) Race, Self-Employment and Upward Mobility: An illusive American dream, Washington, DC: Woodrow Wilson Center Press.

——(2006) 'The urban development potential of Black-owned businesses', Journal of the American Planning Association, 72(2): 227–37.

Black, D., Holtz-Eakin, D. and Rosenthal, S. (2001) 'Racial minorities, economic scale and the geography of self-employment', in W. G. Gale and J. Rothenberg Pack (eds) Brookings-Wharton Papers on Urban Affairs, Washington, DC: Brookings Institution Press.

Blinder, A. S. (1973) 'Wage discrimination: reduced form and structural variables', Journal of Human Resources, 8: 436–55.

Boehm, T. P. and Ihlanfeldt, K. R. (1991) 'The revelation of neighbourhood preferences: an N-chotomous multivariate probit approach', Journal of Housing Economics, 1: 33–59.

Borjas, G. J. (1986) 'The self-employment experience of immigrants', The Journal of Human Resources, 21(4): 485–506.

Borjas, G. and Bronars, S. (1989) 'Consumer discrimination and self-employment', Journal of Political Economy', 97(3): 581–605.

Brimmer, A. (1968) 'Desegregation and Negro leadership', in E. Ginsberg (ed.) Business Leadership and the Negro Crisis, New York: McGraw-Hill.

Dawkins, C.J., Shen, Q. and Sanchez, T.W. (2005) 'Race, space and unemployment duration', Journal of Urban Economics, 58: 91–113.

Dietz, R. D. and Haurin, D. R. (2003) 'The social and private micro-level consequences of home ownership', Journal of Urban Economics, 54: 401–50.

Ellen, I. G. and Turner, M. A. (1997) 'Does neighbourhood matter? Assessing recent evidence', Housing Policy Debate, 8(4): 833–66.

Evans, D. S. and Jovanovic, B. (1989) 'An estimated model of entrepreneurial choice under liquidity constraints', Journal of Political Economy, 97(4): 808–27.

Fairlie, R. W. (1999) 'The absence of the African-American owned business: an analysis of the dynamics of self-employment', Journal of Labor Economics, 17(1): 80–108.

——(2003) 'An extension of the Blinder-Oaxaca decomposition technique to logit and probit models', Yale University Economic Growth Center Discussion Paper No. 873.

——(2005) 'Entrepreneurship among disadvantaged groups: an analysis of the dynamics of self-employment by gender, race and education', in S. C. Parker,

Z. J. Acs and D. R. Audretsch (eds) Handbook of Entrepreneurship, Boston: Kluwer Academic (forthcoming).

Fairlie, R. W. and Meyer, B. D. (1996) 'Ethnic and racial self-employment differences and possible explanations', Journal of Human Resources, 31(4): 757–93.

——(2000) 'Trends in self-employment among white and Black men during the twentieth century', The Journal of Human Resources, 35(4): 643–69.

Fischer, M. J. and Massey, D. S. (2000) 'Residential segregation and ethnic enterprise in US metropolitan areas', Social Problems, 47(3): 408–24.

Gladwin, C. H., Long, B. F., Babb, E. M., Beaulieu, L. J., Moseley, A.,Mulkey, D. and Zimet, D. J. (1989) 'Rural entrepreneurship: one key to rural revitalization', *American* Journal of Agricultural Economics, 71(5): 1305–14.

Glaeser, E. L., Kallal, H., Scheinkman, J. A. and Shleifer, A. (1992) 'Growth in cities', Journal of Political Economy, 100: 1126–52.

Glaeser, E. L. and Vigdor, J. L. (2001) 'Racial segregation in the 2000 Census: promising news', Brookings Institution Center on Urban and Metropolitan Policy Working Paper.

Glazer, N. and Moynihan, D. (1963) Beyond the Melting Pot, Cambridge, MA: MIT Press.

Hamilton, B. H. (2000) 'Does entrepreneurship pay? An empirical analysis of the returns to self-employment', Journal of Political Economy, 108(3): 604–31.

Hout, M. and Rosen, H. S. (2000) 'Self-employment, family background and race', Journal of Human Resources, 35(4): 670–92.

Hurst, E. and Lusardi, A. (2004) 'Liquidity constraints, household wealth, and entrepreneurship', Journal of Political Economy, 112(2): 319–47.

Jencks, C. and Mayer, S. (1990) 'The social consequences of growing up in a poor neighbourhood', in L. E. Lynn, Jr. and M. G. H. McGeary (eds) Inner City Poverty in the United States, Washington, DC: National Academy Press.

Kihlstrom, R. and Laffont, J.-J. (1979) 'A general equilibrium entrepreneurial theory of firm formation based on risk aversion', Journal of Political Economy, 87: 719–48.

Kim, S. (2000) 'Race and home price appreciation in urban neighbourhoods: evidence from Milwaukee, Wisconsin', Review of Black Political Economy, 28: 9–30.

Lancaster, T. (2000) 'The incidental parameters problem since 1948', Journal of Econometrics, 95: 391–414.

Lazear, E. P. and Moore, R. L. (1984) 'Incentives, productivity, and labor contracts', Quarterly Journal of Economics, 99: 275–96.

Lewis Mumford Center (2001) 'Ethnic diversity grows, neighbourhood integration lags behind', Lewis Mumford Center Working Paper.

Light, I. (1972) Ethnic Enterprise in America, Berkeley: University of California Press.

Logan, J. R. (2002) 'Separate and unequal: the neighbourhood gap for Blacks and Hispanics in metropolitan America', Lewis Mumford Center Working Paper.

Lucas, R. E. (1978) 'On the size distribution of firms', Bell Journal of Economics, 9: 508–23.

Meyer, B. D. (1990) 'Why are there so few Black entrepreneurs?', National Bureau of Economic Research Working Paper No. 3537, Cambridge, MA: NBER.

Oaxaca, R. (1973) 'Male-female wage differentials in urban labor markets', International Economic Review, 14: 693–709.

Oliver, M. L. and Shapiro, T. M. (1995) Black Wealth/White Wealth: A new perspective on racial inequality, New York: Routledge.

Oswald, A. J. (1996) 'A conjecture on the explanation for high unemployment in the industrialized nations, Part 1', Working Paper 475, Department of Economics, Warwick University.

——(1997) 'Theory of homes and jobs', Working Paper, Department of Economics, Warwick University.

Quercia, R. G., McCarthy, G. W., Ryznar, R. M. and Can Talen, A. (2000) 'Spatio-temporal measurement of house price appreciation in underserved areas', Journal of Housing Research, 11(1): 1–28.

Wilson, W. J. (1987) The Truly Disadvantaged: The inner city, the underclass, and public policy, Chicago: University of Chicago Press.

Wolff, E. N. (1998) 'Recent trends in the size distribution of household wealth', The Journal of Economic Perspectives, 12(3): 131–50.

6 All Underserved Markets Are Not Created Equal
Why the Private Sector Alone Will Not Address the Capital Needs of Distressed US Communities

Julia Sass Rubin

INTRODUCTION

The economic potential of underserved communities, such as those located in inner-city geographies or populated by people of colour, has received substantial attention over the last decade. Urban scholars have written about the need to invest in such communities for decades (see, for example, Vietorisz and Harrison 1970, Bates 1991, 1994). The issue gained broader awareness, however, after being championed by Harvard Business School professor, Michael Porter. Porter argued that underserved communities should be viewed as markets that are rich in economic opportunities. Those opportunities could best be harvested by profit-driven investors, which would lead to profits for them and economic prosperity for community residents. Porter's thesis has been echoed by others (see The American Assembly 1997, Carr 1999), including a group of researchers at the Milken Institute who have focused specifically on the challenges that underserved communities face in accessing capital. The Milken researchers refer to such communities as 'Emerging Domestic Markets' in order to highlight their economic potential. They argue that information imperfections are keeping profit-driven investors from recognizing what these markets have to offer.

Increasing prosperity in underserved communities is a very worthwhile goal. In the interest of convincing profit-driven investors that such communities have economic merit, however, both Porter and the Milken researchers have oversimplified their message, losing important distinctions in the process. This oversimplification can have damaging consequences for the very communities they are trying to assist. Numerous scholars have addressed the shortcoming of Porter's work (see Boston and Ross 1996, 1997, Bates 1997b, Harrison and Glasmeier 1997, Goozner 1998). This chapter focuses on the limitations of the Milken approach.

My critique is three-fold. First, the Milken researchers treat all underserved communities as interchangeable, not acknowledging that they differ in important ways in the nature and causes of their capital constraints.

These differences matter very much for framing an appropriate response to the problem. Second, the Milken researchers inaccurately claim that underserved communities lack access to capital primarily as a result of information failure, ignoring the numerous other obstacles that raise transaction and operating costs and discourage profit-driven investors from focusing on such communities. Overcoming these additional obstacles requires much more than improved information; it requires subsidy, a fact that the Milken approach obscures and potentially discourages. Third, the Milken researchers' assumption that profit-driven investors can take the lead in meeting the capital needs of underserved communities is unrealistic because it fails to address these additional barriers to investment. Instead, the public sector must initiate a solution by providing the incentives necessary to counter the obstacles and attract profit-driven investors.

My intention in making these critiques is not to discourage profit-driven investors from investing in underserved communities or to brand some geographies and populations as less worthy of such investment. Rather, it is to push for a more sophisticated understanding of what such communities need, one that does not obscure or ignore the complexities of the problems, in order to ensure that these communities are not left behind by either private or public sector investors.

This chapter proceeds as follows. The first section details the specific arguments put forth by the Milken researchers. The second section refutes the idea that underserved communities are homogenous by reviewing the literature on how such populations and geographies differ from each other in the nature and causes of their capital constraints. The third section takes issue with the idea that communities are underserved solely because of information failure. It examines communities that lack access to venture capital, to highlight the numerous other obstacles to investment that such communities must overcome and to argue that such obstacles discourage a solution led by profit-driven investors. The fourth section illustrates some of the limitations of the emerging domestic markets approach via a case study of the CalPERS (California Public Employees Retirement System) California Initiative. The chapter concludes with recommendations for how the public and private sectors can best address the capital needs of underserved communities.

THE EMERGING DOMESTIC MARKETS
IDEA AND ITS ANTECEDENTS

The idea that underserved communities can experience economic prosperity through the efforts of profit-driven investors re-emerged in the mid 1990s, in two influential (and controversial) articles that Michael Porter wrote about the economic potential of inner-city markets (1995, 1997). Porter argued that prior efforts to foster economic development in inner cities had 'been based on heavy subsidies and on distorting or blunting market forces' (Institute for Strategy and Competitiveness 2008). Porter felt that

> A sustainable economic base can be created in the inner city, but only as it has been created elsewhere: through private, for-profit initiatives and investment based on economic self-interest and genuine competitive advantage—not through artificial inducements, charity, or government mandates. (Porter 1995: 55–56)

For Porter, one of the main barriers that kept inner-city markets from developing was a lack of access to capital, especially equity capital. Consistent with his broader theme, he argued that 'the most important way to bring debt and equity investment to the inner city is by engaging the private sector' (Porter 1995: 69).

Porter's ideas had a positive reception at the Milken Institute, a think tank established by former Wall Street financier, Michael Milken. The institute sees its role as using 'capital-market principles and financial innovations to address social and economic challenges, from energy independence to poverty' (Milken Institute 2008). Beginning in the late 1990s, researchers at the institute started focusing on the capital access side of underserved markets, initially as part of a project that the institute did for the Minority Business Development Agency of the US Department of Commerce (Yago and Harrington 1999).

Like Porter, the Milken researchers wanted to 'shift the common viewpoint' about underserved markets in order to convince potential profit-driven investors of their attractiveness (Yago 2007: 1). They felt that terms like 'minority businesses' carried negative associations for these investors (Yago, Zeidman and Abuyuan 2007: 1). They also felt that this terminology was 'statistically inaccurate. If you were looking at states like California or New York, that have diverse population groups, "minority status" is a kind of anachronistic term to describe what's occurring in these demographically- and data-driven markets' (Yago 2007: 1).

In 1999, Milken Institute researchers Michael Harrington and Glenn Yago identified another way of referring to such markets. In a report about the problems faced by minority entrepreneurs in obtaining capital to start and grow their businesses, Harrington and Yago wrote that businesses owned by people of colour represented an '"emerging" and largely untapped domestic market' (Yago and Harrington 1999: 1).

This market was emerging because people of colour were 'experiencing higher rates of population growth than whites' and the businesses owned by people of colour were 'growing even faster than the population in terms of both numbers of new firms and revenues.' However, the growth of this market was 'being constrained by inadequate capital access' (Yago and Harrington 1999: 1).

Harrington and Yago based their 'Emerging Domestic Markets' construct on the international development terminology coined by Antoine van Agtmael of the World Bank (Yago, Zeidman and Schmidt 2003). They hoped to emulate Agtmael's successful reframing of how certain international markets were viewed from being underdeveloped to emerging, as he shifted the emphasis of his analysis from these markets' levels of indebtedness to their levels of growth (Yago 2007).

The initial usage of the emerging domestic markets terminology by Harrington and Yago was in the context of entrepreneurs of colour only. However, Milken researchers broadened the term's application substantially in 2003 and again in 2007 to include:

> ethnic- and women-owned firms, urban and rural communities, companies serving low-to-moderate-income populations, and other small- and medium-sized businesses . . . people of colour (African-Americans, Latinos/Hispanics, Asian Americans/Pacific Islanders and Native Americans), women and low-to-moderate-income communities (LMI) (both businesses located there and firms owned by LMI entrepreneurs). (Yago, Zeidman and Abuyuan 2007: 3)

The Milken researchers argued that all these markets were 'emerging' because they encompassed the fastest growing segments of the US population. Moreover, the growing diversity of the US population 'has increased the range of places in which the new owners live or locate their businesses, leading to demands for capital in a wider variety of locations' (Yago, Zeidman and Abuyuan 2007: 1–2). However, this growth potential was being constrained by unequal access to capital:

> Despite their growth, the ability of [Emerging Domestic Markets (EDM)] businesses to grow their revenue remains constrained. While still marked, the growth rate of EDM firms' sales does not match that of their numbers, indicating smaller size . . . Even after controlling for a variety of factors (e.g., education, experience, industry, location), it is clear from research that EDM firms receive less capital and on less advantageous terms. Without equal access to the full array of financial products on the market, EDM businesses will not grow to their potential. And that would hinder the nation's economic growth. (Yago, Zeidman and Abuyuan 2007: 3–4)

For the Milken researchers, the primary reason 'that emerging domestic markets face capital constraints is information asymmetries—the lack of robust data on the markets. Without comprehensive, reliable demographic and financial information, financial decision makers, business leaders and public policy officials are unable to price risk and evaluate opportunities effectively' (Yago, Zeidman and Abuyuan 2007: 15). The solution they propose is a comprehensive effort 'to build a relational database to pool diverse data, masked to preserve confidentiality' that could be used by banks and other financial institutions to validate the economic potential of underserved markets (Yago, Zeidman, Magula and Sederstrom 2007: 17).

The Milken researchers have worked to expand adoption of the Emerging Domestic Markets framework by setting up the Center for Emerging Domestic Markets at the Milken Institute, to serve as 'a clearinghouse for information, a gathering place for education and networking, and a laboratory for innovation in financing businesses in emerging domestic markets (EDM), whose purpose is to increase the flow of capital to America's emerging domestic markets' (Milken Institute 2008). They also have actively promoted the Emerging Domestic Markets construct through conferences, presentations, research and consulting work (Milken Institute 2008).

Their efforts have paid off with policy makers, practitioners and academics. The Emerging Domestic Markets idea was integral to former California State Treasurer Phil Angelides' 'Double Bottom Line' initiative, which resulted in the state's two largest public pension funds adjusting their investment parameters to place greater emphasis on Emerging Domestic Markets. It also led the California State Assembly to set up an Emerging Domestic Market Advisory Group, 'to create a more efficient financial ecosystem for emerging domestic markets' (California State Assembly 2008).

Practitioners who have adopted the Emerging Domestic Markets idea include the National Association of Investment Companies (NAIC), the trade association of venture capital funds that invest in companies owned by people of colour. NAIC began using the term to refer to their target markets and changed the title of their quarterly publication to 'The Journal of EDM Finance,' with EDM referring to emerging domestic markets. The University of Virginia Darden Business School's Black Business Student Forum has hosted three annual Emerging Domestic Markets Conferences, whose main goal is to promote 'the practical importance of emerging domestic markets . . . [and] reposition these markets as a lucrative business opportunity rather than an exercise in social responsibility' (Darden Business School Forum 2006: 1).

Finally, the Milken researchers have introduced the Emerging Domestic Markets construct into academic discourse, most significantly via a collection of papers by leading scholars that was edited by Yago, Barth and Zeidman of the Milken Institute and published under the title *Entrepreneurship in Emerging Domestic Markets* (2007). The Milken researchers also partnered with the San Francisco Federal Reserve to publish a special issue of the journal *Community Development Investment Review* (2007) on the topic of Emerging Domestic Markets, which included articles by well known business and public policy scholars. Finally, academics regularly cite the numerous Milken Institute publications that promote the idea of emerging domestic markets.

Although the Milken researchers' objective of increasing access to capital in underserved communities is very worthwhile, their approach to reaching this goal is problematic. The second section of this chapter details my first critique of the Emerging Domestic Markets framework: that it treats all underserved communities as homogenous, failing to acknowledge that they differ in important ways in the nature and causes of their capital constraints. These differences matter very much for framing an appropriate response to the problem.

DIFFERENTIATING EMERGING DOMESTIC MARKETS

By placing 'ethnic- and women-owned firms, urban and rural communities, companies serving low-to-moderate-income populations, and other small- and medium-sized businesses . . . people of colour, women . . . businesses located [in low and moderate income communities] and firms owned by [low and moderate income] entrepreneurs' under the Emerging Domestic Markets umbrella, the Milken researchers are implying that all of them lack access to capital at comparable levels and for similar reasons (Yago, Zeidman and Abuyuan 2007: 3). In fact, however, there are significant differences among these populations and geographies in both the nature and causes of their capital constraints.

Take, for example, people of colour and women. Numerous studies have provided evidence that discrimination impedes access to credit for people of colour—particularly for African Americans (Bates 1991, 1997a, Bostic and Lampani 1999, Cavalluzzo et al. 2002, Coleman 2002, 2003, Blanchflower et al. 2003, Mitchell and Pearce 2004, Blanchard et al. 2004, Cavalluzzo and Wolken 2005). The literature has been more mixed, however, when it comes to women's access to credit. Not only has debt capital become significantly more accessible to women entrepreneurs (Greene et al. 2001) but attempts to link discrimination to any continuing limitations in women's access to credit have been inconclusive (Buttner and Rosen 1988, Cavaluzzo and Cavaluzzo 1998, Walker and Joyner 1999, Coleman 2000).

The levels and nature of capital constraints also differ greatly across and within different races and ethnicities. While research that specifically focuses on access to capital is limited, numerous studies have documented how the entrepreneurial experience as a whole varies significantly depending on the race, ethnicity and immigration status of the entrepreneur (Bates 1990, Delgado 1998, Ruiz-Vargas 2000, Carvajal 2004, Mora and Davila 2006). For example, after reviewing the existing literature on Hispanic entrepreneurship, Robles and Cordero-Guzmán (2007) conclude that:

One cannot simply extrapolate and predict similar entrepreneurial patterns without taking into account the country of origin, transnational ties to the home country, location of business (ethnic enclaves versus mainstream markets), and parallel sociodemographic profiles of the group in question. (Robles and Cordero-Guzmán 2007: 22)

Furthermore, research specifically on access to capital for various immigrant communities of colour has documented that both debt and equity capital are available via co-ethnic banks, rotating credit associations and community funds (Bonacich and Modell 1980, Light and Bonacich 1988, Chotigeat et al. 1991, Bates 1994, Greene and Butler 1996, Butler and Greene 1997). Moreover, in at least some of these communities, such capital is potentially more plentiful than for the native-born white communities (Light 2002).

Nor do the distinctions in terms of access to capital depend solely on membership in a specific ethnic community. Chaganti and Greene find that, even within such communities, the availability of capital varies by levels of 'personal involvement of the entrepreneur in the ethnic community instead of [their] reported ethnic grouping' (2002: 1). Similarly, Choi's (2004) study of the Korean immigrant community in Los Angeles demonstrates that because Korean churches act as small business incubators in Koreatown, access to capital is partly determined by membership in specific religious congregations.

In other words, not only do Blacks, Hispanics and Asians differ from each other in their access to capital, but the capital constraints faced by immigrants vary from those of the native born; those of African Americans differ from those of Caribbean Black Americans; those of Puerto Rican Americans differ from those of Cuban Americans; and those of Laotian Americans differ from those of Korean Americans. Additionally, the ease with which individuals within these ethnicities can access capital depends on factors such as their individual attachment to the community and their potential religious affiliation.

In addition to populations, the definition of 'Emerging Domestic Markets' also includes location: whether a community is inner-city or rural. This geographic definition is problematic for two reasons. First, many urban and rural geographies are not actually 'emerging', but instead are experiencing declines in both population and economic well-being (Barkley 2003, Rappaport 2003, Kirschner et al. 2006). Second, as is the case with populations, rural and urban geographies differ from each other on many attributes (Rappaport 2003, Whitener and McGranahan 2003), including their levels of access to capital (Carlson and Chakrabarti 2007). Nor are rural or urban geographies internally monolithic. Although Wall Street and inner-city Detroit are both urban, their economic prosperity and ability to access capital differ dramatically.

The Milken researchers also fail to differentiate between communities that lack access to debt versus those that lack access to equity capital. While some geographies and populations lack access to all forms of capital, debt capital is generally much more readily available than equity. Moreover, the lack of access to equity capital is not just limited to the communities and populations included in the Emerging Domestic Markets framework. The overwhelming majority of all US entrepreneurs are not able to access the levels of equity capital that they need (Maier and Walker 1987, Bates and Bradford 1992).

It could be argued that these are nuanced academic distinctions that are lost on the 'real world' audience that the Milken researchers are trying to influence. However, these distinctions have tremendous relevance for addressing the problem, as demonstrated in the next section of this chapter. The concern is that, by treating underserved geographies and populations as interchangeable, the Milken researchers are communicating to policy makers and investors that the distinctions among these communities are not significant, potentially obstructing solutions to the very problems they are working to address. Rather than analysing underserved communities in the aggregate, as the Milken researchers have done, we must examine each one individually in order to understand exactly what kind of capital—debt or equity—is in short supply and why that is the case. Only then can appropriate solutions be crafted.

In the third section of this chapter, the importance of such a fine-grained approach is demonstrated, focusing specifically on markets underserved by institutional sources of equity, a topic that has received much less scrutiny from the academic community than access to debt. This analysis also highlights the two additional fallacies of the Emerging Domestic Markets approach: that the shortage of capital in underserved communities is primarily the result of information failure; and that profit-driven investors can take the lead in meeting the capital needs of underserved communities.

WHICH MARKETS LACK ACCESS TO INSTITUTIONAL PRIVATE EQUITY CAPITAL AND WHY

Private equity is an asset class that consists of equity investments in companies that are not publicly traded on a stock exchange. Venture capital is a subcategory of private equity that refers to equity investments into young companies, ranging from early stage to expansion.[1] Most institutional venture capital firms are partnerships of professional fund managers who raise money from pension funds, financial institutions, endowments, wealthy individuals and corporations and invest those funds in such a way as to maximise profits for their investors.

Venture capital investments tend to occur in locations with strong deal flow in the form of potential investment opportunities, particularly technology-related investments. In addition to investment opportunities, such locations have the supporting infrastructure—the technological, managerial, legal and financial expertise—that is necessary to take ideas to market (Florida and Kenney 1988a, 1988b, Florida and Smith 1991, 1992).

Venture capital fund managers also prefer to invest in companies that are geographically close to where they are located, to minimise travel time and maximise information (Florida and Kenney 1988a, 1988b, Florida and Smith 1991, 1992, Sorenson and Stuart 2001, Powell et al. 2002, Zook 2005). Areas such as Silicon Valley in California and Route 128 in Massachusetts embody such characteristics and consistently draw a disproportionate share of institutional venture capital dollars. The geographic concentration of the venture capital industry is demonstrated by the fact that, between 2005 and 2007, just 10 states accounted for 85 per cent of all dollars invested.[2] Such geographic concentration has been remarkably consistent for more than two decades (Florida and Kenney 1988a, 1988b, Mason 2007).

Venture capital investments also are highly concentrated by industry and size of investment. Just five industries—software, biotechnology, medical devices and equipment, energy and telecommunications—received 66 per cent of all the dollars invested in 2007 (MoneyTree 2008). Over the last two decades, investments per company have increased as the capitalization of the average venture capital fund grew from $30 million in 1985, to $138 million in 1996, and almost $176 million in 2006 (Onorato 1997, National Venture Capital Association 2008). Since larger investments have comparable transaction costs to smaller ones, venture capitalists have increased their investment sizes in line with their capitalization levels, to reduce transaction costs and increase profits. As of 2007, the average venture capital investment for the venture funds that participate in the PriceWaterhouse MoneyTree Survey was $7,711,962 per company, further limiting venture capital investments to portfolio firms that can absorb fairly large infusions of capital.

The concentration of venture capital investments by geography, industry and size of investment helps explain why, historically, fewer than 3 per cent of all privately held companies in the United States have been able to access venture capital dollars from institutional sources (Maier and Walker 1987, Bates and Bradford 1992).[3] In light of this, the relevant question is which populations and geographies are disproportionately underserved by institutional sources of venture capital.

At present, we lack the data necessary to answer this question. While there is substantial research examining access to debt capital, comparable research on access to equity capital is much more limited for women and virtually non-existent for people of colour. What we know about women's access to equity capital is based on research conducted by the scholars of the Diana Project, a multi-year study of female business owners. They found that women-led firms' share of all equity investments in the US is small, but growing, from 2.4 per cent in 1993 to 4.1 per cent in 1998 (Greene et al. 2001). After eliminating other explanations for this low level of investment in women-led firms, Brush et al. (2001, 2004) conclude that the percentage of equity dollars that goes to women entrepreneurs reflects their historic lack of network commonality with the mainstream venture capital industry, which is primarily male. As a result, the small share of total equity dollars that has gone to women-owned companies has grown as the number of women in the venture capital industry has increased.

Research on access to equity capital for people of colour is based on data from the 1982 Characteristics of Business Owners Survey. Bates and Bradford (1992) analysed that survey and found that African Americans were limited in their access to venture capital, even when controlling for other variables. More recent research on this topic is virtually non-existent.[4] Based on the increase in women's access to equity that occurred in the 1990s, the growth in the number of venture capital funds that focus on entrepreneurs of colour, and the concurrent growth in such funds' capitalization levels, we could assume that access to equity capital is now much less of a problem for African Americans and other people of colour. On the other hand, the large gap that still exists in access to credit for African Americans and Latinos could imply that a similar gap continues to exist in their access to equity capital. More current research clearly is needed to determine which hypothesis is correct.

Some geographies also are disproportionately underserved by venture capital. As Table 6.1 illustrates, 18 states jointly accounted for just 2 per cent of all the dollars invested by venture capital firms between 2005 and 2007, with each state receiving less than $100 million over that three year period. Although these states are primarily rural, venture capital also is in short supply in many urban areas, including most cities outside of the 40 largest US metro areas, as well as in distressed larger cities (Carlson and Chakrabarti 2007).

In contrast to the claims of Emerging Domestic Markets proponents, these populations and geographies are not disproportionately underserved by venture capital as a result of information failure. Information failure may be consistent with Brush et al.'s (2001 and 2004) hypothesis as to why women entrepreneurs lack access to venture capital: they do not share networks with the industry's primarily white and male workforce. However, it is not the central reason why so many rural and distressed urban geographies lack access to venture capital.

Table 6.1   US States That Received $100 Million or Less in Private Equity Dollars

	% of Total Private Equity Dollars Invested 2005 to 2007	% of Total U.S. Population 2000	% of Population That Is Rural 2000	% of People in Poverty 2000 to 2002
18 states	2.0%	11.1%	38.0%	12.5%
Total US			20.0%	11.7%

Sources: PriceWaterhouse MoneyTree Survey and US Census

Rural and distressed urban geographies are disproportionately under-served by venture capital because of the higher transaction and operating costs of investing in these geographies as a result of the numerous obstacles that investors must overcome. Such obstacles include:

- Limited investment opportunities and a lack of profitable investment exits (Barkley and Markley 2001, Barkley et al. 2001, Barkley 2003, Carlson and Chakrabarti 2007, Rubin 2008).
- The absence of a developed investment infrastructure, entrepreneur support networks and entrepreneurial culture (Barkley and Markley 2001, Barkley et al. 2001, Barkley 2003, Hughes et al. 2004, Carlson and Chakrabarti 2007).
- Greater difficulty and travel time for venture capital investors to reach their portfolio companies (Brophy 1997, Barkley and Markley 2001, Barkley et al. 2001, Carlson and Chakrabarti 2007).
- Limited access to specialized workforces and experienced management (Barkley and Markley 2001, Barkley 2003, Carlson and Chakrabarti 2007).
- A lack of understanding of how venture capital works (Barkley and Markley 2001, Barkley et al. 2001).
- An unwillingness to give up company ownership on the part of local entrepreneurs (Barkley and Markley 2001, Barkley et al. 2001, Hughes et al. 2004, Rubin 2008).

Unlike information failure, which can be addressed with better data or improved transparency, these obstacles translate into higher transaction and operating costs that lower the profitability of venture capital investments.

That overcoming such obstacles translates into additional costs for investors is supported by an analysis of the economic models utilised by the venture capital funds that target underserved populations and geographies. With few exceptions, the venture capital funds that focus on women entrepreneurs and entrepreneurs of colour are similar to the rest of the venture capital industry in having a single bottom line of profit maximisation. They view their focus as a form of specialisation, like that practiced by venture funds that invest in biotechnology or telecommunications. As a result of their specialisation, these fund managers are able to access business networks comprised of women entrepreneurs and entrepreneurs of colour and learn about investment opportunities they would otherwise miss. This enables them to profitably overcome information failure in these markets (Bates and Bradford 2002, 2003a, 2003b, 2007, 2008, Bates et al. 2006).

However, the venture capital funds that invest in rural and distressed urban geographies face an additional set of obstacles that increases their transaction and operating costs and lowers their financial returns (see Table 6.2).

Table 6.2   Markets Underserved by Venture Capital

Investment Target	Information Failure	Additional Obstacles to Investment	Need for Subsidy
Rural geographies		Limited deal flow & exits Limited physical & investment infrastructure Less sophisticated entrepreneurs Geographically difficult to reach for investors	To offset transaction and operating costs associated with additional obstacles to investment
Small or distressed urban geographies		Limited deal flow & exits Limited physical & investment infrastructure Less sophisticated entrepreneurs Geographically difficult to reach for investors	To offset transaction and operating costs associated with additional obstacles to investment
Women and minority entrepreneurs	Lack of network access		

Not surprisingly, most of the venture capital funds that do invest in rural and distressed urban geographies have a double bottom line of both social and financial returns, which provides an incentive for them to focus on these challenging markets (Barkley and Markley 2001, Barkley et al. 2001, Barkley 2003, Rubin 2008). Even with a double bottom line, such specialised venture capital funds must take advantage of public sector subsidies to offset the additional transaction and operating costs associated with investing in rural and distressed urban geographies (Barkley and Markley 2001, Barkley 2003, Rubin 2008). Rubin studied 26 double bottom line venture capital funds that invest in rural geographies and found that all of them were capitalized with public sector assistance in the form of direct appropriations, tax credits and mandates (2008).[5]

This highlights the third fallacy of the Emerging Domestic Markets approach: that focusing on the financial opportunities presented by underserved geographies will convince profit-driven investors to take the lead in meeting their capital needs. The problem with this assumption is that profit-driven investors understand that rural and distressed urban geographies present additional transaction and operating costs and have little incentive to absorb these costs as long as high quality investment opportunities are available elsewhere. Oversimplifying the problem or ignoring the economics of underserved markets does not change this fact.

The next section of this chapter illustrates the limitation of the Emerging Domestic Markets approach via a case study of the California Initiative. The initiative, launched by the California Public Employees

Retirement System (CalPERS), the country's largest public pension fund, was designed to bring private equity capital to companies in underserved markets, primarily in California, in order to identify opportunities for financial returns that have been ignored by other sources of investment capital (CalPERS 2001a).

THE CALIFORNIA INITIATIVE

The California Initiative came about in large part as a result of efforts by then California State Treasurer, Phil Angelides, to direct a portion of the investments made by the two largest public pension funds in the state, CalPERS and CalSTRS (California State Teachers Retirement System), to the state's underserved markets. Angelides joined the pension funds' governing boards in 1999, after taking office as State Treasurer. In May 2000, Angelides launched 'The Double Bottom Line: Investing in California's Emerging Markets' initiative by releasing a 36 page report with the same name. The influence of the Emerging Domestic Markets idea was apparent in the title and body of the report, which cited both the Milken researchers and Michael Porter in arguing that investment capital should be directed 'through state programs and the State's pension and investment funds—to spur economic growth in those California communities left behind during the economic expansion of the past decade' (Angelides 2000: 1).

CalPERS approved the California Initiative in June of 2000, as part of its Economically Targeted Investment Program. The Initiative's mission was to:

> invest in traditionally underserved markets primarily, but not exclusively, located in California. The objective is to discover and invest in opportunities that may have been bypassed or not reviewed by other sources of investment capital. These opportunities should offer attractive risk-adjusted returns commensurate with their asset class. (CalPERS 2001a)

In January 2001, CalPERS sent a letter to three hundred investment managers and advisors, inviting proposals for investment by the California Initiative. Following the Emerging Domestic Markets model, the letter defined underserved markets as including:

> urban and rural communities where assets and comparative advantages exist (e.g., available labor pool, lower cost real estate, underutilized infrastructure) conducive to business development. Underserved markets may also pertain to specific consumer groups that have limited access to goods and services that meet their needs. (CalPERS 2001b)

CalPERS did not stipulate how applicants should determine whether a particular market was 'underserved', leaving that decision to individual private equity funds. By doing so, CalPERS hoped to attract proposals from the greatest number of applicants, utilizing the most diverse targeting criteria. CalPERS felt that this increased the likelihood that the California Initiative would produce the kind of strong financial returns that its fiduciary obligations required (Mark 2007).

CalPERS received 67 proposals from potential managers for the California Initiative Program. It evaluated these proposal on the basis of: the operating and investing experience of the principals; the organizations' and individuals' financial performance track record; whether the strategy effectively targeted and capitalized on opportunities in underserved markets; whether the applicants had a California presence and could access the relevant networks; and whether their economics, terms and conditions strongly aligned their interests with those of CalPERS (CalPERS 2001b).

By the summer of 2001, after rigorous due diligence, 10 of the 67 private equity firms that had replied to the request for proposals were selected to receive a total of $480 million in CalPERS investments (Mark 2007) (see Table 6.3). One of the 10 was a fund of funds, the Bank of America California Community Venture Fund, which was selected to sub-allocate $100 million to as many as 15 private equity funds (CalPERS 2007).[6] The remaining nine received direct investments ranging from $10 to $200 million.

As CalPERS had hoped, the investment objectives proposed by the funds were consistent with the broad emerging domestic markets definition of underserved. This left the funds a lot of flexibility in meeting CalPERS' financial objectives. Not surprisingly, none of the private equity funds planned to invest exclusively or primarily in distressed urban and rural geographies and only one of the funds, Pacific Community Ventures, was an overtly developmental fund with an objective of creating wealth in low income communities and achieving both social and financial returns.

Although CalPERS was clear that the California Initiative funds had to offer attractive, risk-adjusted financial returns, it also wanted the Initiative to 'have a meaningful impact on the economic infrastructure of California's underserved markets' (CalPERS 2007). Towards that goal, CalPERS commissioned Pacific Community Ventures' consulting arm to do annual social impact assessments of the nine private equity funds that had received direct funding through the California Initiative.[7] These assessments evaluate the investments using three benchmarks set by CalPERS, which mirror the Emerging Domestic Markets definition of underserved:

1. Providing capital to areas that have historically had limited access to institutional equity capital
2. Employing workers who reside in economically disadvantaged areas
3. Supporting women and minority entrepreneurs and managers (CalPERS 2007: 1)

Table 6.3 California Initiative Round I Funds' capitalization and investment focus

Name/$ Committed	Investment Focus
American River Ventures/$15,000,000	Generate capital appreciation through selective equity investments in seed, start-up, first round and later stage rounds of financing in early stage information technology companies. The Fund will be structured as an SBIC. The fund's focus will be on untapped investments along the Interstate 80 Corridor from San Francisco to Reno, including the North Bay. This market is underserved by private equity capital providers. Historically, angel investors have acted as the primary source of capital for entrepreneurs in this area. The GP will focus on capturing a "first-mover advantage" in this growing and attractive market segment.
DFJ Frontier Fund, L.P./$20,000,000	Invest in entrepreneurial start-ups located in under-represented regions of California with a focus on Sacramento, the Central Valley and the East Bay. Additionally, the fund will provide early stage equity financing to technology firms whose needs lie between venture "angels" and mainstream VC's. DFJ will build strategic relationships with universities and entrepreneurial networks in under-represented areas of Central and Northern California.
Garage California Entrepreneurs Fund, L.P./$10,000,000	Provide seed capital to California-based startups that may fit into one of three underserved categories: 1) Academic—seed-stage companies founded by students, faculty, staff, and/or recent graduates of California universities, 2) Governmental—seed-stage companies founded by employees of California-based government research facilities, and 3) Community—seed-stage companies directly benefiting a disadvantaged community in California.
GCP California Fund, L.P./$50,000,000	Co-invest, on an opportunistic basis, primarily alongside Green Equity Investors III and Green Equity Investors IV funds. Investments will be made through three primary strategies: i) co-investing in appropriate California-based companies that serve under-penetrated urban, rural or ethnic markets; ii) investing directly in smaller transactions that fall below the size of typical Fund investments but which target underserved markets, particularly in California and iii) investing in out-of-state businesses willing to relocate to urban California areas. The Firm's proposed investment strategy will provide middle market companies with access to scarce capital while encouraging the growth of businesses in underserved urban and rural markets.
Nogales Investors Fund I, L.P./$25,000,000	Make equity and equity-related investments in middle market companies located primarily in underserved areas of California and/or that target underserved consumers. The strategy is to source and invest in opportunities that unite corporations and underserved communities and may include attracting South American companies to expand US operations into underserved areas primarily located in California.

(continued)

Table 6.3 (continued)

Opportunity Capital Partners IV, L.P./$25,000,000	Generate significant investment returns primarily by providing acquisition and expansion capital to well-managed companies that operate primarily in the telecommunications, information technology, healthcare, and industrial sectors. Opportunity Capital Partners (OCP) is one of the country's most experienced private equity firms focused on providing attractive returns to its investors by investing primarily in companies in which African-American, Hispanic, and Asian-American entrepreneurs hold significant ownership and management positions or in companies with competitive strategies that focus on providing services and goods to multi-cultural consumer markets. The firm has over 29 years of successful experience in providing capital to these underserved markets and has built a strong brand name. OCP is viewed as a primary source of equity and equity-related financing by its target market of entrepreneurs, financial intermediaries, and co-investors.
Pacific Community Ventures Investment Partners II/$10,000,000	Invest in and develop early and expansion stage enterprises with revenues in the $1 million to $10 million range. The business model aggregates and leverages public and private sector monies, fund investments, charitable contributions and individual as well as corporate pro bono services. Its business advisory services, which links entrepreneurs with experienced, active business executives, adds significant value to portfolio companies and acts as an effective screening mechanism for potential investments. The fund manager has successfully combined vision and values with a comprehensive venture services model. The firm's mission is to provide resources and capital to businesses that have the potential to bring significant economic gain to targeted underserved urban areas. SVCV was conceived in 1998 to provide the tools and strategies of the venture capital industry that would support entrepreneurs, the companies they start, and the people they employ to create wealth in underserved communities. A unique asset of the organization, which distinguishes it from others, is the comprehensive, evolved business advisory services provided to its portfolio companies.
Provender Opportunities Fund II, L.P./$25,000,000	Leverage the firm's established California presence and extensive experience investing in urban-oriented and under-sponsored opportunities. The Fund will focus on adding value to existing under-managed brands or niche entrepreneurial initiatives within the target markets. The Provender investment strategy is based on a focused approach within four industry sectors: Financial Services, Business Services, Consumer Products and Services, and Internet-Related Technologies.
Yucaipa Corporate Initiative Fund/$200,000,000	Build corporate partnerships with retail, distribution, food, manufacturing and commercial products companies that are interested in expanding operations in underserved communities.
Bank of America Capital Access Fund—Fund of Funds/$100,000,000	Pursue a fund-of-funds strategy that will invest in partnerships that are primarily located in California and meet the overall criteria of the California Initiative. Firms may include emerging and niche groups that possess unique networks in underserved areas. A majority of the portfolio funds will focus on private equity investments; however, some funds may include community development real estate investments in which Bank of America's Community Development Group has significant experience.

Source: CalPERS Summary of Recommended Investment Partners, May 14, 2001

These evaluation criteria are very broad, as was the case with the investment criteria CalPERS used to select the California Initiative private equity funds. For example, more than 98 per cent of the zip codes in the United States would quality under the first criterion of having limited access to institutional equity capital.[8] By defining underserved markets so broadly, CalPERS followed the model put forth by Emerging Domestic Markets proponents, which ignores the differences in level of access to capital that exist among underserved communities and the additional challenges that some communities present for investors. While this framing enables the California Initiative's private equity funds to maximize their financial returns by investing in the least challenging geographies, it does not encourage those funds to address the equity capital needs of most underserved communities.

The California Initiative case study highlights both the positive and negative aspects of the Emerging Domestic Markets approach to underserved communities. The Milken researchers' emphasis on the financial opportunities of underserved communities may have contributed to bringing the California Initiative to fruition. However, their broad framing of Emerging Domestic Markets, which treats underserved communities as interchangeable and insists that they lack capital solely as a result of information failure, obscures the need for subsidy to address the challenges that many underserved communities present for investors. Without such subsidies, financial returns driven investors such as CalPERS have little incentive to absorb the additional transaction and operating expenses of investing in these communities.

CONCLUSIONS

In this chapter, I have argued that the Emerging Domestic Markets approach to investing in underserved communities, articulated by researchers at the Milken Institute, has three important limitations. First, it treats the diverse populations and geographies currently underserved by private sector capital providers as interchangeable, ignoring the fact that they differ in important ways in the nature and causes of their capital constraints. It also treats debt and equity capital as interchangeable, despite the very different factors that inhibit access to each form of capital. Second, it wrongly asserts that underserved communities lack access to capital primarily as a result of information failure, overlooking numerous other obstacles that raise the transaction and operating costs of investing in underserved geographies. Third, the Milken researchers' assumption that profit-driven investors can take the lead in meeting the capital needs of underserved communities is unrealistic because it fails to address these additional barriers to investment. As the CalPERS case study illustrates, in the absence of subsidy, financial returns driven investors have little incentive to take on the additional costs of investing in rural and distressed urban geographies.

The first step in meeting the capital needs of disproportionately underserved communities is to identify which communities are underserved and whether they lack access to debt or equity capital. This may require additional research, for example, to determine if entrepreneurs of colour are underserved in their access to equity capital. The second step is to examine underserved communities individually in order to determine why each lacks access to capital. As the analysis of communities underserved by institutional venture capital demonstrates, such communities cannot be lumped together and treated as interchangeable if we want to address what is keeping them from attracting investors.

Finally, the public sector must take the lead in creating an environment that encourages the private sector to help address the capital access needs of underserved communities. For example, in the case of venture capital, such public sector involvement has taken the form of subsidies, via appropriations and tax credits, to offset the higher transaction and operating costs of investing in underserved communities; and mandates, to encourage conventional financial institutions to invest in such markets despite the higher transaction and operating costs.[9] Without such public sector incentives, the private sector is likely to continue by-passing underserved communities.

The desire to use the private sector to address the problems of underserved communities is understandable in light of limited public sector resources and a prevailing political climate that has favoured private sector solutions (Rubin and Stankiewicz 2003). As the current economic crisis demonstrates, however, the need for government intervention cannot be eliminated by ideology or wishful thinking. Whether by limiting negative excesses or by encouraging positive action, government continues to have an important role to play in ensuring a fair and thriving economy.

NOTES

1. The private equity industry also includes firms that invest in large companies to facilitate their restructuring. Since those kinds of transactions are not the focus of this part of the chapter, the term venture capital is used to refer to institutional sources of private equity.
2. This analysis is based on state-level investment data compiled by PricewaterhouseCoopers and the National Venture Capital Association.
3. While few companies qualify for institutional venture capital, many entrepreneurs are able to access equity capital from individual 'angel' investors, family members or personal savings.
4. Yago, Zeidman, Magula and Sederstrom (2007) argue that, because venture capital funds that focus specifically on entrepreneurs of colour control only 1 per cent of all venture capital dollars, entrepreneurs of colour are underserved by institutional private equity. However, this argument provides no documentation for its underlying assumption that specialised venture capital funds are the only ones investing in companies owned by entrepreneurs of colour.

5. Rubin also found that the majority of funds in the study do not focus exclusively on markets with high transaction and operating costs, preferring to invest in a broader region in order to maximise high quality deal flow and minimise expenses. Only 5 of the 26 funds in the study focused exclusively on rural geographies, and these 5 focused primarily on the provision of near-equity and debt rather than equity (Rubin 2008).
6. The exact composition of Bank of America's California Initiative investments is not publicly available. However, the total portfolio of Bank of America's Capital Access Group, which manages those investments, appears to be focused on private equity funds that invest in companies owned and/or managed by women and people of colour. For more information see http://www.bacapitalaccessfunds.com/portfolio/index.asp.
7. The social impact of investments made by the private equity funds that received capital from the Bank of America Capital Access Fund was tracked separately by the Center for Community Capitalism, at the University of North Carolina at Chapel Hill, with funding by the Kauffman Foundation (Ratcliffe 2007).
8. CalPERS defines underserved communities as those 'located outside of [the] 774 United States ZIP Codes—where more than 80 per cent of all private equity in the United States and more than 90 per cent of all private equity in California has been committed' (CalPERS 2008: 15). There are approximately 43,000 zip codes in use in the United States (US Census 2009).
9. For a detailed discussion of public sector efforts to increase access to equity capital for underserved geographies and populations see J. S. Rubin (2008).

BIBLIOGRAPHY

The American Assembly (1997) Community Capitalism: rediscovering the markets of America's urban neighborhoods. Online. Availablehttp://www.americanassembly.org/programs.dir/prog_display_ind_pg.php?this_filename_prefix=comm_capital&this_ind_prog_pg_filename=report (accessed 23 September 2008).

Angelides, P. (2000) The Double Bottom Line: investing in California's emerging markets, ideas to action. June. Online. Availablehttp://www.treasurer.ca.gov/publications/dbl/dbl.pdf (accessed 23 July 2008).

Barkley, D. L. (2003) 'Policy options for equity financing for rural entrepreneurs' in Growing and Financing Rural Entrepreneurship, Federal Reserve Bank of Kansas City, Center for the Study of Rural America.

Barkley, D. L., and Markley, D. M. (2001) 'Nontraditional sources of venture capital for rural America', Rural America, 16(1): 19–26.

Barkley, D. L., Markley, D.M., Freshwater, D., Rubin, J.S. and Shaffer, R. (2001) Establishing Nontraditional Venture Capital Institutions: Lessons learned, Columbia, MO: Rural Policy Research Institute (RUPRI).

Bates, T. (1990) 'Self-employment trends among Mexican-Americans', Census Economic Studies Paper, No. 90–9, August, Washington, DC: US Census Bureau, Center for Economic Studies.

———(1991) 'Commercial bank financing of white- and Black-owned small business start-ups', Quarterly Review of Economics and Business, 31(Spring): 64–80.

———(1994) 'An analysis of Korean Immigrant-owned small business start-ups with comparisons to African-American and non-minority-owned firms', Urban Affairs Quarterly, 30(2): 227–48.

———(1997a) 'Financing small business creation: the case of Chinese and Korean immigrant entrepreneurs', Journal of Business Venturing, 12(2): 109–24.

———(1997b) 'Michael Porter's conservative urban agenda will not revitalize America's inner cities: what will?', Economic Development Quarterly, 11(1): 39–44.

Bates, T. and Bradford, W. (1992) 'Factors affecting new firm success and their use in venture capital financing', The Journal of Small Business Finance, 2(1): 23–38.

———(2002) Venture Capital in Minority Business Investment, report to the E. M. Kauffman Foundation, November, Kansas City, MO: E. M. Kauffman Foundation.

———(2003a) 'Analysis of venture-capital funds that finance minority-owned businesses', Review of Black Political Economy, 32(1): 37–46.

———(2003b) Minorities and Venture Capital: A new wave in American business, Kansas City, MO: E. M. Kauffman Foundation.

———(2007) 'Traits and performance of the minority venture-capital industry', The Annals of the American Academy of Political and Social Science, 613(1): 95–107.

———(2008) 'Venture-capital investment in minority business', Journal of Money, Credit and Banking, 40(2–3): 489–504.

Bates, T., Bradford, W. and Rubin, J. S. (2006) 'The viability of the minority-oriented venture-capital industry under alternative financing arrangements', Economic Development Quarterly, 20(2): 178–91.

Blanchflower, D., Levine, P. and Zimmerman, D. (2003) 'Discrimination in the small business credit market', Review of Economics and Statistics, 85(4): 930–43.

Blanchard, L., Yinger, J. and Zhao, B. (2004) 'Do credit market barriers exist for minority and women entrepreneurs?' Working Paper, Syracuse University.

Bonacich, E. and Modell, J. (1980) The Economic Basis of Ethnic Solidarity, Berkeley: University of California Press.

Bostic, R. W. and Lampani, P. K. (1999) 'Race, geography, risk and market structure: examining discrimination in small business finance', in Business Access to Capital and Credit, Federal Reserve System Research Conference Proceeding, March 1999.

Boston, T. and Ross, C. (1996) (eds) The Review of Black Political Economy, 24(2 and 3).

———(1997) (eds) The Inner City: Urban poverty and economic development in the next century, New Brunswick, NJ: Transaction.

Brophy, D. J. (1997) 'Developing rural equity capital markets', in Financing Rural America, proceedings of a conference sponsored by the Federal Reserve Bank of Kansas City, April 1997.

Brush, C., Carter, N., Gatewood, E., Greene, P. and Hart, M. (2001) Women Business Owners and Equity Capital: the myths dispelled, Report 1, Kansas City, MO: Ewing Marion Kauffman Foundation.

———(2004) Gatekeepers of Venture Growth: the role and participation of women in the venture capital industry, Report 2, Kansas City, MO: Ewing Marion Kauffman Foundation.

Butler, J. S. and Greene, P. G (1997) 'Entrepreneurship and wealth building: from Pakistani/Ismaili enterprise', in Frontiers of Entrepreneurial Research, Wellesley, MA: Center for Entrepreneurial Studies.

Buttner, E. H. and Rosen, B. H. (1988) 'Bank loan officer's perceptions of characteristics of men, women and successful entrepreneurs', Journal of Business Venturing, 3: 249–58.

California State Assembly (2008) 'Emerging Domestic Markets'. Online. Available http://www.assembly.ca.gov/acs/newcomframeset.asp?committee=131 (accessed 24 November 2008).

CalPERS (2001a) 'California Initiative Strategy', presentation to CalPERS Investment Committee, May 2001. Online. Available http://www.calpers.ca.gov/eip-docs/investments/bus-opportunities/ca-initiative-info-packet.pdf (accessed 9 July 2009).

———(2001b) Recommendation memo to investment committee to approve investment strategy and investment partners for the California Initiative, 14 May 2001, CalPERS internal memo.

———(2007) 'Impacting California's Underserved Communities: taking a second look'. Online. Available http://www.calpers.ca.gov/eip-docs/about/press/news/economic-engine/ca-underserved-communities.pdf (accessed 9 July 2009).

———(2008) 'CalPERS California Initiative 2008: creating opportunities in California's underserved markets'. Online. http://www.calpers.ca.gov/eip-docs/about/press/news/invest-corp/item06a-01.pdf (accessed 11 February 2010).

Carlson, C. and Chakrabarti, P. (2007) 'Venture Capital in New England Secondary Cities', New England Community Developments, Federal Reserve Bank of Boston, Issue 1. Online. Available http://www.bos.frb.org/commdev/necd/2007/issue1/venturecap.pdf (accessed 10 August 2008).

Carr, J. (1999) 'Community, capital, and markets: a new paradigm for community reinvestment', Neighborhood Works Journal, 17: 20–23.

Carvajal, M. (2004) 'Measuring economic discrimination of Hispanic-owned architecture and engineering firms in South Florida', Hispanic Journal of Behavioral Sciences, 26(1): 79–101.

Cavalluzzo, K. and Cavalluzzo, L. (1998) 'Market structure and discrimination: the case of small businesses', Journal of Money, Credit and Banking, 30(4): 771–92.

Cavalluzzo, K., Cavalluzzo, L. and Wolken, J. (2002) 'Competition, small business financing, and discrimination: evidence from a new survey', Journal of Business, 25(4): 641–79.

Cavalluzzo, K. and Wolken, J. (2005) 'Small business loan turndowns, personal wealth and discrimination', Journal of Business, 78(6): 2153–77.

Chaganti, R. and Greene, P. G. (2002) 'Who are ethnic entrepreneurs? A study of entrepreneurs' ethnic involvement and business characteristics', Journal of Small Business Management, 40(2): 126–43.

Choi, H. (2004) 'Social capital and community economic development in Los Angeles' Koreatown: faith-based organizations in transitional ethnic community', PhD Dissertation, Los Angeles: University of Southern California.

Chotigeat, T., Balsmeier, P.W. and Stanley, T. O. (1991) 'Fuelling Asian immigrants' entrepreneurship: a source of capital', Journal of Small Business Management, 29(3): 50–61.

Coleman, S. (2000) 'Access to capital and terms of credit: a comparison of men and women-owned businesses', Journal of Small Business Management, 38(3): 37–52.

———(2002) 'The borrowing experience of Black and Hispanic-owned small firms: evidence from the 1998 Survey of Small Business Finances', The Academy of Entrepreneurship Journal, 8(1): 1–20.

———(2003) 'Borrowing patterns for small firms: a comparison by race and ethnicity', The Journal of Entrepreneurial Finance & Business Ventures, 7(3): 87–108.

Darden Business School Forum (2006) 'Premiere "Emerging Domestic Markets" Conference a Success'. Online. Available http://www.darden.virginia.edu/html/news_article.aspx?id=6758 (accessed 6 July 2009).

Delgado, M. (1998) 'Puerto Rican elders and merchant establishments: natural caregiving systems or simply business?', Journal of Gerontological Social Work, 30(2): 33–45.

Florida, R. L. and Kenney, M. (1988a) 'Venture capital, high technology and regional development', Regional Studies, 22(1): 33–48.

——(1988b) 'Venture capital and high technology entrepreneurship', Journal of Business Venturing, 3: 301–19.

Florida, R. L. and Smith, D.F. (1991) 'Venture capital formation, investment, and regional industrialization', Annals of the Association of American Geographers, 83(3): 434–51.

——(1992) 'Venture capital's role in economic development: an empirical analysis', in E. S. Mills and J. F. McDonald (eds) Sources of Metropolitan Growth, New Brunswick, NJ: Center for Urban Policy Research.

Goozner, M. (1998) 'The Porter prescription', The American Prospect, May–June: 56–64.

Greene, P. G. and Butler, J. S. (1996) 'The minority community as a natural business incubator', Journal of Business Research, 36(1): 51–58.

Greene, P. G., Brush, C. G., Hart, M. M. and Saparito, P. (2001) 'Patterns of venture capital funding: is gender a factor?', Venture Capital: An International Journal of Entrepreneurial Finance, 3(1): 63–83.

Harrison, B. and Glasmeier, A. K. (1997) 'Why business alone won't redevelop the inner city: a friendly critique of Michael Porter's approach to urban revitalization', Economic Development Quarterly, 11(1): 28–38.

Hughes, D. W., Mallory, K. and Szabo, M. A (2004) 'Factors influencing venture capital availability in rural states: possible lessons learned from West Virginia', paper presented at the 51st Annual Meeting of the North American Regional Science Association International, Seattle, WA, November.

Institute for Strategy and Competitiveness (2008) Untitled. Online. Available http://www.isc.hbs.edu/econ-innercities.htm (accessed 7 July 2008).

Kirschner, A., Berry, H. E. and Glasgow, N. (2006) 'Changing faces of rural America', in W. Kandel and D. L. Brown (eds) Population Change and Rural Society in the 21st Century, New York: Springer.

Light, I. (2002) 'Immigrant place entrepreneurs in Los Angeles, 1970–99', International Journal of Urban and Regional Research, 26(2): 215–28.

Light, I. and Bonacich, E. (1988) Immigrant Entrepreneurs: Koreans in Los Angeles 1965–1982, Berkeley: University of California Press.

Mark, J. (2007) Interview with author, 24 December 2007.

Maier, J. B. and Walker, D. A. (1987) 'The role of venture capital in financing small business', Journal of Business Venturing, 2(3), 203–15.

Mason, C. (2007) 'Venture capital: a geographical perspective', in H. Landstrom (ed.) Handbook of Research on Venture Capital, Cheltenham, England: Edward Elgar.

Milken Institute (2008) Untitled. Online. Available http://www.milkeninstitute. org/about/about.taf (accessed 7 July 2008).

Mitchell, K. and Pearce, D. K. (2004) Availability of Financing to Small Firms Using the Survey of Small Business Finances, United States Small Business Administration, Office of Advocacy.

MoneyTree (2008) Report compiled by PricewaterhouseCoopers, the National Venture Capital Association and Thomson Financial. Online. Available https://www.pwcmoneytree.com/MTPublic/ns/moneytree/filesource/exhibits/National_MoneyTree_full_year_Q4_2007_Final.pdf (accessed 25 April 2008).

Mora, M.T. and Davila, A. (2006) 'Mexican immigrant self-employment along the US-Mexico border: an analysis of 2000 census data', Social Science Quarterly, 87(1): 91–109.

National Venture Capital Association (2008) Frequently asked questions. Online. Available http://www.nvca.org/faqs.html (accessed 15 March 2008).

Onorato, N. R. (1997) Trends in Venture Capital Funding in the 1990s. US Small Business Administration Office of Advocacy, August. Online. Available http://www.sba.gov/advo/stats/trends_vc.pdf (accessed 15 May 2008).

Porter, M. E. (1995) 'The competitive advantage of the inner city', Harvard Business Review, May–June: 55–71.

———(1997) 'New strategies for inner-city economic development', Economic Development Quarterly, 11(1): 11–27.

Powell, W., Koput, W., Kenneth W., Bowie, J. I. and Smith-Doerr, L. (2002) 'The spatial clustering of science and capital: accounting for biotech firm-venture capital relationships', Regional Studies, 36(3): 291–305.

Rappaport, J. (2003) 'US urban decline and growth, 1950 to 2000', in Federal Reserve Bank of Kansas City Economic Review, Third Quarter. Online. Available http://findarticles.com/p/articles/mi_qa3699/is_200307/ai_n9288994/pg_1?tag=artBody;col1 (accessed 12 May 2008).

Ratcliffe, J. (2007) 'Who's counting? Measuring social outcomes from targeted private equity', Community Development Investment Review, 2(1): 23–37.

Robles, B. J. and Cordero-Guzmán, H. (2007) 'Latino self-employment and entrepreneurship in the United States: an overview of the literature and data sources', The Annals of the American Academy of Political and Social Science, 613(1): 18–31.

Rubin, J. S. (2008) 'Community development venture capital in rural communities', paper presented at the CDFI Fund Research Conference, Washington DC, June.

Rubin, J. S. and Stankiewicz, G. M. (2003) 'Evaluating the impact of federal community economic development policies on their targeted populations: the case of new markets initiatives', paper presented at the Federal Reserve System Biennial Research Conference on Sustainable Community Development, Washington, DC, March.

Ruiz-Vargas, Y. (2000) 'Small business financing sources between immigrants and natives in Puerto Rico', Quarterly Review of Economics and Finance, 40(3): 387–99.

Sorenson, O. and Stuart, T. E. (2001) 'Syndication networks and the spatial distribution of venture capital investments', American Journal of Sociology, 106(6): 1546–88.

US Census Bureau (2009) ZIP Code® Tabulation Area (ZCTA™) frequently asked questions. Online. Available http://www.census.gov/geo/ZCTA/zctafaq.html#Q5 (accessed 9 July 2009).

Vietorisz, T. and Harrison, B. (1970) The Economic Development of Harlem, New York: Praeger.

Walker, D. and Joyner, B. E. (1999) 'Female entrepreneurship and the market process: gender-based public policy considerations', Journal of Developmental Entrepreneurship, 4(2): 95–116.

Whitener, L. A and McGranahan, D. A. (2003) 'Rural America: opportunities and challenges', Amber Waves, February. Online. Available http://www.ers.usda.gov/AmberWaves/Feb03/pdf/feature-rural%20america.pdf (accessed 8 August 2008).

Yago, G. (2007) Emerging Clarity on Domestic Markets. Online. Available http://www.icic.org/site/c.fnJNKPNhFiG/b.3789487/ (accessed 7 July 2008).

Yago, G., Barth, J. R. and Zeidman, B. (eds) (2007) Entrepreneurship in Emerging Domestic Markets: Barriers and innovation, New York: Springer.

Yago, G., and Harrington, M. (1999) Mainstreaming Minority Business: Financing domestic emerging markets, Santa Monica, CA: Milken Institute.

Yago, G., Zeidman, B. and Abuyuan, A. (2007) 'A history of emerging domestic markets', Community Development Investment Review, 3(1): 1–22.

Yago, G., Zeidman, B., Magula, T. and Sederstrom, J. (2007) Emerging Domestic Markets: Increasing capital by improving data, Santa Monica, CA: Milken Institute.

Yago, G., Zeidman, B. and Schmidt, B. (2003) Creating Capital, Jobs and Wealth in Emerging Domestic Markets: Financial technology transfer to low-income communities, Santa Monica, CA: Milken Institute.

Zook, M. A. (2005) The Geography of the Internet Industry, Oxford: Blackwell.

7 Access to Finance in Deprived Areas
Has the Government Lost Interest?

Karl Dayson

INTRODUCTION

Britain's financial services sector has a rich history of innovation, expansion of services and influence (Ferguson 2009). Credit transactions played an important role in the development of modern Britain, and the gradual shift from relational to codified approaches was evident from the fifteenth century onwards (Kermode 1991, Muldrew 1993). By the seventeenth century, letters of credit and rudimentary bank notes were in circulation, in the 1740s Dean Jonathan Swift, the author of *Gulliver's Travels*, started a small loans fund for the tradesmen of Dublin (Hollis and Sweetman 1997), while diversity of ownership emerged in the 1770s with the first mutual building societies[1] (Price 1958, Dayson 2003). Over the next couple of centuries, numerous enterprise and also mutual funding schemes were established, often in specific geographic locations, though it was not until the post-war period that the former became more extensive, while the building societies numbers began to decline. Moreover, the provision of services was not universal and some groups continued to endure some form of financial exclusion.

This chapter explores how the New Labour Government attempted to address the problems faced by entrepreneurs and prospective entrepreneurs. In responding to demands of small business people, New Labour was signalling its difference from the Labour Party of previous decades but it also recognised that firms did struggle to access credit. Having an internationalist outlook, policy makers within the party drew on the burgeoning micro-finance movement in the developing world and the Community Development Finance Institutions (CDFIs) in the US. This global outlook is discussed in the next section of this chapter, following a brief overview of enterprise support in the period leading up to New Labour. In the third section, New Labour's policy of financial support for enterprises is examined, by discussing the relevant policy action reports, the Social Investment Taskforce and the Phoenix Fund. The fourth section reviews the performance of UK CDFIs before suggesting a matrix for understanding their different operational strategies. Finally, the conclusion argues that New Labour's micro-finance policy did not resolve the tension between its economic and social objectives; rather it exposed a lack of understanding about the importance of place, falling to utilise CDFIs as a bridge between the national economy and communities.

In its wilderness years, the Labour Party sought to revitalize their economic and social policies. While their economic policy adopted many of the features of laissez-faire economics (Kitson and Wilkinson 2007), their social policy appeared more nuanced with a combination of redistribution, underclass and inclusion perspectives (Levitas 1998). However, New Labour also followed a classic Labour commitment to modernity,[2] or as some called it, post-modernity (Harvey 1989). This entailed a belief in that Britain's economic prosperity involved an acceptance of deindustrialisation and a greater reliance on the tertiary sector, in particular financial services. In spatial terms it also meant embracing globalisation, even if it resulted in regional inequalities (Theodore 2007). As Kitson and Wilkinson (2007) have argued so persuasively, demand-side economic policy has invariably been absent. Perhaps this is evident in the creation of the Regional Development Agencies (RDAs), which came from the Office of the Deputy Prime Minister (ODPM) and not HM Treasury. Thus local economic development was increasingly delegated to the RDAs or delivered through local regeneration schemes, and criticism of the City and the financial services industry (French et al. 2008) for their perceived role in exclusion and inequality were ignored.

However, during New Labour's first term there was a period when the relationship between inclusion and financial services was accepted with a focus on micro- and small business development. Since the Macmillan report in 1931, it has been recognised that small or micro-sized enterprises tend to be the businesses that experience barriers to growth with respect to sources of finance. This is usually because the most critical stage in the development of any business venture occurs in its first few years, where capital start-up costs are highest. Moreover, the early stages of business growth are also the periods of highest financial risk. Therefore, mainstream financial providers are more cautious in offering loans to start-ups compared to larger, well established enterprises with greater existing assets. In addition, smaller enterprises are disproportionately found in deprived communities who pay more for credit than similar businesses in other locations (Bank of England 2002), while other groups that find access to finance difficult include ethnic minorities (Bank of England 1999), women (Carter et al. 2003) and social enterprises (Smallbone et al. 2001). It is this gap that the CDFIs were expected to cover. Unlike mainstream financial companies, CDFIs[3] 'operate on a non-distributing basis; that is, they do not offer stakeholders substantial financial returns' (Bank of England 2002: 58–59) and should in theory cover their costs through outreach to small enterprises, by offering affordable loans related to an individualised risk assessment. The flexibility and relationship banking offered by CDFIs was considered appropriate in deprived areas (Bank of England 2000).

GLOBAL PERSPECTIVE

UK CDFIs are part of a global micro-finance sector that began in the developing world and spread to the US, before arriving in Europe. Throughout the developing world there are three main debates:

- Are micro-finance providers sustainable?
- Does pursuing sustainability and growth result in disconnection from social mission?
- Are they the most effective way of addressing the needs of deprived communities and micro-entrepreneurs?

According to Copisarow (2000), there are 7,000–10,000 micro-finance institutions worldwide 'out of which no more than 100 to 200 are both profitable and serving thousands of clients' (2000: 14). By contrast, Christen et al. (1994) argued that 'competent' micro-finance entities could be sustainable, though. Johnson and Rogaly (1997) are unsure whether this is likely in all situations. Apart from operational efficiencies (Christen et al. 1994, Gibbons and Meeham 1999) and professionalism (Miller and Andrews 1998), the main reason cited for non-sustainability is the social mission of micro-finance providers, with Hulme and Mosely (1996) arguing that the growth necessary for economic sustainability results in mission drift. Buss (1999) describes this as the principle-agent problem; serving the poorest clients is costly and staff imperceptibly either shift the organisation upmarket or engage in rapid expansion. More philosophically there are doubts about the efficacy of micro-finance in helping the poorest, with Pretes (2002) suggesting that grants not loans may be more effective and Fisher and Sriram (2002) believing that micro-finance cannot alone solve poverty but is only 'a complementary tool within a broader strategy to reduce poverty' (2002: 21), before adding that 'the link between micro-credit and poverty reduction has not been proven' (2002: 26).

Slightly different interpretations of these issues are evident in the US, where micro-finance entities are collectively known as CDFIs. The CDFI sector emerged with the creation of South Shore Bank in Chicago in 1973 (Woodstock Institute 2002) and, by 2007, included over 1,235 organisations. Of these, 508 participated in the annual survey of performance. In 2007 these controlled $17.3 billion of assets and lent $5.3 billion in the year to December. Of the lending undertaken, 38 per cent (by financial value) was for low cost and affordable housing, 44 per cent for small- and medium-sized enterprises (SMEs), 1 per cent for micro-entrepreneurs, 3 per cent for community services and 12 per cent for consumer loans (CDFI Data Project 2007). Most of the funding for the sector is from the CDFI Fund enacted under the 1994 Community Development Banking and Financial Institution Act (CDBFIA). The act matches federal investment with that of the private sector. The latter is mainly from the mainstream banking community, who are obliged under the 1977 Community Reinvestment Act to disclose their activity in all zip codes. This public disclosure of data enables community groups to pressurise the banks to invest in deprived communities, and CDFIs have been an important beneficiary of the banks' response (Johnson et al. 2002). Until 2008, $947 million had been authorised through the CDBFIA.

According to CDFIs they have had an enormous impact in the US. In 2007, they assisted 8,854 businesses, which have created or maintained 34,276 jobs, facilitated the construction or renovation of 57,274 affordable houses, financed the building or renovation of 685 community facilities, provided 14,480 payday loans and helped 7,706 customers to open a bank account (CDFI Data Project 2007). While acknowledging their good work, Dymski (2005) argued that the scale of deprivation meant CDFIs' actual impact had been 'miniscule', while Servon (1999) believed that CDFIs contributed more to the social capital of micro-entrepreneurs than they did financially. By contrast, Shields (1998) stated that CDFIs had been a 'major force' in developing America's poorest communities due to CDFIs' unique characteristics as community owned social financial institutions. However, Benjamin et al. (2004) hold that CDFIs are underperforming when compared to their non-CDFI contemporaries and they struggle to identify indicators of success, hence risk becoming 'ghetto banks' (Martin 1994). This could be because the CDBFIA requires CDFIs to serve targeted areas; hence they face greater risks than other financial institutions (M. Johnson et al. 2002). Yet during the economic crisis it seems CDFIs have managed the downturn better than many, if not most, of the mainstream financial sector. In a speech in November 2008, John Duggan (US Comptroller of Currency) argued that:

> Foreclosure rates within the NeighborWorks network [a CRA funded CDFI] were just 0.21 percent in the second quarter of this year, compared to 4.26 percent of subprime loans and 0.61 percent for conventional conforming mortgages. (http://www.occ.gov/ftp/release/2008–136.htm, accessed 7 September 2009)

It seems that debate in the US concentrates on the extent of the effectiveness and efficiency rather than sustainability of CDFIs, with the instrument of the CDBFIA being used by regulators to ensure the social mission is maintained. Perhaps it is therefore unsurprising that, even after the economic crash in the wake of Lehman Brothers collapse in 2008, CDFIs were seen as significant players in helping deprived neighbourhoods, with President Obama offering the sector $145 million to on-lend.[4]

UK POLICY CONTEXT

As with many aspects of British life the development of micro-finance was strongly influenced by the experience of the US, especially the nomenclature, in which the term CDFI is used to describe the broad social finance sector rather than 'micro-finance' or 'microcredit institution'. The UK's CDFIs have enjoyed extensive support from American CDFI practitioners, and the sector has drawn on the US policy experience. However, the UK has also been shaped by practitioners from Europe, particularly Poland (Copisarow 2000), the developing world and indigenous pre-CDFI provision. This synthesis of perspectives led to a sector that has emerged in an environment with expectations of self-sustainability, while engaged in what American CDFI activists described as the highest risk activity within their model, namely micro-enterprise finance (CDFI Data Project 2007). The reason for this apparent contradiction resides in the former UK Government's ideological commitment to Third Way politics (Giddens 1998): a desire to address unemployment (social democratic impulse), while ensuring any solution does not 'distort' the marketplace (neo-liberal impulse). Consequently, the UK Government did not replicate the US model of imposing reporting obligations on the banks. An irony of this outcome is that the UK now has a more neo-liberal micro-finance policy environment than was present under George W. Bush's Republican-led government.

In the UK, although there was some progress in creating CDFIs in the 1980s and early 1990s,[5] it was with the election of New Labour that national policy to encourage CDFIs was introduced through the Government's social inclusion agenda. Policy was developed through a range of Policy Action Teams, with PAT 3 (HM Treasury 1999a) on enterprise and access to finance and PAT 14 (HM Treasury 1999b) on personal finance.

PAT 14 examined financial exclusion and the policy approach to this problem was summarised by the Treasury Minister, Melanie Johnson:

> The way forward lies in developing new and alternative means to deliver and provide access to financial services as well as ensuring that existing services can reach the whole community. (HM Treasury 1999b: Foreword)

PAT 3 argued that access to finance is more difficult in deprived communities because of the limited amount of personal equity in those localities, which makes them disproportionately reliant on external finance. This is aggravated by a more precarious local economy, the proportionally high cost of making small loans and 'cultural distance', making banks seem unapproachable and disinterested. This is a particular problem for women as they often begin with lower income and assets. PAT 3's strategy for tackling the shortage of finance in deprived communities accepted that, although banks are the main source of external finance, market-based solutions alone could not address all market failures. It suggested that public resources should concentrate on loans rather than grants and proposed that to help achieve this objective CDFIs could 'play a valuable role, by acting as additional sources of credit in the community, focussed on market segments that are not commercial but which offer high social returns' (HM Treasury 1999b: 10), 'strengthen the social and economic fabric of deprived communities' and 'act as a bridge between a deprived community and the mainstream economy' (HM Treasury 1999a: 14).

The community development finance sector received another boost from the implementation of the recommendations of the Social Investment Task Force (SITF), which was also set up in the wake of the policy actions teams, described as the sector's 'wish list' by Affleck and Mellor (2006: 308). The SITF reported in 2000, and its five recommendations aimed 'to obtain higher social and financial returns from social investment, to harness new talents and skills and to address economic regeneration and to unleash new sources of private and institutional investment' (Social Investment Task Force 2003: 3).

The SITF's first recommendation was the introduction of a Community Investment Tax Relief (CITR) that would create an incentive by enhancing the return, to encourage private investment into underinvested communities. The CITR legislation was enacted in 2002 and gives investors in accredited CDFIs a 5 per cent tax relief on the value of their investment for five years. The CITR scheme has already leveraged more than £47 million into the CDFI sector as at October 2008.[6] While there remain some design issues with the scheme, its greatest potential lies in the future when CDFIs increasingly focus on accessing investment rather than grants to grow their portfolios. There has been some criticism of the effectiveness of the scheme but this can largely be attributed to the timing of its introduction: three to five years before effective demand for external capital had grown within the CDFI sector.

The SITF's second recommendation was for the introduction of the community development venture capital model (CDVC) in the UK. CDVC focused on using an equity model (rather than debt-based models which dominate the CDFI sector in the UK) to support business growth in under-invested communities and areas. The first of these was Bridges Ventures launched in 2002 with a €57.2 million fund invested by the Government and private investors. In June 2007, Bridges' second fund of €107 million raised entirely of private institutional and individual investors was successfully completed. The CDVC model has not seen significant growth in the UK, although smaller initiatives by local CDFIs to provide equity or equity-like investments have developed, and two larger, publicly backed organisations—Futurebuilders and Adventure Capital Fund—were launched to provide packages of support including equity-like products to the increasingly enterprising voluntary and community sector.

The Task Force also recommended that charitable trusts and foundations should be given greater latitude to invest in, as well as offer grants to, community development finance institutions. The Charity Commission[7] guidance on social investment followed in 2001, and since then a number of charities have developed investment strategies for CDFIs and other third sector lenders, such as credit unions. These strategies include provision of long-term, subordinated debt at low or no cost, purchase of share capital and mixed packages of risk-taking grant capital, grant support to cover the costs of operations and access to returnable capital.

The fourth recommendation from the task force focused on increasing disclosure from the formal banking sector on their lending activities in deprived areas. The task force recommended voluntary disclosure, and while some banks disclosed some information about their activities, not all have done so. This recommendation has seen the least activity or systemic change. However, as community development finance grows, banks and CDFIs are increasingly finding ways of working together in mutually beneficial ways including indirect investment, product development and delivery (such as delivery of basic bank accounts, savings and budgeting products), and through referrals programmes where retail bank declines are passed to non-bank partners.

The final recommendation from the task force was for further support for the sector with the launch of a trade association dedicated to building a thriving community development finance sector, which would bring economic and social benefit to every disadvantaged community in the UK. The Community Development Finance Association (cdfa) was launched in 2002 and at the time of writing had 76 members representing the majority of the UK's CDFIs, from an initial base of 23.

Following PAT 3 and during the writing of SITR, the Government introduced in 1999 the £30 million Phoenix Fund aimed at CDFIs. This had four components:

1. a challenge fund which gave capital and limited revenue support
2. a development fund for innovative ideas for supporting enterprise
3. a loan guarantee fund to underwrite CDFI borrowing from commercial lenders
4. a network of business mentors for young businesses in deprived communities

The fund was heavily modelled on the US CDFI fund, to support the development of organisations and extend financial services to businesses that were unable to access the finance they required from the commercial banking sector. Between 2000 and 2006, the Phoenix Fund provided more than €60.77 m of grant support to cover existing and emerging organisations. The Phoenix Fund officially ended in March 2006 and new much smaller successor funds have been distributed via the RDAs. In addition the Government hoped that the CITR would help build the capitalisation of the sector to ensure it was sustainable and free from state support.

In the existing literature the emergence of CDFIs can be ascribed to a number of competing ideological arguments that informed New Labour. The 'market failure' perspective believes that the deregulation of financial markets, the desire to minimise costs and risk to help maximise share-holder value, encouraged the mainstream banking sector to withdraw from deprived communities (Leyshon and Thrift 1995, 1996, Rogaly et al. 1999). The second and related argument is that social exclusion caused by neo-liberal economics should be addressed in order to create a cohesive society, but this is best undertaken by non-state actors (Bryson and Buttle 2005). This is because public sector led regeneration has failed as it invariably 'compensated people for being poor' (Social Investment Task Force 2000: 10), rather than promoting latent entrepreneurial talent, thus resulting in the UK having the highest micro-enterprise failure rate in the OECD (Social Investment Task Force 2000). Additionally, public sector loan funds had been poorly managed (Copisarow 2005) with under a half surviving beyond two years (Klett 1994). Moreover, traces of Murray's (1990) underclass debate, which had dominated thinking during the latter stages of the Thatcher Government, were present. Although benefit claimants were the focus of Murray's and Green's (1998) ire, the same arguments could be translated to small business, in that grants and low interest loans encouraged dependency (hence it was no surprise so many state owned funds were never repaid), while 'commercial' credit would encourage a business person to earn money to service the loan. This approach led Affleck and Mellor (2006) to argue that the move from grants to loans was part of the continuing privatisation of the welfare (in this case business welfare) state. Philosophically, this chimed with the brief flowering of New Mutualism, which argued that there were systemic problems with both public and private sector delivery, which cooperatives and other non-profit making organisations could overcome (Mayo and Moore 2001). Although short-lived, New Mutualism reflected a much older strain of Labour ideology, and thus new entities, such as CDFIs, could be introduced as the reawakening of community empowerment (Dayson et al. 1999). Politically these arguments fitted into a Third Way narrative combining the best practice of the private sector, through a socially driven organisation, to address market failure.

UK CDFIS IN PRACTICE

The community development finance sector in the UK encompasses a wide range of social finance organisations providing access to personal finance, micro-finance, small business loans, social enterprise investment and community development venture capital. While the sector is certainly older than the then Labour Government, with the oldest CDFI within the cdfa[8] membership having formed in the mid 1970s, the superficially disparate group of organisations have formed into a discernible sector and been joined by a variety of new institutions, as a result of a broadly supportive policy environment.

Overall, the UK has the most diverse micro-finance sector in Europe (Collin and Thomas 2004) with CDFIs expanding from 11 loan funds with assets of £74 million in 1999 (Rogaly et al. 1999) to at least 57 organisations worth over £397.5 million in 2004 (McGeehan 2005). These organisations made £147 million in loans and investments in 2003–4,[9] up 40 per cent on the previous year (McGeehan 2005). However, although the delinquency and default rates in the UK (8.76 per cent of portfolio suffering 90 or more days without a payment) is better than the average European repayment rate (89.7 per cent) (Vigano et al. 2004), these are still worse than the figures in the US (3.3 per cent overall). Even for US CDFIs that undertake only micro-enterprise lending (less than $35,000 to companies of five or fewer employees), only 5.67 per cent of the portfolio had not paid for at least 30 days and total write-offs were 4 per cent (CDFI Data Project 2007). The impact of delinquency was also cited by Esmée Fairbairn's (2005) analysis of the retrenchment of Street UK (a UK nationwide CDFI), which recorded 90 day delinquency of 12.5 per cent. The review of Street UK also highlighted other challenges faced by UK CDFIs. These include insufficient and inadequate performance data (McGeehan 2005) and too few clients (Copisarow 2005, Esmée Fairbairn 2005). The latter is partially explained as being due to the extent of competition from the mainstream sector forcing CDFIs to serve more difficult cases (Copisarow 2005). The likelihood of this outcome was noted by Rogaly et al. (1999), when they argued that micro-credit that is effective in reaching the unemployed is unlikely to be sustainable. According to Bryson and Buttle (2005) this tension between social mission and sustainability affects all aspects of a CDFI's business, including the loan application process, in which loans are first assessed on social grounds before being examined financially. Consequently, they argue that CDFIs usually serve specified deprived communities resulting in ad hoc provision, which makes it unlikely that they will be a major factor in addressing social exclusion.

While the US provided the impetus for independent CDFIs to arise in the UK, those that initially concentrated on peer lending schemes drew lessons from Poland and the Grameen Bank, Bangladesh (Copisarow 2005, Esmée Fairbairn 2005). However, the majority of CDFIs were engaged in direct lending to micro-businesses and SMEs, and many of these had their antecedents in local authority business loan schemes. These funds became known as 'soft loan schemes', as the lending and collection criteria were weaker than banking standards and, in the main, there were lower expectations of fund performance and recovery of loans. For much of the 1970s and 1980s, soft loan funds were the conventional means to fund businesses, often in tandem with enterprise grants and allowances. However, the survival of these funds averaged less than three years (Klett 1994), and this failure was an additional spur to a more sustainable approach. Today most of the remaining soft loan funds have been incorporated into CDFIs (such as the Warwickshire Fund into the Coventry and Warwickshire Reinvestment

Trust) or have adopted more sustainable characteristics, such as morphing into CDFIs (North West Business Finance as part of Bolton Business Ventures). Often the latter are part of wider business support groups known as Enterprise Agencies, and micro-finance lending forms a subsidiary activity.

Completing the UK sector are CDFIs that serve social, cooperative and charitable enterprises and others that offer personal financial credit (McGeehan 2005).[10] These two sub-sectors have been particularly dynamic, with social enterprise lending being the largest financially and personal credit providers having the most customers. Although not the focus of this chapter, it is worth noting that these two sub-sectors have received more government interest and/or financial support than conventional micro-enterprise lenders.

In summary, the UK has a blended approach framed within a context where micro-credit seeks to serve those most at need, while working towards institutional sustainability, often through support of the Government and other interested agencies. These conflicting dichotomies can be represented by Figure 7.1.

In general UK CDFIs have twin objectives of financial sustainability and delivering social benefit. Figure 7.1 seeks to show the alternative theoretical strategies that are available to a CDFI. It also represents the overall status of CDFIs in the UK.

Box A type CDFIs are driven by a social mission. These types of CDFIs engage in extensive partnership working to ensure they are embedded in the local enterprise support environment. However, their financial management may be underdeveloped or inadequate. This tends to be the status of new CDFIs or those operating in hard-to-serve markets, where outreach is prioritised.

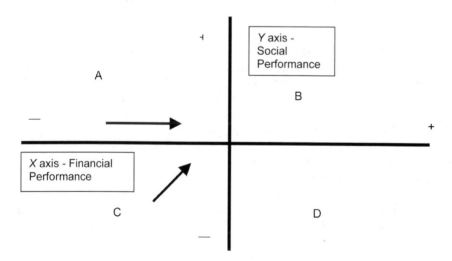

Figure 7.1   Theoretical matrix of UK CDFIs.

Box B could be described as the ideal type. These have strong financial management and levels of self-sufficiency but also pursue a social agenda. They are socially innovative, providing it accords with fiscal stability, though they will not exploit clients financially. To date, with the possible exception of Charity Bank, no UK CDFI fulfils these criteria.

Box C represents the most problematic status, with minimal financial management or too few loans accompanied by high central costs. In addition they display no overt attempts to reach and measure social objectives. The majority of the former soft loan funds could fulfil these criteria.

Box D CDFIs tend to be driven by sustainability. They believe in the need to be profitable in order to make a difference. They may accept the need for social objectives but this is never at the expense of the business. To date, few if any CDFIs are Box D types, though if core funding is removed some may adopt this as a survival mechanism.

Within the UK, most CDFIs are located in either box A and C. In lieu of any statistical frame, it can be estimated that most CDFIs are attempting to improve their self-sustainability, while retaining a strong social ethic. These trends are represented by the two arrows in Figure 7.1.

CDFIS IN THE THIRD TERM OF NEW LABOUR

The cdfa continues to provide an annual report on the performance of CDFIs through a survey of cdfa its members (McGeehan 2008). Overall, the sector continues to grow with £46.5 million levered to 5,442 individuals or businesses in 2007, compared to £27.7 million to 3008 in 2005. However, according to the data the sector is facing a number of challenges. Firstly, respondents stated that access to running costs and access to money for lending remains their greatest concern, though these have fallen from their peak in 2005 and the size and nature of the loan book is of growing interest. Secondly, though the loan portfolio has grown, this has not been spread evenly throughout the sector. When the largest five CDFIs are removed from the data the growth in the sector is more modest, with 1,231 micro-enterprise loans in the in the year to March 2007 worth £10.5 million, compared to 1,464 and £10.4 million in 2005. One explanation is that there are fewer but larger loans being made, and this is inferred by McGeehan as the total loans outstanding is £25 million in 2007, compared to £17.2 million in 2005. This is not supported by the data on lending to small businesses where the outstanding portfolio rose from £5 million to £7.7 million but the number of loans increased sharply from 183 to 455. In fact, lending to social enterprises is the most significant change with the total outstanding portfolio up £10.9 million to £38.2 million. Overall, if we only examine business enterprise lending, though the size of the outstanding portfolio was £40.6 million in 2007 as opposed to just £23.4 million in 2005, the lending undertaken in the two years indicates that growth has risen only a modest 9 per cent (if we assume inflation at 2.5 per cent growth has been a sickly 2 per cent per annum) and the number of customers is down by 14 per cent. Even the total portfolio outstanding figures require closer scrutiny, as 91 plus days delinquency rates are 16.19 per cent for micro-enterprise and 3.49 per cent for small business, while the 31 plus days rates are 26.76 per cent and 7.75 per cent respectively. In such a situation we would expect to see write-off rates at a similar level. Those involved in small enterprise lending averaged 7 per cent but it was only 16 per cent for micro-enterprise lenders, suggesting that the total portfolio outstanding is a less than reliable indicator of the success of the organisation. In addition, while the cdfa collects data on loan portfolio at a given date, it permits CDFIs the freedom to record the write-off only as of the last annual accounts. This opens the possibility that at the time the CDFI declares the total loan portfolio outstanding that they have not written off any bad debts from that portfolio for up to 11 months. It is possible that debts that were up to 90 days in arrears at the time of the last accounts (given that the micro-enterprise delinquency figures at 91 plus days was almost identical to the write-off rate) and remained in arrears during the subsequent year were still included in the total loan portfolio outstanding. On this basis we can assume that CDFIs lending to businesses have found it difficult to write high quality (i.e., not having arrears) loans and that the outstanding loan portfolio is an arbitrary means to assess performance.

Although enterprise lending has continued to prove challenging, the CDFIs have also faced difficulties in the supply of capital. Although RDAs, at 43 per cent, are the highest revenue funders to the sector, their total contribution is a fraction of that provided by the Phoenix Fund and fell by £300,000 in 2005–7, to £2.3 million. Unsurprisingly, given the funding insecurity, the sector has been more aggressive is seeking sustainability and earned more than £6.6 million from loan clients for the year to March 2007 and an additional £7.5 million in other earned income. These changes are evident in the rising interest rates charged, with average figures 4.23 per cent above base rates in 2004, through to 5.19 per cent by 2007. A similar pattern has occurred in loans to small business with rates going from 4.05 per cent above base to 6.41 per cent in 2007. Moreover, the number of CDFIs that charge fees in addition to interest has risen from 44 per cent to 83 per cent of the sector, while the numbers taking security, debentures and personal guarantees are also up (McGeeehan 2008). Consequently, CDFIs, with much lower state support, are passing their deficit in costs of operation on to their client group. It is probable that policy makers expected the sector to produce greater levels of growth and greater efficiency, and while there is evidence for potential improvements in both (Dayson et al. 2008) the reduction in funding has happened before significant management and marketing changes could be made. In essence, the Government decided that the three rounds of the Phoenix Fund, with many CDFIs securing funding only in the last two rounds, was a sufficient period to reach sustainability. As noted above the evidence for this from elsewhere is limited and certainly unlikely for CDFIs concentrating on enterprise lending.

However, the Government's other main policy intervention to support CDFIs, the Community Investment Tax Relief (CITR), seemed to stall (McGeehan 2008, Thiel and Nissan 2008) due to the complexity, its limited application and lack of maturity within the sector. McGeehan argues that risk not returns is the greatest obstacle to investment in CDFIs, which will be ameliorated only by maturity through greater evidence of their lending record. Clearly, risk and specifically the Government's failure to understand its role in the lending process was a significant feature of its policy towards access to finance for small businesses.

From PAT 3 onwards, the Government assumed that there was untapped demand being blocked by capricious bankers (SEU 2001). However, perhaps it was evident that there was an absence of empiricism in policy development when there were no surveys of business needs published alongside, or incorporated within, PAT 3. Without this acknowledgement there was little attempt to conduct a sustained campaign on self-employment and, from the outset, civil servants would privately question[11] whether employment not self-employment was a more appropriate way to tackle economic exclusion. During this policy debate a number of strategic social actors, including think-tanks and those in the voluntary and cooperative sectors, were arguing the benefits of non-governmental provision, particularly where the private sector did not wish to operate. Thus there was a policy symbiosis between the Treasury's demand for greater access to increase economic activity and a desire for a non-profit delivery agent. Fortunately for all sides, the Americans already had a model which could be adopted. As shown above this proved to be deeply problematic but, in the process of designing support mechanisms, issues of demand and risk alleviation were minimised.

In fact, risk was not really considered until the Small Firms Loans Guarantee Scheme (SFLGS) was extended to virtually all business types, which it was hoped would encourage CDFIs to apply for coverage.[12] However, as of April 2008 there were fewer than five CDFIs with approved status. One of the difficulties has been the UK's interpretation of European state-aid rules, with the argument that receiving state support through CITR and a guarantee fund was a double subsidy and therefore in breach of competition law. Though this remains a problem, a number of CDFIs seem to have found mechanisms to ensure they stay within the regulations.

The absence of strategic planning about the exit from Phoenix Fund, beyond an insistence that the responsibility must be transferred to the RDAs, left issues of demand and risk either overlooked, or, as with the SFLGS extension, grafted onto existing arrangements. Instead, most of the RDAs began their control of CDFI support by conducting reviews and commissioning work on demand. Though this work is not in the public domain, feedback from the CDFIs indicate that a thorough evaluation of their performance was a key aspect of the review. Moreover, Thiel and Nissan (2008) argue that VAT registered business are the priority for RDAs and consequently many of the micro-enterprises supported by CDFIs are of only marginal interest. As a result, Thiel and Nissan (2008) stated, RDA support had focused on CDFIs engaged in supporting small businesses. However, across the country the approach of RDAs differed sharply (Thiel and Nissan 2008), though some commonalities were present. Thiel and Nissan's (2008) review of RDA support discusses the problems of diverse delivery, with two (Yorkshire Forward and Advantage West Midlands) at the time wanting to work in a cooperative manner with CDFIs, two others seeking to work via a single partner who would then distribute funds to the other CDFIs in their region (East of England Development Agency and South East England Development Agency) and East Midlands Development Agency seeking to avoid working with CDFIs by creating its own loan funds aimed at small businesses (£10,000 to £30,000 loans) which they indicate will be sustainable in four years. They do accept that CDFIs are needed for micro-enterprise but are not willing to offer any support.[13] The EMDA approach was at the extreme of thinking among RDAs but it does indicate the precarious nature of policy endorsement of CDFIs. After 10 years since CDFIs first came to policy prominence through PAT 3, their continued existence is under threat. However, the EMDA position is not universal and there is goodwill towards the sector in some of the other regions. The tension seems to be the mismatch between the primary focus of a RDA and the Government's policy to overcome barriers to inclusion; or alternatively between economic development and social policy agendas. Intriguingly the Government did not intervene to endorse the role of CDFIs and this may be related to the debate in Whitehall about employment versus self-employment.

CONCLUSION

CDFIs sit across the divide between social and economic policy and in Britain this usually meant favouring the former. From the Government's perspective this involved transferring responsibility to the RDAs, which were focused on economic development. Although the DTI, the previous home, had a business outlook, it was also tasked with a number of social objectives, including improving access to finance; a concern the RDAs were not charged with when the transfer was made. Superficially the transfer was about the reduction in funding as the sector matures and needs less start-up capital. The cdfa and NEF have stressed that the sector was insufficiently developed when the transfer occurred, and that an average funding cut from £7 million per annum from 2000 to 2006 to £2.3 million in 2007 was too severe a burden. But the transfer also enabled the Government to side-step questions about its access to finance policy which had become entrapped between those who wanted greater regulation for the banks (CRA proponents) and those who questioned the continued focus on self-employment as an economic policy.

These tensions are a function of New Labour economic policy, in which a laissez-faire demand side (Kitson and Wilkinson 2007) combines with strategic neo-liberal protectionism, through rejecting increased regulatory control in financial services or customer relations. In this, UK financial service providers have been situated as primary economic agent in both the domestic economy and UK 'global champions'. Within such a position, issues of local responsibility are perceived as historic (French et al. 2008) and anarchistic, due to processes of globalisation and technological change. Moreover, there was rejection of a CRA style legislation that could have located financial institutions within place and space. In this narrative, there is no place for micro-entrepreneurs, despite government rhetoric to the contrary. Thus the state is unwilling to sanction the financial services sector, yet wants to display a message of inclusion for communities. The initial solution for the paradox lay in the development of CDFIs. Fortunately this corresponded to the short-lived New Mutualism discourse and the New Right ideology on benefit dependency, which originally arose during the underclass debate and, by 1999, was extended to businesses and the non-profit sector (Affleck and Mellor 2006, Haugh and Kitson 2007). However, by the beginning of the third-term of the New Labour Government, the emphasis given to small spatially located businesses was displaced by an infatuation with the seemingly perpetual growth of finance and housing related enterprise. In hindsight, this was merely the last gasp of the economic bubble that exploded in popular consciousness with the collapse of Northern Rock. Contributing to this economic immediacy there were debates about the efficacy of CDFIs, in terms of both their performance and whether this was related to a lack of demand among the client group. Rather than re-visit the conceptual framework and justification of UK CDFIs, which would have involved a broadening of their role in community development, they were encased within an economic discourse which resulted in a transfer to the RDAs. This response exposed the Government's intellectual inconsonance and lack of awareness of the role of micro-entrepreneur within a locality. By assuming all entrepreneurs are 'economic actors' who are removed from place, they believed that financial growth was their primary desire. Within this interpretation the concept of local business person being embedded in an intricate web of local social relations, reliant on social capital for work, reputation and identity, was rarely articulated. Therefore, the treatments of CDFIs in the UK and, by extension, micro-entrepreneurs, as well as the free-rider status of the financial services industry, are symbolic of New Labour's policy dichotomy between economic growth and social cohesion, and their economically obsessed interpretation of globalisation.

NOTES

1. The early building societies were pure mutuals, as the membership collectively saved enough until all had built their homes before they were closed down.
2. Both Atlee's 1945 and Wilson's 1963 governments wanted to modernise Britain, the latter famously through the 'white heat of technology'.
3. Community Development Financial Institutions (CDFIs) are a branch of community finance initiatives that focus on loan-based solutions to market failure. The other main branch is credit unions that provide a mutual savings and loans based approach.
4. $45 million already promised was increased to $145 million in Recovery and Reinvestment Act 2009. http://www.cdfifund.gov/recovery/ (accessed: 7 September 2009).
5. Organisations included Hackney Business Venture in 1983, Princes Youth Business Trust in 1986, while Developing Strathclyde and Merseyside Special Investment Fund, which emerged in the 1990s.
6. Question by Margaret Moran MP to Kevin Brennan MP (Chancellor to the Duchy of Lancaster) on the 9 October 2009 column 823W.
7. The regulator of UK charities.
8. Community Development Finance Association, the trade association for social finance organisations in the UK: www.cdfa.org.uk.
9. Period of study was September 2003 to September 2004.
10. These are in addition the UK's credit unions
11. Author's informal conversations with civil servants between 2000 and 2008. Also, a number of CDFIs chief executives, particularly those involved in lender to small- and medium-sized businesses expressed similar views during informal discussions, usually at the cdfa conferences between 2003 and 2007.
12. The Graham Review (2004) recommended extending SFLGS status to CDFIs but the first approval was in 2006/7.
13. Of the other RDAs, One London had placed their approach on hold pending an investigation into the CDFI, Ethnic Mutual; while One North East and the North West Development Agency did not participate in the survey.

BIBLIOGRAPHY

Affleck, A. and Mellor, M. (2006) 'Community development finance: a neo-market solution to social exclusion?', Journal of Social Policy, 35(2): 303–19.
Bank of England (1999) The Financing of Ethnic Minority Firms in the United Kingdom: A special report, London: Bank of England.
——(2000) Finance for Small Business in Deprived Communities, London: Bank of England.
——(2002) Finance for Small Firms: A ninth report, London: Bank of England.
Benjamin, L. Rubin, J. and Zielenbach, S. (2004) 'Community development financial institutions: current issues and future prospects', Journal of Urban Affairs, 26(2): 177–95.
Bryson, J. and Buttle, M. (2005) 'Enabling inclusion through alternative discursive formations: the regional development of community development loan funds in the UK', The Services Industry Journal, 25(2): 273–88.
Buss, T. (1999) 'Micro-enterprise in international perspective: an overview of the issues', International Journal of Economic Development, 1(1): 1–28.

Carter, S., Anderson, S. and Shaw, E. (2003) 'Women's business ownership: a review of the academic, popular and internet literature with a UK policy focus', in D. Watkins (ed.) Annual Review of Progress in Entrepreneurship, Brussels: European Foundation for Management Development.

CDFI Data Project (2007) Providing Capital, Building Communities, Creating Impact: community development financial institutions, Third Ed., Fiscal Year 2003, Washington, DC: CDFI Data Project, Opportunity Finance.

Christen R., Rhyne, E. and Vogel, R. (1994) 'Maximising the outreach of micro-enterprise finance: the emerging lessons of successful programs. A summary of findings and recommendations', paper presented to the Conference on Finance Against Poverty, Reading, February 1995.

Collin, S. and Thomas, W. (2004) 'Overview of the micro-finance sector in western Europe', EMN Working Paper 1, EMN, Paris.

Copisarow, R. (2000) 'The application of microcredit technology to the UK: key commercial and policy issues', Journal of Micro-finance, 2(1): 13–42.

———(2005) Street UK, A Micro-Finance Organisation: Lessons learned from its first three years' operations, Birmingham: Street UK.

Dayson, K. (2003) Carpetbaggers and Credit Unions: a sociology study into the paradox of mutuality in the late twentieth century, PhD thesis, University of Salford.

Dayson, K., Paterson, R. and Powell, J. (1999) Investing in People and Places, Salford: University of Salford.

Dymski, G. (2005) 'New markets or old constraints? Financing community development in the post-"War on Poverty" era', paper presented at the National Economic Association conference, Philadelphia, January.

Esmée Fairbairn (2005) Street (UK): Learning from community finance. A briefing paper, London: Esmée Fairbairn.

Ferguson, N. (2009) The Ascent of Money: A financial history of the world, London: Penguin.

Fisher, T. and Sriram, M. (2002) Beyond Micro-Credit: Putting development back into micro-finance, Oxford: Oxfam.

French, S. Leyshon, A. and Signoretta, P. (2008) '"All gone now": The material discursive and political erasure of bank and building society branches in Britain', Antipode, 40(5): 79–101.

Gibbons, D. and Meeham, J. (1999) 'The Micro-Credit Summit's challenge: working toward institutional financial self-sufficiency while maintaining a commitment to serving the poorest families', Journal of Micro-Finance, 1(1): 131–92.

Giddens, A. (1998) The Third Way: The renewal of social democracy, Cambridge: Polity Press.

Graham Review (2004) Graham Review of Small Firms Loan Guarantee Scheme, London: HM Treasury.

Green, D. D. (1998) Benefit Dependency: How welfare undermines independence, London: IEA.

Harvey, D. (1989) The Condition of Postmodernity, Oxford: Blackwell.

Haugh, H. and Kitson, M. (2007) 'The Third Way and the third sector: New Labour's economic policy and the social economy', Cambridge Journal of Economics, 31(6): 973–94.

HM Treasury (1999a) PAT 3: Enterprise and Social Exclusion, London: HM Treasury.

———(1999b) PAT 14: Access to Financial Services, London: HM Treasury.

Hollis, A. and Sweetman, A. (1997) 'Complementarity, Competition and Institutional Development: the Irish loan funds through three centuries'. Online. Available http://129.3.20.41/eps/eh/papers/9704/9704003.html (accessed 15 June 2008).

Hulme, D. and Mosley, P. (1996) Finance against Poverty, London: Routledge.

Johnson, M., Kemp, J. and Nguyen, A. (2002) 'The Community Reinvestment Act', Kansas Journal of Law and Public Policy, XII(I): 89–123.

Johnson, S. and Rogaly, B. (1997) Micro-Finance and Poverty Reduction, Oxford: Oxfam.

Kermode, J. (1991) 'Money and credit in the fifteenth century: some lessons from Yorkshire', The Business History Review, 65(3): 475–501.

Kitson, M. and Wilkinson, F. (2007) 'The economics of New Labour: policy and performance', Cambridge Journal of Economics, 31: 805–16.

Klett, M. (1994) A Directory of Soft Loan Schemes 1993,1994, Kingston: Small Business Research Centre, Kingston University.

Levitas, R. (1998) The Inclusive Society? Social exclusion and New Labour, Basingstoke: Palgrave Macmillan.

Leyshon, A. and Thrift, N. (1994) 'Access to financial services and financial infrastructure withdrawal: problems and policies', Area, 26: 268–75.

——(1995) 'Geographies of financial exclusion: financial abandonment in Britain and the United States', Transaction of the Institute of British Geographers, New Series, 20: 312–41.

——(1996) 'Financial exclusion and the shifting boundaries of the financial system', Environment and Planning A, 28: 1150–56.

Mayo, E. and Moore, H. (2001) The Mutual State: How local communities can run public services, London: NEF.

McGeehan, S. (2005) Inside Out, London: cdfa.

——(2008) Inside Out 2007, London: cdfa.

Marshall, J. N. (2004) 'Financial institutions in disadvantaged areas: a comparative analysis of policies encouraging financial inclusion in Britain and the United States', Environment and Planning A, 36: 241–61.

Martin, D. A. (1994) 'The President and the cities: Clinton's urban aid agenda', Urban Law, 26: 99–117.

Miller, T. and Andrews, N. (1998) 'Velcro arms, Teflon heart: enhancing livelihoods through community development finance', Ford Foundation paper written for the Foundations Affinity Group on Development Finance, New York, December 2008.

Muldrew, C. (1993) 'Credit and courts: debt litigation in a seventeenth century urban community', Economic History Review, 46(1) :23–38.

Murphy, R. (2003) The Case for an Interest Rate Cap in the UK, Ely: Author published.

Murray, C. (1990) The Emerging British Underclass, London: IAE Health and Welfare Unit.

Pretes, M. (2002) 'Micro-equity and micro-finance', World Development, 30(8): 1341–53.

Price, S. J. (1958) Building Societies: Their origin and history, London: Franey and Co.

Rogaly, B., Fischer, T. and Mayo, E. (1999) Poverty, Social Exclusion and Microfinance in Britain, Oxford: Oxfam.

Servon, L. J. (1999) Bootstrap Capital: Microenterprise and the American poor, Washington, DC: Brookings Institution Press.

SEU (2001) National Strategy for Neighbourhood Renewal, London: Social Exclusion Unit.

Shields, R. W. (1998) 'Community development finance institutions and the Community Development Financial Institutions Act of 1984: good ideas in need of some attention', Review of Banking and Financial Law, 17: 637.

Smallbone, D., Evans, M., Ekanem, I. and Butters, S. (2001) Researching Social Enterprise, Sheffield: Small Business Service.

Social Investment Task Force (SITF) (2003) Enterprising Communities: Wealth beyond welfare, a 2003 update on the Social Investment Taskforce. London: SITF.

Theodore, N. (2007) 'New Labour at Work: long-term unemployment and the geography of opportunity', Cambridge Journal of Economics, 31: 927–39.

Thiel, V. and Nissan, S. (2008) UK CDFIs—From Surviving to Thriving: Realising the potential of community development finance, London: NEF.

Vigano, L. Bonomo, L. and Vitali, P. (2004) 'Micro-finance in Europe', unpublished working paper, Girdano Dell'Amore Foundation & European Foundation Guido Venosta, Milan, Italy.

Woodstock Institute (2002) 'Doing well while doing good: the growth of community development banking, 1992–2001', Reinvestment Alert 18. Online. Available http://woodstockinst.org/document/alert18.pdf (accessed 15 June 2008).

8 Working Life in Rural Micro-Enterprises
Old Forms of Organisation in the New Economy

Susan Baines, Jane Wheelock and Elizabeth Oughton

INTRODUCTION

Rural deprivation is less concentrated and less visible than in towns and cities. People experiencing disadvantage and exclusion in the British countryside are often overlooked because inequalities are obscured by notions of idyllic rural communities (Schucksmith 2000, 2004). Unemployment rates in rural areas are normally lower than in urban areas but these lower rates conceal certain forms of unemployment and underemployment, such as those who work intermittently (Monk et al. 1999, Tryner and Warner 2003). Average earning statistics point to overall rural affluence but they obscure the presence of households living below the poverty line (Tryner and Warner 2003). In addition to precarious, seasonal employment and low incomes, rural disadvantage is characterised by difficulty in accessing a wide range of private and public services including health and care providers, job centres, shops, banks and petrol stations (Lowe and Speakman 2006).

In rural areas micro-enterprises (employing 0–10 people) are more significant providers of employment and services than their urban counterparts (Lowe and Talbot 2000). So-called 'lifestyle businesses' without growth ambition make an important contribution to rural employment (Tryner and Warner 2003). Little is known about the working lives of people dependent on rural micro-businesses for their livelihoods. In this chapter we focus on work and employment in micro-enterprises in rural England.

A HOUSEHOLD APPROACH TO UNDERSTANDING MICRO-BUSINESSES

In the mid 1990s, two of the authors (Jane Wheelock and Susan Baines) conducted a study of micro-businesses in urban England.[1] These micro-businesses were in business services, a sector which had grown rapidly in the previous decade and was generally associated with the development of a new, knowledge-based economy. In accordance with policy concerns of the 1990s, the study focused on business survival and growth. A distinctive feature, however, was that unlike the majority of small business studies it concentrated on links between market and non-market activities inside the business household. Most small business studies emphasised the entrepreneur's personal attributes, attitudes and support needs, a position which has more recently been subject to critique (Hamilton 2006). It was literature on farming rather than on entrepreneurship that helped us to make sense of the urban business owners' behaviour in the last decade of the twentieth century (Baines and Wheelock 1998).

Farming is a sector in which production for the market based on family or household labour and property has long been recognised. The farm can not properly be understood without reference to the family that operates it (Gasson and Errington 1993). Pollack (1985) assessed advantages and disadvantages of family labour in the farm or other micro-business. Family labour offered the benefits of trust, loyalty and lack of opportunism. Its downsides were low levels of appropriate skills within the confines of the family and the danger of conflict, which could spill over from the business into personal relationships or vice versa. Whatmore, taking a feminist perspective to the study of farming labour, noted that terms such as 'the farmer' and 'the self-employed' construct their subject as autonomous individuals where they are better understood as 'rooted in a complex network of unequal family and household relations' (Whatmore 1991: 145). Our research in urban England demonstrated the applicability of that perspective for micro-businesses in sectors not normally thought of in terms of traditional practices or family labour. As in farming families, women and men in the urban micro-businesses we studied participated together but not often under conditions of equality (Baines and Wheelock 1998, 2000). We concluded that the much cited flexibility of micro-businesses characteristically involves a return to distinctly old ways of working (ibid.). These ways of working include long hours, the use of the family home as a workplace, a gender stereotypical division of labour and cooperative, reciprocal values operating at the level of the household. Our findings reflected those of Ram and Holliday (1993) in a more traditional sector. They dubbed the work patterns in Asian-owned clothing firms 'negotiated paternalism'. This was characterised by the input, often unpaid and under-recognised, of female family members.

There were a few non-farming studies conducted before small enterprise became fashionable in public policy or in academic research. These too documented a unity of family household and business enterprise which seemed to contradict the tendency of modern economies towards the separation of labour and capital. Self-employed men (sole traders and small employers) in the construction industry were 'generally dependent upon the unpaid services of their families and the utilisation of domestic assets for business purposes' (Scase and Goffee 1982: 23). The small-scale trader was forced to involve 'his' family in the affairs of the shop (Bechhofer et al. 1974). A precarious economic existence, with heavy reliance on household labour, never ceased to exist for some small traders in industrialised economies. By the mid twentieth century, however, it seemed to represent the reproduction within modernity of something seemingly pre-modern (Clegg 1990). That is why we described new, urban micro-businesses in the 1990s as a re-invented form of the traditional business family (Mariussen et al. 1997, Baines and Wheelock 1998, 2000). In this chapter we report part of a research project in which we turned from the urban to the rural micro-business household. After outlining the context and research approach, we focus upon three separate but inter-linked characteristics for working life in a rural micro-business. These are: work within the household and wider family; the work-family balance; and the participation of non-family members in a micro-business.

A HOUSEHOLD STUDY OF RURAL MICRO-ENTERPRISES

We used in-depth interviews to investigate the kinds of livelihoods rural enterprises support for the women and men who participate in them. Our research was undertaken in remote north Northumberland in the north east of England. Forty-nine people were interviewed in 28 micro-business households. A separate but related study collected survey data on micro-businesses (employing 0–10) across the north east of England[2] reported by Raley and Moxey (2000). This large-scale survey included sole traders and VAT registered and non-registered businesses and attracted responses from nearly 1,300 business owners. All sectors of the rural economy were covered with the exception of farms (farms were surveyed separately but farm diversification businesses were included in the main survey). We used the survey to select micro-businesses started in the 1990s in the most remote part of the region, north Northumberland, for our household interviews. The main criteria for selection were business size and gender of ownership.[3]

A micro-business is formally defined as a businesses employing 0 to 10 (Storey 1994) but there is enormous diversity in their size and capacity to provide a livelihood for owners, their families and employees. Thirteen per cent of survey respondents reported a turnover of less than £10,000 per annum (Raley and Moxey 2000). At the other extreme, there were businesses which created a livelihood for one or more family members in addition to being quite significant employers of non-family labour. In order to ensure that these variations were captured in the north Northumberland sample, we arranged businesses into three size bands which were given the descriptive labels of 'part-time', 'provider' and 'model'. Part-time micro-businesses were very small indeed and did not produce a livelihood for even one person; provider micro-businesses provided an occupation and income for at least one person and sometimes included a family employee or partner or one non-family worker (full-time equivalent); model micro-businesses were employers of more than one (full-time equivalent) non-family wage earner.

We aimed to create a sample equally divided between male and female business owners, although statistically female sole owners are a minority and many women participate in businesses alongside their husbands. Seven businesses out of the 28 in the rural study were formally co-owned by husband and wife but in five of them the business was regarded by both partners as the responsibility of one of them. Of the 28 businesses, 14 were led by a woman, 12 by a man and two by a husband-wife partnership in a fairly symmetrical relationship. Although the sample was initially assembled according to business and owner characteristics, based on the larger survey, the unit of analysis for our qualitative study was the household. Table 8.1 provides an overview of the sample, with summary information about the businesses and households.

The survey of 1,300 rural micro-businesses confirmed that spouses were an important element in the operation of rural micro-businesses and revealed that the next most common form of labour was casual, non-family (Raley and Moxey 2000). In the 28 case study micro-businesses, family work was the norm. Work directly for a micro-business was only one of the ways in which family resources could be significant. Childcare by their parents could, in a minority of cases, enable owners to work for their businesses and sometimes supplement their incomes by earning wages elsewhere. When non-family members were included in micro-businesses it was often as casual, part-time and seasonal workers.

FAMILY WORK FOR NORTHUMBERLAND MICRO-BUSINESSES

Work for rural micro-businesses was overwhelmingly family work. In this section we explore the supply of labour to micro-businesses from within the household and from non-resident family members. We consider how work was divided according to gender and age and examine the extent to which it was commodified.

Survey data revealed that half of the micro-businesses in rural north east England were 'family businesses' in the sense that they included spouses or other family members as either co-owners or employees (Raley and Moxey 2000). Twelve out of the 28 businesses in our qualitative study were 'family businesses' in the narrow sense. The description of a spouse or other family member as a partner, employee or helper did not relate closely to their actual workload or contribution. Ten case study businesses involved family members who were not described as partners or employees. The main family participant was a spouse in all except two of these 10 cases; in both, the owner was single. The informal practical support of spouses could be

Table 8.1 Northumberland Micro-Business Households

Male Owners

Size Band	Micro-Business Activity	Spouse's Occupation or Other Source of Income	Employment in the Micro-Business	Age of Youngest Child in Household
Part-time	Animal care	Own business (food)	Non-family casual	Baby
	Technical writing	Teacher (f-t)	None	3
	Film making	2 p-t jobs	None	13
Provider	Consultancy	Business partner (p-t)	Non-family in past	None
	Manufacture	Business employee (f-t)	Non-family f-t	18
	Manufacture	Office worker (f-t)	None	14
	Construction	Public sector (p-t)	Family f-t	8
	Retail + tourism	Teaching (casual), artist	Non-family p-t	18
Model	Antiques trade	N/A (divorced)	Non-family f-t, p-t & casual	18
	Consultancy	Holiday letting business	Non-family p-t & casual	1
	Food processing	Business partner (f-t)	Non-family f-t	5
	Business services	None	Non-family f-t & p-t	Baby

Female Owners

Size Band	Micro-Business Activity	Spouse's Occupation or Other Source of Income	Employment in the Micro-Business	Age of Youngest Child in Household
Part-time	Tourism (B&B)	Self-employed engineer	None	20
	Tourism (B&B)	Pension, casual work	None	N/A
	Language training	Separated	None	N/A
	Pet boarding	Shop worker (p-t)	Non-family in past	N/A
Provider	Food making	N/A (divorced)	None	14
	Pet boarding	Farmer	Casual	5
	Shop & café	Farm contract worker	Non-family p-t	N/A
	Retail (food)	Chef (f-t)	Non-family p-t seasonal	17
Model	Hairdressing	N/A (divorced)	Non-family f-t & p-t	9
	Retail (village shop)	Oil industry (overseas)	Non-family p-t	7
	Training services	N/A (divorced)	Non-family f-t & p-t	15
	Manufacturing	Public sector	Non-family p-t	11
	Pharmacy	Employed in business	Non-family f-t & p-t	3
	Travel services	Employed in business	Non-family & family f-t & p-t	16

Male-Female Joint Owners

Size Band	Micro-Business Activity	Spouse's Occupation or Other Source of Income	Employment	Age of Youngest Child in Household
Provider	Craft making and sales	Full-time business partners	None	N/A
Provider	Retail (general)	Full-time business partners	Non-family p-t seasonal	12

substantial, up to several hours work every day. Businesses in which family participation was formalised differed from the businesses in the qualitative study as a whole in that they were larger and more likely to have non-family employees. They differed remarkably little in the ways in which family members worked and were rewarded.

Both women and men worked in the micro-businesses run by their spouses, whether or not they themselves had another job or owned another business. Of the 28 business households, 22 contained two adults who were married or cohabiting. Of these 22 couples, there were only three instances in which the partner played no practical role at all in the business. We return to the exceptional cases at the end of this section. Few spouses had specialist skills relevant to the businesses. The most usual contribution of husbands or wives was as an extra pair of hands. Their roles tended to be gender stereotyped (i.e. men for heavy lifting and driving, women for office administration) but they were certainly not rigidly so. There were a few instances of work that were counter to gender typing. For example, the wife of a sawmill owner operated machinery while the husband of a bed and breakfast owner served her guests at breakfast.

Businesses in which spouses participated together were described as joint ventures, where work and rewards were intertwined in such a way that it was not easy to unravel who gave and received what. For example, Nick and Barbara each owned a business in very different sectors that were separate for accounting purposes but regarded by both partners as shared: 'We work together all day, every day, basically'. As in many of the urban micro-businesses from our earlier study, the business project was acknowledged as a joint marital project, where an affective commitment as spouses became additionally an economic commitment (Baines and Wheelock 1998).

In some instances, as in the urban study, situations that respondents described as sharing could be interpreted as the re-confirmation of gendered power roles. Olivia's words, for example, highlight this when talking though her feelings about leaving her job to work in a consultancy business started by her husband after his (enforced) early retirement. They jointly owned the business but both partners referred to it as his. Her work (office administration and book keeping) for his business was less challenging than she had been used to in her former employment. In her view, however, 'the me bit really doesn't come into it, it's always been an us thing'. When she was asked about remuneration for her work she laughed and said jokingly that she would love to see her money!

On a few occasions, business owners revealed that they were conscious of the monetary value of their spouse's contribution because they had thought about, or experienced, situations in which it could be replaced by a market transaction. In such cases a spouse's work was described as a direct alternative to taking on a non-family employee. Maeve's husband, Pete, for example, gave two hours' work to her bakery business every morning despite the fact that he also had a full-time job. Otherwise she would certainly have needed to pay another part-time employee. Wendy could have recruited an employee to replace her husband's work in her village shop if he took a full-time outside job. The couple had discussed this option but felt that as long as he could keep some outside work 'to get away from the place for a little bit' (he did occasional, seasonal farm contracting), it did not make sense for him to earn more money in order to pay a non-family member to work in the shop. Nancy, on the other hand, had taken on a non-family employee when she first started her pet boarding business. Since then she and her husband both reduced the hours they worked in their outside jobs and started to manage the business together with no employees. These were unusual cases in which an economic calculation about a spouse's work was made within the household.

There was high incidence of the participation of teenagers and young adults in their parents' micro-businesses in north Northumberland. There were 16 respondents who had children between the ages of 15 and 21, either resident or partially resident. Only four respondents from that group said that their children took no part at all in the business at the time of the interview. Two respondents reported that younger teenagers also contributed on a small scale. There were variations in the nature, extent and rewards of working for a parent's business but by far the most typical arrangement was casual or occasional work which was remunerated. This was in stark contrast to the non-commoditised relations between spouses in the business.

Most typically, owners' children worked in the businesses for Saturday or holiday jobs, often alongside other casual workers. This was true of sons and daughters. There was just one case in which the very occasional assistance of adult sons was described as 'gratis'. This was a business in which both the parents worked exceptionally long hours for extremely low rewards. In two cases grown-up sons living at home, both with other jobs, worked in return for their board. Only very rarely was work in the parent's business seen as a long-term commitment. The idea of children succeeding their parents in the business was hardly articulated at all. In just three instances this possibility was mentioned but very tentatively indeed. In only one case was a business said to be dependent on the work of the younger generation. Their circumstances were exceptional because the owner had become debilitated by illness and could no longer do the physical work for her bed and breakfast. Overall, older children worked for their parents' business on an *ad hoc* basis, according to the variable need for labour, almost always in return for some reward, usually monetary.

Participation by the older generation in the rural micro-businesses was rarer than for the younger one, and its patterns much more varied. Nevertheless a theme does emerge of some substantial transfers from the older to the younger generation. There were instances where work, a material gift or both from parents was a vital assistance to business start-up. Some of the variation in the participation of elders is explained by the population structure of the rural location. Half the owners were incomers into

Northumberland and did not have close family nearby. In just 12 of the 28 cases there were parents or in-laws living locally. Living a long distance away did not entirely preclude parental support but clearly it made everyday reliance on it impossible. In only two of the 12 households with local parents did the elders play no role at all either in the business or in facilitating work for the business by caring for children. The work of owners' parents (in the business or domestic sphere) was almost never paid for, whether it was occasional or an on-going and onerous commitment. We return to childcare in the next section. Sometimes parents' contribution was a gift and at other times a form of reciprocal exchange was involved. For example, the mother of a hairdresser provided cover for staff who were sick or on holiday and was repaid with a hair cut. The owner of a catering business depended on her mother to work on a much more regular basis. Repayment for the mother's work in this case was care for her animals by the owner's husband. This was an example of a business which certainly would not have been sustainable without intergenerational exchanges; without, in other words, extensions to the boundaries of the household.

It is important in qualitative research to examine cases which seem to be deviant. We turn now to the instances in which family involvement was not present at the time of the interview. There were six such cases. Three of these had been husband-wife businesses in the past. The change to non-participation in each of these three cases was the decision of the spouse and against the owner's will. In two of these instances, withdrawal from the business was associated with marriage break-up. In the other case, the owner's wife had moved from the business into the labour market and explained that she loved the work, the company and having a source of income independent of her husband. He appreciated the extra income she now brought into the household but complained that his work was lonely (he had no employees and his business was in an isolated location). Only one owner described a positive decision to avoid involving his wife in the business. This was a 'ground rule' agreed with his (male) business partner at start-up. The reason he gave was that they did not want worries about the business to impinge on their home lives.

The participation of family members varied enormously in its nature and intensity but our analysis suggests that, for rural business owners, participation by family members is more diverse than for their urban counterparts. Spouses almost always gave some form of assistance to a business owned within the household whether or not they were formally part of the business and whatever their other work or domestic commitments. Older, non-resident family members sometimes made a vital contribution. Decommodified work was typical in both these relationships. In contrast, money was likely to change hands within families for the efforts of young people. In those cases the affective relationship that defines membership of a household has been supplemented by a formal economic one (Wheelock et al. 2003).

THE WORK-FAMILY BALANCE

A micro-business is a form of work organisation in which family members are incorporated in ways not characteristic of other parts of the labour market. Often, but not invariably, work takes place in or near the home. Under such circumstances various patterns of combining work and non-work responsibilities are possible. How rural micro-business owners reconcile work and parenting of young children is the subject of the following section. In a remote, rural location there are particular difficulties associated with managing the workload of a micro-business and caring for young children. These dilemmas were resolved in a variety of ways according to the income needs of the households and according to beliefs about the nature of work, who should perform it and where.

Children of primary school age or younger were present in 10 of the 28 business households, and some of the households with older children had been in business when their children were still young. Who was available to care for children, and when, depended on the demands of all income earning activities within a household. These typically included waged work as well as self-employment (see Table 8.1). Both waged and self-employed work were often seasonal. Both sometimes involved long-distance travel, especially for men. Childcare arrangements were, overall, the responsibility of the mother, whether she was a business owner, was a participant in her husband's business or had an outside job. There were two exceptional cases in which the father was the main carer. In both those instances the mother's income earning capacity was greater than the father's. One woman was a pharmacist and there was a statutory requirement for her to be present on her premises. The other was a teacher whose business owner husband reduced his business activity drastically in order to care for their child while she pursued her career full-time.

Respondents in Northumberland did not complain of lack of formal childcare facilities and there was no suggestion whatsoever that better provision would enhance their ability to manage self-employment, improve their sales or achieve growth and employ others. On the contrary, they often insisted that 'farming out' their children to strangers was unacceptable (Wheelock and Jones 2002). Parents in need of childcare for all or part of their working day typically called upon wider family, especially grandparents. Employees of the business too occasionally helped to care for children. As we discuss in the next section, relationships with employees could be close. This was not therefore thought of as entrusting children to strangers. When there was no resident father, or he was working extremely long hours or working away from home, the children's grandparents were especially important. Two of the three women business owners who were lone parents were entirely dependent on their mothers for childcare. So was a household in which the male owner's business involved frequent long-distance travel. The third lone parent explained how she could manage the work of her home-based food production business without childcare. Her daughters were nine and seven when she started the business and she worked while they were at school and at night when they were asleep. In particularly busy times (demand for her product was seasonal) she could work when they were present, although this caused her some concern about hygiene in the kitchen.

Work which could be flexible enough to be managed around young children was a strong theme in the rural micro-business interviews. Rural respondents tended to idealize that solution. Jenni, who boarded pets, said her baby son could sleep with 17 dogs barking in his ears. Joe remembered that when his three children were young, 'the fact that you had a brat with you when you were doing a delivery to somebody in the van was neither here nor there because it was all part of the fun of it and it enriched their lives to a certain extent'. Not all accounts were so positive, however. Joe's former wife presented a darker picture of the integration of this business into the household. She talked of doing hard physical work (without payment) which involved using dangerous chemicals in the home. Paula's experience, too, revealed some of the pressure that caring for children and working for a business simultaneously can give rise to. She recalled an occasion when her six year old son was sick and she continued to serve in the shop, constantly rushing upstairs to the flat where he lay on the sofa, crying, 'oh mammy please don't go'. She was determined that such a distressing situation would never arise again and took on another part-time employee to free more of her own time for childcare. This was despite her husband's view that the jointly owned business could not afford more non-family employment.

Blurring of boundaries around home and workplace is characteristic of rural micro-businesses and is often described positively by their owners. It can, in some instances, ease the all-pervading modern dilemma of the work-life balance. It is not, however, a cost-free solution.

CHARACTERISTICS OF NON-FAMILY EMPLOYMENT

A fifth of the 1,300 businesses in the large-scale survey used non-family casual labour. Only just over 10 per cent provided full-time, year round, non-family employment. Such stable employment was present in a higher proportion of our 28 cases than in the larger survey. There were seven owners who described the employment of at least one worker as full-time and not subject to laying off due to seasonal or other variations. More typically, employment was both part-time and seasonal, with regular part-timers working varied hours according to need. Additional part-time or casual staff were brought in for particularly busy periods and often worked alongside members of business owners' families.

The nature of working arrangements, and their flexibility for employees as well as the employers, varied enormously. At one extreme, shops in tourist areas took on part-time staff for the short summer season, while a land-based business had a worker employed only in winter. A construction business had a full-time employee (a distant relation of the owner) for most of the year but occasionally laid him off when work was scarce. In a consultancy business, on the other hand, a 'job share' arrangement was created to take into account the family responsibilities of two women employees. One of the largest employing businesses had seven part-time female employees all working different hours. The female owner of this manufacturing business would ideally have liked some of her employees to work full-time and increase production but she recognised that this would not be practical for them because of their childcare needs. She compared their family commitments to her own situation as a mother who had started the business in order to keep a foothold in the world of work while caring for her children. Although she put unusually strong emphasis on the non-work needs of her workers, her personal interest in their welfare was not exceptional.

Sometimes flexibility took forms that would be unlikely in larger organisations. For example, an employee who was a lone parent was allowed to bring her child along to work in an animal care business, and an employer of a secretary described agreeing her working hours around her desire to spend the middle of each day looking after her horse. Employing others, even on a casual and *ad hoc* basis, was often described as a social responsibility. Sometimes respondents commented with regret on the poor quality of the employment they were able to offer. The statements they volunteered about working conditions for their employees included: pay is low; promotion is impossible; customers are demanding and sometimes unreasonable; work is hard and in poor conditions, for example out of doors in winter. Nevertheless, in general, owners were proud of being employers and sometimes said that their employees would have difficulty finding other jobs without having to travel a long distance.

Many businesses were home based, with employees coming into the home. There was therefore quite extreme physical integration of the household and the workplace which usually, although not always, was welcomed by respondents. Trust was important. Sometimes people who were employed both formally and casually in the businesses also undertook household tasks. They were said to help with activities including childcare, taking personal telephone calls, looking after domestic animals and supporting business owners' voluntary and community activities.

The accounts referred to above suggest highly personal, and sometimes very warm, relationships between employer and employee, relationships characterised by trust and mutual respect. Overall these were indeed the characteristics of the employee relationships reported by business owners in rural Northumberland. In this respect they contrast with the awkward and conflict-laden experiences of employing revealed in the qualitative part of our earlier study of urban business service businesses (Baines and Wheelock 1998). There were nevertheless instances of conflict with employees in the rural micro-businesses. Seven respondents reported at least one instance of a sour and unsuccessful relationship with an employee (casual or long-term). The most usual reason for an employment relationship to fail was because the employee did not fit in or was not committed enough to the business.

The largest and most successful business in the study had experienced failed employment relationships several times. Eileen[4] and her husband Greg offered holiday and transport services, and their business had grown slightly out of the 'micro' category by the time of the interview, with 12 full-time and 2 part-time employees. Eileen and Greg had started their business, as was typical, working long hours together. They had recruited early, been forced to lay workers off and then grown again. They described relationships with staff in unusually impersonal terms. Laying people off is something owners of micro-businesses typically describe as extremely distressing (Baines and Wheelock 1998) but Eileen and Greg were matter of fact about it. This was notably the only case in which employment protection legislation was referred to as a problem. Greg claimed that 'it's when you employ people—that's where you get really disillusioned'. At the end of the interview, having described a business which had achieved the kind of growth which policy makers urge upon more micro-business owners, he reflected wistfully on the attractions of having a small and purely family business: '[W]e could have a job for me, a job for my wife, a job for my son and we'd probably have a far better lifestyle and a far better business—maybe one employee'. Highly personal employment relationships, however, were much more typical in the Northumberland study. This is thrown into sharp relief in the worst case of conflict. An employee was said to have stolen from a business. Here the owner expresses her sadness and rage and such a breach of trust:

> I very much believe in being extremely fair, I always, my mother always taught me, it comes from old times of course, they were farming people... but you're quite often, you are let down occasionally, and it's quite often the ones you don't expect. . . . you know, the ones that you've been really kind to, or really trust.

Employment of non-family members could be fraught with conflict because owners and their employees had ill thought-out and incompatible ideas of what the relationship should be like. This emerged as a strong theme in our urban study. In the rural businesses it was less characteristic but did occur in one very particular circumstance. When the owner took over a business and with its existing employees there was almost invariably misunderstanding and sometimes extreme stress.

In Northumberland, business owners who were local, or had lived for many years in the same place, typically used community links to find reliable employees. Sometimes they did not articulate this process clearly. It seemed to have happened as a matter of course. They just knew of someone in the village with the right skills and attitude; 'a good lad', as one said, who happened to need a job. Not all community links which could be activated in this way were quite so local. Contacts in more widely dispersed, rural 'communities' engaged in dog breeding and fox hunting were also mentioned by respondents as sources of reliable information about potential employees. Word of mouth and informal methods of recruitment of this kind seem natural and advantageous to rural business owners and almost certainly contribute to the relative harmony of their employment relationships.

CONCLUSIONS AND DISCUSSION

In this chapter, we have examined three aspects of work for rural micro-businesses. These were family work, the work-family balance and the inclusion of non-family workers.

Family work, especially the work of spouses, was typical of the micro-businesses. Owners and their spouses usually expressed considerable satisfaction with their work and family lives, although there were some dissenting voices. However, the findings suggest some quite negative aspects of working life in rural micro-enterprises. Other studies have shown that the rural self-employed can have very low earnings, indeed that widespread self-employment contributes to rural poverty (Shucksmith 2000). There were 91 survey respondents who worked more than 80 hours per week for a turnover of less than £20,000 per annum (Raley and Moxey 2000). When we take into account the likelihood of unremunerated work from family members, earnings per person are even lower. Some of our case study households were on the margins of economic survival. The Foot and Mouth Disease crisis occurred after our fieldwork but its sudden and devastating impact on many non-farming rural micro-businesses (Bennett and Phillipson 2004) has highlighted their vulnerability.

Rural respondents who were parents usually perceived living in the countryside as good for children. Some thought that the blurring of boundaries around family and work which was typical of small business life was also beneficial to their children, teaching them the work ethic, for example. Formal childcare, of the kind recognised by the National Childcare Strategy, was rarely available but respondents did not complain about this. They believed that childcare should take place within the co-resident parental unit or, failing that, the wider family. Taking care of children within the parental unit sometimes meant working in their presence. Most saw this as positive but some of the accounts they gave suggested that it could be stressful. There may be health and safety concerns in some cases, for example where animals were involved.

Only a few micro-enterprises are providers of jobs for non-family members. Most of the jobs they offer are casual, part-time, seasonal and short term. Owners themselves recognised that working conditions were not always good. Nevertheless, micro-businesses can be quite significant employers in tiny, remote communities where participation in the labour market normally involves travel to market towns or to a distant conurbation. Some owners felt strongly that they were making a contribution to their communities by being employers. Their employment relationships were not free from conflict but overall they tended to be highly personal and sometimes very warm. Micro-businesses' informal recruitment methods, however, can be divisive, exacerbating the exclusion of some individuals and families in rural areas (Monk et al. 1999).

This chapter has added a rural perspective to the topic of enterprise and deprivation. It suggests that both the positive and negative aspects of self-employment and small enterprise highlighted in this volume can be particularly marked in the rural context. There are many satisfactions for rural business owners and their families. We have shown, however, that small business livelihoods in the countryside can be dependent on working practices that look outdated in a modern economy. In particular, we have observed that the participation of family and kin in new businesses recalls the traditional family farm, a form of work organisation considered anachronistic in the very recent past. To express this more conceptually, social relations of the family become re-embedded in the economic institution of the small business (Wheelock et al. 2003). In policy terms the research reported in this chapter warns that the objective of promoting business start-up for disadvantaged people and places (HM Treasury 2008) could potentially have the unintended effect of exacerbating poor working conditions and precarious livelihoods for some vulnerable households. There is a significant and little noted gender dimension to this concern. The reality of working life in rural England is that women participate in small enterprises in ways that do not align with the models of female entrepreneurship and independence the Government is pledged to promote (ibid.). Indeed, the work undertaken by women living in business households is sometimes invisible and frequently not remunerated. Financial independence for women working alongside their husbands can therefore be more, not less, constrained than in wage earning households.

NOTES

1. J. Wheelock and E. Chell, The Business Owner-managed Family Unit: An inter-regional comparison of behavioural dynamics, ESRC Award no. R 000 23 4402.
2. We are grateful to our colleagues from the Centre for Rural Economy for their support and for access to their data.
3. Sample selection was partly directed by a comparative element of the study which is not dealt with in this chapter. We were trying to match, so far as

possible, a sample of male and female business owners and their spouses already interviewed by another research team in rural Norway (see Baines et al. 2003).
4. She was the legal owner of the business, although she made it clear that starting it up had been his idea and business decisions were more likely to be his.

BIBLIOGRAPHY

Baines, S. and Wheelock, J. (1998) 'Reinventing traditional solutions: job creation, gender and the micro-business household', Work, Employment and Society, 12(4): 579–601.
———(2000) 'Work and employment in small businesses: perpetuating and challenging gender traditions', Gender, Work and Organization, 7: 45–55.
Baines, S., Wheelock, J., Oughton, E., Ljunggren, E., Pettersen, L. T. and Magnussen. T. (2003) 'Work and employment in rural, non-farming micro-businesses: a return to old ways of working?', in K. Andersson, E. Eklund, L. Granberg and T. Marsden (eds) Rural Development as Policy and Practice, Helsinki: Helsinki University Press.
Bechhofer, F., Elliot, M., Rushford, M. and Bland, R. (1974) 'Small shopkeepers: matters of money and meaning', Sociological Review, 22(4): 465–82.
Bennett, K. and Phillipson, J. (2004) 'A plague upon their houses: revelations of the foot and mouth disease epidemic for business households', Sociologia Ruralis, 44: 261–84.
Clegg, S. (1990) Modern Organizations: Organization studies in the post-modern world, London: Sage.
Gasson, R. and Errington, A. (1993) The Farm Family Business, Wallingford, Oxon: CAB International.
Hamilton, E. E. (2006) 'Whose story is it anyway? Narrative accounts of the role of women in founding and establishing family businesses', International Small Business Journal, 24(3): 253–71
HM Treasury (2008) Enterprise: unlocking the UK's talent. Online. Available http://www.berr.gov.uk/files/file44992.pdf (accessed August 2009).
Lowe, P. and Speakman, L. (eds) (2006) The Ageing Countryside: The growing older population of rural England, London: Age Concern.
Lowe, P. and Talbot, H. (2000) 'Policy for small business support in rural areas: a critical assessment of the proposals for the small business service', Regional Studies, 34(5): 479–85.
Mariussen, Å., Wheelock, J. and Baines, S. (1997) 'The family business tradition: modernisation and reinvention? Some contrasts between Britain and Norway', International Studies of Management & Organization, 27(3): 64–85.
Monk, S., Dunn, J. Fitzgerald, M. and Hodge, I. (1999) Finding Work in Rural Areas: Bridges and barriers, York: Joseph Rowntree Foundation.
Pollack, R. A. (1985) 'A transaction costs approach to families and households', Journal of Economic Literature, 23(3): 581–608.
Raley, M. and Moxey, A. (2000) Rural Micro-Businesses in the North East of England: Final survey result, Newcastle upon Tyne: Centre for Rural Economy, University of Newcastle.
Ram, M. and Holliday, R. (1993) 'Relative merits: family culture and kinship in small firms', Sociology, 27(4): 629–48.
Scase, R., and Goffee, R. (1982) The Entrepreneurial Middle Class, London: Croom Helm.

Shucksmith, M. (2000) Exclusive Countryside? Social inclusion and regeneration in rural Britain, York: Joseph Rowntree Foundation.
——(2004) Social Exclusion in Rural Areas: A review of recent research, London: DEFRA.
Storey, D. (1994) Understanding the Small Business Sector, London: Routledge.
Tryner, A. and Warner, S. (2003) Rural Economies: Stepping stones to healthier futures, Cheltenham: Countryside Agency.
Whatmore, S. (1991) Farming Women: Gender, work and family enterprise, Basingstoke: Macmillan.
Wheelock, J. and Jones, K. (2002) '"Grandparents are the next best thing": informal childcare for working parents', *Journal of Social Policy* 31(3): 441–63.
Wheelock J., Oughton, E. and Baines, S. (2003) 'Getting by with a little help from your family: towards a policy relevant model of the working household', *Feminist Economics*, 9(1): 19–45.

Entrepreneurship, Social
Exclusion and Worklessness

Simon Pemberton

INTRODUCTION

Over the last 10 years the task of regenerating the UK's most deprived neighbourhoods has focused upon jobs; through investment in such activities,
individuals are then able to work themselves out of poverty and social exclusion (Kleinman 2000). As part of taking this agenda forward, there has been
a considerable emphasis by successive Labour governments on promoting
the role of enterprise for job creation and to address benefit dependency in
the most deprived areas of the UK and for the most marginalised groups
(Marlow 2006). Such an approach involves viewing enterprise as part of a
broader social agenda that positively correlates new business formation with
increased levels of employment and economic activity (Potter 2005).
  A key difference between current approaches to tackling social exclusion
and benefit dependency in the UK through enterprise and those adopted by
previous Conservative administrations in the 1970s and 1980s is a greater
desire for policy integration with other sectors in order to match local
employment programmes with required investment in local services, environmental standards and housing, as well as direct engagement with the
private sector. Hence entrepreneurship, 'the process of recognising and pursuing opportunities with regard to the alienable and inalienable resources
currently controlled with a view to value creation' (Chell 2007: 18), is no
longer simply viewed as a natural response to industrial restructuring/dein-
dustrialisation within the UK (Carter and Jones-Evans 2006).
  Such thinking also relates to Porter's (1995) work in the United States on
inner-city areas and the need for disadvantage to be addressed by the private sector rather than government subsidy. More broadly it also relates to
neo-liberalist conceptions of the relationship between the state, civil society
and the market, and the need for government to 'steer' and regulate private
sector interests, whilst supporting public (state) intervention in areas of
market failure (Diamond and Liddle 2005). Nevertheless, whilst various
governments may be committed to neo-liberalist approaches, there is a lack
of homogeneity in how they have developed associated governance processes and the implications for approaches to tackle issues such as social
exclusion (Grover 2002).

In this respect, the model that has been pursued in the UK has been one involving economic participation that is supportive of income maintenance to address social exclusion through supply-side approaches (Peck and Theodore 2000, Grover 2002, Theodore 2007). Consequently, interventions focused on skills and educational development, social capital enhancement, improving housing and infrastructure and addressing health and crime problems, as well as developing enterprise and improving access to economic opportunities have been prioritized, most notably through the Government's National Strategy for Neighbourhood Renewal (NSNR) (Social Exclusion Unit [SEU] 2001). This set out minimum standards or 'floor targets' to be achieved in order to reduce the disparities between the most and least deprived areas of the UK on all of these themes (ibid.).

Yet the real potential for enterprise policies among increasingly diverse and excluded populations arguably remains poorly understood (Marlow et al. 2003). The Government identified that the three most relevant causes of worklessness, encapsulating both the unemployed and the economically inactive and driving social exclusion in deprived communities, have been: the changing nature and location of jobs; 'residential sorting'; and (negative) 'area effects' (SEU 2004b). Less attention has been paid to date, through either the NSNR or other approaches, to how enterprise relates to each of these areas, and the effectiveness of (supply-side) policy responses that promote enterprise as a solution therein. The rest of this chapter explores such issues in more detail, by briefly analysing the concepts of social exclusion and worklessness, followed by a consideration of the role of entrepreneurship as a panacea to such issues. Recent policy approaches of relevance are then explored, followed by critical reflection of the preceding discussion and implications for the future nature and scale of enterprise policy discussed.

SOCIAL EXCLUSION

The concept of social exclusion originated in France in the mid 1970s to describe the condition of certain groups on the margins of society who were cut off from both employment and the income safety net of the welfare state. During the 1980s and 1990s, the term became increasingly adopted by European Union (EU) member states, given its appeal across the political spectrum; it promotes equality through tackling deprivation and lack of rights while supporting a cohesive society (Eisenschitz and Gough 2006).

In the transition from the EU to the UK, the term has been increasingly concerned with exclusion from the labour market, and whilst poverty underpins social exclusion it covers a much wider range of issues than inadequacy of income. The Social Exclusion Unit (SEU), set up by the Government in 1998 to address such issues, defined the term as 'what can happen when people or areas suffer from a combination of linked problems such as unemployment, poor skills, low incomes, poor housing, high crime environments, bad health and family breakdown' (SEU 2004a: 7). Nevertheless, such a definition does not focus on the processes that create the problems identified in the definition (Cameron and Davoudi 1998).

Whilst Atkinson (1998) usefully highlights three main elements within the concept of social exclusion—relativity (exclusion from a particular society in a particular place at a particular time), dynamics (a set of processes rather than a static condition) and agency (those excluding and those excluded), reference to Ruth Levitas' work (2005) on 'discourses' of social exclusion identifies that social divisions within society are generally treated as abnormal, as the aim of government policy in the UK has been re-integration into the labour market at the expense of devaluing unpaid work and downplaying issues of 'in-work' poverty. Indeed, Levitas (2005) notes the emphasis by the Government on 'social integrationist' discourses (SID) of exclusion (from the labour market), and to a lesser degree 'moral underclass' discourses (MUD), at the expense of broader (and more controversial) 'redistributionist' discourses (RED). This, she claims, has given rise to a simplistic view of a 'comfortable majority and excluded minority' (Kleinman 2000: 55), requiring welfare-to-work pathways to foster inclusion. Consequently, Levitas et al. (2007) have called for a greater recognition of the complex manner in which multiple forms of disadvantage are experienced, and which are often reinforcing, as a result of broader inequalities of income and power within society and that 'deep exclusion' may be articulated at both an individual and community level.

To summarise briefly, it is evident that defining, interpreting and operationalising the concept of social exclusion is not straightforward given the conflicting perspectives being espoused. Notwithstanding this, the Labour government in the UK, despite the fragility of analysis underpinning the term, promoted a policy agenda focused on the re-engagement of individuals with the labour market (Marlow 2006). Included within this agenda has been the encouragement of entrepreneurship to address concentrations of worklessness and it is to this concept that attention now turns.

ENTREPRENEURSHIP AS A RESPONSE TO WORKLESSNESS

Given successive Labour governments' emphasis on 'welfare to work' programmes to reduce benefit dependency (for example, through the 'New Deal' options), self-employment has been recognised as a suitable mechanism by the Government to support 'hard to reach' individuals back into work (Eisenschitz and Gough 2006). Such thoughts were initially set out in the third (of 18) Policy Action Team (PAT) reports[1] (HM Treasury 1999) that were produced in order to provide essential building blocks for the development of the NSNR.

The PAT 3 report focused particularly on the success of business support in serving the most deprived communities and identified that 'there is a vital role that enterprise can play in helping to renew our poorest and most marginal communities' (ibid., Foreword). In addition, it recognized that 'promoting enterprise to expand employment opportunities can build confidence and capacity and offer a route out of (social) exclusion through economic opportunity' (HM Treasury 1999: 6). This is in line with Porter's (1995) work on releasing the capacity of the private sector to regenerate inner-city areas.

One of the key findings that emerged from the PAT 3 report was that there was a lack of entrepreneurship in areas subject to high levels of worklessness, which can broadly be defined as 'those unemployed or economically inactive and [who are eligible for], or in receipt of, working age benefits' (SEU 2004a: 12). This, it suggested, was due to a lack of appropriate business support and a lack of finance available, especially for social enterprise formation and development (HM Treasury 1999). In this respect, social enterprises were defined as businesses run for a social objective, rather than for the sake of profit distribution to shareholders, that could help in strengthening the social and economic fabric of deprived communities, for example, by the provision of services that are not profitable enough to attract private sector firms and through the provision of training and experience to people who may otherwise be unemployed (ibid.).

Building upon this work the NSNR that was launched in 2001 highlighted the 88 most deprived districts in England and the concentrations of deprivation and worklessness that existed within each of these areas and set out plans to reduce the disparities between such areas and the rest of the country (SEU 2001). Of particular relevance were actions, supported by a national Neighbourhood Renewal Fund (NRF), to reduce the barriers to employment in the three crucial areas of childcare, skills and transport, whilst attempting to 'make work pay' through tax credits, the minimum wage and benefit supplements. Enterprise 'floor targets', focused on achieving minimum standards for all (but with an emphasis on underperforming groups such as lone parents, BME [black and other minority ethnic] groups, the over 50s and those with no qualifications) and reducing the disparities between the most and least deprived area, were used as a tool to support such actions and specified the general need to 'develop more enterprise in disadvantaged communities' (Office of the Deputy Prime Minister [ODPM] 2004: 12).

Despite such ambitions and the fact that the NSNR set out national targets to promote jobs and enterprise in deprived areas, the Government acknowledged in 2004 that results had been mixed and that although some progress had been made on tackling broader issues of deprivation, 'concentrations of worklessness had largely been missed' (SEU 2004a: 7; see also National Evaluation report of the Impact of the NRF, Department of Communities and Local Government, Communities and Local Government

[CLG] 2008a). Indeed, the SEU report drew attention to the significant variation in worklessness rates within regions and highlighted that, in the worst affected 1 per cent of streets, more than half of all adults were out of work and on benefits and, in some places (especially the north west, north east, Yorkshire and Humber), almost all adults in certain streets were out of work and on benefits (SEU 2004a: 3). In 2009, around 2.6 million people were claiming 'sickness-related' benefits (incapacity benefit or income support, with this figure rising to 5.2 million if job seekers allowance is included), and around a fifth of these claimants lived in the most deprived 10 per cent of neighbourhoods in England (Department of Work and Pensions [DWP] 2009).

The implicit link made by the Government between high levels of worklessness and low levels of enterprise was also stated through reference to statistics which suggested that self-employment in areas with the highest concentrations of worklessness was half the rate of England as a whole (SEU 2004b: 3). However, the way in which enterprise can be defined and measured can vary, and whilst some commentators such as Lloyd and Mason (1984) and Mole et al. (2002) have concurred that there is a deficit in 'enterprise culture' in areas subject to high levels of worklessness and deprivation, a whole range of other supply- and demand-side factors are also important in terms of determining levels of entrepreneurship within deprived areas. These include: population change; housing, including affordability and tenure (as an asset to support access to finance); levels of economic activity; disposable income; business skills, qualifications and managerial experiences of local residents; the local political context; and associated business support infrastructure (see Keeble and Walker 1994 and Slack 2006 for further details).

As a consequence, Armington and Acs (2002), amongst others, have pointed out that if some of the most deprived and affluent districts in England are taken (according to the Government's own indices of deprivation of 2000, 2004 and 2007), the relationship between business formation rates and the deprivation rankings of areas such as Liverpool and Manchester (most deprived) and Wokingham and East Sussex (least deprived) is not clear-cut. Given the variety of factors influencing levels of entrepreneurship by Keeble and Walker (1994) listed above, this finding should not be wholly surprising.

Other observers have argued that greater emphasis should be placed upon the quality of businesses created rather than an over pre-occupation with the quantity of those developed in workless neighbourhoods (Marlow et al. 2003). This is because the promotion of enterprise per se could be counterproductive to addressing social exclusion if not managed in an appropriate and flexible manner. Indeed, even the PAT 3 report noted that although self-employment is one avenue into work and can provide a good opportunity for people in deprived areas to move into productive activity, 'it will not be the right option for everyone' (HM Treasury 1999: 12).

Such questions over the potential benefits and problems associated with self-employment as a panacea for addressing worklessness need to be explored in more depth. The following sections set out to answer important, but frequently neglected, questions over the nature of individuals who reside in such areas, their propensity and ability to generate and participate in enterprise activities and the role of different types of enterprise (vis-à-vis other policies focused more broadly on enhancing skills or human capital) in responding to key causal processes of worklessness.

CHARACTERISTICS OF WORKLESS INDIVIDUALS AND IMPLICATIONS FOR ENTERPRISE SOLUTIONS?

Characteristics of Workless Individuals and Assessing the Impact of Different Enterprise Initiatives

Before moving on to discuss the characteristics of workless individuals, a note of caution needs to be expressed which relates back to definitions of worklessness: given that the term covers the economically inactive (as well as the unemployed actively seeking work), it must be appreciated that it therefore can relate to students, those looking after the family or home, those who are permanently sick or disabled as well as 'other inactive' people (Pemberton and Mason 2007). Consequently, there is a need for local understanding of the groups who may need to be targeted in areas with high concentrations of worklessness and the propensity of enterprise policy to make an impact.

Given this caveat, in general terms it has been identified that individuals who live in concentrations of worklessness tend to be from groups who are known to perform poorly in the labour market. For example, almost half the working-age population in concentrations of worklessness have no qualifications and 50 per cent of all households have at least one person with a limiting long-term illness (coupled with an associated higher proportion of carers). BME groups are more than twice as likely to live in such areas compared to the population as a whole (SEU 2004b). Indeed, for certain BME groups, such as Pakistanis and Bangladeshis, their current employment rate (43 per cent, 2007) is significantly lower than the national UK average of 73 per cent (CLG 2007). Individuals are also likely to have low aspirations for employment and education, to have narrow travel horizons and to suffer from intergenerational exclusion (SEU 2004b).

It is pertinent therefore to consider: (a) the likely impact of different forms of enterprise on workless individuals residing in deprived communities; and (b) the degree to which they can respond to key drivers of worklessness. In terms of the former, relatively little research has been undertaken on this topic although a key study worthy of reporting was one conducted by the former ODPM (ODPM 2003).

   The research involved an analysis of existing evidence relating to the impact of different types of enterprise as well as the effectiveness of policies, which directly or indirectly promote business regeneration of workless (and deprived) areas. Four broad types of enterprise were included: start-up businesses, social enterprises, BME businesses and inward investment. Various kinds of 'deprived areas', for example inner-city areas, coalfields, coastal areas and remote rural areas, were also considered.

   Research undertaken by Van Stel and Storey (2004) has called into question the relationship between the development of start-up businesses and their contribution to addressing the needs of deprived areas. Indeed, the ODPM review found that 'only a small minority of small firms create the majority of additional jobs (in deprived or workless areas)' (ODPM 2003: 1). However, on a more positive note it was argued that the ability to start a business created opportunities for many who might normally be excluded from the labour market, such as refugees or those moving from unemployment. But the extent to which self-employment can reduce unemployment, it was suggested, 'was not known although there are higher rates of involuntary closure amongst previously unemployed people, especially if they were long-term unemployed' (ibid.: 1).

   A further important point raised was that the extent to which firms located in deprived areas had owners and employees from these areas was unknown, 'although it is likely to depend on the sector of the business and the types of skilled labour that the business required' (ibid.: 1). It was also stated that the extent to which firms provided jobs also depended on the extent to which they displaced jobs in other similar firms. Reference was also made to the fact that many new firms in the UK are concentrated in low value-added sectors and that the quality of jobs (in terms of wages and conditions) was lower in small firms. Moreover, Marlow (2006) has indicated that if policy encourages growth in sectors with low human capital requirements then, along with forcing the non-subsidised out of the market, there is also the possible failure of entrants themselves upon removal of subsidies, leading to a downward spiral of enterprise confidence and subsequently reinforcing levels of worklessness within particular localities.

   Finally, it was suggested by the ODPM (2003) that small firms benefited the residents of deprived or workless areas through the provision of services that might not otherwise be available; however, the review noted that 'the extent to which residents and businesses in deprived areas use these local services is not known' (ibid.: 1).

   With regards to social enterprises, the ODPM review was less detailed. Although there is much evidence from this sector concerning credit unions, workers' cooperatives and local exchange trading schemes (LETS) and that a key strength includes community involvement and addressing areas of market failure through focusing on achieving social objectives, the review simply noted that there 'was very little information available on the impact of these organisations and no comparisons of their impact compared to conventional enterprises' (ibid.: 1–2).

In terms of BME businesses, Harding (2002) has suggested that the Government has embarked on a number of initiatives to increase BME enterprise, such as the development of the Phoenix Development Fund and the Community Finance Initiative and tailored support through Business Links, although the ODPM (2003) argued that there was little empirical evidence currently available to support the claim that both BME groups— and these schemes therein—were important in regeneration. Neverthe-less, the fact that deprived areas have an over-concentration of ethnic minorities was referred to, as was the propensity of certain BME groups (such as the Chinese and Pakistani community) to be self-employed.

However, the fact that BME enterprises are often concentrated in partic-ular sectors with localised markets and lower growth prospects may impact on their contribution to job creation. Issues of institutional racism, 'islama-phobia', intergenerational succession, access to finance and the nature of business support may also impinge upon their development potential (Mer-seyside Social Inclusion Observatory [MSIO] 2005). With regards to the latter, research by Smallbone et al. (2001) indicated that the inadequacy of existing local market intelligence and local databases, an over-emphasis on product-oriented support that fails to meet BME enterprise requirements and a lack of confidence and trust in those delivering support by BME owner-managers were key difficulties that needed to be addressed. On the other hand, financial barriers of relevance appear to impact disproportion-ately upon some types of BME groups more than others, and especially those that are more prone to worklessness—for example, African Carib-beans—and their lack of access to bank finance at start up (ODPM 2003).

On a more positive note, recent work by Ram and Carter (2003) has indi-cated that second- and third-generation differences are emerging with respect to BME enterprise and that younger members of BME communities are less likely to remain in traditional sectors and seek to 'break out' with specific skills in management consultancy, IT and financial services. Consequently, BME enterprise policy may need to be more flexible in order to support later BME generations to become self-employed in some of the sectors described above, as well as targeting first-generation BME unemployed individuals into work. This is particularly of relevance for certain BME females, for example, those from the Muslim community, who are frequently more prone to work-lessness as a result of cultural factors impacting upon their ability to work outside the home (ibid.). Both interventions will require better data collection, collation and interpretation on the nature and impact of BME enterprise.

Inward investment into deprived areas was referred to by the ODPM (2003) as a way of generating new investment and jobs, though it was acknowledged that most studies 'have considered the impact at a regional scale rather than looking at its impact on local neighbourhood regenera-tion' (2003: 2). They also identified a lack of evidence on the extent to which forms of inward investment for which the availability of large supplies of labour is important (for example, call centres), have provided jobs for people from deprived or workless neighbourhoods (ibid.).

In sum, the ODPM (2003) review concluded that very few studies had been concerned with assessing the contribution of enterprise to reducing worklessness and addressing social exclusion. It also pointed out that there was negligible evidence relating to the extent and nature of entrepreneurship in these areas, as well as a lack of information on the effects of policies aimed at encouraging entrepreneurship. Furthermore, from this analysis it appears that most types of businesses have yet to fully achieve the potential for employing individuals in areas with high concentrations of worklessness.

Enterprise Policy and Drivers of Worklessness

In essence perhaps the lack of evidence of the tangible impact of enterprise policy on workless neighbourhoods can be related to a rather uncritical analysis of how enterprise can respond to the key 'drivers' of worklessness.

The first key driver relates to changes in the nature and location of jobs, as in certain instances concentrations of worklessness have been created when a main local employer or industry has closed down (SEU 2004b). It has been claimed by the Government that areas, employers and individuals can adapt to such changes through (amongst other interventions) enterprise-led approaches (ibid.). However, given the typical characteristics of individuals living in such areas, such as a preponderance of individuals from 'hard to reach' groups, who may also have a lack of qualifications and suffer from a limiting long-term illness, it can often be difficult for these individuals to adapt and gain new qualifications and experience and develop the motivation and expertise to start new businesses. Whilst psychosocial theories (Jahoda 1982, Warr and Jackson 1985) regarding the impact of job loss on the individual have been developed to explain how individuals may respond to being out of work, they are less relevant to explaining patterns of worklessness in areas where not being in employment is the norm (SEU 2004b).

The Government has also suggested that a lack of access to employment may be a more relevant issue influencing worklessness in some places, with the presence of the informal economy additionally making formal work less attractive, especially when combined with benefits. However, from an enterprise perspective, fostering an enterprise culture in areas with high concentrations of worklessness may be difficult in terms of overcoming 'access' difficulties; as could sustaining social enterprises created to support access to broader employment opportunities. In addition, problems have also been noted in terms of legitimately formalizing enterprise activities that have traditionally operated informally (Williams 2005).

A second factor identified as contributing to concentrations of worklessness relates to residential sorting, with the housing market grouping the most disadvantaged individuals together according to individuals' access to financial resources and subsequent ability to move in to, or out of, deprived areas (SEU 2004b). Housing policy can unintentionally exacerbate residential sorting; for example, social housing is increasingly used by workless individuals who are sometimes housed together in the same street or on the same estate. In this respect, it may be difficult to generate self-employment given the development of what some commentators describe as a 'culture of worklessness' or intergenerational influences that may develop within such localities (Theodore 2007). This point also relates to a third driver of worklessness—area effects—where it is argued that once people live in an area with many people out of work, their chances of finding work can be reduced simply because of where they live. This is due to place effects, such as poor infrastructure or variation in the quality of local services, or people effects, which may relate to limited information about employment opportunities or area-based discrimination by some employers, due to the high concentration of workless individuals within a neighbourhood (SEU 2004b).

The emphasis on measuring the impact of enterprise-led programmes on concentrations of worklessness and deprivation in quantitative economic terms, rather than considering wider, more qualitative social issues of relevance to achieving such ambitions may also be contributing to the lack of clarity over the impact of enterprise in deprived areas. Analysis of contemporary policy interventions introduced by the UK Government can help to elucidate this point, especially the Local Enterprise Growth Initiative (LEGI) and the Working Neighbourhoods Fund (WNF). Indeed, each can be critically analysed in terms of: the degree to which they accept or challenge the assertion that increasing enterprise will alleviate worklessness and broader issues of social exclusion; and the extent to which they prioritize different types and scales of entrepreneurship, or alternative policy interventions as a solution to worklessness problems for specific groups.

RECENT UK GOVERNMENT INTERVENTIONS: THE PRIORITISATION OF A BROADER AGENDA?

Convery (2006) highlights three significant initiatives introduced in the UK recently that have been supportive of addressing worklessness and social exclusion through enterprise-led approaches. First, 15 City Growth Pathfinders have been piloted in a number of urban locations focused on creating a favourable environment conducive to business growth. Second, he notes that the Local Authority Business Growth Incentive (LABGI) scheme has been introduced to allow local authorities to retain a portion of any uplift to their business rates resulting from an improvement of their business tax base. Third, he identifies the Local Enterprise Growth Initiative (LEGI) as providing a substantial funding source to local authorities to promote business development in deprived areas. Given the latter's prominence within UK Government policy, it is appropriate to briefly focus upon this policy intervention in greater detail.

The Local Enterprise Growth Initiative (LEGI)

LEGI was announced in the 2005 Budget, and guidance identified that it was:

> crucial to ensure that local authorities and their partners are provided with opportunities to stimulate economic growth through enterprise development in their most deprived areas, to help narrow the gap on key indicators like worklessness between those areas and the rest of the country. (Neighbourhood Renewal Unit [NRU] 2006a: 5)

In total £418 million has been allocated to the programme, delivered jointly between CLG, HM Treasury and the Department of Trade and Industry (DTI) until 2010/11 (CLG 2008b). There are three national level outcomes:

- to increase total entrepreneurial activity among the population in deprived local areas;
- to support the sustainable growth—and reduce the failure rate—of locally owned business in deprived areas; and
- to attract appropriate inward investment and franchising into deprived areas, making use of local labour resources (CLG 2008b: 4).

The first outcome is concerned with the quantity of business formation in deprived areas and a presumption that such enterprise will develop in situ. However, this may prove difficult to achieve in reality, especially where concentrations of deprivation and worklessness are situated on peripheral residential estates some distance from industrial estates, business parks or city centres. Convery (2006) therefore suggests that LEGI may be in danger of over-concentrating on areas of disadvantage, although the second outcome attempts to address this issue; reducing the failure rate of businesses by boosting local demand for activities and services produced by new enterprises. Nevertheless, success in achieving this objective will be dependent upon 'success' in other areas, such as addressing in-work poverty, local housing environments, population stability and enhancing levels of economic activity. Finally, LEGI also prioritizes inward investment into deprived areas, with a focus on linking local (workless) labour to such opportunities. However, the difficulties in undertaking such activity have already been outlined.

In the first round of LEGI, 10 bids were awarded a total of £126 million funding (over three years) following 55 applications involving 70 of the 91 eligible local authorities in England (NRU 2006a). A consistent theme of the successful bids was the value of social enterprise as a means of both promoting enterprise and tackling issues around deprivation through the creation of social businesses (NRU 2006b). In the second round, all eligible local authorities that were unsuccessful in the first round, plus those that did not bid, were invited to submit; the Government was 'particularly interested' in bids from local authorities that had the lowest rates of enterprise formation and were furthest from meeting their enterprise targets (ODPM 2006). Ten authorities, eight of which located in northern England, were subsequently successful with their applications (NRU 2006c) and were awarded £153 million for the period 2007/08 to 2009/10 (CLG 2008b).

Analysis of both the successful and unsuccessful Round 1 and Round 2 bids indicates rather familiar solutions to the problems identified, including access to finance, investment readiness, business education, social enterprise formation, grassroots outreach, women and BME entrepreneurs, mentoring or coaching, business incubation workspace and access to procurement. Hence, it is possible to note the 'traditional' economic or business solutions proposed and less detail on how far these activities need to be re-aligned to engage individuals who typically reside in workless or socially excluded neighbourhoods.

To further exemplify some of the above issues, it is useful to focus briefly on one particular LEGI programme in England: the Sefton/Liverpool Enterprise Growth Initiative (SLEGI) (see Figure 9.1). This is because the area arguably presents the greatest economic regeneration challenge currently in the UK as three of its Super Output Areas[2] fall within the top 10 most deprived in the country. The rate of worklessness for this area was around 34.1 per cent in 2007, as opposed to a regional average of 14.8 per cent and a Great Britain average of 11.9 per cent. Self-employment rates are currently

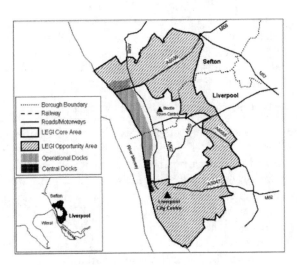

Figure 9.1   Map of Sefton Liverpool Enterprise Growth Initiative (SLEGI).

around 6 per cent, as opposed to figures of 9.4 per cent nationally and this is attributed to a clear weakness in enterprise culture (Liverpool City Council, 2009; The Mersey Partnership, 2009; Liverpool City Council 2006).

Four 'work streams' totalling £20.5 million are presented in respect of 'unlocking enterprise' to address worklessness and the broader social exclusion of individuals within the SLEGI area. There is an emphasis on young people, and especially those not currently in any employment, education or training, as well as business development and inward investment activities. However, in contrast to national guidance, there is partial reference to the nature of individuals residing within the area, although the focus is still predominantly enterprise orientated. It is recognized that a poorer quality labour supply puts local businesses at a disadvantage, with 37.6 per cent of the economically active in the SLEGI area currently having no qualifications or a Level 1 qualification (compared with a figure of 24.5 per cent for Great Britain), whilst highly qualified people form a lower proportion of economically active adults in the SLEGI area—12.2 per cent, compared with 28.6 per cent in Great Britain (ibid.).

Thus, a number of key points emerge from both the national and local analysis. Firstly, unlocking enterprise to address worklessness (vis-à-vis other types of interventions) is espoused as a key intervention required. Second, that there is subsequently a need for more detail on the actual characteristics and needs of those who are workless as the types of activity being proposed will clearly have a differential (and varying) impact on addressing barriers to entrepreneurship depending upon the group or individual in question (see CLG 2008b). Finally, in the context of the SLEGI area, most of the 'drivers' of worklessness highlighted earlier are evident and thus proposing to link workless neighbourhoods to opportunities in the wider Liverpool area (the so-called 'Zone of Opportunity') is a welcome move, although there may still need to be the development of further 'radical' approaches which consider the importance of the relative (broader) scales of intervention for successful (enterprise) policy, as well as other related policy interventions required, such as skills development (see below).

The Working Neighbourhoods Fund

Bringing the story up to date, reference to the recently launched Working Neighbourhoods Fund (WNF), developed within the context of on-going welfare reform and the development of a competitive workforce, is useful for generally confirming the above conclusions. Set up in 2007 in order to tackle persistent problems of worklessness in 65 of the most deprived areas of England, this new fund has replaced the NRF, and includes a 'reward' element for local authorities and communities that are 'most successful in tackling worklessness and increasing skills and enterprise levels' (CLG 2007: 3). One and a half billion pounds are available between 2008/09 and 2010/11 through the new Area Based Grant (ABG) and, like Government thinking about the LEGI, it specifies a clear link between entrepreneurship and worklessness through the development of Local Area Agreements (LAAs). These are to set locally agreed priority targets (up to 35) between all partners in the Local Strategic Partnership (the 'partnership of partnerships' within a locality) over a three year period.

Interestingly, though, it is the increased emphasis on skills that potentially sets this new approach apart. Building upon the City Strategy Pathfinders that were introduced to tackle low employment rates through joining up employment and skills provision, there is recognition through the WNF of the nature of human capital in deprived areas and how this may vary. In turn, it is argued that this may subsequently impact upon individuals' abilities to enter employment or self-employment; in the 10 per cent most deprived neighbourhoods in England, it is reported that over a quarter of individuals have no qualifications at all. Furthermore, there also appears to be more of an emphasis on involving local communities themselves in addressing levels of worklessness in the most socially excluded neighbourhoods. Peer support and peer pressure are two factors identified as being important to such efforts, along with a reiteration of the potential of social enterprise and the introduction of Skills Health Checks and Action Plans for one million workless people and low skilled individuals in employment from 2010 to 2011 (ibid.).

CONCLUDING THOUGHTS: THE NEED FOR GREATER CRITICAL REFLECTION AND IMPLICATIONS FOR THE NATURE OF POLICY INTERVENTIONS, THEIR INTEGRATION AND SCALE

In the UK, it is clear that there has been increasing emphasis on tackling worklessness and social exclusion through neighbourhood renewal processes in the most deprived areas than was the case hitherto. In conceptual terms, however, the preceding analysis reveals that the way in which worklessness and entrepreneurship have been linked in a UK context involves a supply-side emphasis on worker motivation, skills and attitudes (dovetailing with the Government's 'supply-side fundamentalism'; see Peck and Theodore 2000) and a focus on individual failings as contributing to levels of worklessness and lack of entrepreneurship, rather than broader, macroeconomic forces (Theodore 2007). Such an approach involves an acceptance of high levels of worklessness—and lower levels of entrepreneurship—as a cultural 'way of life' in many disadvantaged areas. In contrast, demand-side analyses, which focus on the quality of the types of businesses supported or created, are largely absent.

This is somewhat problematic as both the availability of (self-)employment opportunities in an area and the quality of such opportunities are equally important in determining the effectiveness of government policy.

Hence through drawing upon Theodore's (2007) arguments, it can be suggested that much greater consideration needs to be given to local economic development and social economy initiatives that support 'quality' entrepreneurial activities combined with suitable training initiatives that acknowledge the nature of human capital within neighbourhoods. In this way, these types of interventions can be suitably tailored to the specific needs of those defined as workless. This has, to an extent, begun to be realised by the Government, which has identified such issues in its recent national review of worklessness in the UK (CLG 2009).

The emphasis on 'quality' entrepreneurship and the specific needs of particular groups which has been recognised throughout this chapter needs to be returned to, as over the last five years there has been considerable weight placed by the UK Government on encouraging social groups under-represented in entrepreneurial activity to consider self-employment. Rouse and Kitching (2006) note that such efforts have been justified on the grounds of social inclusion, economic competitiveness and reducing welfare dependency (the 'poverty alleviation' paradigm). As already alluded to, however, a degree of caution is required for a number of reasons, not least because of the relative paucity of information on both the positive and negative impact of different types of enterprises on workless individuals. For example, a recent evaluation of the self-employment option of the Government's New Deal programme targeting workless individuals concluded that policies encouraging such groups into self-employment may have significant personal and financial consequences (Kellard et al. 2002). Consequently, the business survival rates of companies created by those previously unemployed are often fairly limited and can contribute to increased debt and financial hardship (ibid.).

Furthermore, along with BME groups, women have been particularly targeted by entrepreneurship policy, and especially those residing in disadvantaged areas, including lone parents. This focus relates to the recognition by the Government of their potential contribution to the UK economy (Shaw et al. 2001). However, the general nature of targeting by support agencies towards 'other' women from higher socio-economic backgrounds at the expense of those residing in areas of worklessness has been identified as a barrier to self-employment (Fielden and Dawe 2004). But more fundamentally, Grover (2007) notes that there may be a broader 'rationality mistake' occurring, in that attitudes to self-employment for women (and lone parents therein) have been structured through economic rationalities rather than gendered moral rationalities. In this way, it is suggested that, from the government's perspective, the only value associated with other forms of work—such as reproductive work—is where it is delivered through childcare enterprises (ibid.).

Even if such an approach is uncritically accepted, there are still problems. Rouse and Kitchen (2006) move on to note that entrepreneurial support has largely ignored the role of childcare in entrepreneurship policy and consequently they argue that this issue has been both a cause and consequence of business failure. It has also meant that tensions have emerged in relation to the development of low profit businesses by such individuals in disadvantaged areas as a result of enterprise programmes, and their ability to succeed in the medium to long term, given the lack of childcare support and the (low value) nature of business activity therein (also see Bond and Kersey 2002).

Enterprise policy may therefore need a longer intervention period to address deep-rooted (and frequently intergenerational) problems, especially in the absence of a fuller debate on 'quality' issues, the specific needs of workless individuals (especially those highly dependent on benefits, and certain 'equalities' groups), poor mobility in labour markets and low skills levels. Indeed, it may actually be more appropriate to increase enterprise in deprived areas by focusing on existing small businesses rather than on those who are workless. In this way, existing businesses would be supported in order to provide more local opportunities targeted at those out of work, rather than to support workless residents to develop businesses which may have only a limited chance of succeeding and which, at best, may return only low profits.[3]

The Government itself acknowledged that the spatial level of intervention required to address concentrations of worklessness will be different in different places: '[S]ometimes the answer will lie in a neighbourhood, but often the solution will need action across a city or region' (SEU 2004b: 8).[4] The need for greater horizontal integration (across partners) is highlighted, as the lead role and responsibility for business (and skills) development will now rest with local government. Nonetheless, the 'double devolution' agenda in the UK (Davies 2008) means that vertical integration in policy and governance relations also needs consideration as power is additionally expected to be devolved down to neighbourhoods and individuals, as well as to local businesses.[5]

Despite the rhetoric of a broader social agenda for enterprise in addressing worklessness and social exclusion, it is evident in a UK context that closer institutional and policy integration across a range of sectors is still required (North and Syrett 2008). It also needs to be taken forward in a way which does not simply relate to pursuing the development of local enterprise or social enterprise per se. Instead, the chapter has highlighted that a greater understanding of what we mean by 'social exclusion' and 'worklessness', and the relative scales of intervention required to address the varying needs of those workless—including self-employment (as well as access to existing opportunities), housing, childcare and training issues— is pre-requisite for determining 'what works' for (enterprise) policy and how and where agencies need to work more closely together to be effective. Without such an approach, concurring with recent work by Marlow (2006), there is a risk that the benefits of enterprise may at best be of limited value and at worst, exacerbate difficulties for the most marginalized individuals residing within workless neighbourhoods.

NOTES

1. PAT Report 3: Enterprise and Social Exclusion (HM Treasury 1999).
2. (SOAs—an administrative geography covering between 1,000 and 1,500 population).
3. The job linkage issue has arisen in a different context through another recent study conducted by the Institute of Public Policy Research (IPPR 2006) in the UK. This concluded that initiatives centred on creating (self-)employment opportunities in the most deprived areas were frequently misguided, as the most disadvantaged do not always live in such neighbourhoods. This implies that solutions to the employment needs of deprived areas may need to be found at the sub-regional or regional scale, rather than at the local level and more emphasis should therefore be placed upon linking workless neighbourhoods to areas of economic opportunity.
4. Such thoughts are also reflected within the Government's Sub-National Review of Economic Development and Regeneration (SNR) in the UK conducted in July 2007 (HM Treasury 2007). This highlighted the need for greater horizontal integration (across partners) as the lead role and responsibility for business (and skills) development will now rest with local government. Consequently, the Working Neighbourhoods Fund, the LEGI grant and LABGI receipts will all need to be integrated with a local authority's other functions, as regulatory agencies, substantial purchasers and employers in their own right, and as providers of political leadership (Convery 2006, CLG 2009).
5. It is expected that enterprise support offered locally aligns neatly with the regional economic strategies of the Regional Development Agencies. The use of LAAs by LSPs, as well as new Multi Area Agreements (MAAs) between two or more top-tier or unitary local authorities, their partners and government will be an important tool to secure such integration across a range of geographical scales (for initiatives such as LEGI and the Working Neighbourhoods Fund). More specifically—and in line with the UK Government's review of worklessness (CLG 2009)—they should help to facilitate 'city region' targets with pooled local and regional funds (for example, Work and Skills integrated budgets), promote Worklessness Assessments, help Job Centre Plus to work in partnership with the Learning and Skills Councils (LSCs) and employers in developing broader approaches to tackling worklessness (including the production of Work and Skills Plans) and also help raise pan city-region issues for social enterprises to target in order to support their development and sustainability (CLES 2006).

BIBLIOGRAPHY

Atkinson, A. B. (1998) 'Social exclusion, poverty and unemployment', in A. B. Atkinson and J. Hills (eds) Exclusion and Opportunity, CASE Paper 4, London: London School of Economics, Centre for Analysis of Social Exclusion.
Armington, C. and Acs, Z. J. (2002) 'The determinants of regional variation in new firm formation', Regional Studies, 36(1): 33–45.
Bond, M. and Kersey, D. (2002) 'Expanding childminding provision in areas of deprivation', Local Economy, 17: 303–12.
Cameron, S. and Davoudi, S. (1998) 'Combating social exclusion: looking in or looking out?', in A. Mandanipour, G. Cars and J. Allen (eds) Social Exclusion in European Cities, London: Jessica Kingsley.

Carter, S. and Jones-Evans, D. (2006) Enterprise and Small Business, 2nd Edition, London: Prentice Hall.

Centre for Local Economic Strategies (CLES) (2006) What Difference Can City Regions Make? Manchester: CLES.

Chell, E. (2007) 'Social enterprise and entrepreneurship: towards a convergent theory of the entrepreneurial process', International Small Business Journal, 25(5): 5–26.

Communities and Local Government (CLG) (2007) The Working Neighbourhoods Fund, London: CLG.

———. (2008a) Impact and Outcomes of the Neighbourhood Renewal Fund, London: CLG.

———. (2008b) LEGI: National Baseline—Executive Summary, London: CLG.

———. (2009) Stepping up to the Challenge: The Government's response to tackling worklessness—a review of the contribution and role of English local authorities and partnerships, London: CLG/DWP.

Convery, P. (2006) 'Local Enterprise Growth Initiative', Local Economy, 21(3): 316–27.

Davies, J. S. (2008) 'Double-devolution or double dealing? The local government paper and the Lyons review', Local Government Studies, 34(1): 3–22.

Department of Work and Pensions (DWP) (2009) Working Age Client Group Data, May 2007. Online. Available http://www.dwp.gov.uk (accessed 20 July 2009).

Diamond, J. and Liddle, J. (2005) The Management of Regeneration: Choices, challenges and dilemmas, London: Routledge.

Eisenchitz, A. and Gough, J. (2006) Spaces of Social Exclusion, London: Routledge.

Fielden, A. and Dawe, A. (2004) 'Entrepreneurship and social inclusion', Women in Management Review, 19(3): 139–42.

Grover, C. (2002) 'Welfare reform, accumulation and social exclusion in the United Kingdom', Social Work and Society, 4(1): 78–91.

———(2007) 'The Freud Report on the future of welfare to work: some critical reflections', Critical Social Policy, 27: 534–45.

Harding, R. (2002) Global Economic Monitor (GEM) National Report: Focus on inclusion, London: GEM.

HM Treasury (1999) Enterprise and Social Exclusion, NSNR Policy Action Team (PAT) 3 Report, London: HMSO.

———(2007) Review of Sub-National Economic Development and Regeneration, London: HMSO.

Institute of Public Policy Research (IPPR) (2006) City Leadership: Giving city regions the power to grow, London: IPPR.

Jahoda, M. (1982) Employment and Unemployment: A social-psychological analysis, Cambridge: Cambridge University Press.

Keeble, D. and Walker, S. (1994) 'New firms, small firms and dead firms: spatial patterns and determinants in the United Kingdom', Regional Studies, 28(4): 411–27.

Kellard, K., Legge, K. and Ashworth, K. (2002) Self-Employment as a Route off Benefit, Research Report 177, Leeds: Department of Work and Pensions (DWP).

Kleinman, M. (2000) 'Include me out? The new politics of place and poverty', Policy Studies, 21(1): 49–61.

Levitas, R. (2005) The Inclusive Society? Social exclusion and New Labour, Basingstoke: Palgrave.

Levitas, R., Panatzis, C., Fahmy, E., Gordon, D., Lloyd, E. and Patsios, M. (2007) The Multidimensional Analysis of Social Exclusion, London: Cabinet Office.

Liverpool City Council (2006) Local Enterprise Growth Initiative Application. Online. Available http://www.neighbourhood.gov.uk/publications.asp?did=1873 (accessed 28 February 2008).

————(2009) City of Liverpool Key Statistics Bulletin, Issue 6, March 2009. Liverpool: Liverpool City Council.

Lloyd, P. E. and Mason, C. M. (1984) 'Spatial variation in new firm formation in the UK: comparative evidence from Merseyside, Greater Manchester and South Hampshire', Regional Studies, 18(3): 207–20.

Marlow, S. (2006) 'Enterprising futures or dead-end jobs? Women, self-employment and social exclusion', International Journal of Manpower, 27(6): 588–600.

Marlow, S., Westall, A. and Watson, E. (2003) Who Benefits?, London: New Economics Foundation and Prowess.

The Mersey Partnership (2009) Economic Review 2009. Liverpool: The Mersey Partnership.

Merseyside Social Inclusion Observatory (MSIO) (2005) Economic Market Research: Black and Minority Ethnic (BME) study in Wirral's NRAs, research report produced for Wirral's Thriving Local Economy Partnership, MSIO, University of Liverpool, Liverpool.

Mole, K., Greene, F. and Storey, D. J. (2002) 'Entrepreneurship in three English counties', Working Paper, Centre for Small and Medium Sized Enterprises, Warwick Business School, Warwick.

Neighbourhood Renewal Unit (NRU) (2006a) Enterprise and Economic Opportunity in Deprived Areas: Local Enterprise Growth Initiative (Round 2 Guidance, June 2006). Online. Available http://www.neighbourhood.gov.uk/publications.asp?did=1809 (accessed 28 February 2008).

————(2006b) Local Enterprise Growth Initiative: Key themes in successful Round 1 proposals. Online. Available http://www.neighbourhood.gov.uk/displaypagedoc.asp?id=1796 (accessed 28 February 2008).

————(2006c) £157 million to kick start enterprise in deprived areas, Announcement of Funding, NRU Press Notice, 6 December 2006. Online. Available http://www.neighbourhood.gov.uk/page.asp?id=1869 (accessed 28 February 2008).

North, D. and Syrett, S. (2008) 'Making the links: economic deprivation, neighbourhood renewal and scales of governance', Regional Studies, 42(1): 133–48.

Office of the Deputy Prime Minister (ODPM) (2003) Business-led Regeneration of Deprived Areas: A review of the evidence base, Research Summary 5, London: ODPM.

————(2004) Briefing Note on Changes to PSA 1 and Floor Targets as a Result of the Spending Review 2004 (SR04), London: ODPM.

————(2006) 'Multi-million pound boost for deprived areas', ODPM News Release 2006/0030, 23 February 2006. Online. Available http://www.neighbourhood.gov.uk/news.asp?id=1714 (accessed 28 February 2008).

Peck, J. and Theodore, N. (2000) 'Beyond "Employability"', Cambridge Journal of Economics, 24: 729–49.

Pemberton, S. and Mason, J. (2007) 'Uncovering the invisible minority: Irish communities, economic inactivity and welfare policy in the United Kingdom, European Planning Studies, 15(10): 1439–59.

Porter, M. (1995) 'The competitive advantage of the inner city', Harvard Business Review, 73: 55–71.

Potter, J. (2005) 'Entrepreneurship policy at a local level: rationale, design and delivery', Local Economy, 20(1): 104–10.

Ram, M. and Carter, S. (2003) 'Paving professional futures: ethnic minority accountants in the UK', International Small Business Journal, 21(3): 55–71.

Rouse, J. and Kitching, J. (2006) 'Do enterprise support programmes leave women holding the baby?', Environment and Planning C: Government and Policy, 24: 5–19.

Shaw, E., Carter, S. and Brierton, J. (2001) 'Unequal entrepreneurs: why female enterprise is an uphill business', Policy Paper, The Industrial Society, London.

Slack, J. (2006) 'The new entrepreneur scholarships: self-employment as a means to tackle social deprivation', Local Economy, 20(6): 447–55.

Smallbone, D., Ram, M., Deakins, D. and Baldock, R. (2001) Accessing finance and business support by ethnic minority businesses in the UK, paper presented to the Public Policy and the Institutional Context of Immigrant Businesses Conference, Liverpool, March.

Social Exclusion Unit (SEU) (2001) A New Commitment to Neighbourhood Renewal: A national strategy action plan, London: Cabinet Office.

———(2004a) Breaking the Cycle, London: Office of the Deputy Prime Minister.

———(2004b) Jobs and Enterprise in Deprived Areas, London: Office of the Deputy Prime Minister.

Theodore, N. (2007) 'New Labour at work: long-term unemployment and the geography of opportunity', Cambridge Journal of Economics, 31: 927–39.

Van Stel, A. J. and Storey, D. J. (2004) 'The link between firm births and job creation: is there a Upas Tree effect?', Regional Studies, 38(8): 893–909.

Warr, P. and Jackson, P. (1985) 'Factors influencing the psychological impact of prolonged unemployment and re-employment', Psychological Medicine, 15: 795–807.

Williams, C. (2005) 'The undeclared sector, self employment and public policy', International Journal of Entrepreneurial Behaviour and Research, 10(4): 26–37.

10 The Hidden Enterprise Culture

Colin C. Williams

INTRODUCTION

The aim of this chapter is to evaluate the prevalence in deprived neighbourhoods of a 'hidden enterprise culture' composed of enterprises and
entrepreneurs operating in the informal economy. Potentially, this is an
important issue when considering enterprise and enterprise development in
deprived areas. If it is indeed the case that a large hidden enterprise culture
exists in such communities, then it might well be that deprived communities are far more enterprising and entrepreneurial than so far portrayed and
that facilitating the legitimisation of this hidden enterprise culture could be
an important way forward for enterprise development.

In order to evaluate this, the chapter will firstly review the existing literature on this topic so as to reveal that few studies so far have sought to evaluate the prevalence of a hidden enterprise culture. Following this, and in order
to start to fill this gap in understanding, attention will turn towards a survey
of the extent and nature of the informal economy in deprived and affluent
urban and rural English localities. This will reveal that although the informal
economy is not concentrated in deprived neighbourhoods and informal economic activity in deprived neighbourhoods is less oriented to entrepreneurial
endeavour than in affluent areas, a greater proportion of entrepreneurs and
established self-employed engage in the informal economy in deprived than
affluent areas. The result is a call to reposition the hidden enterprise culture
more centre-stage in discussions of enterprise and entrepreneurship than has
so far been the case, especially in deprived communities.

Before commencing, however, it is necessary to set out the working definitions of both the informal economy and entrepreneurship adopted in this
chapter. So far as the informal economy is concerned, or what has been
variously called the 'underground', 'undeclared', 'shadow', 'cash-in-hand' or
'hidden' economy or sector, this chapter follows the strong consensus in the
literature by defining such endeavour as the paid production and sale of goods
and services that are legitimate in all respects besides the fact that they are
unregistered by or hidden from the state for tax or benefits purposes (Thomas
1992, Portes 1994, European Commission 1998, Williams and Windebank
1998, Marcelli et al. 1999, Renooy et al. 2004, Evans et al. 2006, Katungi
et al. 2006, OECD 2000a, 2000b, 2002). The only illegitimate aspect of
the informal economy, therefore, is that the transactions are unregistered or

hidden from the state for tax or social security purposes. Transactions involving illicit goods and services (for example, drug trafficking, gun-running) are not part of the informal economy and neither are unpaid exchanges.

When defining entrepreneurship, however, no such consensus exists. Indeed, it has long proven a problematic and elusive concept which Hull et al. (1980) likened to 'hunting the heffalump'. Here, therefore, the working definition adopted is that an entrepreneur is somebody who is actively involved in starting a business or are the owner-manager of a business that is less than 36 months old (Reynolds et al. 2002, Harding et al. 2005). This definition, although excluding aspects sometimes included (for example, intrapreneurship) is fit for the purpose for which it is here intended, namely studying whether those starting-up business ventures participate in the informal economy.

ENTREPRENEURSHIP AND THE INFORMAL ECONOMY

Until now, although the literature on entrepreneurship has seldom examined the issue of informal work practices amongst entrepreneurs, the literature on the informal economy has analysed the prevalence of entrepreneurs in the informal economy, albeit not in terms of whether informal entrepreneurship is more prevalent in the informal economies of some populations and not others.

Informal Work Practices amongst Entrepreneurs

An old adage is that if you scratch an entrepreneur, you will find a 'spiv' (Burns 2001: 4). Indeed, popular culture often depicts the entrepreneur as a rogue who does not always play by the rulebook. Yet despite the commonality of such a narrative, this representation is largely absent from the vast literature on entrepreneurship. Instead, the strong and broad agreement throughout the entrepreneurship literature is that the entrepreneur should be depicted in a positive, wholesome and virtuous manner. Put another way, there is an overwhelming tendency to engage in celebratory odes to entrepreneurship by portraying the entrepreneur more as an ideal type or object of desire, rather than as a descriptive subject. For evidence, one perhaps needs to look no further than the recurring narrative that entrepreneurs are 'economic heroes' (Cannon 1991), even 'super heroes' (Burns 2001: 24). As Burns (2001: 1) proclaims, they are 'the stuff of "legends" . . . held in high esteem and held up as role models to be emulated'. This virtuous and wholesome depiction is present, furthermore, across all theoretical approaches to entrepreneurship (see Cunningham and Lischeron 1991: 47). Whether the 'great person' school is adopted, which views them as born rather than made and reads them as possessing a 'sixth sense' along with intuition, vigour, energy, persistence and self-esteem and contrasts them with 'mortals' who 'lack what it takes', or instead the more socially constructed approaches are advocated of the classical, management, leadership or intrapreneurship schools, all commonly portray the entrepreneur as a positive and wholesome figure possessing virtuous attributes that 'lesser mortals' do not. Such a virtuous representation, as Jones and Spicer assert,

> offers a narrative structure to the fantasy that coordinates desire. It points to an unattainable and only vaguely specified object, and directs desire towards that object . . . One secures identity not in 'being' an enterprising subject but in the gap between the subject and the object of desire. This lack is central to maintaining desiring. (Jones and Spicer 2005: 237)

For further evidence of the dominance of this ideal-type depiction, one has only to consider the qualities, attributes and traits commonly attached to the entrepreneur. Although each of the above schools champions certain qualities over others, argue over whether particular traits are applicable or not, and debate what emphasis should be given to which qualities or sets of qualities, near enough all list only wholesome, positive and virtuous attributes, traits and qualities when depicting the entrepreneur. Table 10.1 summarises the qualities which Burns (2001: 27) finds most lists attribute to entrepreneurs, along with their antonyms. These qualities construct a wholesome and virtuous heroic figure, as can be clearly seen when such attributes are inverted to depict the dualistic opposite, the 'non-entrepreneur'.

However, it is perhaps the work of Berglund and Johansson (2007) that provides the most solid evidence of how the entrepreneurship literature is

Table 10.1   Qualities of Entrepreneurs and Their Antonyms

Qualities of Entrepreneurs	*Antonym*
Need for independence	Dependent
Need for achievement	Lack will to achieve
Internal locus of control	Believe in destiny
Ability to live with uncertainty	Cannot live with uncertainty
Take measured risks	Avoid risks
Ability to be opportunistic	Fail to take opportunities
Innovative	Lack ability to innovate
Self-confidence	Lack confidence
Proactive	Reactive
Decisive	Indecisive
Higher energy	Lack energy
Self-motivated	Lack ability to motivate themselves
Vision and flair	No vision or flair

Source: Derived from Burns (2001: 27)

dominated by a wholesome ideal-type depiction of the entrepreneur. They conduct a discourse analysis of how entrepreneurship is portrayed in a prominent handbook of entrepreneurship, 10 of the most frequently cited articles in *Journal of Business Venturing* and, finally, articles appearing in special issues of *Entrepreneurship and Regional Development* and *Entrepreneurship Theory and Practice*. Table 10.2 summarises their findings. It shows that the category of entrepreneurship contains all that is often seen to be positive,

Table 10.2 Words and Phrases Used to Describe Entrepreneurship and Their Opposites

Words That Describe Entrepreneurship	Opposite Words
Market activity	Doing things that are not traded
Development	Stagnation, decline
(Economic) growth	(Economic) stagnation, decline
Change	Stability
Dynamic	Static, passive
Innovation	Routine, traditional, habitual
Technological change	Human stability
Private sector	Public sector
Creation	Destruction
Risk	Safety
Risk-taking	Risk-avoidance
Venture capital	Resources without risk
For profit	Non-profit
Uncertainty	Certainty
Managing	Taking orders, or failing
Opportunity perception	Blindness to opportunity
See and act on opportunities	Letting opportunities slip away
Driving force	Restraining force
Information	Unawareness
Knowledge	Ignorance, foolishness, delusion
Discovery	Undiscovered
Exploit	Preserve, maintain
Acting	Hesitate, doubt
Strategic	Untactical, ill-advised
Creativity	Unimaginative, dearth of ideas
Process	On-the-spot account

Source: Berglund and Johansson (2007: Table 1)

182 Colin C. Williams

virtuous and wholesome in contemporary societies and economies while the non-entrepreneur is a receptacle into which is cast all that is negative.

Given the dominance of this wholesome, virtuous and positive ideal-type depiction of the entrepreneur, it is therefore perhaps of no surprise to find that forms of entrepreneurship that do not conform to this ideal-type are seldom discussed in the entrepreneurship literature. Indeed, when forms of entrepreneurship are pinpointed that do not conform to this ideal-type depiction, such as entrepreneurs operating in the informal economy, the usual response is to either reposition them outside the boundaries of entrepreneurship, ignore them, depict them as temporary or transient, or simply consign them to the margins by portraying them not as 'mainstream' entrepreneurship. Put another way, the ideal-type depiction currently has what can be described only as a firm grip in determining what is considered entrepreneurship and what is deemed unworthy of consideration. Indeed, it is perhaps for precisely this reason that so little attention has been paid to the notion of a hidden enterprise culture of entrepreneurs operating in the informal economy. To draw attention to such a facet of entrepreneurship would sully and tarnish the overwhelmingly clean and wholesome ideal-type representation of the entrepreneur.

For some decades, nevertheless, a small tributary of thought in the entrepreneurship literature has sought to contest the dominance of this wholesome ideal-type depiction of the entrepreneur. Some commentators, for example, have sought to foreground various more negative attributes associated with entrepreneurship. Perhaps best known in this regard is the study by Kets de Vries (1977), who argues that entrepreneurs are the product of unhappy family backgrounds, particularly situations in which the father is a controller and manipulator, remote and often seen as a deserter. The classic study of entrepreneurs as people who do not always play by the rulebook, meanwhile, is Collins et al. (1964), partially corroborated by Bhide and Stevenson (1990). Indeed, in recent years, as the emotive attachment to achieving this fantasy state of being has gathered pace, so too have the attempts to tarnish the wholesome and virtuous ideal type (for example, Fournier 1998, Deutschmann 2001, Armstrong 2005, Jones and Spicer 2005, 2006). It is important to recognise, however, that this more critical literature remains only a small backwater in the entrepreneurship literature. On the whole, those seeking to move beyond celebratory textbook odes and towards understanding the more negative aspects of the lived practices of entrepreneurs have been in the minority. The outcome is that the prevalence of informal work practices amongst entrepreneurs has been seldom investigated in the entrepreneurship literature.

Entrepreneurship in the Informal Economy

To review what is currently known about the relationship between the informal economy and entrepreneurship, therefore, it is necessary to move beyond the literature on entrepreneurship and to investigate the equally large body of literature on the informal economy, which is perhaps less constrained by the ideal-type depiction of the entrepreneur and more open to examining the lived practices of entrepreneurship. Analysing this literature, it becomes quickly apparent that in most countries and regions of the world, a large proportion of all economic activity takes place in the informal economy: some 48 per cent of non-agricultural employment in North Africa is estimated to be in the informal economy, 51 per cent in Latin America, 65 per cent in Asia and 72 per cent in sub-Saharan Africa (International Labor Office [ILO] 2002b). Such a finding has been reinforced by many other studies (Williams and Windebank 1998, Schneider and Enste 2000, Renooy et al. 2004, Williams 2004, Bajada and Schneider 2005, Chowdury 2006, Fernandez-Kelly and Shefner 2006, Guha-Khasnobis and Kanbur 2006, Guha-Khasnobis et al. 2006).

Analysing the structure of this informal labour market, this literature has gradually recognised that those engaged in the informal economy are not only low paid waged employees working under 'sweatshop-like' conditions but also own-account or self-employed workers. In sub-Saharan Africa, for example, some 70 per cent of informal workers have been found to be self-employed rather than waged employees, 62 per cent in North Africa, 60 per cent in Latin America and 59 per cent in Asia (ILO 2002b). This, in turn, has led to greater interest in the relationship between entrepreneurship and the informal economy.

On the whole, this has so far taken the form of displaying how many of the self-employed engaged in the informal economy display entrepreneurial qualities. At first, this re-reading of the informal self-employed as a hidden enterprise culture and as displaying entrepreneurial qualities emerged in a third world context (De Soto 1989, 2001, Franks 1994, Rakowski 1994, Cross 2000, ILO 2002a, Browne 2004). As the ILO (2002a: 54) for example states, the informal economy represents 'an incubator for business potential and . . . transitional base for accessibility and graduation to the formal economy' and depict informal workers as showing 'real business acumen, creativity, dynamism and innovation'. In more recent years, this depiction of informal workers as a hidden enterprise culture has also begun to take hold in the literature on the informal economy in Western economies (Renooy et al. 2004, Small Business Council 2004, Snyder 2004, Williams 2004, 2006, Evans et al. 2006). Until now, however, this informal economy literature has not sought to evaluate what proportion of new business ventures start up wholly or partially in the informal economy. Nor has it sought to analyse whether this hidden enterprise culture is more prevalent in some populations than others. Given these gaps in understanding, as well as the lack of evidence on the prevalence of informal work practices amongst entrepreneurs, a survey is reported below that has sought to start to make some headway in terms of understanding the extent of this hidden enterprise culture.

EXAMINING THE HIDDEN ENTERPRISE CULTURE IN ENGLAND

Given this lack of evidence on whether there is a large hidden enterprise culture of enterprises and entrepreneurs operating in the informal economy, and whether entrepreneurship is more prevalent in the informal economies of some areas rather than others, case study evidence is here reported from a survey of English localities conducted between 1998 and 2002. Using the Index of Multiple Deprivation (ODPM 2000), which ranks all neighbourhoods according to their level of multiple deprivation, maximum variation sampling was used to select a range of affluent and deprived urban and rural localities for investigation (see Table 10.3). Although the outcome is that this sampling method does not provide a nationally representative sample, it does avoid the pitfall of studying only one particular locality-type and consequently being unable to decipher whether their findings are unique to this locality-type (Leonard 1994) and how the hidden enterprise culture differs across localities.

Having selected a diverse range of localities for investigation using maximum variation sampling, a spatially stratified sampling technique (Kitchen and Tate 2001) was then used to select households for interview in each district. If there were some 1,000 households in the district and 100 interviews were sought, the researcher called at every 10th household. If there was no response or an interview was refused, then the 11th household was visited, then the 9th, 12th, 8th and so on. This provided a spatially stratified sample of each district.

To gather data, a relatively structured face-to-face interview schedule was designed. Firstly, background information was gathered on the households in terms of the age, gender, employment status and work history

Table 10.3   Overview of Locations Studied in the English Localities Survey

Area-Type	Locality	Number of Interviews
Affluent rural	Fulbourn, Cambridgeshire	70
Affluent rural	Chalford, Gloucestershire	70
Deprived rural	Grimethorpe, South Yorkshire	70
Deprived rural	Wigton, Cumbria	70
Deprived rural	St Blazey, Cornwall	70
Affluent suburb	Fulwood, Sheffield	50
Affluent suburb	Basset/Chilworth, Southampton	61
Deprived urban	Manor, Sheffield	100
Deprived urban	Pitsmoor, Sheffield	100
Deprived urban	St Mary's, Southampton	100
Deprived urban	Hightown, Southampton	100

Source: English Localities Survey

of household members as well as the gross household income, including whether any household member had started up a business venture in the past 36 months. Secondly, and adopting a gradual approach to addressing this sensitive topic of participation in informal work, questions were asked about the type of labour the household last used to complete a range of 44 common domestic tasks followed by questions on whether they had conducted any of these 44 tasks for other households and, if so, whether they had been paid or not and whether they had been paid 'cash-in-hand'. Third and finally, a range of open-ended questions were then asked on informal work concerning its nature, including for those who had started up a business venture in the prior 36 months, whether their transactions had been wholly or partly conducted in the informal economy and their motives for engaging in informal work. Although this interview schedule therefore collected data on a whole array of informal work, such as off-the-books waged employment and people who conducted paid favours on a one-off basis for kin, friends and neighbours and who are not seeking to expand this into some business venture, the focus below is solely upon both those who have started up business ventures in the past 36 months and the more established self-employed who operate in the informal economy.

Before analysing these findings, however, the validity of this method needs to be briefly discussed since it might be believed that collecting reliable data on the informal economy is a difficult, if not impossible, task. In this survey, akin to many previous studies collecting data on informal work in the context of overall household work practices (Pahl 1984, Leonard 1994, MacDonald 1994), the finding was that respondents displayed little reticence in openly talking about their informal practices. Although such endeavour might be hidden from the state authorities for tax and social security purposes, it was openly discussed by respondents in much the same manner as they discussed their voluntary unpaid activity for others. Moreover, the total amount customers reported spending on off-the-books work in each locality in these countries approximated to what suppliers of informal work reported having received. There is thus little evidence either of suppliers under-reporting such work, or of customers falsely allocating economic activity to informal work when this was not the case. The results are reported below.

THE PREVALENCE OF A HIDDEN ENTERPRISE CULTURE IN ENGLAND

In order to evaluate the prevalence of a hidden enterprise culture of enterprises and entrepreneurs operating in the informal economy, especially in deprived neighbourhoods, the spatial variations in the informal economy will be evaluated firstly. Secondly, the prevalence of entrepreneurship in the informal economy will be examined, followed finally by the prevalence of informal work practices amongst entrepreneurs.

Spatial Variations in the Informal Economy

For many decades, a 'marginality thesis' prevailed which held that the informal economy was concentrated amongst marginalised populations, whether these be poor nations, deprived localities and regions, lower income socio-economic groups or women (for example, Castells and Portes 1989, De Soto 1989, Lagos 1995, Maldonado 1995, ILO 2002a). In recent decades, however, a wealth of literature has refuted this marginality thesis (for reviews, see Williams and Windebank 1998, Williams 2004).

This English localities survey reinforces this critique of the marginality thesis which argues that informal work is not concentrated in deprived populations. Starting with the consumption side of the equation, the finding is that informal work is more likely to be used by those who live in affluent English areas. As Table 10.4 demonstrates, this is the case in both urban and rural areas. Analysing where the consumption of informal work is rife, therefore, the finding is that such work is more prevalent in affluent than deprived areas. This is perhaps no surprise.

Is it the case, however, that even if the consumption of informal work is rife in affluent areas, the suppliers are concentrated in deprived neighbourhoods? There is, after all, a perception that even if the populations of affluent areas consume more informal work in the form of gardening services, domestic cleaners and home maintenance services, the workers performing such tasks are likely to come from more deprived areas. Contrary to such assertions grounded in the marginality thesis, Table 10.5 demonstrates that this assumption about the supply of informal work is

Table 10.4   Percentage of Everyday Tasks Undertaken Using Informal Work in England: By Locality-Type

Area	% of the 44 Tasks Last Conducted Using Informal Work	No. of Households Surveyed
All areas	5.5	861
Rural areas	5.0	350
Urban areas	5.8	511
Lower income rural areas	5.6	210
Lower income areas—Southampton	4.4	200
Lower income areas—Sheffield	5.4	200
Higher income rural areas	4.1	140
Higher income suburb—Southampton	6.5	50
Higher income suburb—Sheffield	11.2	61

Source: English Localities Survey

Table 10.5   Participation in Informal Work in England: By Area

Area-Type	Sample Size	% of Total Sample	% of all informal work identified:	Average Pay/ Informal Task (£)	Average Household Income per Annum from Informal Work (£)
All	861	100	100		
Urban lower income	400	47	22	90	46
Rural lower income	210	24	16	25	47
Urban higher income	111	13	37	1,665	435
Rural higher income	140	16	25	564	921

Source: English Localities Survey

incorrect. People living in households in affluent areas conduct a disproportionate share of all informal work and also receive much greater monetary rewards than those living in lower income areas. This applies in
both the urban and rural environment.

Take, for example, lower and higher income urban areas. Households in
affluent areas, despite being only 11 per cent of the sample, conduct 37 per
cent of all informal work. The average amount received by a household in
a deprived urban neighbourhood compared with a household in an affluent
suburb for conducting a task on an informal basis was £90 compared with
£1,665; the average hourly wage rate for informal work was £3.40 compared with £7.50; and the mean annual household income from informal
work was £46 compared with £435. This significant geographical disparity
in the rewards gained from informal work, moreover, also pertains when
only those who engage in such work are analysed. For the 40 per cent of
households in lower income neighbourhoods who participate in the informal economy, the mean annual household income from such work was
£115 compared with £2,420 in the 18 per cent of households who supplied
such work in affluent suburbs. The monetary rewards from informal work,
therefore, are heavily skewed towards the populations of affluent suburbs.

Deprived areas, in sum, have smaller informal economies than more
affluent areas. Whether it necessarily follows that deprived areas also have
smaller hidden enterprise cultures is now investigated. This is because it
might be the case that although deprived areas have smaller informal economies, those engaged in informal work are far more engaged in entrepreneurial
forms of informal endeavour than their counterparts in affluent areas. To
investigate whether this is the case, attention now turns towards the nature
of the informal economy in deprived and affluent areas and an investigation
of the prevalence of entrepreneurship in the informal economy in these two
area types.

THE PREVALENCE OF ENTREPRENEURSHIP
IN THE INFORMAL ECONOMY

Although Pedersen (2003) finds that 1 in 13 people in the UK declare that they engage in informal work, until now, few have investigated the types of informal work that they conduct and whether the forms of informal work conducted markedly vary across locality-types. The finding of this survey is that by no means all informal work can be construed as enterprising and entrepreneurial. As Table 10.6 displays, some 18 per cent of the informal work undertaken by respondents was informal waged employment conducted as an employee on a cash-in-hand basis for a formal or informal business and a further 49 per cent was composed of paid favours conducted for friends, acquaintances and kin, mostly on a one-off basis and not as part of a strategy to develop an enterprise. Just 11 per cent of the informal work reported was informal entrepreneurship (informal work conducted on an own-account basis as part of a business venture that is less than 36 months old) and 22 per cent was informal self-employment (informal jobs conducted by the established self-employed as part of their business). Just one-third of all instances of informal work reported were therefore conducted on an own-account basis by early-stage or more established self-employed people as part of their business. As such, only a relatively small segment of the informal economy can be represented as a hidden enterprise culture. The vast majority (some two-thirds) is either informal waged employment or paid favours conducted for others but not as part of a strategy to develop an enterprise.

There are also some marked variations between affluent and deprived localities in the prevalence of entrepreneurship in the informal economy. While the nature of the informal economy in deprived areas is more orientated towards informal waged employment and paid favours, in affluent areas it is more orientated towards off-the-books transactions by business start-ups and the established self-employed. In other words, representing the informal economy as a hidden enterprise culture is much more akin to the lived experiences of affluent than deprived populations. As such, the emergent depiction of informal work in the informal economy literature as a hidden enterprise

Table 10.6   The Anatomy of Informal Work in Affluent and Deprived English Localities

	Higher Income Areas	*Lower Income Areas*	*All Areas*
Informal waged employment	1	19	18
Informal entrepreneurship	27	9	11
Informal self-employment	60	8	22
Paid favours	12	64	49

Source: English Localities Survey

culture can be seen as an attempt to re-represent the informal economy through the lived practices of affluent rather than deprived populations.

In sum, this research suggests that caution is required when reading the informal economy as a hidden enterprise culture, especially with regard to deprived areas. To do so is not only to impose on to deprived populations a representation of the informal economy that is not applicable to them but also to seek to represent this work from a perspective more in keeping with affluent than deprived populations. This current tendency in the informal economy literature, put bluntly, marginalises the lived experiences of those living in deprived areas.

The Prevalence of Informal Practices amongst Entrepreneurs

Even if this survey indicates the need for caution when discussing the prevalence of entrepreneurship in the informal economy, especially in deprived neighbourhoods, it is a very different finding when it comes to examining the prevalence of informal work practices amongst entrepreneurs.

In the 811 households composed of 1,320 working-age adults, this survey identified 91 people (6.9 per cent of the surveyed working-age population) who had started up a business in the past three years. Of these 91 entrepreneurs, 70 (77 per cent) reported that they had conducted some or all of their trade on an informal basis. Although this is a relatively small sample and the sample frame skewed towards deprived neighbourhoods, this finding that over three-quarters of entrepreneurs engage in informal transactions raises questions about the validity of the wholesome ideal-type depiction of entrepreneurs in the entrepreneurship literature. Indeed, comparing the findings of this survey with other nationally representative surveys of entrepreneurship in the UK, there is tentative evidence that these findings might not be too far from the norm. The 2001 Global Entrepreneurship Monitor survey of the UK identifies that 6.5 per cent of the working age population can be classified as early-stage entrepreneurs (Harding et al. 2005) compared with 6.9 per cent in this study. In consequence, and in the absence of other evidence, this finding that some three-quarters engage in the informal economy can be thus seen as a very tentative preliminary signal that a significant proportion of business start-ups in England engage in informal work.

Turning to the more established self-employed, it is similarly the case that of the 81 identified (8.1 per cent of the surveyed working-age population) who had an established business, 60 (74 per cent) reported that they conduct some or all of their trade in the informal economy. Again, therefore, around three-quarters of the more established self-employed engage in informal transactions. The clear implication, in consequence, is that the cleansed and pure ideal-type depiction of entrepreneurs as always playing by the rulebook is not the lived practice. Below, and to start to unpack this, each group is taken in turn.

The Participation of Entrepreneurs in the Informal Economy

Of the 91 early-stage entrepreneurs identified in this survey, less than a quarter (23 per cent) reported that they operated wholly legitimate enterprises and did not engage in informal transactions. Some 57 per cent, meanwhile, had registered their business but conducted a portion of their trade off-the-books and 23 per cent had not registered their business and conducted all of their trade on an informal basis. As such, some 77 per cent of all entrepreneurs were working in the informal economy.

Who are these informal entrepreneurs? Table 10.7 reports their characteristics. Before doing so, it is important to highlight that there is again some tentative evidence that the results may not be too far from the norm. Of all the entrepreneurs identified in this survey, just 4 per cent were unemployed or economically inactive at the time they established their business. The majority (75 per cent) were employees in employment and 21 per cent registered self-employed. This profile of the employment status of entrepreneurs is very similar to broader national representative surveys of the profiles of those starting up business ventures in the UK. The Small Business Service (2006), for example, identify that 5 per cent are unemployed, 80 per cent employees in employment and 13 per cent self-employed. There is therefore little difference between this survey and wider more nationally representative surveys.

Table 10.7   Characteristics of Informal Entrepreneurs

	% of Entrepreneurs:		% of Surveyed Population (n = 1,320)
	All (n = 91)	Informal (n =70)	
Employment status:			
Employee in employment	75	70	30
Self-employed	21	26	7
Non-employed	4	4	63
Location:			
Deprived urban areas	48	51	46
Deprived rural areas	24	28	24
Affluent urban areas	18	13	13
Affluent rural areas	10	8	17
Household employment status:			
Multiple-earner household	70	74	28
Single-earner household	20	16	24
No-earner household	10	10	48

Source: English Localities Survey

Turning to the profiles of informal entrepreneurs, the first important point to note is that there is no marked difference with entrepreneurs more generally. Just 4 per cent of entrepreneurs participating in off-the-books practices were unemployed when setting up their business venture, whilst the majority were either employees in employment (70 per cent) or self-employed (26 per cent). They are also markedly more likely to live in a multiple wage earner household. Some 70 per cent of all entrepreneurs and 74 per cent of informal entrepreneurs live in multiple-earner households compared with just 28 per cent of the surveyed population as a whole. Meanwhile, while entrepreneurs as a whole are more likely to be found in urban areas in general, and affluent urban areas more particularly, entrepreneurs engaged in informal practices are more likely to be in deprived areas. Indeed, a greater proportion of the entrepreneurs surveyed in deprived areas engage in informal practices than in affluent areas. Some 85 per cent of entrepreneurs surveyed in the deprived areas engage in the informal economy compared with just 60 per cent in affluent areas.

Contrary to the depiction in the marginality thesis, however, entrepreneurs operating in the informal economy are not concentrated in marginalised populations. Instead, and as Table 10.8 reveals, these entrepreneurs are polarised at the two ends of the income spectrum in that they are concentrated in both the poorest and most affluent households in terms of gross household income. In the lowest quartile of households, surveyed in terms of gross household income, 34 per cent of the informal entrepreneurs are found clustered, whilst in the highest quartile of households surveyed are found 40 per cent of all informal entrepreneurs.

Examining the differences in the character of the informal entrepreneurs in the highest and lowest income households, meanwhile, Table 10.8 shows that entrepreneurs operating registered enterprises but conducting a portion of their trade in the informal economy are concentrated in the highest income quartile of households, whilst those entrepreneurs surveyed working wholly in the informal economy are heavily concentrated in the lowest income

Table 10.8 Distribution of Informal Entrepreneurs: By Gross Household Income

	Household by Gross Income			
	Lowest Quartile	Lower Quartile	Upper Quartile	Highest Quartile
% of sample	25	25	25	25
% of all entrepreneurs (n = 91)	29	5	22	44
% of informal entrepreneurs (n = 70)	34	7	19	40
% of wholly illegitimate (n = 18)	61	11	6	22
% doing portion off-the-books (n = 52)	29	6	23	46

Source: English Localities Survey

households. This, however, is not the only difference in the character of informal entrepreneurs in the highest and lowest income households. Those in the highest quartile in terms of gross household income were also more likely to be in formal employment or registered self-employed (95 per cent of the informal entrepreneurs surveyed) and to use their formal occupation to engage in relatively well-paid informal self-employment related to their formal job. Those in the lowest quartile in terms of gross household income, in stark contrast, often do not have a formal occupation that they can use to engage in informal own-account work. Instead, entrepreneurs in this quartile generally engage in lower paid forms of informal entrepreneurship.

The Participation of the Established Self-Employed in the Informal Economy

Turning to the 60 established self-employed that conduct some or all of their trade in the informal economy, only 9 (15 per cent) operated wholly in the informal economy and these were nearly all people also in formal employment or classified as 'economically inactive'. The vast majority (85 per cent) conduct only a portion of their trade in the informal economy and these on the whole are registered self-employed. The established self-employed engaged in informal work thus possess a very different employment profile

Table 10.9   Characteristics of the Established Self-Employed

	% of Established Self-Employed:		% of Surveyed Population (n = 1,320)
	All (n = 81)	*Informal* (n = 60)	
Employment status:			
Employee in employment	16	15	30
Self-employed	81	80	7
Non-employed	5	5	63
Location:			
Deprived urban areas	40	45	46
Deprived rural areas	24	25	24
Affluent urban areas	20	15	13
Affluent rural areas	16	15	17
Household employment status:			
Multiple-earner household	75	70	28
Single-earner household	21	25	24
No-earner household	4	5	48

Source: English Localities Survey

to informal entrepreneurs. As Table 10.9 displays, some 80 per cent are run by the registered self-employed, 15 per cent by formal employees operating their self-employed enterprise on the side and 5 per cent by the registered unemployed. This finding that most are the registered self-employed is reinforced in many other studies (O'Higgins 1981, Pahl 1984, General Accounting Office 1994, Small Business Council 2004).

The intimation, therefore, is that as informal entrepreneurs become more established, they leave their formal employment and become registered self-employed. Indeed, the employment histories of the 60 established self-employed reinforce this finding. Of the 48 defining their employment status as registered self-employed, 30 had been previously employees in employment while the remainder had been continuously self-employed. This is thus tentative evidence of a transition from employment to self-employment amongst informal entrepreneurs as their businesses become more established. Such a finding reinforces the evidence elsewhere that those starting up enterprises tend to be people in waged employment, often depicted as straddling the legitimate and off-the-books economy as a 'risk-reduction strategy' (McCormick 1998), and that it is only later in the development of the enterprise that they might become fully self-employed and leave their waged employment (for example, Reynolds et al. 2002).

Analysing the differences between affluent and deprived neighbourhoods, meanwhile, the finding is that a greater proportion of the established self-employed in deprived areas (82 per cent) engage in the informal economy than in affluent areas where just 62 per cent of the self-employed participate in the informal economy. Similar to business start-ups, therefore, the vast majority of the established self-employed reported that they engage in the informal economy, thus countering the wholesome ideal-type depiction of entrepreneurs.

Breaking down the more established self-employed engaged in the informal economy, two distinct groups can be identified: the 'transitional' self-employed, who are in the process of formalising their businesses; and 'serial' informal economy traders, who have no intention of fully legitimising their activities.

Transitional Business Ventures. Of the 60 established self-employed engaged in the informal economy, 23 were in the process of transforming their businesses into legitimate enterprises. Although at various stages of doing so, these self-employed share a commitment to formalisation. An example of such a 'transitional' venture is Justin, a young man in his early twenties, registered as self-employed and running a rapidly growing car valet business with a number of employees. As a young teenager, he had washed cars one Saturday morning at a charity event with his local scout group and following this, had continued doing so at weekends. Knocking on doors and offering his services, he had quickly built up a regular clientele and carried on doing this throughout his school years. By sixteen years old, he had a well-formulated plan of what he wanted to do for a living. Rather than continue with his education, he left school using the money accumulated to purchase a van and equipment to set up as a car valet. Five years after starting up, he now employs three people and is currently seeking to reduce the share of his turnover from domestic customers and expand the proportion from the more commercial side of his operation, such as used car dealers and car maintenance garages for whom he provides a valet service. Although he continues to conduct a portion of his work on a cash-in-hand basis for domestic customers, especially long-standing clients, he has over the years formalised a greater share of his business and is intending to be in his words 'more or less fully legit' within the next year or so.

Serial Users of Informal Practices. The remaining 37 established self-employed engaged in informal transactions have no intention of formalising their business practices. An example is a business run by a husband and wife team, Tony and Mo. They own a number of picture framing and mirror retail shops. Most trade is on-the-books. However, whenever close social contacts ask for pictures to be framed or mirrors, they nearly always do so off-the-books. As Mo put it, 'You would never make any profit if you put everything through the books'. Although normally it was friends, neighbours and acquaintances offered an off-the-books rate this sometimes expanded a little further, especially when money was tight. Having recently bought a new house, their response had been to conduct more informal transactions than normal for a wider range of customers. This couple, therefore, were serial and on-going users of off-the-books transactions and it was heavily embedded in their trading practices.

It is not solely the registered self-employed, however, who run established enterprises that conduct trade in the informal economy. Nine of the 60 self-employed with established businesses that trade in the informal economy were formal employees operating their enterprises in addition to their formal employment. An example is Martin who works for a garage door installation company. Alongside his formal employment, he had his own long-standing 'parasitic' wholly off-the-books business venture. When visiting clients for his company, he would whenever appropriate give them a quote for the company doing the job and another for him doing the job privately at the weekend or in the evening. Unlike others starting up a business on the side, he had no intention of leaving his formal job since this gave him the necessary contacts for his own micro-enterprise. In one sense, this can be seen as an example of 'intrapreneurship', albeit not of a sort so far quoted in any textbooks on entrepreneurship.

CONCLUSIONS

This chapter has sought to understand whether there exists in deprived neighbourhoods a 'hidden enterprise culture' composed of enterprises and entrepreneurs operating in the informal economy. This is potentially an important issue when considering enterprise in deprived areas. If a large hidden enterprise culture exists that is not recorded in official data, then it might well be that deprived communities are far more enterprising and entrepreneurial than so far assumed. Reporting the results of face-to-face interviews with 811 households in affluent and deprived urban and rural areas about their participation in the informal economy, this chapter has revealed that not only is the informal economy smaller in deprived areas than affluent areas but to depict the informal economy as a hidden enterprise culture is to represent the informal economy through the lived experiences of affluent rather than deprived populations. This current tendency in the informal economy literature thus marginalises the lived experiences of those living in deprived areas.

However, although this chapter therefore finds little evidence to support current attempts to re-read the informal economy as a hidden enterprise culture, especially in deprived populations, it does find that the majority of entrepreneurs engage in the informal economy, especially in deprived neighbourhoods. This survey therefore identifies a marked discrepancy between the textbook celebratory odes to the entrepreneur that construct a virtuous ideal-type depiction of entrepreneurs and the lived realities of entrepreneurship. Until now, despite entrepreneurs being commonly represented as risk-takers, it has been seldom questioned whether this means that they always keep to the rules. Notable by its absence from most literature on entrepreneurship has been the notion that these risk-takers might weigh up the probability of being caught and the level of punishments and decide to do some or all of their business in the informal economy. This survey, nevertheless, reveals that some three-quarters of all entrepreneurs and the same proportion of established self-employed conduct some or all of their transactions in the informal economy.

Consequently, the depiction of enterprise culture as composed of entrepreneurs playing by the rulebook in their business lives is called into question. Although most literature on entrepreneurship might adopt a gleaming 'whiter-than-white' depiction of entrepreneurs, such entrepreneurship is here tentatively asserted to perhaps represent just the tip of the iceberg. Beneath the surface, so far largely ignored, there does indeed seem to be a large hidden enterprise culture composed of entrepreneurs who do not always play within the bounds of the law. Of course, not all entrepreneurs engage in the informal economy and it is not the intention here to suggest that they do. Portraying entrepreneurs as always flouting the law is as erroneous as suggesting that they are always virtuous and follow the rulebook. The point is that the lived practice of entrepreneurship is for some not as wholesome and legitimate as portrayed in ideal-type depictions.

Until now, in sum, most attention when examining the hidden enterprise culture has been on the prevalence of entrepreneurship in the informal economy. Relatively little attention has been paid to the prevalence of informal transactions amongst entrepreneurs. This chapter, however, reveals that it is this latter issue that is perhaps the more relevant issue, especially so far as deprived populations are concerned. Now required, therefore, are some nationally representative surveys to further evaluate whether this potentially important facet of enterprise culture is more widely the case by evaluating the proportion of business start-ups that are wholly legitimate ventures, the share that are registered enterprises conducting a portion of their trade off-the-books and the percentage that are wholly unregistered enterprises conducting all of their trade in the informal economy. If this chapter stimulates such research to be pursued and greater engagement of the entrepreneurship literature with the lived practices of entrepreneurship, then it will have achieved its main objective. If it also results in a little more caution in the informal economy literature when depicting the informal economy as a hidden enterprise culture, and greater pause for reflection on the appropriateness of such a re-representation, especially with regard to deprived populations, then it will have fulfilled all of its objectives.

BIBLIOGRAPHY

Armstrong, P. (2005) Critique of Entrepreneurship: People and policy, Basingstoke: Palgrave Macmillan.
Bajada, C. and Schneider, F. (eds) (2005) Size, Causes and Consequences of the Underground Economy: An international perspective, Aldershot: Ashgate.
Berglund, K. and Johansson, A. W. (2007) 'Constructions of entrepreneurship: a discourse analysis of academic publications', Journal of Enterprising Communities, 1(1): 77–102.
Bhide, A. and Stevenson, H. H. (1990) 'Why be honest if honesty doesn't pay?', Harvard Business Review, 68(5): 121–29.
Browne, K. E. (2004) Creole Economics: Caribbean cunning under the French flag, Austin: University of Texas Press.
Burns, P. (2001) Entrepreneurship and Small Business, Basingstoke: Palgrave.
Cannon, T. (1991) Enterprise: Creation, development and growth, Oxford: Butterworth-Heinemann.
Castells, M. and Portes, A. (1989) 'World underneath: the origins, dynamics and effects of the informal economy', in A. Portes, M. Castells and L.A. Benton (eds) The Informal Economy: Studies in advanced and less developing countries, Baltimore: John Hopkins University Press.
Chowdury, U. (2006) Informal Sector in a Developing Economy, New Delhi: Anmol.
Collins, O. F., Moore, D. G. and Unwalla, D. B. (1964) The Enterprising Man, East Lansing: Bureau of Business and Economic Research, Michigan State University.
Cross, J. C. (2000) 'Street vendors, modernity and postmodernity: conflict and compromise in the global economy', International Journal of Sociology and Social Policy, 20(1): 29–51.
Cunningham, J. B. and Lischeron, J. (1991) 'Defining entrepreneurship', Journal of Small Business Management, 29(1): 47.
De Soto, H. (1989) The Other Path: The economic answer to terrorism, London: Harper and Row.
———(2001) The Mystery of Capital: Why capitalism triumphs in the West and fails everywhere else, London: Black Swan.

Deutschmann, C. (2001) 'Capitalism as religion? An unorthodox analysis of entre-preneurship', European Journal of Sociology, 44(3): 387–403.

European Commission (1998) Communication of the Commission on Undeclared Work, Online. Available http://europa.eu.int/comm/employment_social/empl_esf/docs/com98–219_en.pdf (accessed 1 November 2009).

Evans, M., Syrett, S. and Williams, C. C. (2006) The Informal Economy and Deprived Neighbourhoods: A systematic review, London: DCLG.

Fernandez-Kelly, P. and Shefner, J. (eds) (2006) Out of the Shadows: Political action and the informal economy in Latin America, University Park: Pennsylvania State University Press.

Fournier, V. (1998) 'Stories of development and exploitation: militant voices in an enterprise culture', Organization, 61(1): 107–28.

Franks, J. R. (1994) 'Macroeconomic policy and the informal economy', in C. A. Rakowski (ed.) Contrapunto: The informal sector debate in Latin America, Albany: State University of New York Press.

General Accounting Office (1994) Tax Administration: IRS can better pursue non-compliant sole proprietors, 2 August, GAO/GGD-94-175, Washington, DC: General Accounting Office.

Guha-Khasnobis, B. and Kanbur, R. (eds) (2006) Informal Labour Markets and Development, Basingstoke: Palgrave Macmillan.

Guha-Khasnobis, B., Kanbur, R. and Ostrom, E. (eds) (2006) Linking the Formal and Informal Economy: Concepts and policies, Oxford: Oxford University Press.

Harding, R. (2003) Global Entrepreneurship Monitor: Business start-up activity, London: London Business School.

Harding, R., Brooksbank, D., Hart, M., Jones-Evans, D., Levie, J., O'Reilly, J. and Walker, J. (2005) Global Entrepreneurship Monitor United Kingdom 2005, London: London Business School.

Hull, D., Bosley, J. J. and Udell, G. G. (1980) 'Renewing the hunt for the Heffalump: identifying potential entrepreneurs by personality characteristics', Journal of Small Business, 18(1): 11–18.

International Labor Office (2002a) Decent Work and the Informal Economy, Geneva: International Labor Office.

———(2002b) Women and Men in the Informal Economy: A statistical picture, Geneva: International Labor Office.

Jones, C. and Spicer, A. (2005) 'The sublime object of entrepreneurship', Organization, 12(2): 223–46.

———(2006) 'Outline of a genealogy of the value of the entrepreneur', in G. Erreygers and G. Jacobs (eds) Language, Communication and the Economy, Amsterdam: John Benjamins.

Katungi, D., Neale, E. and Barbour, A. (2006) People in Low-Paid Informal Work: Need not greed, York: Joseph Rowntree Foundation.

Kets de Vries, M. F. R. (1977) 'The entrepreneurial personality: a person at the crossroads', Journal of Management Studies, February: 34–57.

Kitchen, R. and Tate, N. (2001) Conducting Research in Human Geography: Theory, practice and methodology, London: Prentice Hall.

Lagos, R. A. (1995) 'Formalising the informal sector: barriers and costs', Development and Change, 26(1): 110–31.

Leonard, M. (1994) Informal Economic Activity in Belfast, Aldershot: Avebury.

MacDonald, R. (1994) 'Fiddly jobs, undeclared working and the something for nothing society', Work, Employment and Society, 8(4): 507–30.

Maldonado, C. (1995) 'The informal sector: legalization or laissez-faire?', International Labour Review, 134(6): 705–28.

Marcelli, E. A., Pastor, M. and Joassart, P. M. (1999) 'Estimating the effects of informal economic activity: evidence from Los Angeles County', Journal of Economic Issues, 33(3): 579–607.

McCormick, D. (1998) 'Fundis and formality: very small manufacturers in Nairobi', in M. Schatzberg (ed.) The Political Economy of Kenya, New York: Praeger.

O'Higgins, M. (1981) 'Tax evasion and the self-employed', British Tax Review, 26: 367–78.

ODPM (2000) Index of Multiple Deprivation, London: Office of the Deputy Prime Minister.

OECD (2000a) Reducing the Risk of Policy Failure: Challenges for regulatory compliance, Paris: OECD.

———(2000b) Tax Avoidance and Evasion, Paris: OECD.

———(2002) Measuring the Non-Observed Economy, Paris: OECD.

Pahl, R. E. (1984) Divisions of Labour, Oxford: Blackwell.

Pedersen, S. (2003) The Shadow Economy in Germany, Great Britain and Scandinavia: A measurement based on questionnaire surveys, Copenhagen: The Rockwool Foundation Research Unit.

Portes, A. (1994) 'The informal economy and its paradoxes', in N. J. Smelser and R. Swedberg (eds) The Handbook of Economic Sociology, Princeton: Princeton University Press.

Rakowski, C. (1994) 'The informal sector debate, Part II: 1984–1993', in C. A. Rakowski (ed.) Contrapunto: The informal sector debate in Latin America, Albany: State University of New York Press.

Renooy, P., Ivarsson, S., van der Wusten-Gritsai, O. and Meijer, R. (2004) Undeclared Work in an Enlarged Union: An analysis of shadow work. An in-depth study of specific items, Brussels: European Commission.

Reynolds, P., Bygrave, W. D., Autio, E. and Hay, M. (2002) Global Entrepreneurship Monitor: 2002 Executive Monitor, London: London Business School.

Schneider, F. and Enste, D. H. (2000) 'Shadow economies; size, causes and consequences', Journal of Economic Literature, 38(1): 77–114.

Small Business Council (2004) Small Business in the Informal Economy: Making the transition to the formal economy, London: Small Business Council.

Small Business Service (2006) Small Business Survey, 2005, Sheffield: Small Business Service.

Snyder, K. A. (2004) 'Routes to the informal economy in New York's East Village: crisis, economics and identity', Sociological Perspectives, 47(2): 215–40.

Thomas, J. J. (1992) Informal Economic Activity, Hemel Hempstead: Harvester Wheatsheaf.

Williams, C. C. (2004) Cash-in-Hand Work: The underground sector and the hidden economy of favours, Basingstoke: Palgrave Macmillan.

———(2006) The Hidden Enterprise Culture: Entrepreneurship in the underground economy, Cheltenham: Edward Elgar.

Williams, C. C. and Windebank, J. (1998) Informal Employment in the Advanced Economies: Implications for work and welfare, London: Routledge.

11 Locating Enterprise and Placing Wealth

Entrepreneurship and Place-Based Enterprises in Depleted Communities

Doug Lionais

INTRODUCTION

The region continues to be of central importance for both economic and social development studies and policy (Pike 2007). The region is conceptualised as being the location of, among other things, entrepreneurial competitive advantage (Keeble 1997, Audretsch and Keilbach 2004) and deprivation and socio-economic exclusion (Miles and Tully 2007). This chapter examines the role of business enterprise in a particular type of region—the depleted community—in which we find localized concentrations of economic exclusion. Depleted communities are areas where, despite economic decline, people remain attached to the community.

Within depleted communities, enterprise is often proposed as a way out of depletion. There are at least two approaches in which enterprise is proposed to address depletion. In the first approach, the establishment of high growth enterprises is a way for underperforming regions to develop clusters of innovative technology-based firms. This approach is an attempt to mimic successful regions in the new global economy, thus the numerous forms of Silicon Island/Glen/Fen and so on trying to replicate the success of Silicon Valley (Hospers and Benneworth 2005). The second approach seeks to establish social enterprises that are specifically organised to involve deprived and excluded populations. This approach is evident in the rise of the social economy or the third sector (Borzaga and Defourny 2001a, Haugh and Kitson 2007).

Each approach, however, has its inherent contradictions. The high growth enterprise approach finds its roots in Birch's (1987) study of job creation in America. Birch found that the majority of new jobs in the economy were created not by the large industrial employers but by small and medium-sized business. New business starts, fast growing gazelles in particular, became an important target for regional development policy, thus the attempts to replicate exemplary regions of the new economy such as Silicon Island. Although the development of such an exemplary region is based on a complex array of historically and spatially contingent factors (Saxenian 1994, Kenney 2000), many regions attempted to wholly re-create its success by focusing on only a few of the identified characteristics of such regional systems (Feldman et al. 2005). Incentives such as venture capital funding, university links and social networks of the type associated with dynamic cluster economies were unfurled to attract entrepreneurial firms and to encourage start-ups. The contradiction is that these policies attempt to attract entrepreneurs to economic environments quite unlike those found in successful regions. Successful regions have excelled because they relate strongly to growth mechanisms that are dominant in the current economy (Hudson 2001). High growth, high technology firms are unlikely to locate in depleted communities that, by definition, lack an institutional constitution that relates to economic growth mechanisms.

The social economy approach has its own contradictions. The social economy re-emerged in the 1980s as a response to widening economic divergence in Western societies. The collapse of Fordism and the retrenchment of the welfare state left a vacuum in which an empowered third sector emerged as a provider of jobs and welfare. Social enterprises play a specific role within a social economy comprised of a various non-profit organisations. Social enterprises are proposed as entities that can address depletion and exclusion by involving those who are excluded in the production process. Beyond using excluded groups in their operation, social enterprises are also expected to use democratic processes, build social capital and remain self-sufficient by using the market mechanism. The commitment of social enterprises to meeting the social needs of its clients, however, presents a contradiction. The social obligations of social enterprise require investments in time and money which detract from its ability to remain financially sustainable (Amin et al. 2002). Social enterprises are designed to compensate for market failures yet they are expected to be profitable by selling their products on the market. As a result, most social enterprises never achieve self-sustainability; instead they remain dependent on government or other support. The potential for social enterprises that are themselves dependent on wealth redistribution to transform depleted communities is questionable.

In both of these cases, there is a contradiction between the organisational form (profitable and sustainable business enterprise) and the context of operation (depleted communities). On the one hand is policy that suggests depleted regions need to remake themselves in the image of a high tech boomtown. This ignores the real gaps and obstacles to such development that exist in depleted communities. On the other hand is policy that suggests depleted communities can support only particular forms of social enterprise that focus on the unmet social needs of the locality. Location plays an important role in each of these cases and, yet, the relationship between enterprise and depleted communities is not always clear. This chapter will bring light to these issues.

The first section of this chapter examines the process of uneven development and the creation of depleted communities with particular attention to the implications of depletion for enterprise development. The second section explores the experience of high growth firms that choose to locate in depleted communities. In this section, the location decision process of the entrepreneurs and their assessment of their environment after starting operations are examined. In the third section, the experience of place-based businesses is examined. The place-based business is a form of social enterprise that grounds wealth creation in specific, strategically selected places. In this section, the focus is on the relationship between structure and place in place-based business. Finally, the last section compares the experience of the two types of firms and their relationship to the depleted community, probing the connection between both forms of enterprise and deprivation and exclusion.

UNEVEN DEVELOPMENT, DEPLETED COMMUNITIES AND ENTERPRISE

Uneven development is the defining spatial characteristic of capitalism (Smith 1990). It is the outcome of inherent contradictions and processes within capitalism. At its root, uneven development is the product of concentrations of capital; capital centralizes through processes of accumulation and investment into productive capital in particular spaces that are considered to possess economic advantage. Centralization of capital, however, creates crisis by inflating costs and lowering profitability. Capital can find solutions to these crises by shifting idle capital out of production in its current form and delegating it to new uses (Harvey 1982). Capital can seek a spatial fix by investing in new productive spaces (where labour is cheaper for instance) and by selling to new markets. Capital can also seek a technological fix by investing in new, productive machinery and research and development. New productive processes and investments, however, will also entail new location logics. Thus a technological fix inevitably leads to a new spatial outcome.

Uneven development, through technological and spatial fixes, is a process of investment and devaluation (Smith 1990). Investment into a location as a space of production and consumption can create growth and profitability for capital. However, as profitability decreases, capital devalues its investment by moving capital to new spaces. Devaluing a location prepares it, given time, for new rounds of investment as the structures and institutions which lead to declining profits are destroyed. Uneven development, therefore, is not only a description of diverse development rates for different regions but also includes the active destruction of places and the cultures and social relationships embedded in them.

Contrarily, capital investment is also involved in the making of place. Capital investment in locations of production attracts labour and develops new locally embedded economic and social relationships. What type of investments are made in what kinds of locations depends to a large extent on the historical context of particular locations and their role in the spatial division of labour (Massey 1995). As populations embed themselves in productive locations, they make alternative demands on space. Society invests in space for the purposes of creating social rather than productive value. Thus processes of place production where people assign social meaning and build social relationships around particular locations often follows from capital investment in locations as spaces for profitable production (Hudson 2001). A 'sense of place' can emerge as people develop attachments to place and both imbue their places with identities and form identities in relation to them. Thus, places can become locations of high social value as well as high economic value.

The process of uneven development has both economic and social impacts. The strength of the social value people attach to place creates different impacts when the see-saw of uneven development tilts to devaluation. Figure 11.1 demonstrates a simplified model of the types of places that emerge given different levels of valuation by capital and society. Dynamic places (upper right quadrant) emerge when location is valued highly as both a profitable space and as meaningful social space. Such places tend to have histories spanning generations where the social relationships have developed to construct strong identities of community. Dynamic places have also been able to continuously re-invent themselves as attractive places for both capital and people.

Alternatively, some spaces are highly valued as locations of capital accumulation but do not have high values of social meaning (upper left quadrant). New industrial sites, such as mining and resources towns, are typical of this type. Places such as these have not developed strong identities and social meanings. They tend to have limited demographic profiles (mainly working-age males) and their populations are contingent upon the economic value found in the location. For instance, in mining towns in the Canadian north there is a direct correlation between the price of the mineral being mined and the population of the town. When the prices are down

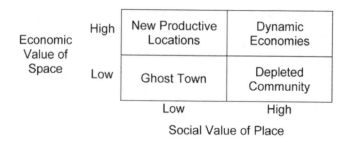

Figure 11.1   Typologies of economic and social space.

and labour is not required, unemployed persons leave because there is no social attachment to place. Fort McMurray in Alberta, Canada, fuelled by the Tar Sands development, is the premiere destination of this type in the country. Large populations of young males from across Canada are attracted by the high salaries to work the oil patch. They rarely establish themselves permanently; rather, they fly back and forth for periods ranging from a few months to a few years (Stewart 2008).

When such places lose their economic viability, the workers move on to new locations of capital accumulation or return 'home' to the places where they find social meaning. When this happens, these frontier towns are deserted and become ghost towns (lower left quadrant). The lack of social meaning provides little purpose to remain in the face of economic devaluation. In this quadrant we may also find places where people remain not out of choice but due to an inability to move out of the location. Economic hardship may create structural inertia for residents who cannot mobilise what few economic assets they have. Such places may actually attract those who are excluded from the mainstream economy because they offer affordable spaces for living for those on the economic margins and provide the potential for a sense of community based on common experiences of exclusion. Vancouver's infamous downtown eastside represents such a community for some (Taylor 2003).

Finally, in the lower right quadrant, we find places that maintain high valuations as social places; these are locations with a strong sense of place, place identity and place attachment. Yet these places have been abandoned by private capital; they no longer provide profitable spaces for capital accumulation. These spaces are *depleted communities*, places to which people remain attached despite the economic signals to leave. With a strong sense of place informing personal identity, there is reluctance to sever such ties to location. That is, while economically depleted, these areas retain strong social bonds between people and between people and place. Furthermore, the value in these social bonds can offset problems associated with economic decline and marginalization.

Table 11.1 suggests that the long-term success of a place is dependent upon both economic valuations of space as well as social valuations of place. Social relations, reciprocity and community found in strong social places can, at least in the short term, act as an alternative support system for people in their places. In the long term, however, depleted communities require some sort of economic regeneration in order to sustain themselves. In the absence of effective regeneration, depleted communities develop a whole host of social problems including unemployment, poverty, crime and social tension. Economic exclusion takes its toll on the community. Over time, the community becomes less and less capable of developing productive growth mechanisms on its own.

Regeneration in depleted communities is a difficult and complex task for multiple reasons. First, no two regions are alike. The potential for

regeneration is dependent on, among other things, the extent of the depletion the community faces, the strength of the social ties within the community and the quality of local leadership. There are questions of both
capacity and willingness at a community level. Furthermore, regions do
not independently control all of the factors of development. Regions are
embedded in a global system of capital production. Although regions have
a degree of agency in their economic development, the ability of regions to
grasp the opportunities of the broader system depends on how the local
socio-economic system aligns itself with the organisation of specific production processes and networks (Lagendijk et al. 2000, Henderson et al.
2002). Peripheral regions hold a tenuous position within the production
system and 'may be endangered if they are unable to secure and hold down
a place in circuits of value creation, circulation and appropriation' (Hudson
2002: 263). It is doubtful that regions that play a role of routine production rather than knowledge production can build the capacity to become a
sustainable region in the global system. A part of the problem here is identified by Smith (1990) in that the see-saw movement of capital is much less
evident at the national and global scale. Regions waiting for the see-saw to
tip back in their direction, or trying to tip it that way, face a balance that is
heavily weighted towards urban agglomerations. Deindustrialised regions
in particular are faced with a predicament. Such regions often cannot, or
are unwilling to, compete on 'weak' competitive factors, such as low wages,
nor on 'strong' factors, such as knowledge production (Hudson 2002).

In short, depleted communities that have not found a role in the new
economy face significant obstacles to development. Using conventional
thinking, we would not expect businesses to locate in depleted communities except to exploit cheap resources and labour. To others (see Spear et
al. 2001), however, the concentration of excluded individuals in depleted
communities suggests the need for specific forms of social enterprise to deal
explicitly with these groups. Depleted communities are locations where,
under one set of logic, despite the enterprise approach to development, we
would not expect to see any entrepreneurial firms locate and under another
set of logic, we expect to see particular types of social firms establish themselves to meet the need of the poor and the excluded. Under either approach
the context of the location is expected to have a strong influence on the
firms that do locate in depleted communities. In the following two sections
I look at the relationship between enterprise and the depleted community.

LOCATING HIGH GROWTH ENTERPRISES

Despite the obstacles for entrepreneurial development found in depleted
communities, entrepreneurial approaches are still promoted as means for
local communities to gain a foothold in the global economy. Since the work
of Birch (1987), the small business sector has been understood to be the

main engine of job creation and economic growth. Peripheral regions suffer from the lowest start-up rates (Mason 1991). Low firm start-up rates in the periphery are understood to be due to a lack of the appropriate mix of factors that promote the level of entrepreneurship seen in successful regions (Malecki 1997). Benneworth (2004) argues that such a factor approach, based on exemplar regions (the Silicon Valleys), is not able to recognize factors that lead to entrepreneurial process in the periphery. That is, it is not that entrepreneurship is neither impossible nor non-existent in the periphery but that current entrepreneurial and location theories have not paid sufficient attention to the periphery and the particular forms of entrepreneurship that emerge there. On the contrary, depleted communities are regional contexts to which entrepreneurship can adapt through innovative processes (Johnstone and Lionais 2004). The very qualities of the periphery, Benneworth concludes, can be the basis for emergent entrepreneurial cultures. In this section I explore how the entrepreneurial process unfolds within the context of the depleted community. The location choice of entrepreneurs is used to gain an understanding of how location and enterprise are related.

Traditional location theory is based on a production function analysis of location in terms of minimizing input and output costs (McCann and Sheppard 2003). Under this theory, firms would locate in the most advantageous locations for profitability. Traditional location theory, however, assumes a static economy with known input and output costs. Dynamic markets, limited knowledge and entrepreneurial processes of 'creative destruction' (Schumpeter 1942) do not easily fit into classical location theory.

More contemporary theories of firm location stress the importance of clusters (Porter 1990) and agglomerations (Amin and Thrift 1992). Under this concept, firms will locate near other firms with similar technological specializations in order to take advantage of knowledge spill-overs. Clusters of inter-related firms share resources and untraded interdependencies (Storper 1995). The close interaction and sharing of knowledge in clusters in turn drives innovation and makes clusters fertile ground for new start-ups. Within clusters, localised social networks are valued as mechanisms of knowledge transfer, including information leading to opportunity identification for new entrepreneurs (Sorenson 2003).

Under either approach, there is little hope for depleted communities unless they can lower their cost factors or increase the quality of their knowledge networks. Depleted communities are neither places with strong entrepreneurial cultures nor are they locations in which external entrepreneurs would see locating as advantageous. Thus, given the obstacles to development that exist in depleted communities, traditional forms of entrepreneurship would not be likely (Johnstone and Lionais 2004).

Entrepreneurial decision making, however, is influenced by a broad range of internal and external factors and not solely based on economic advantage. Location theories assume that the goal of enterprise is to maximize profit. Entrepreneurship researchers, however, have long demonstrated that entrepreneurs are less motivated by economic return than they are by other factors, such as need for independence and need for personal development (Scheinberg and MacMillan 1988, Birley and Westhead 1994). Given this understanding of entrepreneurship, Stam (2007) calls for a more evolutionary approach to location theory, one that recognises the human agency involved in the decision process. According to Stam, all entrepreneurial decisions are shaped by both personal preferences and external opportunities and incentives. In other words, entrepreneurial decision making is socially embedded (Granovetter 1985, 1995) and includes both economic and non-economic factors. Personal and non-financial motivations apply to location decisions as well as initial decisions to engage in entrepreneurial activity. Galbraith and De Noble (1988), for instance, indicate that entrepreneurs, although not insensitive to the quality of the business environment, place high importance on ambience or personal lifestyle desires when making location decisions.

While endogenous entrepreneurship in depleted communities is not likely, it is not completely absent either. Entrepreneurs may make a personal choice to locate in a 'poor' business environment. This was the basis of a study conducted in 2007 on entrepreneurs in a Cape Breton, Canada. Cape Breton has experienced a collapse of its traditional industries in coal mining, steel making, fishing and forestry. Despite the economic decline, Cape Breton maintains a strong sense of place and identity and its populace displays strong place attachment. Therefore, Cape Breton exemplifies the definition of depleted community (Johnstone and Lionais 2004). The 2007 study examined the factors that went into the location choice of locally based innovative firms. The firms in this study were controlled to include firms that targeted external markets and to exclude firms dependent on local natural resources. Thus the entrepreneurs in the study had no 'natural' reason to locate in the community and would have had to make a conscious choice in determining that Cape Breton is where they would choose to locate their business.

In the study, the entrepreneurs were asked to rank a list of 31 factors in terms of their importance for selecting the local community for their business location. The list of business location factors were adopted from Karakaya and Canel's (1998) study on business location decisions of fast growing firms in New England and New York. In addition to the factors used by Karakaya and Canel, several factors relating to quality of life were added: proximity to extended family members, proximity to an area of natural beauty, personal attachment to local culture/heritage and safe area to raise children. The mean score for the top 10 rated factors is reported in Table 11.1.

Three of the top 5 and 4 of the top 10 factors for choosing to locate in Cape Breton were related to quality of life rather than business cost factors. Places that provided a safe area for families, proximity to extended family, cultural ties and natural beauty ranked high for these entrepreneurs. In other words, personal factors rather than business-related factors were the most

Table 11.1   Average rating of business location factors *(0 = not important, 1= important, 2=very important, 3=extremely important)*

Rank	Business Location Factor	Mean Score
1	Safe area to raise children	1.71
2	Availability of skilled labour	1.61
3	Proximity to extended family members	1.59
4	Personal attachment to local culture/heritage	1.59
5	Local investment incentives	1.56
6	Proximity to an area of natural beauty	1.53
7	Availability of capital financing	1.50
8	Transportation facilities	1.39
9	Availability of local airport	1.33
10	Availability of low cost labour	1.33

important concerns for these entrepreneurs operating in a depleted community. Proximity to an extended family and cultural ties serve to anchor the entrepreneurial process because of the local connections of the entrepreneur.

When all 31 factors measured were grouped into categories we see confirmation of this finding. Figure 11.2 demonstrates the average scores of each category of factors. Quality of life ranks highest of all location decision factors.

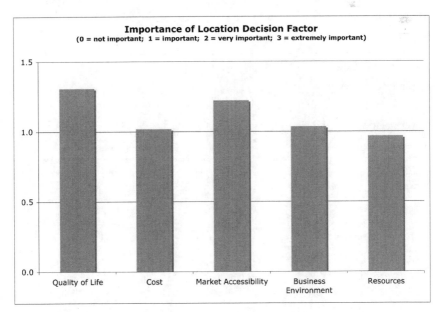

Figure 11.2   Average rating of business location factors—grouped.

While Figure 11.2 shows that quality of life factors rank highest for entrepreneurs located in a depleted community, economic factors are also important. Market accessibility ranked high. This is important as the firms in the study targeted external markets. Thus there is a degree to how distant they could be to their markets.

Once located, enterprise must deal with the environment in which it is situated. The local context can assist or obstruct a firm's growth. The firms within the study were asked to identify the main obstacles and advantages for growth that were particular to the local area. Tables 11.2a and 11.2b summarise the most common obstacles and advantages respectively.

In terms of obstacles to business growth in depleted communities, these firms identify 'distance to market' as a main concern. This suggests that while accessibility was a significant factor for selecting location, firms in Cape Breton still feel distant from their markets. The ability to attract high skilled labour to the area and the lack of leadership from government were also seen as major impediments to growth.

One purpose of the study was to identify whether entrepreneurial firms in depleted communities used factors of 'depletion' or factors of 'community' to cope with the economic context in which they located. The responses in Tables 11.2a and 11.2b above show that both are determinants. Community support is cited as the most common advantage for business growth. Quality of life also ranks high as a factor that promotes growth. Both of these components can be associated with sense of place and social institutions embedded in the locality. On the other hand, low employee turnover

Table 11.2a   Obstacles to business growth (percentage of firms)

Obstacle	%
Proximity to Market	38.9%
Human Resources	33.3%
Local Attitudes and Culture	33.3%
Government Policy and Operations	33.3%
Access to Financing	27.8%

Table 11.2b   Advantages for business growth (percentage of firms)

Advantage	%
Community Support	33.3%
Employee Turnover	27.8%
Quality of Life	27.8%
Cost of Labour and Operations	22.2%

and low cost of labour and operations were also cited as strong advantages of the local area. These factors can be attributed to the depleted nature of the economy, which keeps prices low and employees with few other options for movement. Thus, firms use both factors of depletion and community to cope with the obstacles associated with operating in a depleted economy.

The study reported above considers one particular depleted community using a relatively small group of firms. Therefore, there are limits to how much this particular experience can be generalised. Given that limitation, however, there are three conclusions that we can draw from this analysis. First is that entrepreneurial location in this depleted community is based on assets of 'community'. It seems reasonable to expect the same of other depleted communities. Entrepreneurs who choose to locate in depleted communities likely do so because of the quality of life and sense of place attachment associated with the community. Many of the entrepreneurs in the study above were expatriate Cape Bretoners, who had developed their skills and ideas elsewhere and then returned 'home' to form their enterprise. Thus personal motivations rooted in meaningful social relationships rather than rational business criteria dominated location decision factors. Modern understandings of economic activities are typically stripped of non-economic relations; the economy isolated as its own sphere of purely market logic. This study demonstrates otherwise. The social connection between the entrepreneur and the community represents a social purpose for these enterprises.

Second, despite the 'community' basis for entrepreneurial location decisions in depleted communities, what allows entrepreneurial firms to exist in such locations has as much to do with depletion as it does community. In particular, enterprises in this study relied on the low cost of labour, low employee turnover (due to lack of competing employment opportunities) and low cost of operations to offset disadvantages of the location, such as distance to markets and the availability of skilled labour. The growth that these firms were experiencing was as much a component of being located in a weak economy as it was a product of community.

Furthermore, the third conclusion that can be drawn is that a strong local community can hinder the growth of entrepreneurial firms as well as help it. Community attitudes and culture were cited as obstacles to development in these cases. Common complaints reported by entrepreneurs were: expectations of failure; lack of innovative thinking; and distrust of entrepreneurs. These sentiments within the community are related to the working class culture and its traditional distrust of business. In part, this is due to the historical role of the community as a location of blue-collar work. Resistance to entrepreneurial activity can thus be a significant part of the social composition of depleted communities.

Finally, the relationship between high growth entrepreneurial businesses and local groups of excluded and deprived individuals is indirect at best. Although entrepreneurs choosing to locate in depleted communities may be doing so for social reasons, the motivation is usually personal. The purpose is to maintain a personal quality of life and live within a desired familial and cultural setting, rather than as a means to help develop the community or serve a particular group of excluded individuals. As a consequence, there is no explicit connection between the firms and those suffering from the disadvantages of depletion. Entrepreneurial firms provide employment in areas where opportunities for employment are lacking, but there is no evidence in this study that firms wish to target specific groups of excluded individuals to bring into the firm. Blackburn and Ram (2006) examine the limitations entrepreneurial firms have in addressing social exclusion. They conclude that social exclusion is a multifaceted concept with complex social and individual causes and, in such a context, entrepreneurial development may have an effect on those on the cusp of marginality but it is unlikely to impact those who are most excluded in society. Furthermore, Blackburn and Ram question whether enterprises are the most appropriate organisational form for delivering social inclusion policy. All of these findings are reflected in this case. It is difficult to understand how entrepreneurial firms operating in depleted economic contexts can also take on the responsibility of social inclusion and remain competitive. Rather, these firms have an indirect effect on exclusion by altering, in whatever modest way, the economic and cultural make-up of the community. That is, they contribute to a more vibrant economy, provide employment and contribute to creating an entrepreneurial culture (Benneworth 2004, Berglund and Johansson 2007). Locating enterprises in a depleted community demonstrates the potential for alternate business purposes and the development in such places. It suggests that a different future is possible.

PLACING WEALTH IN THE SOCIAL ECONOMY

An alternative to the high growth entrepreneurial approach to regenerating depleted communities is the social economy approach. The social economy is an emerging phenomenon of related socio-economic activities that address social and economic inequalities. Moulaert and Ailenei (2005) argue that interest in the social economy rises with crises in society. The current interest in the social economy is a response to the increasing dominance of neo-liberal policy and the retrenchment of the welfare state. This has led to dual problems of increasing economic divergence and the reduction of public support for the excluded.

The social economy has become a favoured policy for regenerating depleted communities (Neamtan and Downing 2005). This has come from two directions. Not only is the social economy a grassroots movement of development, but it is also used by the state to devolve responsibility for development to the regions (Amin et al. 2002). Regions that are unable to ground mechanisms of growth in the mainstream economy are offered the social economy as an alternate means to development.

As the social economy has gained prominence and continues to be promoted as a panacea for lagging regions, it has also attracted more critical analysis. Amin et al. (2002, 2003) have asked whether or not the social economy can deliver on its promises. Those promises include: meeting the needs of the excluded, increasing civic engagement, pursuing social justice and supporting a counter-culture of needs-based economics. Beyond these expectations, the social economy is also expected to be self-reliant and sustainable. In short, the social economy is expected to be an alternative to the mainstream economy. Instead, Amin et al. (2003) find that the social economy provides an alternative and impoverished form of welfare provision.

Bringing light to arguments Amin et al. use supports this conclusion because they are directly related to the potential impact that social enterprise may have on depleted communities. First is the ability of social enterprise to be self-sustaining. Amin et al. (2002) argue that the discourse of enterprise has been adopted by the social economy as a means to legitimate its activities. Yet very few social enterprises ever become self-sufficient because most are reliant on public funding to support their core operations. Hayton (2000) reports that many organisations adopt the rhetoric of enterprise in order to legitimise their activities and access targeted funding programs but that they never achieve self-sufficiency (nor intend to). Rather than becoming an alternative form of wealth creation, social enterprises engage in processes of wealth redistribution. The focus on meeting social needs such as deprivation and exclusion conflicts with the self-sustainability of social enterprise. The tension between social goals and profitability leads to processes of isomorphism (Laville and Nyssens 2001), and most organisations remain dependent on outside support.

The second argument is the role of geography and how it is understood in the social economy. Amin et al. (2003) argue that 'the local' is used uncritically in social economy debates; it is usually meant to refer to 'a small, definable territory and a homogenous resident population'. In this context, the social economy is a means for local, depleted communities to use their own resources to address their own distinct, territorial problems. The assumption in play here is that local problems are rooted in their own locality. As noted above, however, local depletion is an outcome of uneven development. Local depletion is as much a part of global economic forces as it is of local development. In contrast, the social economy has tended to treat the local as a bounded territory with complete agency in determining its own destiny. Amin et al. (2003) argue that such a localised social economy, where the term 'social' is associated with localized areas of poverty and exclusion, is not likely to result in a 'socialized economy' but rather to the establishment of a 'second class economy' that dwells on the peripheries of capitalism.

A more nuanced conception of locality understands places as relational entities that are defined by the numerous internal and external relationships that coalesce around particular places. Thus while location certainly plays a role in combating uneven development and the socio-economic problems it causes, social economic practices need not and, more prescriptively, *should* not be constrained by territory. Rather, the key process of economic development is the (re)building of relationships, both within and external to, the local. Social enterprise as a closing-in, a circling of the wagons around the community, blocks the potential for the community to build valuable connections outside itself and, in so doing, to engage in and ground global value chains within the local.

PLACE-BASED BUSINESS

The role of social enterprise in addressing the problems of a depleted community is therefore a complex one. There are tensions between the need to address social need and to create wealth. There are also tensions around ensuring that the enterprise is rooted in the community but that it does not limit itself to the community. While most social enterprises, on analysis, play a welfare replacement role, there are a few examples that provide more innovative models that address the concerns listed above. Two such models are the Mondragon Cooperative Corporation and New Dawn Enterprise, explored below. What differentiates these is that they shift the 'social' from meeting needs to grounding wealth creation in their community. That is, they use geography rather than social needs as their means of being social. These are examples of place-based business.

Place-based businesses are profit-oriented enterprises that are 'rooted' to particular places. For place-based business, profitability is instrumental for the achievement of the social goal. Wealth that is created is returned to the community; therefore, place-based businesses are a mechanism to combat uneven development. They ground circuits of value production in depleted communities. Focusing on wealth creation also suggests that place-based business can go beyond the local. Given the economic conditions within depleted communities, place-based businesses would be severely limited because they would be contained to the depleted community. Growth and profitability, in the long run, would require finding markets and supply chains from outside the community. Therefore place-based businesses would appear to address the two critiques of the social economy noted above: they create wealth and they are not limited by the local. Place-based businesses have a social purpose embedded in a productive business form. They differ from traditional business forms in that the social purpose is formalised with the socio-legal structure of the enterprise. Two examples follow.

Mondragon Cooperative Corporation

The Mondragon Cooperative Corporation (MCC) is a complex of worker cooperatives and related organisations headquartered in the Basque country of Spain. In 2008, the MCC had over 90,000 employees, €4.35 billion in sales and €33.5 billion in assets (MCC 2009). The MCC complex includes operations in industrial manufacturing, financial services, distribution and research, training and education. It operates 250 different business and support entities with branches in 12 countries worldwide. In a sector noted for its small firms and limited capacity (Borzaga and Defourny 2001b), the MCC stands out as a large, diverse and successful example of a social purpose enterprise.

The MCC began with a single stove factory in 1956 when an enterprising priest encouraged a group of engineering students to form their own company in the local area. At that time, the Basque country was suffering from the repercussions of the Second World War and the Spanish Civil War. Unemployment reached up to 50 per cent in Mondragon (Mathews 1999). The priest, Father José Arizmendiarrieta, believed that the only way to address the problems of social exclusion he saw around him was not through charity but through production. He preached that engaging people in employment and creating wealth was the best way to transform the community.

This foundational purpose of the organisation is embedded in its sociolegal structure. It is through this structure that the MCC establishes its social purpose and grounds itself within the community. Up until the 1980s, the Mondragon cooperatives were loosely affiliated through its bank, the Caja Laboral Popular. Between 1984 and 1995, a series of cooperative congress meetings led to the formation of the MCC as a coordinating body for the cooperatives and the establishment of the regulations and principles of the organisation (MCC 2001). Each member company must agree to abide by the MCC's regulations and principles by signing a contract of association. The basic principles of Mondragon include:

1. Open membership
2. Democratic organisation
3. Worker sovereignty
4. Instrumental or subordinate nature of capital
5. Participation in management
6. Wage solidarity
7. Cooperation between cooperatives
8. Social transformation
9. Universal nature
10. Education

Local commitment is built into the principle of social transformation. For the MCC, social transformation means building a 'freer and more just society' (MCC 2001). It achieves this goal through 'reinvesting the majority of its profits, supporting community development initiatives, co-operating with other Basque social and economic institutions and promoting local culture and a social security policy based on solidarity and responsibility' (MCC 2001: 37). This principle ideologically identifies Mondragon as a community-based organisation. The MCC's rooting in the Basque community is further articulated in the mission statement where it is identified as a business with 'deep cultural roots in the Basque Country' (MCC 2001: 37).

MCC's contract of association also sets out how a cooperative can distribute its surpluses. The MCC is rooted to the local community through its profit distribution system. The 'Congress Regulations' stipulate how member firms must distribute their profits (MCC 2003). A minimum of 10 per cent goes to an educational and cultural fund, a minimum of 20 per cent is delegated to a cooperative reserve fund and a maximum of 70 per cent is returned to the worker-members' accounts. The reserve fund ends up on the equity side of the balance sheet. The proportion of equity in the reserves, though fluctuating year to year, accounts for approximately half of the equity in the MCC. The reserve fund serves to anchor the cooperative in the Basque community. The fund is used to pursue the purpose of the organisation and represents the community's stake in the organisation.

The MCC is an example of business enterprise used as a tool to address the depletion of the community. While exclusion and deprivation were acute problems in the region at the time the cooperatives began, the route to transformation was based on sound business principles and interaction (trading) between the region and the wider context. The transformation from depletion to success in the Basque region, and particularly in the smaller towns and villages where MCC operates, is a result of this focus on producing wealth rather than addressing social need directly. That is, MCC addresses the causes rather than the roots of depletion (Lionais and Johnstone 2009).

New Dawn Enterprises

New Dawn Enterprises is a community business corporation located in Cape Breton, Canada. It currently has assets of over $12 million (Canadian) and over 150 employees. New Dawn primarily operates in service industries such as housing, health care, real estate and vocational training. Started in 1976 by a group led by community business entrepreneur, Greg MacLeod, New Dawn was a response to the economic depletion the community was experiencing (Johnstone and Lionais 2004).

Like MCC, New Dawn's social purposes and grounding are formalised in its legal structure. New Dawn's purposes are formalised through the Memorandum of Association. The primary purpose of New Dawn established in the memorandum of association is to 'promote and establish ventures that contribute to the creation of a self-supporting community'. The community is formally identified as Cape Breton. The memorandum also ensures that the profits that the enterprise makes are directed towards this purpose. This is accomplished by ensuring that no individual can financially gain from the operation of the business or through its dissolution. For instance, clause 'c' of the memorandum ensures that any profits realized would be reinvested in the organization to further its purposes. Taken together, New Dawn's memorandum of association institutionalizes a social purpose and establishes the organisation as a place-based business.

New Dawn has had less of a transformative impact on its community than the MCC has. In fact, its impact has been fairly modest. Yet, the model remains interesting in that it demonstrates the potential for a different approach to business; one that is rooted to particular places. In the New Dawn model, all of the surplus is reinvested back into the firm. The result is a maximum capitalization of profits and potential future growth within the community; the firm becomes a way to capture circuits of capital.

As this section shows, several differences can be drawn out between place-based business and traditional social enterprise. First, compared to traditional social enterprise, the place-based business has a different relationship with the community. Social enterprise typically serves existing social needs of marginalised populations. By definition, the markets that social enterprise serve are market failures. The need arises because private capital has not found a way to profitably serve the need. Social enterprise intervenes to serve the need in the absence of any other actor, historically the nation state. This raises questions concerning whether the social economy can serve these needs effectively and be self-sustaining or profitable.

Place-based business, on the other hand, focuses on wealth creation. MCC, for instance, operates in highly competitive and complex markets. New Dawn has tended to focus on local services but must compete with private firms within that market. In some senses, the products or services offered by place-based business are incidental; the purpose is to serve the community by creating wealth. Wealth creation and accumulation serves a social purpose by creating employment and generating more capacity within the community.

Second, wealth created by place based business is rooted through its legal structure. Both New Dawn and the MCC use the legal structure to spell out their social purpose (local development) and to ensure that wealth is locked into the community. Thus place-based businesses are formally rooted into the community rather than casually; they are place-based in the sense that they are immovable. This is different to the entrepreneurial firms examined in the previous section. Entrepreneurial firms are not formally tied to the community, as place-based firms are.

Third, place-based enterprises differ in their relationship with excluded and deprived populations. The place-based businesses outlined here operate very much like the private sector firms discussed earlier. They do not attempt to address existing social needs. Rather, they deal with the causes of geographically concentrated exclusion and inequality. Place-based business addresses inequality in the sense that it attempts to rebalance the forces of uneven development and create economic activity where it is lacking.

Place-based business grounds wealth-creating mechanisms in communities where they are lacking. In this way, they address the causes of depletion and exclusion rather than the symptoms.

CONCLUSIONS

Enterprise development and the social economy continue to be proposed as regeneration strategies for depleted communities. Yet the promise each holds is very different. High growth entrepreneurship emphasizes interaction in competitive global markets based on high tech innovations. The vision for the community is idealized as a Silicon Valley-esque mixture of dynamic firms and an expanding creative class (Florida 2002). The social economy, on the other hand, emphasizes local markets based on need. The vision for the social economy is idealised as localised communities of care and self-help based on small-scale service industries rooted to sensitivities of social justice, culture and tradition.

Both approaches have their associated problems, particularly in the context of the depleted community. Enterprise development approaches suffer from a host of problems related to fragmented activities and a factor-based approach (Lichtenstein et al. 2004). As a result, incentives based on analysis of strong entrepreneurial regions get applied to peripheral regions in equal fashion. Entrepreneurship and enterprise development is generalised as a uniform process. Lacking in this approach is an appreciation for the role of geography and local context in the entrepreneurial process. The local is absent in this approach. In contrast, the social economy is overly focused on the local. Providing for local needs traps the social economy in a wealth redistribution role. Rather than building the capacity of the region, this form of social economy sets depleted communities on a path of dependency. The role of geography is again underemphasised in this approach. The role of the community within greater economic structures is ignored.

In contrast, the approach taken here is to explore the relationship between the local, the enterprise and the wider global context. The depleted community, I argue, has an impact on the forms of enterprise operating within that context. In the cases examined here, both entrepreneurial firms and place-based firms are embedded in the local community. They are embedded prior to start-up, the local community playing an important role in the start-up decisions of the enterprises. In both cases, the social aspects of the local community motivated the location choice, as a place holding an attractive quality of life for the entrepreneurs and as a place in which enterprise was seen as a means of sustaining a meaningful community for place-based business.

The ways in which these firms are embedded in the community and the community in them, alters the ways in which they act. Although the enterprise forms explored above come from two very different conceptual worlds—the profit-driven entrepreneurial firm and the needs-based social enterprise—they are more alike than dissimilar. The high growth firms for instance, through their entrepreneurs, pursue a quality of life based in a peripheral depleted community distant from the creative cities they are expected to be attracted to. There are more social factors in the entrepreneur's decision process than seen elsewhere. The place-based businesses have the opposite movement. While they are based on a community purpose, the enterprises here use a profit-oriented approach that is much different to typical social enterprises. In both cases the firms locate for social purposes but operate as wealth generators.

The similarities between these forms of enterprise suggest that the context of the depleted community has an important role in determining the characteristics of enterprises that emerge in such places. Yet again we find that geography matters (Massey 1984) and that the economy is enacted in different ways in different places. In this case, the experience of both types of firm suggests that development in depleted communities builds on the strength of the community. In both cases, successful development depended on the degree to which people were willing to insert place attachment into enterprising activity. Communities where there are strong senses of place can leverage those social values into economic value through local enterprise. From a policy perspective, this suggests that depleted communities seeking to develop their economies can build on place attachment as well as providing more traditional incentives for enterprise development. Quality of life and strength of community can be the basis for starting and attracting entrepreneurial activity.

Furthermore, the findings here suggest that enterprising activity is not necessarily profit-driven. Both types of enterprise examined above are socially motivated; driven by individual desires to be located within a particular community in the first case and by a social desire to improve the community as a whole in the latter. This is in contrast to mainstream conceptions of the firm, abstracted from the individuals involved, as a purely profit-seeking organization. The examples here demonstrate that social purpose organizations can exist in a multitude of forms, including entrepreneurial forms and socially driven corporations.

While social concerns are essential for these forms of enterprise, profitability or the creation of surplus remains central. There is, however, a distinction between profitability as means or as an end that is demonstrated by both examples. In both cases, to greater and lesser extents, profitability is instrumental rather than intrinsic. Producing surplus is a serious concern but profit maximisation is not necessarily so. Profit maximisation would in most cases lead to alternative location choices. Therefore, in these cases, the location of the business and the social value embedded in place is more important than profitability. Once the location decision is made, wealth creation and profitability are imperative for achieving organizational goals. That is, once located in the community, profitability becomes a means to achieve the social purpose of the enterprise. The difference between the two forms is that the social purpose of the entrepreneurial firms is individually formed and informally structured and the purpose of the place-based enterprise is socially formed and formally structured.

This brings us to the relationship between enterprise and exclusion. As noted above, neither approach directly addresses exclusion and deprivation. Neither case assumes the responsibility of caring for excluded populations. This is not to contend that wealth creating enterprises cannot have an impact on exclusion and deprivation; however, exclusion and depletion are symptoms of deeper processes of uneven development. Local patterns of exclusion and depletion are outcomes of a lack of value creating mechanisms in the community. Businesses, both entrepreneurial and place-based, can participate in creating and grounding circuits of value creation within a community. The impact on exclusion is in this sense more preventive than reactive. By creating more vibrant economies grounded within the locality, these firms counteract processes of depletion that lead to exclusion and deprivation.

Although business has a role to play in addressing the root causes of depletion, they are not appropriate organizational tools for dealing directly with existing deprivation and exclusion. Blackburn and Ram (2006), as already noted, demonstrated the limitations of entrepreneurship and small firms in combating exclusion. Addressing existing depletion is more properly the role of an advanced welfare system.

This leads to my final point. Business and enterprise certainly have a role in addressing social and economic inequality. In identifying that role, however, it may be more instructive to ask how inequality and exclusion are produced in the first place. As noted earlier, processes of uneven development are inherent in the capitalist system. Rather than looking at ways in which the provision of welfare can be colonized by market structures, perhaps it is better to find ways to run an economy that produces less need for welfare provision. A more equitable economy will need to produce wealth in ways that does not concomitantly produce greater inequality. Therefore business and enterprise do have a role.

Place-based businesses, as outlined above, are interesting examples that may be instructive in this regard. Place-based businesses are capable of significant wealth creation but also distribute that wealth in more equitable ways. As such these forms represent the potential not only for firms to play a role in particular forms of depleted communities but as examples of business organization that can be both successful and social. Given that the Basque country is now one of the fastest growing regions in Spain, the MCC demonstrates that principled social purpose organisation can be successful in a variety of socio-economic contexts. Developing similar forms of growth-oriented, social-purpose firms presents the potential for economic growth and equality and the possibility of an altered (social) economy.

BIBLIOGRAPHY

Amin, A., Cameron, A. and Hudson, R. (2002) Placing the Social Economy, London: Routledge.

———(2003) 'The alterity of the social economy', in A. Leyshon, R. Lee and C. C. Williams (eds) Alternative Economic Spaces, London: Sage.

Amin, A. and Thrift, N. (1992) 'Neo-Marshallian nodes in global networks', International Journal of Urban and Regional Research, 16(4): 571–87.

Audretsch, D. and Keilbach, M. (2004) 'Entrepreneurship capital and economic performance', Regional Studies, 38(8): 949–59.

Benneworth, P. (2004) 'In what sense "regional development"?: Entrepreneurship, underdevelopment and strong tradition in the periphery', Entrepreneurship and Regional Development, 16: 439–58.

Berglund, K. and Johansson, A. W. (2007) 'Entrepreneurship, discourses and conscientization in processes of regional development', Entrepreneurship and Regional Development, 19(6): 499–525.

Birch, D. (1987) Job Creation in America: How our smallest companies put the most people to work, New York: Free Press.

Birley, S. and Westhead, P. (1994) 'A taxonomy of business start-up reasons and their impact on firm growth and size', Journal of Business Venturing, 9: 7–31.

Blackburn, R. and Ram, M. (2006) 'Fix or fixation? The contribution and limitations of entrepreneurship and small firms to combating social exclusion', Entrepreneurship and Regional Development, 18: 73–89.

Borzaga, C. and Defourny, J. (eds) (2001a) The Emergence of Social Enterprise, London: Routledge.

———(2001b) 'Social enterprises in Europe: a diversity of initiatives and prospects', in C. Borzaga and J. Defourny (eds) The Emergence of Social Enterprise, London: Routledge.

Feldman, M. P., Francis, J. and Bercowitz, J. (2005) 'Creating a cluster while building a firm: entrepreneurs and the formation of industrial clusters', Regional Studies, 39: 129–41.

Florida, R. (2002) The Rise of the Creative Class: And how it's transforming work, leisure, community and everyday life, New York: Basic Books.

Galbraith, C., and De Noble, A.F. (1988) 'Location decisions by high technology firms: a comparison of firm size, industry type and institutional form', Entrepreneurship Theory and Practice, 13: 31–48.

Granovetter, M. (1985) 'Economic action and social structure: the problem of embeddedness', American Journal of Sociology, 91: 481–510.

———(1995) 'The economic sociology of firms and entrepreneurs', in A. Portes (ed.) The Economic Sociology of Immigration, New York: Russell Sage Foundation.

Harvey, D. (1982) The Limits to Capital, Oxford: Basil Blackwell.

Haugh, H. and Kitson, D. (2007) 'The Third Way and the third sector: New Labour's economic policy and the social economy', Cambridge Journal of Economics, 31(6): 973–94.

Hayton, K. (2000) 'Scottish community business: an idea that has had its day?', Policy and Politics, 28(2): 193–206.

Henderson, J., Dicken, P., Hess, M., Coe, N. and Yeung, H. W. C. (2002) 'Global production networks and the analysis of economic development', Review of International Political Economy, 9(3): 436–64.

Hospers, G.-J. and Benneworth, P. (2005) 'What type of regional policy for Europe? Theoretical reflections and policy lessons from Sardinia', Intereconomics, 40(6): 336–44.

Hudson, R. (2001) Producing Places, London: Guilford Press.

220   *Doug Lionais*

———(2002) 'Changing industrial production systems and regional development in the new Europe', Transactions of the Institute of British Geographers, 27: 262–81.

Johnstone, H. and Lionais, D. (2004) 'Depleted communities and community business entrepreneurship: revaluing space through place', Entrepreneurship and Regional Development, 16: 217–33.

Karakaya, F., and Canel, C. (1988) 'Underlying dimensions of business location decisions', Industrial Management and Data Systems, 98(7): 321–29.

Keeble, D. (1997) 'Small firms, innovation and regional development in Britain in the 1990s', Regional Studies, 31(3): 281–93.

Kenney, M. (ed.) (2000) Understanding Silicon Valley: Anatomy of an entrepreneurial region, Palo Alto: Stanford University Press.

Lagendijk, A., Giunta, A. and Pike, A. (2000) 'Introduction: scalar interdependencies between industry and territory', in A. Giunta, A. Lagendijk and A. Pike (eds) Restructuring Industry and Territory: The experience of Europe's regions, London: TSO.

Laville, J.-L. and M. Nyssens (2001) 'The social enterprise: towards a theoretical socio-economic approach', in C. Borzaga and J. Defourny (eds) The Emergence of Social Enterprise, London: Routledge.

Lichtenstein, G., Lyons, T. S. and Kutzhanova, N. (2004) 'Building entrepreneurial communities: the appropriate role of enterprise development activities, Journal of the Community Development Society, 35(1), 5–24.

Lionais, D. and Johnstone, H. (2009) 'Building the social economy using the innovative potential of place', in J. J. McMurtry (ed.) Living Economics, Toronto: Emond Montgomery.

Malecki, E. (1997) Technology and Economic Development, London: Longmans.

Mason, C. (1991) 'Spatial variations in enterprise: the geography of new firm formation', in R. Burrows (ed.) Deciphering the Enterprise Culture: Entrepreneurship, petty capitalism and the restructuring of Britain, London: Routledge.

Massey, D. (1984) 'Introduction: geography matters', in D. Massey and J. Allen (eds) Geography Matters!: A reader, Cambridge: Cambridge University Press.

———(1995) Spatial Divisions of Labour: Social structures and the geography of production, London: MacMillan.

Mathews, R. (1999) Jobs of Our Own: Building a stakeholder society, Sydney: Pluto Press.

MCC (2001) The History of an Experience, Mondragon: Mondragon Cooperative Corporation.

———(2003) Congress Regulations, Mondragon: Mondragon Cooperative Corporation.

———(2009) MCC 2008 Annual Report, Mondragon: Mondragon Cooperative Corporation.

McCann, P. and Sheppard, S. (2003) 'The rise, fall and rise again of industrial location theory', Regional Studies, 37(6/7): 649–63.

Miles, N, and Tully, J. (2007) 'Regional development agency policy to tackle economic exclusion? The role of social capital in distressed communities', Regional Studies, 41(6):855–66.

Moulaert, F. and Ailenei, O. (2005) 'Social economy, third sector and solidarity relations: a conceptual synthesis from history to present', Urban Studies, 42(11): 2037–53.

Neamtan, N. and Downing, R. (2005) Social Economy and CED in Canada: Next steps for public policy, Montreal: Chantier de l'économie sociale.

Pike, A. (2007) 'Editorial: whither regional studies?', Regional Studies, 41(9): 1143–8.

Porter, M. (1990) The Competitive Advantage of Nations, New York: Free Press.

Saxenian, A. (1994) Regional Advantage: Culture and competition in Silicon Valley and Route 128, Cambridge: Harvard University Press.

Scheinberg, S., and MacMillan, I. C. (1988) 'An 11-country study of motivations to start a business', in B. A. Kirchoff, W. A. Long, W. E McMullan, K. H. Vesper and W. E. Wetzel (eds) Frontiers of Entrepreneurship Research, Wellesley, MA: Babson College.

Schumpeter, J. A. (1942) Capitalism, Socialism, and Democracy, New York: Harper and Brothers.

Smith, N. (1990) Uneven Development: Nature, capital and the production of space, Oxford: Blackwell.

Sorenson, O. (2003) 'Social networks and industrial geography', Journal of Evolutionary Economics, 13: 513–27.

Spear, R., Defourny, J., Favreau, L. and Laville, J.-L. (eds) (2001) Tackling Social Exclusion in Europe. The contribution of the social economy, Aldershot: Ashgate.

Stam, E. (2007) 'Why butterflies don't leave: locational behavior of entrepreneurial firms', Economic Geography 83(1): 27–50.

Stewart, S. (2008) 'Why Cape Breton shakes in the echo of this distant boom', Globe and Mail, 29 January.

Storper, M. (1995) 'The resurgence of regional economies, 10 years later: the region as a nexus of untraded interdependencies', European Urban and Regional Studies, 2(3): 191–222.

Taylor, P. (ed.) (2003) The Heart of the Community: The best of the Carnegie Community Newsletter, Vancouver: New Star Books.

12 Discursive Chasms

An Examination of the Language and Promotion of Social Enterprise

Carole Howorth, Caroline Parkinson and Matthew MacDonald

INTRODUCTION

Social enterprises have been attracting widespread interest over the last decade, particularly as a 'solution' to social exclusion and a means of developing sustainable communities. In the UK, the encouragement of social enterprises is viewed as a central tenet of regional development strategies, especially in areas of deprivation. People running social enterprises are held up as vital to the economy, and a commitment to the development and growth of the social enterprise sector is being emphasised by policy makers at all levels. There has been a mushrooming of events, articles, books, journals, websites and specialist associations which reflect a growing interest in the social enterprise sector.

The way forward for social enterprises is couched in the language of business and enterprise. Pomerantz (2003: 26) expresses a widely held view in writing 'The key to social enterprise involves taking a business-like, innovative approach to the mission of delivering community services.' There appears to be an assumption that social enterprises will take on the existing business model. For example, 'Social enterprises must see themselves as businesses, seek to become more professional and continuously raise their standards of performance and their ambitions' (DTI 2002). And social enterprises are encouraged to be part of the mainstream economy: social enterprise should 'become part of the solution to reviving and strengthening local economies' but 'should not be seen as a side show to the real economy' (NWDA 2003). However, Parkinson and Howorth (2008) argue that the emphasis on replicating existing business models restricts the potential for social enterprises to develop new or innovative models that combine the best of 'social' and 'enterprise'.

The people who run social enterprises are often called 'social entrepreneurs', and there is an expectation that they will combine 'entrepreneurial flair with a commitment to giving something back to the community' (Michael 2006). Thus, there exists an interesting juxtaposition of business and entrepreneurship with commitment to a community and giving something back. This is our starting point and the focus of this chapter.

The activities currently labelled social entrepreneurship and social enterprise have been around for hundreds of years. However, the re-badging of social activity in terms of entrepreneurship and the current rhetoric used to promote the concept may neglect the ideological and political influences at its roots. Panepento (2007) notes that, in the US, the adoption of social enterprise by existing non-profit organisations not only alters service delivery models but can also lead to distraction from a charitable mission. The move towards social enterprise as a strategy can dramatically alter the relationship with beneficiaries, staff, funders, partners and society as a whole. Philips (2006) observes that social enterprises rely heavily on mission for recruiting staff, involving beneficiaries, establishing partnerships and engaging with wider society. The dilution of charitable purpose by the introduction of notions of enterprise could undermine trust in a charity (Paxton et al. 2005). Panepento's conclusion is that because of this, social enterprise may be eventually self-defeating.

The shift towards social enterprise and the changing values that underpin organisations are reflected in the language used. Discourses determine the production of power and knowledge and they set the boundaries of debate. Language itself can thus be a source of inclusion and exclusion. This chapter considers how the language of business and entrepreneurship is employed, and held up as being the way forward, for social enterprises. It explains how this provides the potential for discursive tension between policy makers, funders and support agencies, on the one hand, and the social enterprise organisations and individuals on the other; paradoxically for activities aimed at reducing social exclusion, it can lead to exclusion of those who do not buy in to the prevailing discourse. Of concern is that social entrepreneurs who feel most ill-at-ease with business language may well be those who have a higher commitment to social aims and often the greatest potential to make a difference.

The chapter explores the concepts and language that are central to people managing social enterprises and those working with and advising them, in order to understand whether the entrepreneurship paradigm prevails at the grassroots level of social enterprise. It is structured as follows. A brief historical review reveals that social enterprises have been around in deprived communities for hundreds of years. We show how the same activity has existed under different labels across time but that in recent years the enterprise discourse has dominated. A brief historical review starting in the seventeenth century reveals that the discursive shift from patriarchal discourses about reforming the deserving (as compared to an undeserving) poor to greater emphasis on community-led initiatives was couched in discourses of self-help and mutuality. In the section that follows, an understanding of the roots of social enterprise in deprived communities is shown to be important. It explains how discourse analysis has been employed in more recent years to analyse the language used and how it can highlight areas of potential tension and misunderstanding between social entrepreneurs, advisers, policy makers and others. The conclusion explains that by adopting a critical stance, we are able to understand better the effects and impact of particular policies and activities.

HOW HAS LANGUAGE AND ACTIVITY CHANGED OVER TIME?

MacDonald and Howorth's (2008) analysis across three hundred years discovered examples of all forms of social enterprise that are included in modern definitions; for example, work integration schemes, state service delivery under contract, micro-finance with social aims and fair trade. They trace the roots back to the seventeenth century in the UK, when, instead of traditional poor relief, wealthy people started to provide bequests and endowments for the setting up of particular institutions or for particularly defined groups of the poor. Jordan (1959) indicates that this quickly became a social norm and developed into what Owen (1965) terms 'associated philanthropy' as wealthy people began to pool their resources and set up associations to help the poor. MacDonald and Howorth (2008) suggest that it is within this tradition that the first quasi-social enterprises can be identified.

One such example is the organisation set up by Thomas Firmin (see Owen 1965), who was the head of a philanthropic association that provided the unemployed with raw materials for 'continuing their usual occupations', stockpiled corn and coal to be sold at cost at times of hardship and, by the 1670s, provided employment for 2,000 or so spinners, flax-dressers, weavers and others. In a similar spirit to current social enterprises, Firmin argued that profit was there merely to mitigate and make more efficient the input of charitable funds (Owen 1965: 19).

Much of the quasi-social enterprise activity in the seventeenth and eighteenth centuries was patriarchal and the language reflects a missionary zeal for 'improving' the lower classes. This can be seen in, for example, Thomas Bray's proposal for providing 'lewd women' with alternative employment and training.[1] There was still evidence of this in the nineteenth century; the first resolution of the Family Welfare Association of Manchester and Salford, established in 1833, stated that 'the condition of the working classes might be alleviated or removed . . . by affording them the encouragement derived from a more active manifestation of the sympathy of the wealthier classes, and the advantages of their advice' (Gaddum 1974: 5). One of many examples highlighting that welfare was secondary to improvement and reform is provided in the following aims: 'the encouragement of frugality and forethought, the suppression of mendacity and imposture, and the occasional relief of sickness and unavoidable misfortune' (Gaddum 1974: 5).

MacDonald and Howorth (2008) indicate that these first quasi-social enterprises were all relatively short-lived, but they provide early examples of trading and business practice to alleviate social need and to provide service under contract on behalf of the state. The language betrays the patriarchal emphasis of voluntary associations on attempting to find strategies that met both perceived social needs and their desired moral improvements in beneficiaries.

The first recorded examples of working class associations, rather than philanthropy of the wealthy, and the first instances of social enterprise being recognised by the UK government were Industrial and Provident Societies. It has been argued that pressure to impose state control on working class associations stemmed from a fear of revolution (Hobsbawm 1962, MacDonald and Howorth 2008); the first Register of Friendly Societies was set up in 1846 (Gorsky 1998) and the first Industrial and Provident Societies Act (IPSA) was introduced in 1852. The Acts highlight an emphasis on the needs of members. For example, from the 1852 Act, 'various Associations of Working Men have been formed for the mutual Relief, Maintenance, Education and Endowment of the Members, their Husbands, Wives, Children, or Kindred, and for procuring to them Food, Lodging, Clothing, and other Necessaries, by exercising or carrying on in common their respective Trades or Handicrafts' (from the 1852 Industrial and Provident Societies Act, in Hudson 2001: 7).

Although there is a clear shift towards activity stemming out of the community rather than patriarchal attempts at reform, the language continued to be couched in dependence and charitable aims with little reference to enterprise or business concepts. The shift towards enterprise language does not appear until the late twentieth century.

The term 'social enterprise' first started to appear in the early 1990s, following an increased emphasis on enterprise generally. In the US in 1993, Harvard Business School launched their Social Enterprise Initiative. Similar initiatives were happening in Europe at about the same time. However, initially in Europe 'enterprise' and 'entrepreneurship' were less prominent. For example, in 1991, the Italian parliament created a specific legal entity for 'social cooperatives' (Defourney and Nyssens 2006). Similar initiatives took place in a variety of European countries and under various labels. In the UK, social enterprise took off in 2002 with the launch of the Social Enterprise Coalition and the Social Enterprise Unit, both aimed at promoting social enterprises throughout the country (Defourney and Nyssens 2006).

Within the current prevailing discourse, social enterprises can be perceived as organisations using entrepreneurial processes for social purpose. However, many contest the positioning of social enterprise activity within a mainstream enterprise discourse. They would locate social enterprise activity within community or economic development, where it has a political agenda of alternative democratic structures and processes. Wallace (1999) traces the development of the current social purpose enterprise paradigm in the US through various movements, from community activism and leadership, civic emancipation, economic empowerment through self-sufficiency, political mobilisation for neighbourhood improvement and self-reliance.

Pearce (2003) traces the history of the movement in the UK back to the 1970s Job Creation Programme, when the focus was on community development and the cooperative movement. Haughton (1998) situates the UK movement within sustainable regeneration, itself a response to the failure of top down urban policy approaches throughout the 1980s.

The discourse of social enterprise is arguably the result of a wholesale shift over the last decade, particularly in the UK, from the community to the social era (Pearce 2003, Drucker 1994). The topic has seen a radical and rapid discursive shift through various agendas, including some mentioned above, to the social economy and social entrepreneurship.

This chapter argues that this is not simply a case of semantics but that the language reflects underpinning agendas. The following sections consider the importance of examining language and discuss previous studies that have examined discourses within this particular context.

THEORETICAL UNDERSTANDING

Studies in many areas of social policy and social science have used discourse analysis to explore relational, ideological and political struggles (see for example Atkinson 1999, Collins 1999, Hastings 1999, 2000, Stenson and Watt 1999, Jacobs 2004). Discourse and narrative methods have also been used in entrepreneurship research but to a more limited extent (for example, Ahl 2004, Hjorth and Steyaert 2004, Lindh de Montoya 2004) and in social entrepreneurship (Howorth et al. 2008, Parkinson and Howorth 2008).

There has been particular interest in the enterprise culture, with its various meta rhetorics and discourses, since Thatcherism in the UK in the 1980s. The enterprise discourse is often portrayed as hegemonic, assuming a Foucauldian stance that language is a reflection of power relations, struggles and dynamics (Foucault 1972, see also du Gay 1991, 2004, Jones and Spicer 2005). For Foucault, discourses are 'practices that systematically form the objects of which they speak' (Foucault 1969, quoted in Parker 1999), and determine how power and knowledge are produced. Sets of discursive practices delimit the boundaries of debate (Foucault 1972) and become self-policing.

The apparent hegemony of the enterprise discourse is perpetuated in the popular media. Here, entrepreneurs are held up as heroes with special qualities or as quick-witted wheeler-dealers. Anderson (2005) points to the persistent power of the heroic entrepreneurial metaphor. Nicholson and Anderson (2005) propose that the myth embodied in cultural beliefs, popular literature and journalism becomes self-perpetuating; mystery is created around the myth of the entrepreneur and perpetually reinforced. The mystery shrouding the myth grows; the myth becomes shorthand and eventually 'the uncorrected "collective memory"' (Nicholson and Anderson 2005:

166). The discourse of the enterprise culture, independent of the rise in interest in collective processes, can be seen as re-asserting individualism (Nicholson and Anderson 2005).

Dictionary definitions validate this common understanding of an entrepreneur, referring to someone who undertakes an enterprise or business with the chance of profit or loss.[2] This definition encompasses pro-activity, risk and the entrepreneurial process and emphasises the profit motivation. Considering that the roots of social enterprise activity, as discussed above, were in collective activity with strong social or charitable aims, it is not surprising that Parkinson and Howorth (2008) show that the use of terms such as 'entrepreneur' and 'enterprise' is resisted or dismissed by those on the ground.

Parkinson and Howorth (2008) review recent studies that have challenged the hegemony of the enterprise discourse. They provide examples of the Foucauldian perspective and its antecedents being criticised for assuming that the individual is slave to ideologies or discourses and is powerless to resist the 'call' (Cohen and Musson 2000, Jones and Spicer 2005). That view of the individual is seen as too deterministic, leaving no room for individuals to resist and find their own alternative discourses. The focus instead is on how people appropriate or re-write the discourse to make sense of their specific realities; a reflection of the interest in entrepreneurship as a socially embedded and constructed phenomenon rather than an economic reality. Interest is in the relationship between meta discourses and their use at the micro level.

Various studies show people reproducing idealised views of entrepreneurs and being entrepreneurial, while simultaneously challenging and rewriting the enterprise discourse (Cohen and Musson 2000, Fletcher 2006). Cohen and Musson (2000) show that, contrary to the hegemonic view, people are able to discriminate between discourses and appropriate them to their circumstances. In the struggle between competing discourses, elements of the business or enterprise discourse are appropriated and others rejected. People find relevance in the enterprise discourse through their own reading of it (Cohen and Musson 2000). Consequently, meaning cannot be solely constructed by those in positions of power to exclude or include certain groups, since this is also alterable by the subjects of the discourse.

Similarly, Fairclough (1989, 1992, 1995) suggests that discourse is more than reflective of social power situations, in that language use influences, as much as it is influenced by, social practice. Discourse must therefore be studied in reference to the social and political context (Fairclough and Wodak 1997). Critical discourse analysis includes situations, objects of knowledge and the social identities of, and relationships between, people and groups of people (Weiss and Wodak 2003). Language is constitutive of meaning, the 'prism through which we conceptualise the world' (Jacobs 2004: 819) and is seen as a social practice shaping, and shaped, by social relations and structures.

In a similar context, Moulaert et al. (2007) looked at the tension between the hegemonic regime of urban development and counter-hegemonic forces attempting to transform the urban governance mechanisms. They found that the hegemonic discourse was neither omnipotent nor self-fulfilling in practice (Moulaert et al. 2007: 206) and that policy and practice remains pragmatic in the face of the rapid advance of neo-liberal logic (Moulaert et al. 2007: 202). Instead, 'counter-hegemonic forces' make up part of the patchwork of local agents, and through social innovation can actually permeate macro structures (Moulaert et al. 2007: 202). They also found that these forces are strongest within local communities, where the gap between practice and the 'grand discourse' is widest and where the connection to path dependency is stronger. As Begg (2002) notes, it is at the local level that discourse is challenged and reproduced.

In terms of enterprise policy, this indicates the power of communities or groups to author their own futures, in spite of social reproduction of asset-poor communities by the state through the potentially hegemonic discourse of enterprise. This empowerment is a powerful tenet of social regeneration and social inclusion initiatives, as well as social enterprise.

An examination of the language and promotion of social enterprise can provide, therefore, an insight into the power relations at play. The following section reveals the findings of recent studies. We argue that it is important to consider the effects of the entrepreneurship discourse, particularly in an already highly contested realm such as the social or community. It is noted that in practice 'enterprise' and 'entrepreneurship' are often used interchangeably, although 'enterprise' is more commonly associated with policy and practice, whereas 'entrepreneurship' appears more frequently in academic and media articles. Our review therefore considers both terms. The following section considers studies of discourses around social entrepreneurship, although there is inevitably some overlap with social enterprise.

THE ENTREPRENEURSHIP DISCOURSE IN 'SOCIAL' ENTREPRENEURSHIP

It appears that there is an unquestioned application of the entrepreneurship paradigm to social activity that we have shown was until very recently located within other, equally dominant, discourses of the modern western world. A reading of principal writings and documents in the last five years reveals heroic claims that social entrepreneurship works in the most problematic areas of society where markets and other policy initiatives have failed, that social entrepreneurs are 'unsung heroes' and 'alchemists' who can build things with limited resources. Pearce (2003) argues that the changing language represents a discursive shift: from political engagement to problem fixing; from collective action to individual entrepreneurs; and from democratic structures to a focus on social purpose. The charge is that in the rise of the social enterprise agenda, community has been sidelined discursively and complex values and meanings behind the social ignored.

This has happened in two main ways. Firstly, as has been the case with entrepreneurship, stronger emphasis is placed on individuals, rather than the collective (Holmquist 2003, Cho 2006), to bring about social change. This has resulted in a sense of elitism, reflected in current preoccupations with, for example, how to identify those with the most potential. If the 'everydayness' or 'prosaics' of entrepreneurship (Steyaert 2004) are important for understanding its ubiquitous potential, rather than as the privilege of the few, then 'empowering the many' in the community context is important (Pearce 2003: 69). Parkinson and Howorth (2008) argue that, instead, the monological aspect of the entrepreneurial turn (Cho 2006) that promotes individual agency is reproducing a focus on people who have a special ability to spot opportunities (Robinson 2006). Social entrepreneurs in many studies are understood either in comparison with, or in contrast to, their private sector counterparts (see for example Shaw et al. 2001, Perrini and Vurro 2006). This is now critiqued by some (Haugh 2006), and a new focus is emerging on social entrepreneurial processes and opportunity identification, where agency is conceivable as collective.

Secondly, a tension around using entrepreneurial involvement to fill social gaps is noted (Perrini and Vurro 2006). Throughout the discourse, social entrepreneurship is overtly posited as the panacea to failure in market and state mechanisms, as discussed in our introduction. In this, it is explicitly manoeuvred into a technocratic function of serving underserved parts of society, where people engaged in social entrepreneurship take on a palliative role (Cho 2006). This managerially defined position, marked by a general emphasis on performance, impact, efficiency and sustainability, detracts from a more political-ideological function. It simultaneously disarms the 'third sector' of radical approaches to civil society and maintains the distance between the state and parts of society served by social entrepreneurship (Cho 2006).

Entrepreneurship as applied to social entrepreneurship reinforces the old. While there is still no consensus on the definition of an entrepreneur or entrepreneurship, concepts are being carried over wholesale to the study of social entrepreneurship. For example, Covin and Slevin's framework of proactivity, risk management and innovativeness at the level of the firm (Covin and Slevin 1991) has recently been employed in social entrepreneurship research (Weerawardena and Sullivan Mort 2005), the suggestion being that the existence of these three factors is evidence of acting entrepreneurially. As with 'mainstream' entrepreneurship before it, the promotional rhetoric (Dees 2004) has led to a research focus characterised by functionalist and positivist approaches. Paradoxically, given its collective and political-ideological roots, the study of social entrepreneurship might be more prone now to individualistic and economic presumptions than 'mainstream' entrepreneurship, where such perspectives have long since been questioned. It is important to be aware that the philosophy underpinning the approach taken by researchers and policy makers can affect what is investigated and discovered. This in turn influences the direction and development of our theories and understanding.

The remainder of this section presents two empirical studies that have attempted to capture understandings by analysing the discourse around social entrepreneurship and social enterprise.

The Language of Social Entrepreneurs

Parkinson and Howorth (2008) examine the interplay between the meta rhetoric of enterprise and on-the-ground constructions; in other words how far the entrepreneurship discourse is meaningful, or otherwise, to individuals engaged in social entrepreneurship. They selected their subjects by asking others to identify social entrepreneurs, and interestingly all those identified were individuals managing social enterprises.

Different responses to the entrepreneurship rhetoric were expected. Parkinson and Howorth highlight the probability that many 'social entrepreneurs' have never delved into academic research. Individuals whose frame of reference was a populist view of entrepreneurship were expected to talk in terms of individual, heroic traits and characteristics. Interviewees who embraced entrepreneurial language and terms, on the other hand, were expected to talk about being proactive, managing risks, innovation, opportunities and the start-up and development process. Alternatively, social entrepreneurs could adopt a frame of reference more closely aligned with community action than business or entrepreneurship. This would be exhibited in language around community and local issues and could be in addition or as an alternative to entrepreneurship. Those who felt most ill-at-ease with business language might be those with a higher commitment to social aims.

Parkinson and Howorth (2008) examined the language of social entrepreneurs by comparing the actual words and key concepts used by nominated social entrepreneurs in comparison to those used in general speech (the British National Corpus of Spoken English) and those used by private sector entrepreneurs. They found that the interviewees framed their roles relatively more in concepts of groups and affiliations, obligation and necessity, government, helping and hindering, social actions and general work or employment concepts. They were significantly less likely to talk about selling, business or personal belongings. Where used, the word 'business' was directly linked with negative connotations such as 'dirty', 'ruthlessness', 'ogres', 'exploiting the black economy', 'wealth and empire building' and 'treating people as just second class'. There was vehement rejection of the term social entrepreneur and frequent avoidance of the word 'social' in association with both 'entrepreneur' and 'enterprise' as if the two did not belong together.

Metaphoric and other figurative language used by the interviewees mainly portrayed the role of social entrepreneurs as protectors and champions: shepherding; fighting the lost battle; expedition and nurturing. Alternative identities emerged of community activists, managers and caretakers. Notably but perhaps not surprisingly, the interviewees did not use language around heroes, risk or innovation. Parkinson and Howorth (2008) suggest that the interviewees appeared to have low affinity to heroic conceptualisations of the entrepreneur but that there might be some affinity with the entrepreneur as saviour (Nicholson and Anderson 2005). Their interviewees responded to questions about them being social entrepreneurs by openly dismissing the concept, with statements such as: 'it's amusing!', 'it's ridiculous!', 'too posh . . . I'm working class'.

Parkinson and Howorth (2008) conclude that social entrepreneurs operating in the UK adopt multiple frames of reference to construct and articulate their realities. They suggest that these resonate closely with discourses that compete with, and ultimately re-appropriate meaning to, elements of the entrepreneurship discourse. The ideological and cultural meanings centre around three main tenets: the social entrepreneurs' positions within the ideological struggle between local government and community; need-driven action, anchored firmly in the present and immediate past; and collective action for local change.

The analysis suggests that the activities labelled under social entrepreneurship reappear as political, dependent on their 'in between' position to exist, rather than as economic entities in their own right. The in-between position may be between community and the 'system' from a political perspective; between localities and wider institutional structures; between need (as a result of state/private sector failure) and opportunity (from the same failure); or between ideologies and social values and the attainment of social change towards those values.

In concluding, Parkinson and Howorth highlight that there was a strong collective logic dominating the language used by the respondents in their study. These particular 'social entrepreneurs' appeared to draw their legitimacy from other (social and moral) sources than the entrepreneurship discourse. Although labelled as social entrepreneurs, they did not 'buy in' to the identity imposed on them externally. The social entrepreneurs were seen operating literally in a different world of meaning (Paton 2003), driven by discourses of social need and moral duty. The analysis presented a complex picture of the interviewees as agents and stewards in collective, locally situated processes. It highlighted a preoccupation with social, local and human concepts. Social entrepreneurs were also significantly more likely to use words conventionally associated with the project of community development or regeneration than entrepreneurship.

Interestingly however, their study also showed an overuse of the words enterprise and entrepreneur and the key concept business. Further analysis revealed that this was often as a negative comparator, against which to define status or activity differently. This highlights the importance of analysing language in context. Notably, the social entrepreneurs in this study did not talk about the building blocks of entrepreneurship that might be associated with a conventional reading of the enterprise discourse, including innovation, risk, proactiveness, market and opportunities, profit or personal drive.

The study showed how the enterprise discourse became altered, combined with other discourses, particularly those of management, leadership and, not least, community development or activisim. It was argued that the enterprise discourse is not only appropriated but assimilated under these other discourses. For example, opportunity recognition and starting new activities was evident but redefined in relation to social need rather than opportunity. Engagement with these moments of need was also often presented as reactive or happenstance, rather than proactive. In another example, failure of the enterprise was conceptualised in terms of failing to protect the community, letting them down. Also, success was articulated in terms of recognition and resilience, rather than performance.

Most strikingly, their study found that the social entrepreneurs seemed to draw their legitimacy as activists, guardians or indeed entrepreneurs from a sense of social morality, rather than from the entrepreneurship discourse directly, as might be expected from 'mainstream' entrepreneurs. As evidenced in other studies, such as Cohen and Musson (2000), what may be emerging is a 'modified' social construction of entrepreneurship that strongly resists the hegemony of the enterprise discourse by drawing elements from other discourses to make sense of micro-realities. At the same time it allows the enterprise discourse to work in an apparently hegemonic way, even though it is contested.

Clearly, Parkinson and Howorth studied only a small group of individuals in a specific context but the analysis did produce some interesting insights into the way individuals make sense of the social enterprise agenda around them. A related study by Howorth et al. (2008) compared the language used by different groups involved in social enterprise activity in a deprived community in order to provide insights into the development of enterprise solutions.

The Language of Social Enterprise in Deprived Communities

Howorth et al.'s (2008) study was of individuals connected with social enterprise in a defined UK area of deprivation (IMD definition). They position their study in respect of Bordieu's concept of symbolic violence, suggesting that explicit use of a business dominated discourse of social entrepreneurship could risk subordinating the very people and activities in deprived communities that the policy is overtly attempting to support.

Interviews were held in 2006 with 10 individuals; three enterprise support workers, three managers of social enterprises with varying experience, one local entrepreneur involved in starting up a social venture and two community leaders, who were involved in activities labelled as social enterprise. In addition, they analysed a recorded steering group meeting of the local social enterprise support agency. The analysis, presented briefly here, considered three groups: support workers, social enterprise managers and community leaders.

Analysis of the support workers' texts revealed strong beliefs about inclusion and exclusion in social enterprise, reinforced by discursive practices. They displayed a polarised conceptualisation of social enterprise, in which sustainable enterprising activities were positively framed in contrast to negative funding dependency and 'funding junkies'. Enterprise was conceptually framed as the antidote to dependency and complacency, used particularly in reference to helping existing organisations to make the transition out of the apparently dead-end social sector into the more positive arena of enterprise. While mainly reproducing government rhetoric, the support workers nonetheless showed some resistance to policy level assumptions about social enterprise in their communities.

In the social entrepreneurs' texts, enterprise was defined as freedom and independence from funding regimes. Funding was negatively framed, as it was by the support workers. However, enterprise was equally negatively reproduced, for creating friction with social objectives and pressure to become business-like. The speakers detached themselves from the individual entrepreneurial identity put forward by the support workers, preferring to portray their roles in the social entrepreneurship process as one of building and expanding.

Finally, in the community leaders' texts, business and enterprise concepts were far less prevalent, unsurprisingly, with the interviewees preferring to talk about their projects or social ventures and, more prominently, the people affected. Sustainability was re-written as tenacity and longevity, often in reference to their own influence or the community. This was reflective of a more political narrative overall, in which enterprise was subjugated under discourses of community or social action. In keeping with this, the speakers attached themselves to a more radical entrepreneurial identity, in which their roles were perceived as fighting and battling on behalf of people in their specific communities.

The authors concluded that the community leaders remained more focused on social aims because they were less exposed to the social enterprise discourse. Equally, the enterprise discourse and business and management language were less prominent in the social entrepreneurs' excerpts than the support workers'. Where they did use enterprise or business terminology, it was discursively demarcated as separate from the dominant discourse of social need. Overall, business discourses were more prevalent among interviewees who were closer to policy makers, particularly support workers, and vice versa.

In this study, Howorth et al. (2008) explore whether the application of the enterprise discourse to the social sphere, in the guise of the social enterprise agenda (and the micro-rhetoric of 'sustainability' in particular) could have the potential to lock out certain players and activities. At the level of the support workers, the focus on enterprise was seen to negate the social values and ideologies seen elsewhere as important (for example, social ownership, community action and development). The discourse of enterprise presented by social enterprise policy was believed to be allowed to work dominantly and to delimit discussion of social value. Exclusionary effects were seen to potentially lock out less business-minded people or activities that do not comply with the legally constituted forms of social enterprise organisation.

However, Howorth et al. also examine how far the residual lock-out effect on the two groups working 'on the ground' is resisted and the rhetoric of becoming business-like or sustainable is prevented from violating social values. They contend that, while the enterprise discourse might reinforce conventional understandings and the popular myths around entrepreneurship, in other ways it is contested and appropriated at every level studied. The support workers focused on existing organisations becoming more business-like, with emphasis on money and viability, yet challenged ideologies at the heart of these perspectives. The social entrepreneurs and leaders echoed the imperative of becoming business-like but established clear discursive boundaries between being business-like and their main *raison d'être* of serving important social needs.

To return to Bordieu's theory of symbolic violence, the rhetoric as it is interpreted and enacted by the support workers was indeed seen to reinforce inequitable social relations within poor areas and (for example) 'people on the estate', who were positioned as not business-like, therefore not enterprising, and in need of fixing by external intervention. In the process, welfarism and social regeneration objectives that were clearly forefront for the social entrepreneurs and community leaders were backgrounded by a neo-liberal view of enterprise as a tool of economic regeneration. However, they also revealed competing world views that undermine this subordination effect. As Moulaert et al. (2007) and Begg (2002) indicate, it was at the micro level, the furthest removed from the state, that the discourse was most clearly contested. At an individual level people effectively resisted the discourse (through either appropriation or negation) by defaulting to the dominant popular myth of the entrepreneur or enterprise and then demarcating boundaries between that world and theirs.

These findings expand on similar themes that were identified in the first study. Drawing these studies together it would appear that the activities of social entrepreneurs as constructed on the ground do not relate to many of the concepts conventionally associated with entrepreneurship, at either surface or discursive levels; and that a distinct chasm between these and the dominant concepts in the rhetoric around social enterprise and social entrepreneurship is developing.

CONCLUSIONS

We are not suggesting that activity in the social or community context should not be classed as entrepreneurial or indeed that the reality of the modern environment in which social enterprises and entrepreneurs operate does not necessitate the adoption of certain practices and discourses, including sustainability and business management. However, by adopting a critical stance, we are able to understand better the effects and impact of particular policies and activities.

Parkinson and Howorth (2008) suggest that the conceptual assumptions in the dominant entrepreneurship discourse, critiqued by many entrepreneurship researchers, may constitute an even wider chasm when applied to people and processes in the domain labelled social entrepreneurship. It appears that political engagement and collective action still have currency to those operating on the ground and that democratic structures may be equally as prominent as the focus on social activity. It is also a reminder that discursive shifts, driven by policy makers, funders, the sector and academics alike, do not necessarily infiltrate ideology at the level where the action is located. Therefore, while the questions of how to back the winners may become accepted, to many they may propagate a focus that is difficult to contest and could influence the use of resources. If the entrepreneurial turn promotes a monological perspective (Cho 2006), it presents a challenge to policy that applies it to social gaps and social change (Perrini and Vurro 2006) and to research from a management or entrepreneurship discipline that fails to take account of the political sociology of the field.

It is important to note that we are not suggesting that these initiatives are wrong or that they are intrinsically flawed. What we are suggesting is that the policy drive may bring with it a particular discourse that is limited. It is possibly restrictive in that it could reduce the entrepreneur who operates in a depleted community (and his or her voice) to being a passive recipient of the dominant policy discourse. It takes little if any account of the contested space that is policy formation, or the contested space that is entrepreneurship and business in deprived communities.

By locking into this narrow, particular view of enterprise the social regenerative potential from initiatives that manifest in new forms of social or local enterprise may be lost. No account is taken of effects on family and kinship, the raising of aspirations and self-esteem and the impact on the community psychology that prevails in localised neighbourhoods. In fact, the structured discourse not only acts as an exclusive narrative but it brings into play individual actors as part of an economic response, at the expense of local politics and alternative ideals about the meaning of enterprise (Gibson-Graham 1996).

The studies reviewed in this chapter help to provide a better understanding of the application of the entrepreneurship paradigm in a highly socialised environment. However, there is need for further research. In the field of social entrepreneurship, there is a distinct lack of high level research that develops critical and conceptual analysis, with much of the research until recently tending to provide descriptive statistics and illustrative case studies. The approaches reviewed here combine grounded, interpretive perspectives of phenomenological enquiry with the socially critical framework of critical discourse analysis. These approaches appear to have considerable potential for providing insights into the moving target of entrepreneurship within this highly contested field. They also take the view that meaning is produced in context and respect the contextuality of individuals in particular sub-regions at a specific time in history. Although the studies do not aim at generalisation, they provide interesting insights for future researchers to develop.

NOTES

1. Bray, T. (1698) A General Plan of a Penitential Hospital for Employing and Reforming Lewd Women, Publisher unknown (in Owen 1965: 35) as an unrealised proposal of the time for a social enterprise approach to relieving a disadvantaged group.
2. See for example Concise Oxford Dictionary, 9th edition.

BIBLIOGRAPHY

Ahl, H. (2004) The Scientific Reproduction of Women's Entrepreneurship: A discourse analysis of research texts on women's entrepreneurship, Copenhagen: Copenhagen Business School Press.
Anderson, A. R. (2005) 'Enacted metaphor: the theatricality of the entrepreneurial process', International Small Business Journal, 23(6): 585–603.
Atkinson, R. (1999) 'Discourses of partnership and empowerment in contemporary British urban regeneration', Urban Studies, 36(1): 59–72.
Begg, I. (2002) Urban Competitiveness: Policies for dynamic cities, Bristol: The Policy Press.
Cho, A. H. (2006) 'Politics, values and social entrepreneurship: a critical appraisal', in J. Mair, J. Robinson and K. Hockerts (eds) Social Entrepreneurship, Basingstoke: Palgrave Macmillan.
Cohen, L. and Musson, G. (2000) 'Entrepreneurial identities: reflections from two case studies', Organization, 7(1): 31–48.
Collins, C. (1999) 'The dialogics of community: language and identity in a housing scheme in the West of Scotland', Urban Studies, 36(1): 73–90.
Covin, J. G. and Slevin, D. P. (1991) 'A conceptual model of entrepreneurship as firm behaviour', Entrepreneurship Theory and Practice, 16(1): 7–26.
Dees, G. (2004) 'Rhetoric, reality and research: building strong intellectual foundations for the emerging field of social entrepreneurship', paper presented at the 2004 Skoll World Forum on Social Entrepreneurship, Oxford, March.
Defourney, J. and Nyssens, M. (2006) 'Defining social enterprise', in M. Nyssens (ed.) Social Enterprise, London: Routledge.
Drucker, P. (1994) 'The age of social transformation', Atlantic Monthly, 274: 53–80.

DTI (2002) Social Enterprise: A strategy for success, London: Department of Trade and Industry.

du Gay, P. (1991) 'Enterprise culture and the ideology of excellence', New Formations, 13: 45–61.

———(2004) 'Against 'enterprise' (but not against "enterprise" as that would make no sense)', Organization, 11(1): 37–57.

Fairclough, N. (1989) Language and Power, London: Longman.

———(1992) Discourse and Social Change, Cambridge: Polity Press.

———(1995) Critical Discourse Analysis: The critical study of language, London: Longman.

Fairclough, N. and Wodak, R. (1997) 'Critical discourse analysis', in T. van Dijk (ed.) Discourse as Social Interaction, London: Sage.

Fletcher, D. E. (2006) 'Entrepreneurial processes and the social construction of opportunity', Entrepreneurship and Regional Development, 18(5): 421–40.

Foucault, M. (1972) The Archaeology of Knowledge, New York: Pantheon Books.

Gaddum, J. (1974) Family Welfare Association of Manchester and Salford: A short history 1833–1974, Manchester: Family Welfare Association.

Gibson-Graham, J. K. (2006) The End of Capitalism (as We Knew It): A feminist critique of political economy, Minneapolis: University of Minnesota Press.

Gorsky, M. (1998) 'The growth and distribution of English friendly societies in the early nineteenth century', Economic History Review, 51(3): 489–511.

Hastings, A. (1999) 'Analysing power relations in partnerships: is there a role for discourse analysis?', Urban Studies, 36(1): 91–106.

———(2000) 'Discourse analysis: what does it offer housing studies?, Housing, Theory and Society, 17: 131–39.

Haugh, H. (2006) 'Social enterprise: beyond economic outcomes and individual returns', in J. Mair, J. Robinson and K. Hockerts (eds) Social Entrepreneurship, Basingstoke: Palgrave Macmillan.

Haughton, G. (1998) 'Principles and practice of community economic development', Regional Studies, 32(9): 872–77.

Hjorth, D. and Steyaert, C. (2004) Narrative and Discursive Approaches in Entrepreneurship, Cheltenham: Edward Elgar.

Hobsbawm, E. (1962) The Age of Revolution: Europe 1789 to 1848, London: Abacus.

Holmquist, C. (2003) 'Is the medium really the message? Moving perspective from the entrepreneurial actor to the entrepreneurial action', in C. Steyaert and D. Hjorth (eds) New Movements in Entrepreneurship, Cheltenham: Edward Elgar.

Howorth, C., Parkinson, C. and Southern, A. (2008) 'Does enterprise discourse have the power to enable or disable deprived communities?', in D. Smallbone, H. Landstrom and D. Jones Evans (eds) 4th RENT anthology, Cheltenham: Edward Elgar.

Hudson, R. (2001) Producing Places, London: Guilford Press.

Jacobs, K. (2004) 'Waterfront redevelopment: a critical discourse analysis of the policy-making process within the Chatham Maritime Project', Urban Studies, 41(4): 817–32.

Jones, C. and Spicer, A. (2005) 'The sublime object of entrepreneurship', Organization, 12(2): 223–46.

Jordan, W. K. (1959) Philanthropy in England, 1480–1660: a study of the changing pattern of English social aspirations, London: Allen & Unwin.

Lindh de Montoya, M. (2004) 'Driven entrepreneurs: a case study of taxi drivers in Caracas', in D. Hjorth and C. Steyeart (eds) Narrative and Discursive Approaches in Entrepreneurship, Cheltenham: Edward Elgar.

MacDonald, M. and Howorth, C. (2008) 'Social enterprise experiments in England: 1660–1908', paper presented to the Social Enterprise Research Conference, London South Bank University, July.

Michael, A. (2006) 'Securing Social Enterprise's Place in the Economy'. Online. Available http://www.sbs.gov.uk/sbsgov/action/news (accessed 12 February 2007).

Moulaert, F., Martinelli, F., Gonzalez, S. and Swyngedouw, E. (2007) 'Introduction: social innovation and governance in European cities: urban development between path dependency and radical innovation', European Urban and Regional Studies, 14(3): 195–209.

Nicholson, L. and Anderson, A. R. (2005) 'News and nuances of the entrepreneurial myth and metaphor: linguistic games in entrepreneurial sense-making and sense-giving', Entrepreneurship Theory and Practice, 29(2):153–72.

NWDA (2003) Social Enterprise Survey, Warrington: North West Development Agency.

Owen, D. (1965) English Philanthropy 1660–1960, Cambridge, MA: Harvard University Press.

Panepento, P. (2007) 'Charities' business ventures hard to sustain, study finds', Chronicle of Philanthropy, 19(17): 47.

Parker, I. (1999) Critical Textwork: An introduction to varieties of discourse and analysis, Buckinghamshire: Open University Press.

Parkinson, C. and Howorth, C. (2008) 'The language of social entrepreneurs', Entrepreneurship and Regional Development, 20(3): 285–309.

Paton, R. (2003) Managing and Measuring Social Enterprises, London: Sage.

Paxton, W., Pearce, N., Molyneux, P. and Unwin, J. (2005) The Voluntary Sector Delivering Public Services: Transfer or transformation? York: Joseph Rowntree Foundation.

Pearce, J. (2003) Social Enterprise in Anytown, London: Calouste Gulbenkian Foundation.

Perrini, F. and Vurro, C. (2006) 'Social entrepreneurship: innovation and social change across theory and practice', in J. Mair, J. Robinson and K. Hockerts (eds) Social Entrepreneurship, Basingstoke: Palgrave Macmillan.

Philips, M. (2006) 'Growing pains: the sustainability of social enterprises', Entrepreneurship and Innovation, 7(4): 221–30.

Pomerantz, M. (2003) 'The business of social entrepreneurship in a "down economy"', Business, 25(3): 25–30.

Robinson, J. (2006) 'Navigating social and institutional barriers to markets: how social entrepreneurs identify and evaluate opportunities', in J. Mair, J. Robinson and K. Hockerts (eds) Social Entrepreneurship, Basingstoke: Palgrave Macmillan.

Shaw, E., Shaw, J. and Wilson M. (2001) Unsung Entrepreneurs: Entrepreneurship for social gain, Durham: University of Durham Business School.

Stenson, K. and Watt, P. (1999) 'Governmentality and the "social"', Urban Studies, 36(1): 189–201.

Steyaert, C. (2004) 'The prosaics of entrepreneurship', in D. Hjorth and C. Steyeart (eds) Narrative and Discursive Approaches in Entrepreneurship, Cheltenham: Edward Elgar.

Wallace, S. (1999) 'Social entrepreneurship: the role of social purpose enterprises in facilitating community economic development', Journal of Developmental Entrepreneurship, 4(2): 153–75.

Weerawardena, J. and Sullivan Mort, G. (2005) 'Investigating social entrepreneurship: a multi-dimensional model', Journal of World Business, 41: 21–35.

Weiss, G. and Wodak, R. (2003) Critical Discourse Analysis: Theory and interdisciplinarity, Basingstoke: Palgrave Macmillan.

13 Can the Market Deliver the Goods?
A Critical Review of the Social Enterprise Agenda

Geoff Whittam and Kean Birch

INTRODUCTION

The encouragement of social enterprises and social entrepreneurship has become a central part of policy agendas across different levels of governance from the European Union, through the national UK state (for example, DTI 2002) to the Scottish government (for example, Scottish Executive 2006a, 2006b). Within this chapter we want to critically evaluate the conceptual underpinnings of these policy initiatives. Although there is confusion over the usage of terms such as social enterprise and social entrepreneurship (see Birch and Whittam 2009), for the purposes of our argument here, we use the definition adopted by the Social Enterprise Coalition:

> A social enterprise is not defined by its legal status but by its nature: its social aims and outcomes; the basis on which its social mission is embedded in its structure and governance; and the way it uses the profits it generates through trading activities. (NEF/SAS 2004: 8)

Importantly, the definition embraces two of the fundamental issues we wish to focus on within this chapter, namely the market orientation and the governance structure of social enterprises. Additionally, we argue that the concept of social capital, observed by policy makers as a key objective to renew communities of deprivation, is misunderstood and that sustainable social enterprise, again an objective of policy, has become narrowly focused to mean the financially sustainability of social enterprises themselves.

Social enterprise represents the pursuit of market mechanisms to resolve problems that have been created by this same mechanism. It is the market that produces inequalities, regional imbalances and a morality that does not necessarily promote social justice. It could be argued that we have a scenario where, in the words of Blackburn and Ram (2006: 77), '[p]aradoxically, then, we are looking at the system of regulated capitalism to solve a problem that it has generated'. A key policy instrument introduced by the state to promote the market orientation of social enterprise is the introduction of a competitive process in public procurement contracts. The objective of this policy is to 'create markets' by encouraging competition amongst social enterprises and thus reducing the impact of existing market failure. However, as traditional economic theory informs us, the promotion of increasing competition can result in uncompetitive markets once one organisation has gained a 'first mover' advantage over its potential rivals.

In the recent past, there have been many examples of how attempts to embed social enterprises into the market system through public procurement contracts have had undesirable consequences. We have observed the workforce of *Shelter*, the national charity established to help the homeless, going on strike in a dispute over the imposition of inferior contracts introduced by the *Shelter* management team in an attempt to remain competitive. *Quarriers*, a 130 year old Scottish based charity providing a variety of services to vulnerable people and families, had their first strike, again over pay and conditions. *Quarriers* offered their workforce a below inflationary pay rise citing that they could not afford more due to insufficient monies received through winning a local authority contract. These are not isolated incidents but they illustrate the potentially dire consequences of subjecting social enterprise organisations to the discipline of the market.

By its very name, social enterprise implies a governance structure based on 'an entrepreneur'. We want to question whether this mode of governance is the most appropriate for delivering many of the potential benefits of a social enterprise. The problem is that one of the established motives for entrepreneurs is to be one's own boss; a motivation which can prove problematic for the development of the social capital necessary for social enterprise to successfully achieve sustainable economic development at a local level. For example, it has been argued that the Community Interest Company (CIC), introduced in the UK in 2005, is 'hierarchically controlled through the agency of the "good" regulator, rather than democratically controlled by their own stakeholders and retain a unitarist orientation' (Ridley-Duff 2007: 389). In order to illustrate this point, we draw on the work of Mark Granovetter to analyse the problems associated with the establishment of social capital by an entrepreneurial model based on the classic capitalist firm.

The chapter will first highlight the problems of definition with the key terms of social enterprise and social entrepreneurship, before identifying policy developments within Scotland. We focus on Scotland because the latest initiatives there reflect similar initiatives in other countries and the general principles underpinning the policy are applicable elsewhere. Next, we critically evaluate the rationale for policy developments in terms of a traditional economic approach to gain an understanding of the competitive process. This is further developed to examine the utilisation of social entrepreneurship and social capital to promote regeneration in deprived communities.

DEFINITIONS: WHAT IS SOCIAL ENTERPRISE
AND SOCIAL ENTREPRENEURSHIP?

Across the social economy, but particularly within the social enterprise component, there is a stress on entrepreneurialism and enterprising activity generally. For example, the UK government *Social Enterprise Strategy* highlights the role they can play in 'helping to drive up productivity and competitiveness' (DTI 2002: 8), whilst the OECD (1999) places clear emphasis on the 'entrepreneurial spirit' of such organisations. In more recent policy discussions, the UK government presents social enterprise as a 'diverse and enterprising way of tackling social and environmental issues' (Small Business Service [SBS] 2005a: 7); one which contributes to the Public Service Agreements (PSA) targets 6 and 7 directed at creating an 'enterprise society' (SBS 2005b: 2). The role of social entrepreneurship in the social economy appears to be yet another confusingly conflated concept. It is not clearly defined in the social enterprise discourse, apart from a claim by the European Commission (EC) that social economy organisations are 'flexible and innovative'.[1]

The academic discussion of social entrepreneurship actually focuses more on the individual characteristics of people involved in the social economy. In his definition, Gregory Dees (2001: 2) draws upon previous research on market-based entrepreneurs in the wider economic, management and business literature (for example, Say, Schumpeter, Drucker, Stevenson) that described entrepreneurs as people who 'mobilize the resources of others to achieve their entrepreneurial objectives'. The social entrepreneur can therefore be defined as someone who acts as a change agent in the social sector by:

1. Adopting a mission
2. Pursuing new opportunities to achieve that mission
3. Continually innovating, adapting and learning
4. Avoiding limitations of current resources
5. Being concerned with accountability to their clients and community (ibid.: 4).

This follows on from earlier definitions of the 'public entrepreneur' who seek to affect to resolve a particular social problem (Waddock and Post 1991), although this vision has a limited applicability to the current social economy and enterprise model because it is concerned with single events or actions (such as Live Aid) that may achieve a limited result since they do not necessarily deal with the causes of problems, only their symptoms. A more relevant explanation of social entrepreneurship seeks to explain the combination of innovative ideas and risk-taking with a bridging role within the community, bringing various groups together across public and private sector organisations (Purdue 2001, Grenier 2002). Thus a particularly important characteristic in social entrepreneurship is the ability to collaborate with many disparate groups, maintain that network and develop and use it as needed in the pursuit of the social objective (Johnson 2000).

It is this bridging role that provides social entrepreneurship with a link to sustainability, especially in terms of community empowerment and the promotion of social ends. Amin et al. (2002), for example, found that the success of social ventures depended upon their leadership. Within policy discourse, the provision of products and services to excluded groups is only one aspect of social entrepreneurial activity; the other is the provision of work and through such activity empowering people to build up their 'social capital' (ibid. 2002). In their review of the social economy, the Scottish Executive (2003) emphasise the role that the social economy generally has in developing social capital, although without exploring the definition or usage of the concept. It is this aspect of social entrepreneurship, developing social capital, that represents an important policy intervention; social economy and social enterprise strategies are directed at providing products, services and employment to deprived regions and areas, supposedly assisting in producing regional sustainability in 'weak' development terms relating to economic growth (see Chatterton 2002), and 'strong' development terms in relation to social cohesion (Giddings et al. 2002; Hopwood et al. 2005). This will be explored more thoroughly in subsequent sections.

POLICY INITIATIVES IN SCOTLAND

The overall policy for regeneration in Scotland is outlined in the policy document *People and Place Regeneration Policy Statement* (Scottish Executive 2006a). Policy is orientated towards promoting the state as an 'enabler' rather than a provider as the following quote illustrates:

> Where the private sector is willing and able to invest in the effective and sustainable transformation of an area then the opportunity should be grasped. Our approach to regeneration will seek to act as a catalyst, or lay the foundations, for private sector activity. (Scottish Executive 2006a: 5).

This strategy is further shown in the comment that 'much needs to be done to ensure that private sector players, such as developers, banks and the construction industry, view Scotland as 'open for business on regeneration' (Scottish Executive 2006a: 21). The orientation of this regeneration strategy is in line with other key objectives of the Scottish Executive which seeks to grow 'the economy in a sustainable way', creating prosperity which 'gives us the means to tackle poverty and disadvantage' (Scottish Executive 2006a: 3). The concept of sustainability is used in a narrow economic way (see Birch and Whittam 2009 for further discussion) and, indeed, when the concept is applied to social enterprises, it can be interpreted as sustainable to the individual organisation rather than at the community level.

Such policy documents complement earlier statements by the Scottish Executive, such as *Better Communities in Scotland Closing the Gap* (Scottish Executive 2002), which outlined the role of social enterprise in regeneration; elements of this have been reviewed by a public consultation, *A Social Enterprise Strategy for Scotland* (Scottish Executive 2006b). The title of the 2002 document is significant for its recognition of 'core' and 'periphery' development, noting that some communities have been 'left behind' and therefore that the regeneration strategy seeks to build 'a better Scotland, where a child's potential, and not their background or postcode, will decide their future' (Scottish Executive 2002: 4). The way this is to be achieved is by ensuring '"core public services" have as much effect as possible in disadvantaged areas and through the development of "social capital"—the skills, confidence, support networks and resources—that they need' (Scottish Executive 2002: 9). A key component in delivering these two objectives is the social economy because 'social economy organisations are particularly effective in working with excluded and disadvantaged people' and '[t]he social economy has a crucial role in our agenda of Closing the Opportunity Gap' (Scottish Executive 2004: 1). A part of this process is to be achieved by excluded groups themselves through initiatives such as seedcorn funding that, 'with its emphasis on enterprise sustainability, will allow us to harness the entrepreneurial potential that exists within disadvantaged communities but that often goes untapped' (Scottish Executive 2004: 7). The recent consultation identifies current thinking, utilising a broad definition of social enterprise as 'businesses which compete in the open market for contracts or sales but combine trading with social, community or environmental aims' (Scottish Executive 2006b: 1). However, we find the Department of Trade and Industry (DTI) definition, 'Social enterprises are businesses with primarily social objectives whose surpluses are principally reinvested for that purpose in the business or in the community, rather than being driven by the need to maximise profit for shareholders or owners', being used on other pages of the consultation (ibid.: 4). Notwithstanding this discrepancy, the consultation identifies social enterprise in terms of a trading income of at least 50 per cent of overall income (25 per cent for new social enterprises), which can be obtained from contracts with public or private organisations and service level agreements.

It is evident from this policy discourse that the social economy agenda, encompassing both social enterprise and social entrepreneurship, is strongly influenced by objectives covering both market failure and social inclusion. The former appears to be driven by the Government's conceptualisation of sustainable development in 'weak' terms (growth and sustainability as compatible), whilst the latter is driven by social objectives drawn from concerns with community regeneration. Morin et al. (2004) suggest that the 1994 Commission on Social Justice set up by then Labour Party leader, John

Smith, had an enormous influence on later Labour Party policy, especially in relation to such regeneration programmes. As part of this regeneration policy, communities were meant to be empowered through engagement, although the degree to which this happened was variable (Purdue 2001). However, we would argue that this framing of market failure and social exclusion produces problematic regeneration outcomes because there is a particular emphasis on social entrepreneurship and social enterprise that ignores the embeddedness of individuals and organisations in social networks that can constrain their effectiveness in empowering communities.

CRITIQUE OF POLICY INTERVENTIONS

One reading of the rationale for policy intervention to encourage the establishment and development of social enterprise, as defined by the DTI, is reducible to market failure; for example, '[s]ocial enterprises create new goods and services and develop opportunities for markets where mainstream business cannot, or will not go' (DTI 2002). However, it can be argued that implicit within this perspective is the desire to extend market-based activities or the commodification and adoption of market solutions to areas which were previously designated as the responsibility of the state (Fasenfest et al. 1997, Mathiason 2005). In particular, the role of social entrepreneurship has been extended to social markets in areas such as housing, health and education. Whilst not all social goods are and can be marketed, and there is indeed some 'blocking' (Walzer 1983) of some exchanges, the boundaries are flexible and there is a movement towards market solutions for the provision of goods and services in these areas over the last two decades.

Additionally, market failure is seen as the result of the inability of the market to account for fairness or redistributive justice, alongside the negative effects of externalities produced by private firms; for example, pollution, poor amenities (OECD 1999). The social economy is therefore able to provide services or products that would otherwise not be available in particular places (and not over the whole economy when the state would presumably intervene with public provision). A further aspect of the development of the social economy has focused on social exclusion, which concentrates on aspects of social cohesion that are constituted within specific places (ibid.). A key feature of this policy intervention is 'empowering individuals and communities, encouraging the development of work habits and increasing employment diversity' according to the *Social Enterprise Strategy* (DTI 2002: 21). Another element in this process is sustainability through local wealth creation, such as the recycling of money from employment through local services and organisations so that they can produce more employment that then produces more local wealth (ibid.). Through the dual-purpose process of service provision and employment amelioration, to counter market failure and social exclusion respectively, the social economy should therefore empower the community or locality in which it is situated (Amin et al. 2002, 2003). However, there are two problems with this approach to regeneration, which we will outline briefly below. The first is whether (social) entrepreneurship can alleviate deprivation and encourage community empowerment; the second is whether market solutions can be deployed in such situations altogether.

First, we noted in the introduction the comment by Blackburn and Ram (2006: 77) that '[p]aradoxically, then, we are looking at the system of regulated capitalism to solve a problem that it has generated'. They then proceed to challenge the notion that the promotion of business ownership is necessarily the best way to tackle social exclusion on the grounds that small business tend to have inferior social provision for employees compared to larger firms and public sector organisations. Johnstone and Lionais (2004) suggest that what they call 'community business entrepreneurship' maybe a way to overcome this paradox. At the same time, they acknowledge that 'uneven development' is a product of the capitalist system leading to 'less-favoured', 'peripheral' or 'de-industrialised' regions, resulting in what they call 'depleted communities', 'where the economy is in decline and the resources of the area, according to profit-seeking capital are "used-up"' (ibid.: 218). Depleted communities are nevertheless communities where individuals still live, have an emotional attachment and are therefore not ghost towns. However, as we explore below, there is a problem with a redevelopment strategy dependent on 'community business entrepreneurship' which seeks to utilise 'locally referent networks of social relations with a common culture and attachment to place' (ibid.: 219). The problem of embeddedness may well limit the ability of networks to fully exploit the opportunities that such a regeneration strategy may well offer.

Second, traditional economic theory suggests that the benefit of promoting a competitive market economy is that an allocative efficient solution can be achieved in situations of scarcity. For example, the desire to achieve more than normal profits drives enterprises to be ever more innovative in their delivery of goods and services. This results in lower costs being achieved and if these cost savings earned in the product market are passed on to consumers in the final goods markets then society benefits because of lower prices. However, if one enterprise manages to secure an advantage over a rival, through securing a government contract for example, then there is the possibility that the successful enterprise may be able to exploit this advantage on a more permanent basis by exploiting internal economies of scale that can be achieved only as a result of winning the government contract in the first place (for a fuller discussion of this see Oughton and Whittam 1997). Through the securing of a long-run cost advantage, the successful enterprise can use this advantage to create barriers to entry for other organisations. That is, potential entrants will either have to produce on an equivalent scale to achieve the same unit cost of production or, more likely, will have to reduce internal costs (wages, service quality for example) in order to compete. However, if the long run cost of the 'successful' enterprise can act as a barrier to entry then potential rivals may well exit the market, leading to imperfect competition and the consequences of monopoly conditions in the delivery of certain goods and services.

The problematic nature of this issue is further highlighted with the adoption of a contestable market approach in the promotion of social enterprise initiatives to deliver public goods and services. In essence, this approach involves competition for the market, as opposed to competition in the market. The traditional economic approach to the promotion of the competitive process is to encourage the development of perfect markets or, where this is not possible due to the existence of a natural monopoly producing market failure, then the second best option (the promotion of competition for a market) has to be adopted. This approach is evident in the break-up of previous nationalised industries such as the railways. An element of 'natural monopoly' exists over the infrastructure of the railways such as the track and stations thereby competition through the awarding of franchises occurred for the right to operate train services utilising the rail infrastructure. The competition as such exists for the right to operate rail services on the natural monopoly of track and stations. Such an approach has been utilised by local authorities in the awarding of contracts and service level agreements through a competitive process to social enterprise organisations to provide goods and services for those in deprived areas. Basing the social enterprise agenda on competition for the market, as opposed to in the market, results from the nature of the funding resources underpinning the delivery of services by social enterprises, which necessarily impacts on the ability of social enterprise to contribute to regeneration.

SOCIAL CAPITAL AND THE REGENERATION OF DEPRIVED COMMUNITIES

Social entrepreneurship is placed at a crucial juncture in this policy vision, between the community and the achievement of the social objective. It plays a central role here because the communities in which social enterprise and the social economy are meant to have the greatest impact tend to entail several barriers to participation: they lack material resources; they lack wide or strong networks;[2] they lack relevant skills; and they have to work within specific institutional boundaries (such as tax credit or benefit systems) (see Williams et al. 2003: 156). Of these, the lack of social networks, usually referred to as social capital, has been highlighted within both policy and academia as an important method to empower communities (Chanan 1999, Smallbone et al. 2001, Scottish Executive 2003, Arthur et al. 2004). The social economy is supposed to be a means to encourage the development of social capital by encouraging mutualism within communities through grassroots empowerment based on 'active participation' and a 'stakeholder society' (Amin et al. 2002). In a somewhat circular conceptualisation, social entrepreneurship is supposed to provide the means to achieve this mutualism through the social economy.

Although the role of social entrepreneurship and the promotion of social capital in pursuit of sustainable development are conceptualised in a variety of ways throughout the literature, their relationship can be theorised in terms drawn from economic sociology that challenge the links being made between them. To illustrate the role of the social entrepreneur (or social entrepreneurship) to social capital, we can outline several popular concepts of social capital and show how social entrepreneurship fits within this framework. The first thing to note is that social capital, despite its meta-theoretical claims, is a diverse concept that cuts across disciplines and consequently understandings. According to Michael Woolcock (1998), it was first identified in the work of Jane Jacobs and Pierre Bourdieu and developed by James Coleman, Ronald Burt and Robert Putnam, amongst others. It has several different definitions that contradict and contrast with each other; for example, it has been presented as individual (Bourdieu) and community (Putnam) based, as well as functional (Coleman) and consequentialist (see Quibria 2003). The concept itself has been strongly criticised by other authors (see Fine 2001 for a critique), although this has not stopped its growing popularity.

By drawing on work in economic sociology we want to show how social capital can be helpfully conceived in terms that cover all these aspects and therefore make it difficult to present any one of them as being an adequate rationale for policy action. On the other hand, the complexity of the ensuing concept means that working with this in policy making would also be problematic. To start with, social capital can be seen as the structure of a network (the bridge) as well as its construction or development (the bridging process) (Fine 2001). We can split the first of these into two types by considering the difference identified by Granovetter (1973, 1985) between 'strong' and 'weak' ties. Strong ties represent those that bind people together into a homogenous group that holds similar views and norms of behaviour; these then produce conformity to group conventions by group actors. Weak ties represent those that connect heterogeneous people together across different groups; this enables access to diverse information and contacts. Social entrepreneurship sits uncomfortably between these two positions because of the role it occupies. In the original formulation by Granovetter (1973), he outlined how invention occurred on the fringes of social networks (where there are less weak ties) because of the possible costs that such activity could have to the groups and people involved; whilst diffusion and innovation resulted from core network positions (such as social entrepreneurship) after initial investment had been made by others. As a bridge between different groups, social entrepreneurship plays a crucial role in diffusing invention across networks because it occupies a pivotal position within those networks and consequently it provides access to networks (linking social capital) that the more marginal groups lack. However, because of this position, social entrepreneurship restricts the empowerment of communities because it creates structural limits that maintain the difference between groups.

In contrast, a community consists of 'strong' ties between people that enable every person within that group to access everyone else in that group, at least in purely network terms. Several authors have also highlighted the importance of power in these relationships (Devine-Wright et al. 2001, Robison and Flora 2003, Rydin and Holman 2004). Within this structure then, as opposed to a process where power resides, there is a means for community accountability through both formal and informal means. The structure leads to the integration of people into a group that creates institutions of obligation enforcement through shared norms, expectations and mutuality, whilst also enabling every person access to everyone else (Woolcock 1998, Purdue 2001, Johnston and Percy-Smith 2002, Robison and Flora 2003). We can stylistically define the social capital that such a community has as a strong yet closed network (bonding), one that socially fragments society generally because it does not link different communities together. Their strength is a consequence of their permanence, which is largely inherited rather than earned, covering similar people drawn from similar locations and holding similar norms. It is therefore the group itself that holds social capital, reiterating the position of academics like Robert Putnam and Francis Fukuyama (see Woolcock 1998, Quibria 2003).

Social entrepreneurship can therefore be positioned as a response to the exclusivity and closed structure within community networks. It operates as a linking capacity between groups, bringing together agendas and resources in the pursuit of particular projects; such 'gate-keepers' draw on a range of different capacities within the community (Purdue 2001). It is therefore a version of weak networks that connect disparate groups and enables social cohesion by stopping fragmentation. Because social entrepreneurship pursues projects, it is a temporary process that provides links dependent upon the individual capabilities of the entrepreneur or entrepreneurial organisation involved. The social capital inherent within social entrepreneurship can be characterised in contrast to that inherent within communities. This implies that the promotion of the former will be detrimental to the retention of the latter.

Social entrepreneurship that seeks to empower the community through the promotion of social capital particular to entrepreneurialism, or enterprise more generally, would break down the existing social capital in a community by loosening the ties that bind, increasing diversity and promoting social atomisation generally. However, social entrepreneurship that seeks to empower communities by combining community and entrepreneurial social capital results in the entrepreneur acquiring a gate-keeper role that enables greater control and power over setting agendas, distributing resources and making decisions. To achieve this, entrepreneurs ensure ties are routed through themselves, so that they control the implementation of strategy and resources for their own (or the community's perceived) ends. Thus social entrepreneurship depends upon the maintenance of difference between groups that leads to the escalation of group atomisation, except where they are brought together for purposes outlined by the entrepreneur.

This raises a further point, namely the motivation of the entrepreneur. Given that the desire to be one's own boss can be an important motivation behind starting a business (Hisrich 1986, Caird 1991), it follows that many entrepreneurs may well not be interested in building social capital for the community. The sharing of information, contacts, resources etc. can be seen by the entrepreneur as a dilution of control. It is therefore important to overcome the problems associated with both bonding and linking social capital; for example, with bonding social capital there is a difference between social capital based on trust, understanding, compassion and inclusion and that based on fear, mistrust, hate and a desire to protect a group from the outside (Wilson 1997). Such negative social capital can lead to the prevention of innovation and other types of social capital. Rydin and Holman (2004: 123) suggest a new form of 'bracing' social capital needs to be conceptualised to overcome this problem. 'Bracing' social capital, which captures 'the idea of a kind of social capital that is primarily concerned to strengthen links across and between scales and sectors but only operates within a limited set of actors', would go beyond the restrictive categories of 'bonding' and 'linking'. This widens the concept of sustainability from a narrow financial perspective to sustainability in terms of a local community, where developing social capital will be seeking to build capacity in terms of skills and abilities within a given locality. Consequently, the role of social entrepreneurship has to be reconsidered so that it does not either lead to the break-down of existing community relations nor the establishment of new networks in which power is centred on an individual or organisation who sets the agenda for local regeneration.

CONCLUSIONS

Aside from the concerns about the relationship between social entrepreneurship and social capital, there are a range of other criticisms that can be levelled at policy decisions promoting social enterprise or entrepreneurship. First, social enterprise organisations have been encouraged because they adopt trading activities as their main revenue source, enabling sustainable development. This is an important issue only where government or public bodies do not wish to continue funding such services in the future, through either direct control or grant funding (Mathiason 2005). One consequence of this is that there is less need for strong networks to exist because social enterprise does not necessitate that an organisation maintain a link with a particular community or place (Eikenberry and Kluver 2004). Secondly, and following on from the first issue, the new emphasis on market solutions re-orients activities to business concerns that impact upon the organisational, cognitive and institutional environment within which social enterprise organisations operate. Furthermore, the shift becomes self-fulfilling as the original change is justified on the basis of the shifting environment that then replicates business concerns (see Ferraro et al. 2005); social means are thereby replaced by economic means, whether or not the ends are social or economic. Therefore the possibility that emancipatory or empowering approaches to regeneration and development are undertaken is lessened, being replaced by entrepreneurial-based approaches that are subsequently reinforced. A recent example of this is the new organisational form of the CIC. It illustrates a lack of government interest in challenging or changing ownership forms, especially where these are social or cooperative ownership (Arthur et al. 2004). Finally, the whole question of inequality and its effects is ignored. The ability to provide opportunities for some people means that those opportunities have to be withheld from other people. In other words, the concentration of employment and wealth in specific places is not simply the result of endogenous characteristics of each area, especially when we consider the role of social capital, an essentially relational or network concept, and the consequence of too much inclusion. The promotion of social entrepreneurship could mean that only certain individuals and groups receive the benefits of social capital, whereas others are left with either none or the remnants that the included are willing to share.

In the preceding discussion we have highlighted the ever-increasing popularity of social entrepreneurship as a potential solution to achieve regeneration and social inclusion. What we have sought to do is highlight the rationale for this popularity and some of the obstacles that may prevent desirable policy outcomes. In particular, we have questioned whether a market-based solution is appropriate to resolve problems created by the market in the first place. We have noted the importance of understanding the differences between 'strong' and 'weak' ties in networking relations that are at the heart of social capital. Indeed, weak ties are individually atomising and therefore drive the process of marketization as people need to rely increasingly on their connection with others through formal exchange processes—whether trust-based or not—rather than familial or social relationships. We have further identified a potential conflict of promoting social entrepreneurship whereby social enterprise organisations or social entrepreneurs may seek to limit the development of social capital within a locality due to the desire of the entrepreneur to maintain control of a particular project.

To overcome the potential problems highlighted in this chapter so far, there is a need for clarity of purpose for policy makers. The differing interpretations of social capital, social enterprise and social entrepreneurship need to be made explicit. In particular in relation to achieving regeneration from the development of social capital perhaps the perception of social capital as a 'public good' needs to be fully understood. Coleman (1990) argues that social capital is not the private property of any of the individuals who benefit from it. Whilst this is undoubtedly true, the key aspect of a 'public good' that is ignored is excludability. Whilst social capital may not be the property of one individual, it is the property of the group and the group can exclude others from access; thereby the analogy with the 'public good' argument falls. If we utilise Putnam's description of social capital then we can observe social capital being utilised in a similar fashion to Fukuyama, who identifies differing levels of trust in differing societies, and society as a whole will benefit. In this context, individuals cannot be excluded and, hence, social capital does take on the attribute of a public good.

NOTES

1. http://europa.eu.int/comm/enterprise/entrepreneurship/coop/index.htm (accessed November 2005).
2. There is a need to highlight the difference between types of network relationships here because, as a local authority officer responsible for social economy in their region said in an interview, several deprived communities have very strong bonds with each other (September 2005).

BIBLIOGRAPHY

Amin, A., Cameron, A. and Hudson, R. (2002) Placing the Social Economy, London: Routledge.
———(2003) 'The alterity of the social economy', in A. Leyshon, R. Lee and C. Williams (eds) Alternative Economic Spaces, London: Sage.
Arthur, L., Keenoy, T., Smith, R., Scott Cato, M. and Anthony, P. (2004) 'People versus pounds: the prospects for radicalism in the UK social economy', paper presented at the Crises Conference on Innovation and Social Transformation, Montreal University, 11–12 November.
Birch, K. and Whittam, G. (2009) 'Critical survey: the third sector and the regional development of social capital', Regional Studies, 42(3): 437–50.
Blackburn, R. and Ram, M. (2006) 'Fix or fixation? The contributions and limitations of entrepreneurship and small firms to combating social exclusion', Entrepreneurship and Regional Development, January: 73–89.
Caird, S. (1991) 'The enterprising tendency of occupational groups', International Small Business Journal, 9: 75–81.
Chanan, G. (1999) 'Employment policy and the social economy: promise and misconceptions', Local Economy, 13(4): 361–68.
Chatterton, P. (2002). '"Be realistic: demand the impossible". Moving towards "strong" sustainable development in an old industrial region', Regional Studies, 36(5): 552–61.
Coleman, J. S. (1990) Foundations of Social Theory, Cambridge, MA: Harvard University Press.
Dees, J. G. (2001) 'The meaning of "social entrepreneurship"', CASE, Duke University. Online. Available http://www.fuqua.duke.edu/centers/case/documents/dees_SE.pdf (accessed November 2005).

Devine-Wright, P., Fleming, P. and Chadwick, H. (2001) 'Socio-psychological perspective', Impact Assessment and Project Appraisal, 19(2): 161–67.

DTI (2002) Social Enterprise: A strategy for success, London: Department of Trade and Industry.

——(2004) Business Plan 2004–2007, London: Department of Trade and Industry.

ECOTEC (2003a) Guidance on Mapping Social Enterprise: Final report to the DTI Social Enterprise Unit, London: Department of Trade and Industry.

Eikenberry, A. and Kluver, J. (2004) 'The marketization of the nonprofit sector: civil society at risk?', Public Administration Review, 64(2): 132–40.

Fasenfest, D., Ciancanelli, P. and Reese, L. (1997) 'Value, exchange and the social economy: framework and paradigm shift in urban policy', International Journal of Urban and Regional Research, 21(1): 7–22.

Ferraro, F., Pfeffer, J. and Sutton, R. (2005) 'Economics, language and assumptions: how theories can become self-fulfilling', Academy of Management Review, 30(1): 8–24.

Fine, B. (2001) Social Capital versus Social Theory, London: Routledge.

Fukuyama, F. (1995) Trust: The social virtues and the creation of prosperity, London: Penguin.

Giddings, B., Hopwood, B. and O'Brien, G. (2002) 'Environment, economy and society: fitting them together into sustainable development', Sustainable Development, 10: 187–96.

Granovetter, M. (1973) 'The strength of weak ties', American Journal of Sociology, 78(6): 1360–80.

——(1985) 'Economic action and social structure: the problem of embeddedness', American Journal of Sociology, 91(3): 481–510.

Grenier, P. (2002) 'The function of social entrepreneurship in the UK', paper presented to the ISTR Conference, Cape Town, July.

Hisrich, R. D. (1986) 'The woman entrepreneur: characteristics, skills, problems, and for success', in D. L. Sexton and R. W. Smilor (eds) The Art and Science of Entrepreneurship, Cambridge, MA: Ballinger.

Hopwood, B., Mellor, M. and O'Brien, G. (2005) 'Sustainable development: mapping different approaches', Sustainable Development, 13: 38–52.

Johnson, S. (2000) Social Entrepreneurship Literature Review, Edmonton: University of Alberta, Canadian Centre for Social Entrepreneurship.

Johnston, G. and Percy-Smith, J. (2003) 'In search of social capital', Politics and Policy, 31(3): 321–34.

Johnstone, H. and Lionais, D. (2004) 'Depleted communities and community business entrepreneurship: revaluing space through place', Entrepreneurship and Regional Development, May: 217–33.

Mathiason, N. (2005) 'Social enterprise: business phenomenon of the century', The Guardian, 20 November.

Morin, M., Simmonds, D. and Somerville, W. (2004) 'Social enterprise: mainstreamed from the margins?' Local Economy, 19(1): 69–84.

NEF/SAS (2004) Unlocking the Potential, London: New Economics Foundation/Shorebank Advisory Services, The Social Enterprise Coalition.

OECD (1999) Social Enterprises, Paris: Organisation for Economic Co-operation and Development.

Oughton, C. and Whittam, G. (1997) 'Competition and cooperation in the small firm sector', Scottish Journal of Political Economy, 44(1): 1–30.

Purdue, D. (2001) 'Neighbourhood governance: leadership, trust and social capital', Urban Studies, 38(12): 2211–24.

Quibria, M. (2003) 'The puzzle of social capital: a critical review', Asian Development Review, 20(2): 19–39.

Ridley-Duff, R. (2007) 'Communitarian perspectives on social enterprise', Corporate Governance, 15(2): 382–92.

Robison, L. and Flora, J. (2003) 'The social capital paradigm: bridging across disciplines', American Journal of Agricultural Economics, 85(5): 1187–93.

Rydin, Y. and Holman, N. (2004) 'Re-evaluating the contribution of social capital in achieving sustainable development', Local Environment, 9(2): 117–33.

Scottish Executive (2002) Better Communities in Scotland: Closing the gap, Edinburgh: Scottish Executive.

———(2003) A Review of the Scottish Executive's Policies to Promote the Social Economy, Edinburgh: Voluntary Issues Unit, Scottish Executive.

———(2004) Future Builders in Scotland: Investing in the social economy, Edinburgh: Scottish Executive.

———(2006a) People and Place: Regeneration policy statement, Edinburgh: Scottish Executive.

———(2006b) A Social Enterprise Strategy for Scotland: A consultation, Edinburgh: Scottish Executive.

Small Business Service (2005a) 'Social enterprise: emerging priorities', report of working group meeting with Alun Michael, London: Small Business Service.

———(2005b) GHK Review of the Social Enterprise Strategy: Summary of findings, London: Small Business Service.

Smallbone, D., Evans, M., Ekanem, I. and Butters, S. (2001) Researching Social Enterprise, London: Small Business Service.

Waddock, S. and Post, J. (1991) 'Social entrepreneurs and catalytic change', Public Administration Review, 51(5): 393–401.

Williams, C., Aldridge, T. and Tooke, J. (2003) 'Alternative exchange spaces', in A. Leyshon, R. Lee and C. Williams (eds) Alternative Economic Spaces, London: Sage.

Wilson, P. A. (1997) 'Building social capital: a learning agenda for the 21st century', Urban Studies, 34(5–6): 745–60.

Woolcock, M. (1998) 'Social capital and economic development: toward a theoretical synthesis and policy framework', Theory and Society, 27: 151–208.

14 Micro-Enterprise and Cooperative Development in Economically Marginalized Communities in the US

Jessica Gordon Nembhard

INTRODUCTION

The International Cooperative Alliance (ICA) used 2005, the United Nation's Year of Micro-Credit, as a stage to highlight the role cooperative enterprises have played for over a century in providing micro-finance and supporting micro-enterprise throughout the world. Launching the theme, 'Micro-finance is our business: Co-operating out of poverty' at the International Day of Cooperatives on 2 July 2005, the ICA claimed that 'cooperatives are amongst the most successful micro-finance institutions' (ICA 2005a: 1). While cooperatives have a history of financing small-scale economic activity, providing financial services to the underserved and helping members 'take advantage of social capital in situations where financial capital is scarce', this is not for what they are best known. Worker cooperatives allow members to own and govern their own company but also are not the most familiar type of cooperative. Cooperatives are better known for pooling members' resources to own agricultural marketing boards and processing plants, and to operate consumer-owned retail stores (particularly grocery) and utilities.

The purpose of this chapter is to explore how well cooperative enterprises serve the micro-finance needs and the micro-enterprise development of low income people in the US. In order to better understand micro-enterprise development and micro-financing as anti-poverty tools in the US, this chapter compares and contrasts micro-enterprise development through traditional micro-enterprise and commercial financial institutions and then through cooperative ownership and cooperative financial institutions.

This chapter addresses first why reduction or alleviation of poverty is important; what is at stake and to whom does it matter. The second section summarizes recent findings about (1) micro-financing and micro-entrepreneurship among low income people in the US; and (2) what we know about cooperatives and cooperative micro-enterprises owned by low income communities in the US, including the non-market and economic accomplishments of both approaches. In the third section, the author then compares and contrasts the benefits and impacts of the two broad strategies for community economic development and poverty reduction. The chapter ends with some conclusions about the strengths and replicability of cooperative micro-entrepreneurship and micro-financing and some reflections on policy implications and potential areas for policy advocacy.

WHY IS POVERTY REDUCTION NECESSARY?

Poverty, particularly in the US and particularly among women, children and low income people of colour, is cyclical and persistent. While the pervasiveness and scope of poverty varies with business cycles, the poor are always with us and there is a steady population in abject poverty. Even when income inequality narrows, for example, wealth inequality gaps remain wide, worldwide. Poverty has economic, social and moral costs, not just for those who experience it, but also for the entire society (see Sherman 1994, for example). There is worldwide recognition of the need to alleviate poverty and for alternative poverty-reduction strategies (Davies et al. 2008, Birchall 2003, ICA and ILO 2005).

World wealth inequality is increasing.[1] The richest 2 per cent of adult individuals own more than half of all global wealth assets, with 1 per cent of adults owning 40 per cent of global assets in the year 2000. The richest 10 per cent of adults accounted for 85 per cent of the world's total wealth (Davies et al. 2008: 7). The bottom 50 per cent of the world's adult population owned only about 1 per cent of global wealth. The wealthiest tenth's average net worth grew to three million dollars by 2004, up another 6 per cent since 2001, and up 76 per cent since 1995 (in 2004 dollars) (United for a Fair Economy 2006b).[2] The poorest quarter by net worth fell from an average net worth of $50 in 2001 to–$1,400 in 2004 (better than1998 at–$2,100, although some subgroups increased wealth slightly during the last three years).

In the US in 2001, the top 10 per cent of wealth holders owned 70 per cent of all wealth and 1 per cent owned 33 per cent of the wealth, leaving 90 per cent of wealth holders (on the bottom) with only 30 per cent of the wealth (Collins et al. 2005). By 2004, median wealth declined for families in the bottom 40 per cent of the income distribution (Bucks et al. 2006), and the debt burden increased, especially for the middle class. US savings rates (personal savings as a percentage of disposable personal income) have been on the decline, over the past 20 years, declining from 4.3 per cent in 1998 to 1.4 per cent in 2003, for example (Collins et al. 2005). While the most recent statistics have not yet been published, with the housing crisis that began in 2008 in the US and the financial crisis of 2008–9 which spread worldwide, we know that both income and wealth have been decreasing for the most vulnerable as well as for the middle class, as housing foreclosures and unemployment have risen over the past three years.

Wealth and Race

The US racial wealth gap is larger than the income gap, hovering around 60 per cent. The average African American household owns at best about 15 per cent (or 15 cents of every dollar) of the wealth the average white household owns (Gordon Nembhard and Chiteji 2006). The value of assets owned by the median white family grew from 2001 to 2004 but fell for the median family of colour. There was essentially no change (no significant increase) in the median net worth of African Americans from 2001 to 2004 as measured by the SCF, which over-samples the wealthy (Bucks et al. 2006). If measured by the Survey of Income and Programme Participation (SIPP), which over-samples those who rely on government transfers (so better represents the wealth holdings of low income people), in 2000 African American households held US$8,044 of median net worth but by 2002 held only US$5,446 (Gottschalck 2008: 13–14). Greatest wealth losses were in home equity—and this trend has significantly increased from 2007 to the end of the decade, particularly for families of colour. Similarly for Latinos, wealth holdings decreased significantly between 2000 and 2002, to $7,950 (Gottschalck 2008: 13–14), with declining home ownership. In comparison, median net worth for 'non-Hispanic whites' (a US term for whites with no Hispanic background) increased between 2000 and 2002, to US$87,056 according to SIPP measurements (Gottschalck 2008: 13–14). See Table 14.1.

Women's Wealth Inequality

Women's wealth inequality is also a particular challenge. Chang (2006) uses the 2001 Survey of Consumer Finances (both individual and household data) and finds large gender gaps between men and women of similar household types; and that single parenting matters a great deal in wealth accumulation. Never-married women under the age of 65, for example, whose incomes almost reach parity with men, have only 15 per cent of the wealth of men, whether or not they have children (the 2004 data show little change in this gap). In addition, data about women of colour suggest that they experience greater barriers to wealth accumulation than white women and that gender wealth inequality may be greater among non-white men and women than among whites (Chang 2006: 118), though

Table 14.1   Median Net Worth in 2002 in US Dollars (SIPP)

African American	$5,446
Latino	$7,950
White	$87,056

Source: Gottschalck 2008 (Table 6)

the absolute numbers are much smaller. Black separated and divorced men held US$22,700 of wealth in the 2001 SCF compared with Black separated and divorced women who held only US$3,050. Black never-married men held median net worth of US$120, compared with median net worth of US$50 for never-married Black women (Chang 2006: 117). In many cases, women are left to raise African American children but often have the fewest resources, not just lower incomes but much less wealth.[3]

Poverty rates have stabilized at about 12.3 per cent in the US, after rising continuously since 2001 (DeNavas-Walt et al. 2007).[4] The economic status of low income people and, in particular, low income people of colour and women is precarious. For women of colour especially, poverty rates have increased again, starting in 2008. Control over income and assets is thus of paramount importance (see Johnson 1997) for women's livelihoods and those of their families.

Involvement in and ownership of cooperatives, as well as micro-businesses, are one response to gaining control over assets and income; rational actions that enable individuals to take charge of their economic futures, engage in family friendly economic activity and assert their influence and energy into an economic process that provides a variety of positive returns. The following two sections provide a review of the two approaches to community economic development and poverty reduction: micro- and cooperative enterprise.

MICRO-ENTERPRISE AND COOPERATIVE ECONOMIC DEVELOPMENT

Micro-Entrepreneurship and Micro-Lending: Types, Who They Serve, Accomplishments

About 20 million of the 22 million small business owners in the US operate micro-enterprises, a very small business with five or fewer employees that 'requires US$35,000 or less in start-up capital and that does not have access to the traditional commercial banking sector' (Edgcomb and Klein 2005). According to Edgcomb and Klein, 5.13 million are women-owned micro-enterprises. African Americans own 650,000 and Latinos, 800,000 micro-enterprises. Business owners with personal incomes less than US$10,000 comprise 4.3 million and 1.7 million are owned by low income self-employed individuals. Micro-entrepreneurship programmes served an estimated 150,000 to 170,000 people in the US in 2000, at a relatively low median cost per client (Field US 2005a). A 2003 study finds that the micro-enterprise median loan loss rate is 7 per cent (Field US 2005a).

While the micro-finance industry and support organizations produce substantial research and evaluation of micro-enterprise programmes, each programme is different, and unique in different ways, which makes it difficult to make generalizations across studies (Business Research Division 2004, Edgcomb and Klein 2005). It is also difficult to make inferences from these studies about how much exactly was gained from the micro-enterprise itself; what is the exact causal effect. However, the results are generally positive and encouraging about both the effects of training in micro-entrepreneurship and the effects of micro-enterprise ownership on participants. Social and economic benefits accrue from programmes in rural and urban areas (Business Research Division 2004: 70), such as empowerment and self-sufficiency (Business Research Division 2004: 70), leadership and social capital development and skill acquisition.

Benefits and Impacts of Micro-Enterprises

Micro-enterprises offer many social and economic benefits to the community and individuals. They promote individual business development and asset ownership, often in cases where the entrepreneur has no other opportunities. As such, they 'can play a role in the revitalization of local economies' (Edgcomb and Klein 2005: 2). They provide jobs, 'enabling people to stay in their communities in spite of structural changes in local economies' (Field US 2005b: 2). While most of the businesses remain small, generating an average of 1.5 jobs, some of the businesses have had stellar growth and increase local employment (Field US 2007a: 1). They also develop a 'pipeline of entrepreneurial talent' (Field US 2007a: 2).

Most studies in the US find that micro-enterprise ownership increases household income and decreases poverty to some extent; in some cases as a key component of household income and in others as a complement to wages or as supplemental income. Micro-entrepreneurs 'appear more adept at sustaining employment, as they can move between self- and wage employment, focusing on whichever is more remunerative and appropriate given local economic conditions and their family situation' (Field US 2007a: 1).

Micro-business development as a strategy has had some successes, especially when combined with low wage work or income transfers. Elaine Edgcomb, in an e-mail note to the author (November 2000), summarises findings from the Aspen Institute's *Micro-enterprise and the Poor: Findings from the Self-Employment Learning Project Five Year Survey of Micro-entrepreneurs*, 1999: seventy-two per cent of very poor micro-entrepreneurs experienced household income gains and 53 per cent of them moved out of poverty; the micro-business contributed about 37 per cent of the increase in income and an increase in assets of US$18,706 on average; reliance on public assistance declined. Edgcomb notes that other studies have similar results. More recent studies continue to find high levels of success.[5]

Finally, there is some evidence to suggest that micro-entrepreneurship has had some success in increasing the assets of low income entrepreneurs, achieving increased savings levels, business equity, business net worth and access to credit (Edgcomb and Klein 2005, Field US 2005b: 3, Field US

2007b).[6] However, some report declines in net worth, probably because debt increased (Field US 2005b: 3).

Recent studies suggest that micro-enterprise development strategies have been successful in reaching the low income entrepreneurs. Studies reported by the Aspen Institute's FIELD programme in 2005 find that a majority of micro-entrepreneurs are from groups targeted by the 'industry': women (65 per cent), people of colour (55 per cent), low income people (59 per cent started with incomes at or below 80 per cent of area median income), people with disabilities and those who experience barriers to accessing commercial credit (Edgcomb and Klein 2005). Significantly, business survival rates are comparable to general business survival rates with similar characteristics and owners (Field US 2005a).

Among women, entrepreneurship is indeed growing. Women-owned businesses increased in the 1990s and, during most of the period, sales in these businesses increased (see Simms 2002, also Williams 2000, on the rapid growth of businesses owned by women of colour in Massachusetts). Some women-owned businesses do quite well, particularly the larger, corporate businesses in non-traditional industries (such as wholesale trade, business services, auto dealerships and manufacturing), industries in which minority women are less likely to be owners (Simms 2002: 2–3). Most women-owned businesses, however, are small and in the service or retail sectors, concentrated in specialty retail operations such as jewellery and book stores, and do not earn revenues even proportionate to their percentage of ownership of businesses. Seventeen per cent of all women-owned businesses are owned by women of colour (33.9 per cent Black, 36.5 per cent Latina, 26.8 per cent Asian and Pacific Islander, and 5.8 per cent Native American or Alaskan Native; Simms 2002: 2).

A key challenge is to further develop and strengthen women's business ownership, which has been one of the missions of many of the micro-lending and micro-business development programmes in the US and throughout the world. Ownership is a central facet of cooperative economic development, explored in the following section.

Cooperatives: Types, Who They Serve, Accomplishments

Cooperatives are companies owned by their members; the people who use their services and formed the company for a particular purpose. Cooperatives are created to satisfy a need for a quality good or service at an affordable price, a product that the market is not adequately providing. They are also created to develop an economic structure to engage in the needed production or to facilitate more equal distribution of the gains. The ICA defines a cooperative as 'an autonomous association of persons united voluntarily to meet their common economic, social and cultural needs and aspirations through a jointly owned and democratically controlled enterprise' (International Cooperative Alliance 2005b: 1).

According to the ICA, cooperatives employ more than 100 million people internationally and have more than 800 million individual members. In the US, about four in 10 people or 120 million members are served by cooperatives. According to the National Cooperative Business Association (NCBA), almost 10,000 credit unions in the US serve 84 million members and hold assets greater than US$600 billion in 2005. There are 6,400 housing cooperatives, 3,000 farmer-owned cooperatives, 1,000 mutual insurance companies, 900 rural electric cooperatives, 270 telephone cooperative, 250 purchasing cooperatives and about 300 worker cooperatives (NCBA 2005).

Cooperatives are usually classified in three categories: consumer-owned, producer-owned or worker-owned (or a hybrid of some combination of the stakeholders). In the first, consumers form a buying club or cooperative business to supply, for example, fresh produce, vegetarian foods, electricity, eco-fuels, pharmaceuticals, childcare or financial services. Cooperative retail enterprises such as natural-food grocery stores and rural energy cooperatives are some of the most numerous and successful examples. Cooperative financial institutions such as credit unions are some of the most widely used cooperatives, providing affordable and accessible financial services to underserved communities. Second, in the producer-owned model, producers form cooperatives to jointly purchase supplies and equipment or to jointly process and market their goods. Agricultural cooperatives are some of the largest and most profitable of cooperatives.

In the third category, workers use the cooperative ownership model to jointly own and manage a company for themselves, to save a company that is being sold off or closed down or to start a company that exemplifies workplace democracy and collective management. Worker-owned businesses offer economic security and democratic economic participation to employees and provide decent jobs and environmental sustainability to communities (from Gordon Nembhard 2008; see also Haynes and Gordon Nembhard 1999, Gordon Nembhard 2002, 2004b). Cooperative ownership is growing in the provision of social services such as home health care, health care, drug rehabilitation, childcare and in the area of fair trade.

Cooperatives, particularly worker-owned cooperatives, are a form of democratically owned economic enterprise that gives members control over their own income and wealth and stimulates the local economy, addressing insufficiencies and lack of access. Cooperatives are characterized by pooling of resources, joint ownership, democratic governance, and sharing risks and profits in the production, distribution, or acquisition of affordable high quality goods and services. Cooperative businesses operate according to a set of internationally agreed values and principles that have evolved over the past 150 years: voluntary and open membership; democratic control by members (based on 'one member, one vote' rather than voting according to number of shares of stock owned); members' economic participation (returns based on use); autonomy and independence (self-help organizations controlled by members); continuous education, training and information; cooperation among cooperatives; and concern for community (see Thordarson 1999, International Cooperative Alliance 2005b).

Cooperative enterprise outcomes are generally not well documented, and a general paucity of industry data is noted.[7] However, research on the effectiveness and benefits of cooperative business ownership is increasing. Some of the main impacts are outlined below.

Benefits and Impacts of Cooperative Enterprise

Cooperative economic development is proving to be successful in urban as well as rural areas around the world, developing and surviving as a response to market failure and economic marginalisation (see Fairbairn et al. 1991). They tackle a range of issues such as: community control in the face of transnational corporate concentration and expansion; pooling of resources and profit sharing in communities where capital is scarce and incomes low; and increased productivity and working conditions in industries where work conditions may be poor, and wages and benefits usually low (Gordon Nembhard 2008). The United Nations (UN) and the International Labour Organization (ILO) have recently recognised the potential of cooperative enterprises for economic development and poverty reduction (International Labour Conference 2002, Birchall 2003).

There is evidence to suggest that cooperatives increase productivity and create value, particularly where employee ownership and control exists. Levine and Tyson (1990: 202), for example, surveyed the research and found that 'both participation and ownership have positive effects on productivity'. Levine and Tyson also point out that many researchers note the superior working conditions in cooperatives. Logue and Yates (2005) find that worker cooperatives and employee-owned firms have survival rates that equal or surpass conventional firms, and a combination of conventional and non-traditional economic returns. They 'place more emphasis on job security for employee-members and employees' family members, pay competitive wages (or slightly better than their sector), provide additional variable income through profit-sharing, dividends or bonuses, and offer better fringe benefits' (2005: ix). In addition, worker cooperatives often support community programmes and facilities such as health clinics and schools.

The author's own preliminary research on the benefits of cooperative ownership finds that cooperatives fill gaps left by market failure and that successful cooperatives have income and wealth benefits for their members that spill over into their communities. Cooperatives tend to promote increased civic engagement (see for example Gordon Nembhard 2000, 2002, 2004b, Gordon Nembhard and Blasingame 2002, 2006), helping to empower communities to create new economic structures and infrastructures that meet their myriad needs, based on their particularities and experiences. The small, democratically governed cooperatives in particular, whose members are often low income, work to broaden and democratize business and home ownership, allow members to pool resources and skills to enable them to be owners and to achieve economies of scale and higher efficiencies.

There is less research on why and how a particular population of people uses cooperative ownership for their own economic advancement. The experiences of subaltern populations as economically marginalised communities with strong social solidarity provide additional socio-economic and cultural conditions from which to build relevant, viable and relatively unique cooperative economic enterprises. Because subaltern peoples are discriminated against in mainstream labour, capital and housing markets, they often have to rely on one another and work together. Subaltern populations often have little personal wealth and are excluded from much of mainstream prosperity and economic stability. Cooperatives have played an important role in advancing the rights and prospects of African Americans. African Americans have a long and strong history of cooperative ownership, especially in reaction to market failures and economic racial discrimination (see Gordon Nembhard 2004a). However, it has often been a hidden history and one thwarted by racial discrimination (and white supremacist violence).

Almost all cooperators agree that the commitment to democratic participation, economic cooperation and the provision of specific affordable, high quality goods and services are what make them different from other businesses. Democratic participation and democratic economic decision making are considered major benefits of being a member of a cooperative and a major accomplishment of cooperatives, particularly small cooperatives (see Gordon Nembhard 2004b for a full discussion of cooperative benefits).

Many new urban cooperatives include in their mission improving the quality of life and community empowerment. Most members of cooperatives and leaders feel that the benefits their cooperative gives to the community are empowering. Jobs are anchored in the community and local products supported. The pooling of resources is empowering. Many cooperatives also tend to utilise local suppliers, share resources with other cooperatives and with community organizations and residents.

Finally, there is some evidence that worker cooperatives and other employee-owned enterprises pay wages that are competitive with, or better than, locally prevailing wages and include profit sharing, bonuses and dividends that other companies usually do not offer. Worker cooperatives also tend to offer better fringe benefits than conventional companies in their field (Logue and Yates 2005). The employee ownership index, for example, outperformed the overall stock market during 1997 and since has tended to converge toward the broad stock market indicators (Logue and Yates 2005). A review of the literature shows that cooperatives and substantially employee-owned companies also have greater productivity (Logue and Yates 2005, Levine and Tyson 1990, Krimerman and Lindenfeld 1992).

One worker cooperative, Cooperative Home Care Associates (CHCA) in NYC, with over 700 member-owners, provides several asset-building opportunities for its member-owners (most of whom are low income and many of whom relied on public assistance before working at CHCA). CHCA pays annual dividends in profitable years averaging 25 per cent of initial equity investment (or US$250) and leads the industry in above average wages, benefits, career ladder, leadership training, advocacy and low turnover (Gordon Nembhard 2004a, Shipp 2000, Glasser and Brecher 2002, Inserra et al. 2002). CHCA's worker-owners also receive a US$10,000 life insurance benefit, and most owners contribute to a 401(k) plan (to which the co-op also contributes an average of US$100 per employee in profitable years) (CHCA 2008). As of October 2008 the value of its 401(k) plan exceeded US$2.5 million, and 234 worker-owners accumulated more than US$4,000 in their accounts (CHCA 2008). CHCA also aids its employee-owners to establish checking and/or savings accounts. Seventy per cent of CHCA's employees use direct deposit into savings or checking accounts but before joining the company 73 per cent had not had a checking account and 79 per cent did not have a savings account (CHCA 2008). The cooperative also provides small no-interest loans and allows cashing out vacation days to help members with cash flow problems. In addition, CHCA helps about 30 per cent of its worker-owners to receive the Earned Income Tax Credit and Child Tax Credit and promotes free income tax preparation services (CHCA 2008).

Cooperative Micro-Finance

Financing and capitalization are issues, particularly for small cooperatives in low income communities. Even though cooperatives address some level of financing by helping members pool their resources and leverage other resources, it is difficult for cooperative businesses to raise all the money needed through member equity.[8] There are a variety of fund-raising strategies and loan agreements used to augment member's equity. Low income cooperatives in particular often combine member equity with loans and grants, for start-up and expansion, which come from both traditional lending institutions and sector specific sources. A few successful worker cooperatives in the US have started to set up revolving loan funds and development funds and services to help create new worker cooperatives.[9]

Credit unions have been used historically not just to provide financial services to underserved communities but also for business development and to fund cooperative development. This model was used historically in the Black community (see for example Pitts 1950) and is also the model practiced very successfully in Spain by the Mondragon Cooperative Corporation.[10] William Jackson's research on US credit unions empirically confirms credit union pro-consumer behaviours. Credit unions exhibit a pricing asymmetry that lowers the interest expense associated with deposits but also lowers the interest revenue associated with loans over the interest rate cycle, 'consistent with a strategy of maintaining constant margins between average deposit rates and average loan rates' (Filene Research Institute 2006: 1). Keeping loans affordable and providing as high a return on savings as possible is important at any period of time and for every demographic but is particularly important for low income households and those denied access to traditional financing.[11]

Credit unions whose mission is to promote community economic development, such as Community Development Credit Unions (CDCUs), provide access to affordable commercial and mortgage loans to help low income communities develop affordable housing and small locally owned businesses. CDCUs in the US serve low income populations with 'fairly priced loans', financial savings and transaction services at a 'reasonable cost' (National Federation of Community Development Credit Unions 2008). The 1.4 million members (predominantly low income and of colour) hold an average deposit of $3,789 (CDFI Data Project 2006). Memberships, assets, shares and net worth of CDCUs grew, expanding at rates greater than those of most mainstream credit unions over the past several years (Gemerer 2008). While delinquency rates are starting to increase, they are still below industry average. In 2006, CDCUs opened an estimated 78,774 new accounts to people who were previously unbanked. As of the end of 2006, an estimated 1,889 members accumulated $1.8 million toward specific wealth-building savings goals through CDCU IDA (Individual Development Account) programmes (CDFI Data Project 2006). The expanse of CDCUs is particularly important to people of colour who suffer from credit market discrimination and even may be less likely to receive a micro-credit loan. More research is needed to document this.

The above descriptions of micro-enterprise and cooperative economic development strategies reflect how they are often treated as completely separate approaches. The next section will tease out areas of similarity and construct an argument for greater policy recognition of collective aspects of micro-enterprise.

COMPARING MICRO-BUSINESS AND COOPERATIVE BUSINESS

As seen in the sections above, micro-business development has had some successes, especially as a strategy combined with low wage work or income transfers. Some studies in the US find that micro-enterprise ownership increases profits and household income. Jonathan Feldman (2002: 69) summarises that 'to the extent that micro-enterprises reduce unemployment and pay more than income subsidies, they can contribute towards reducing inequality.' Owning a business, or business equity, is certainly an important component of the wealth portfolio. For low income people and women, owning a business is an important asset but also an important income generator. Micro-enterprise ownership develops entrepreneurship, economic independence and leadership, allowing groups to turn work and opportunities in the informal sector into business ownership more in the formal sector of the economy. However, as Feldman goes on to argue, these successes are tempered when examined in greater depth.

Feldman postulates that 'the income levels and gains by workers and firms linked to micro-enterprises may still be considerably less than those of average workers and firms' (2002: 92). Women-owned businesses, for example, are not generally the big profitable businesses. All businesses as well as businesses that are jointly owned between two spouses, had higher annual receipts than women-owned businesses (Simms 2002: 2). Most women small business owners increase their incomes, but if amounts are analysed the increase is often only incremental. They also do not always accumulate much wealth from their entrepreneurship. Their economic situation may stabilize but business ownership is always risky. Overall, even though micro-businesses tend to experience longer average sustainability than traditional small businesses, probably because of the supports that accompany their development, they are still precarious.

Smallness is a disadvantage and 'isolated micro-enterprises may often be confined to relatively "underdeveloped" or labour-intensive sectors that require relatively low skills but are relatively spatially fixed' (Feldman 2002: 92). In addition 'scarce resources and limited cost recovery have affected the [micro-finance] industry's ability to reach larger numbers of micro-entrepreneurs' (Edgcomb and Klein 2005: 2). While generally considered to be a successful development strategy, there are not enough resources to support or help all micro-entrepreneurs, reducing the impacts micro-business ownership could have. Studies suggest that access to capital and follow-up services (US Department of Health and Human Services 1994), services such as entrepreneurship training, mentoring and networking (NED&LC 1998), more time to develop a business and greater access to computers and computer training (Dumas 2001) are necessary if this strategy is to live up to its potential for low income women and people of colour.

Moreover, the global nature of the economy advantages large-scale, multinational or networked economies and actively disadvantages small-scale, stand-alone firms. Their small size can of course be an advantage in that micro-business owners can sometimes suspend business activity for a time and start up again when they want or need to without incurring new costs of entry or transactions costs. This makes micro-business more flexible, even as it is vulnerable to the vagaries of the market. Generally, however, small stand-alone businesses struggle to survive in an increasingly global economy and struggle to provide employees (and owners) with livable wages, full benefits and job ladder opportunities. Only about 50 per cent of low income entrepreneurs have health insurance, for example, according to one study (Field US 2005a). In addition, their small scale often limits their profitability as well as their ability to gain market share and grow.

There are many similarities between the micro-business development programmes and cooperative business development models. Shared risk and social and economic networking in particular stand out as common to both. At the same time, cooperative businesses tend to suffer from similar challenges to small businesses. Often the work is gruelling and endless, the return is small and growth is difficult; and cooperatives are challenged additionally by developing trust and effective strategies for democratic governance.

As seen, however, the cooperative model offers additional protection against the isolation, constraints and market vagaries described above. Cooperative ownership provides control over capital, participation and management expertise similar to business ownership in general, but with shared risks and returns to owners rather than lenders. In a cooperative, members share ownership responsibilities, so duties and stresses about a specific business are spread over a group rather than a single owner or competing owners. Collective wisdom and sense of solidarity increase productivity and peace of mind. Feldman summarises that cooperative ownership—democratic management and profit sharing—tends to redirect profits for reinvestment in the firm to promote training, and reduces the possibility that mangers take advantage of their lower status, less skilled or less professionally secure co-workers (Feldman 2002: 161). He also notes that 'governance systems that lead to improved worker participation can improve product quality, competitiveness and therefore growth (Feldman 2002: 162). The pooling of capital into cooperative businesses increases resources and increases scale, which is particularly important to the sustainability and affordability of micro-businesses. Many women-owned cooperatives in particular also develop job ladder mobility for increased opportunities within the enterprise.

At a more social level, cooperatives encourage interaction, teamwork, inter-cooperation, and giving back to one's community. They also develop social ties among members and between members and the community—a sense of solidarity (see Shipp 2000, Gordon Nembhard and Haynes 2002). Cooperators develop social capital skills, so that networking and working together become the norm, and the skills to facilitate this are developed in all members (see Shipp 2000, Gordon Nembhard 2004b). Cooperative members and employee owners become used to the transparency and accountability in their own organizations (through open-book policies, 'one member, one vote', shared management and so on). They come to expect transparency and accountability and help re-create this in civil society and political arenas (Gordon Nembhard and Blasingame 2002). Many members become more active in their communities in general, taking on leadership roles both in their cooperatives and in voluntary and community organizations (this was found especially with women members and in communities of colour; see Weiss and Clamp 1992, Nippierd 1999, Mammen and Paxson 2000, Gordon Nembhard 2004b for examples). In addition, citizen activism and advocacy often can be effective countervailing forces that increase democracy and participation (see Gordon Nembhard 2004b, Gordon Nembhard and Blasingame 2002 for further discussion of this).

The major difference between the two approaches, for the purposes of this chapter, is that micro-business development models do not officially recognise collaboration—the benefits from collaboration and the pooling of resources and risks—the official cooperative principles and cooperative ownership structures that increase job ladder mobility and increase growth while maintaining worker-owner control. Rather than competing strategies, however, these might better be viewed as complementary strategies.

Feldman (2002) suggests several changes in the focus of micro-enterprise development (see Feldman 2002: 145) but, most importantly for this chapter, more emphasis on collaborative aspects of micro-enterprise. He argues that through 'the creation of strategic alliances and networks' ethnic micro-enterprises can overcome the disadvantages of their small size and build resources using the 'complementary capacities' of their affiliates (p.150). In addition smaller firms can develop and supply labour to larger affiliate firms in a cluster of interlocking enterprises that support each other. Also working with universities and other community organizations, members of small enterprises can increase their own skills and those of their employees and build organizational capacities, while increasing the quality of their networks. Higher quality networks provide job ladder and career mobility opportunities. Increasing an entrepreneur's skills and human capital often coincides with an ability to make a larger equity investment which increases the likelihood of success (Feldman 2002). Also job ladders can be built by 'extending labour saving technology and advanced technologies' (p. 157). Finally, investment in highly technical and highly skilled businesses, and the ability to own and operate a high tech company, is more lucrative—achieving entree into high paid niches and modernising a firm (p. 154). Better pooling of resources can enable entrepreneurs to enter more lucrative industries.

One example of networks in practice is peer lending. Many micro-enterprise studies find that 'peer lending' or 'solidarity circles,' which provide a 'more cohesive, supportive environment' than the individual loan programmes for micro-businesses, 'is a better community development strategy than an individual lending programme' (NED&LC 1998: 34). The former Executive Director of Coalition for Women's Economic Development contends that 'inherent in [the peer lending] model is community risk, community solidarity and community empowerment' (NED&LC 1998). Creating a pool or team of businesses that screen each other and take responsibility for each member paying back the loan has been proven very successful both for the micro-entrepreneurs and for the lenders. This lowers risks and transactions costs for the lenders. In addition, peer lending uses the sense of solidarity, responsibility and trust among the group to strengthen and support micro-enterprise development. The study by the University of Colorado School of Business (Business Research Division 2004: 63), for example, finds that 'lending groups can serve as a mechanism for peer support and networking, two vital components to successful entrepreneurship.' Colorado micro-enterprise service providers use peer boards and alliances that facilitate discussion among emerging and small business owners who 'solve their issues together with other micro-enterprise owners' (p. 61). Cooperative businesses do this organically—pooling of resources, learning together and joint decision making are major components of a cooperative business. Here strategies to develop both kinds of firms, and some aspects of training, could be joined to support both forms of business ownership.

Feldman builds on this in his suggestion that a franchise cooperative model is the best strategy to strengthening the micro-enterprise model. Feldman suggests that the constraints felt by micro-enterprises can be overcome by various forms of collaboration, using innovation and alternative ways to organise resource development. Franchise cooperatives interlink small business owners and cooperatives into federations and associations or networks which share marketing, training, supply procurement, distribution, financing and other activities, similar to marketing cooperatives and other kinds of producer cooperatives. 'The ability of ethnic micro-enterprises to benefit from training, innovation and progressive governance systems will be enhanced if such micro-enterprises are part of larger entrepreneurial networks' (Feldman 2002: 107).

Franchises can provide scale economies to support training, and promote the adoption of technologies. 'Franchise cooperatives' (Feldman's term) add the democratic governance and shared ownership components of cooperatives to other small businesses, and provide economies of scale (Feldman 2002: 164). Feldman notes that cooperatives tend not to franchise but that this is an important strategy with great potential. Versions of the cooperative franchise model include the Mondragon Cooperative Corporation in Spain (MacLeod 1997, Mondragon Cooperative Corporation 2006), and the Association of Arizmendi Cooperatives bakeries in the Bay Area of California in the US (Marrafino 2009).

Another model in which networks and micro-enterprise operate to the benefit of low income communities is the extended family. Extended family members are often essential in micro-enterprise development and to a micro-business' success. Some communities use their extended families as a source of social capital and economic support which aids business development and wealth accumulation. Robles (2006) finds this in Latino families and suggests that the expansion of social networks is likely to play a critical role in determining wealth accumulation among Latinos. Extended families are also important in Native American, Asian American and Native Hawaiian, and African American communities. They can be another mechanism to reduce the burden of child rearing on one family or a single parent; and also are an economic resource and a source of additional finances. Policies that recognise and empower extended family networks are therefore also wealth enhancing, and potential business development policies.

Cooperatives re-create the extended family among unrelated members so that business ownership collectivizes work, and creates another kind of extended family—often just as functional. The joint ownership of enterprises that provides such collective work, services and supports not only stabilizes income but provides opportunities for asset building to a wider group of people. Cooperatives magnify the effectiveness of micro-enterprise, and mitigate many of the challenges that plague and hinder micro-enterprise development and success.

In conclusion, it appears that many similarities already exist between the micro-business development programmes and cooperative business development models. Micro-ownership as a collective enterprise is seen to address many of the issues facing sole proprietor micro-enterprise ownership, such as risk, scale and isolation. The main difference between the two approaches, as argued here, is that micro-business development models mostly do not officially *recognise* collaboration. Embracing some of these cooperative principles and structures can magnify the effectiveness of micro-enterprise, and mitigate many of the challenges that plague and hinder micro-enterprise development and success. Rather than competing strategies, these might better be viewed as complementary strategies that are already making a difference to communities and people.

CONCLUSIONS

While micro-enterprises and cooperatives share many qualities, this chapter has argued that the collective/peer-to-peer aspects of cooperative enterprise could strengthen the micro-enterprise offering; 'micro-ownership as a collective enterprise'. As seen, many of the elements that support and strengthen micro-enterprise development are the collective, peer-to-peer components of the programmes, where micro-business cohorts help each other and are responsible for each others' loans. While effective, these elements are not necessarily recognised as such. These are important and well celebrated elements of cooperative ownership.

The cooperative approach offers advantages, which it could be argued solve in many ways the limitations of the sole proprietor micro-enterprise model. They spread risk and share resources so that responsibility and training is not a burden on any one entrepreneur. Cooperatives are governed democratically, and profits are shared equitably with a view to both the good of the business as well as the needs of members, their families and their communities. Members work together, problem solve together and share responsibility for the business and its assets and liabilities—thus lessening some of the stresses of business ownership, and capitalizing from multiple viewpoints and on joint responsibilities. Cooperative enterprises are also a particularly effective and responsive way for subaltern populations, for whom the market system does not often work favourably, to participate economically. They have played an important role in forwarding the rights and prospects of certain populations for a long time already. Connecting micro-enterprise development and micro-lending strategies with cooperative ownership would help make the model more useful to even more people and their communities.

To strengthen the case being built in this chapter, however, more evidence and documentation of cooperatives' impacts are needed. The successes within certain populations, for example, are often anecdotal and isolated, little understood and even less documented—particularly as part of an economic development strategy and a larger economic independence movement. Much better data about cooperative enterprises and their development would contribute to our understanding of the potential for increasing the scale of cooperative business ownership and cooperative franchising.

Over the centuries cooperative businesses have provided important and innovative structures for economic solidarity, independence and democracy, particularly for marginalised communities. The twenty-first century can witness exponential growth in this model if we maximize its strengths and intelligently address the remaining challenges.

NOTES

1. Davies et al. 2008 explain the difficulty in gathering and comparing data globally on wealth holdings within countries (particularly in the developing world) and across countries. Their estimates are carefully made, based on all available information. Also see Bucks et al. 2006 and Gottschalck 2008 for an explanation of wealth data in the United States.
2. United for a Fair Economy (UFE) using data from the Federal Reserve's Survey of Consumer Finances
3. There are no comparable wealth statistics specifically about Latinos.
4. The 2006 rate though lower than 2005 remains higher than the late 1990s. Rates for children (17.4 per cent), children under six (20 per cent) and female-householder single parent families (28.3 per cent) remain high. The poverty levels of Latinos (20.6 per cent) and Blacks (24.3 per cent) are much higher than the average and for whites (8.2 per cent) (DeNavas-Walt et al. 2007). Browne (1999) notes that Latinas and African American women continue to face the greatest risk of poverty. During the late 1970s and early 1980s, the labour market looked much better for women of colour (better than for their male counterparts). However, by the end of the 1980s, advancement for African American women had at best stalled and Latinas continued to show some economic mobility but at a slower pace (also see Badgett and Williams 1994, Browne 1999). 'Women of color are increasingly responsible for supporting their families at a time when all individuals at the bottom of the income distribution are slipping further behind those at the top' (Browne 1999: 1).

5. In one study the average household income of participants increased by 19 per cent (from US$32,743 to US$38,859) after an average of two years (Field US 2005a). Welfare recipients increased household income by 87 per cent over two years, from US$10,114 to US$18,952 (Field US 2005a). The Field study found that 36 per cent of the 24 per cent of participants who began the programme living in poverty experienced a net increase in income above the poverty line (Field US 2005a). Another study found that household income increased by 91 per cent and 72 per cent of 133 low income entrepreneurs reported income growth, with some of them achieving levels above poverty (Field US 2005b:1). Studies also find that low income participants, particularly those relying on government assistance, significantly reduced their welfare receipts over two to five years (Field US 2005a).

6. In one study, 37 per cent of clients increased savings and median savings were US$2,000. On the other hand, some reported increased net worth while others reported declines in net worth, probably because debt increased (Field US 2005b: 3). Note that in some studies average assets held by participants was US$10,000 after two and a half years; business assets were over US$4,000 after two years; and business net worth averaged about US$4,000 after two years in two studies (Field US 2007b). In addition Edgcomb and Klein (2005) find that, after five years, participants held median household assets of US$13,140; home ownership increased from 14 per cent to 22 per cent (2005: 70). These levels are still low if compared to the average white family in the US, however.

7. In the US, cooperatives and their sectors, and the cooperative industry in general, do not maintain extensive records or data sets. The US Department of Agriculture maintains some data and analyses the agricultural cooperative sector. The National Cooperative Business Association and National Cooperative Bank (NCB) keep some statistics about US-based cooperatives. The credit union sector collects the best data. We have the least systematic data about worker cooperatives.

8. Members contribute to the equity from their own savings or earnings through a membership fee or initial investment. The cooperative holds their equity share in an internal account and usually disburses dividends based on share value and patronage. Cooperatives, like other businesses, often need more capital than their members can contribute on their own.

9. See for example Maraffino 2009 and Worker Ownership Fund n.d. Also the Federation of Southern Cooperatives/Land Assistance Fund (a non-profit organization that supports rural cooperative development and land acquisition/retention) raises funds (from private and government sources) to provide technical services, loans and a revolving loan fund to its cooperative members; and includes a network of credit unions serving rural Black communities (Federation of Southern Cooperatives/Land Assistance Fund 2002, Gordon Nembhard 2004a).

10. Mondragon's Credit Union, Caja Laboral, is heavily involved in cooperative development, research and development and other financial supports for its network of cooperatives (see MacLeod 1997, Thomas 2000). Mondragon also supports a university and other educational institutions which promote cooperative development in addition to meeting traditional educational needs (see Mondragon Cooperative Corporation 2006).

11. Credit Union National Association (CUNA) reports that in the 12 months ending December 2007, US credit unions provided nearly US$11 billion in direct financial benefits to the nation's 87 million members—'equivalent to US$126 per member or US$239 per member household' (CUNA 2008a).

Credit union members hold an average member deposit of US$6,897 (CDFI Data Project 2006). In CUNA's document, 'Benefits of Credit Union Membership', the trade organisation also calculates that credit unions provide an average saving of US$181 per year on a US$25,000 new automobile loan, and that 'those who use the credit union extensively—often receive total financial benefits that are much greater than the average.' In the past four years, both loan and savings growth of credit unions has increased while delinquencies remained low and relatively flat (CUNA 2008b).

BIBLIOGRAPHY

Badgett, M., Lee, V. and Williams, R. M. (1994) 'The changing contours of discrimination: race, gender and structural economic change', in M. Bernstein and D. Adler (eds) Understanding American Economic Decline, Cambridge: Cambridge University Press.

Birchall, J. (2003) Rediscovering the Cooperative Advantage: Poverty reduction through self-help, Geneva: Cooperative Branch, International Labour Office.

Browne, I. (ed.) (1999). Latinas and African American Women at Work, New York: Russell Sage Foundation.

Bucks, B. K., Kennickell, A. B. and Moore, K. B. (2006) 'Recent changes in US family finances: evidence from the 2001 and 2004 Survey of Consumer Finances', Federal Reserve Bulletin, A1–A38.

Business Research Division (2004) Analysis of Micro-Enterprise Business Segments in Colorado, Boulder: Leeds School of Business, University of Colorado at Boulder.

CDFI Data Project (2006) 'Providing Capital, Building Communities, Creating Impact', Community Development Financial Institutions, 6th Edition. Online. Available http://www.natfed.org/files/public/CDP_FY_2006_Joint_Publication.pdf (accessed 1 December 2008).

Center for the Study of Cooperatives (1998) Proceedings from the Women in Cooperatives Forum, November 7–8, 1997, Saskatoon, Saskatchewan (Canada): Center for the Study of Cooperatives, University of Saskatchewan.

Chang, M. L. (2006) 'Women and wealth', in J. Gordon Nembhard and N. Chiteji (eds) Wealth Accumulation and Communities of Colour in the US: Current issues, Ann Arbor: University of Michigan Press.

Collins, C. and Yeskel, F. with United for a Fair Economy and Class Action (2005) Economic Apartheid in America, New York: New Press.

Cooperative Home Care Associates (CHCA) (2008) 'Helping low income New York City residents develop assets', presentation and mimeo at the Annie E. Casey Foundation conference, 'Expanding Asset Building Opportunities through Shared Ownership', Baltimore, 2 December.

Credit Union National Association (CUNA) (2007) The Benefits of Membership, Economics and Statistics Department report. Online. Available http://www.cuna.org (accessed December 2007).

——(2008a) 'The Benefits of Credit uUnion Membership'. Online. Available http://www.cuna.org (accessed 7 November 2008).

——(2008b) 'US Credit Union Profile: Mid-Year 2008', Economics and Statistics Department report. Online. Available www.cuna.org (accessed 7 November 2008).

Curl, J. (2003) 'A History of Worker Cooperation in America'. Online. Available http://www.red-coral.net/WorkCoops.html (accessed 6 March 2003).

Davies, J. B., Sandstrom, S., Shorrocks, A. and Wolff, E. N. (2008) 'The world distribution of household wealth', Discussion Paper No. 2008/03, Helsinki,

Finland: United Nations University World Institute for Development Economics Research (UNU-WIDER).

DeNavas-Walt, C., Proctor, B. D. and Smith, J. (2007) 'Income, poverty, and health insurance coverage in the United States: 2006', Current Population Reports P60–233 (US Census Bureau), Washington, DC: US Government Printing Office.

Dumas, C. (2001) 'Evaluating the outcomes of micro-enterprise training for low income women: a case study', Journal of Developmental Entrepreneurship, 6(2): 97–128.

Edgcomb, E. L. (2000). E-mail note to the author, November.

Edgcomb, E. L. and Klein, J. A. (2005) Opening Opportunities, Building Ownership: Fulfilling the promise of micro-enterprise in the United States, Washington, DC: Aspen Institute, FIELD.

Fairbairn, B., Bold, J., Fulton, M., Ketilson, L. H. and Ish, D. (1991) Cooperatives & Community Development: Economics in Social Perspective, Saskatoon, Saskatchewan: University of Saskatchewan Center for the Study of Cooperatives (revised 1995).

Federation of Southern Cooperatives/Land Assistance Fund (2002) 35th Anniversary—2002 Annual Report, East Point, GA: FSC/LAF.

Feldman, J. M. (2002) 'From micro-enterprise to franchise cooperative: a new model for ethnic entrepreneurship', in J. M. Feldman and J. Gordon Nembhard (eds) From Community Economic Development and Ethnic Entrepreneurship to Economic Democracy: The cooperative alternative, Umea, Sweden: University of Umea. (National Institute for Working Life).

Field US (2005a) 'Fast Facts & Highlights', Field US Stats and Stories. Online. Available http://fieldus.org/Stories/FastFacts.html (accessed 3 February 2008).

——(2005b) 'Micro-enterprise: making a difference', FIELD Funder Guide, Issue 2, Washington, DC: Aspen Institute.

——(2007a) 'Making the economic development connection', FIELD Funder Guide, Issue 9, Washington, DC: Aspen Institute.

——(2007b) 'Micro-enterprise programmes as asset builders', FIELD Funder Guide, Issue 10, Washington, DC: Aspen Institute.

Filene Research Institute (2006) 'A Comparison of the Deposit and Loan Pricing Behaviour of Credit Unions and Commercial Banks', review of W. E. Jackson III (2006) A Comparison of the Deposit and Loan Pricing Behavior of Credit Unions and Commercial Banks. Online. Available http://filene.org/publications/detail/a-comparison-of-the-deposit-and-loan-pricing-behavior-of-credit-unions-and-commercial-banks (accessed 5 August 2009).

Freedom Quilting Bee (2002). Online. Available http://www.ruraldevelopment.org/FQBhistory.html (accessed 30 September).

Gemerer, G. (2008) Financial Trends in Community Development Credit Unions: A statistical analysis (January 1–December 31, 2007), New York: National Federation of Community Development Credit Unions.

Glasser, R. and Brecher, J. (2002) We Are the Roots: The organizational culture of a home care cooperative, Davis: University of California Center for Cooperatives.

Gordon Nembhard, J. (2000) 'Democratic economic participation and humane urban redevelopment', Trotter Review: 26–31.

——(2002) 'Cooperatives and wealth accumulation: preliminary analysis', American Economic Review, 92(2): 325–29.

——(2004a) 'Cooperative ownership in the struggle for African American economic empowerment', Humanity and Society, 28(3): 298–321.

——(2004b) 'Non-traditional analyses of cooperative economic impacts: preliminary indicators and a case study', Review of International Co-operation, 97(1): 6–21.

————(2008) 'Cooperatives', in W. A. Darity (ed.) International Encyclopaedia of the Social Sciences, 2nd Edition, Farmington Hills, MI: Macmillan Reference US (Thomson Gale).

Gordon Nembhard, J. and Blasingame, A. (2002) 'Economic dimensions of civic engagement and political efficacy', Working Paper, Democracy Collaborative-Knight Foundation Civic Engagement Project, University of Maryland, College Park.

————(2006) 'Wealth, civic engagement and democratic practice', in J. Gordon Nembhard and N. Chiteji (eds) Wealth Accumulation and Communities of Colour in the US: Current issues, Ann Arbor: University of Michigan Press.

Gordon Nembhard, J. and Chiteji, N. (2006) 'Introduction', in J. Gordon Nembhard and H. Chiteji (eds) Wealth Accumulation and Communities of Colour in the US: Current issues, Ann Arbor: University of Michigan Press.

Gordon Nembhard, J. and Haynes Jr, C. (2002) 'Using Mondragon as a model for African American urban redevelopment', in J. M. Feldman and J. Gordon Nembhard (eds) From Community Economic Development and Ethnic Entrepreneurship to Economic Democracy: The cooperative alternative, Umea, Sweden: University of Umea. (National Institute for Working Life). [Excerpted from 'A Networked Cooperative Economic Development: Mondragon as a Model for African American Urban Redevelopment', unpublished working paper, 2002.]

Gottschalck, A. O. (2008) 'Net worth and asset ownership of households: 2002', in Current Population Reports P70–115 (April), Washington, DC: US Census Bureau.

Haynes, C., Jr and Gordon Nembhard, J. (1999) 'Cooperative economics—a community revitalization strategy', The Review of Black Political Economy, 27(1): 47–71.

Holyoke, G. J. (1918) The History of the Rochdale Pioneers, 10th Edition, New York: Charles Scribner's Sons.

Inserra, A., Conway, M. and Rodat, J. (2002). Cooperative Home Care Associates: A case study of a sectoral employment development approach, Washington, DC: Aspen Institute Economic Opportunities Programme.

International Cooperative Alliance (ICA) (2005a) 'Message from the International Cooperative Alliance', 83rd ICA International Cooperative Day, 11th UN International Day of Cooperatives, 'Microfinance is our business—co-operating out of poverty', Geneva, Switzerland, July 2.

————(2005b) 'What Is a Co-op?', Geneva, Switzerland: International Cooperative Alliance, July 29. Online. Available http://www.ica.coop/coop (accessed 24 August 2006).

International Cooperative Alliance and International Labour Office (ILO) (no date, c. 2005). 'Cooperating out of Poverty: the Global Cooperative Campaign Against Poverty', Geneva, Switzerland. Online. Available http://www.coop.org/outofpoverty/campaign.pdf (accessed 23 August 2006).

International Labour Conference (2002) 'Recommendation 193: recommendation concerning the promotion of cooperatives', International Labour Office. Online. Available http://www.ilo.org/coop (accessed 23 August 2006).

Jackson, W. E., III (2006) A Comparison of the Deposit and Loan Pricing Behavior of Credit Unions and Commercial Banks. Online. Available http://filene.org/publications/detail/a-comparison-of-the-deposit-and-loan-pricing-behavior-of-credit-unions-and-commercial-banks (accessed 6 December 2009).

Johnson, R. (1997) 'Poor women, work, and community development: a reflection paper', Mimeo, Jamaica Plain, MA: Cooperative Economics for Women.

Krimerman, L. and Lindenfeld, F. (eds) (1992) When Workers Decide: Workplace democracy takes root in North America, Philadelphia: New Society.

Levine, D. and Tyson, L. (1990) 'Participation, productivity and the firm's environment', in A. Blinder (ed.) Paying for Productivity: A look at the evidence, Washington, DC: Brookings Institution Press.

Logue, J. and Yates, J. (2005) Productivity in Cooperatives & Worker-Owned Enterprises: Ownership and participation make a difference!, Geneva, Switzerland: International Labour Office.

MacLeod, G. (1997) From Mondragon to America, Sydney, Nova Scotia: University College of Cape Breton Press.

Mammen, K. and Paxson, C. (2000) 'Women's work and economic development', The Journal of Economic Perspectives, 14(4): 141–64.

Marraffino, J. (2009) 'The replication of Arizmendi Bakery: a model of the Democratic Worker Cooperative Movement', Grassroots Economic Organizing (GEO) Newsletter, 2(3).

Mondragon Cooperative Corporation (2006) 'The History of an Experience'. Online. Available http://www.mcc.coop/ing/quienessomos/historiaMCC_ing.pdf; and 'Economic Data: Most Relevant Data'. Available http://www.mcc.coop/ing/magnitudes/cifras.html (both accessed 31 January 2006).

National Cooperative Business Association (NCBA) (2005) 'About Cooperatives' and 'Statistics'. Online. Available http://www.ncba.coop (accessed 23 August 2006).

National Economic Development & Law Center (NED&LC), and Coalition for Women's Economic Development (CWED) (1998) The Challenge of Micro-Enterprise: The CWED story, Oakland, CA: NED&LC.

National Federation of Community Development Credit Unions (2008) 'What Is a CDCU?' Online. Available http://www.natfed.org (accessed August 18 2008).

Nippierd, A,-B. (1999) 'Gender issues in cooperatives', Journal of Cooperative Studies, 32(3): 175–81.

Pitts, N. A. (1950) The Cooperative Movement in Negro Communities of North Carolina: A dissertation, Studies in Sociology 33, Washington, DC: Catholic University of America Press.

Reynolds, B. J. (2001) 'A history of African-American farmer cooperatives, 1938–2000', presentation to the annual meeting of the NCR-194, USDA/RBS/Cooperative Services. Mimeo, US Department of Agriculture. Online. Available http://www.agecon.ksu.edu/accc/ncr194/Events/2001meeting/Reynolds01.pdf(accessed [date]).

Robles, B. (2006) 'Wealth creation in Latino communities: Latino families, community assets and cultural capital', in J. Gordon Nembhard and N. Chiteji (eds) Wealth Accumulation and Communities of Color in the US: Current issues, Ann Arbor: University of Michigan Press.

Sherman, A. (1994) Wasting America's Future: The Children's Defense Fund report on the costs of child poverty, Boston: Beacon Press.

Shipp, S. C. (2000) 'Worker-owned firms in inner-city neighborhoods: an empirical study', Review of International Co-operation, 92–93(4/99–1/00): 42–46.

Simms, M. C. (2002) 'Women-owned businesses in 1997: a step in the right direction', paper presented at the Allied Social Sciences Association Meetings, Atlanta, January 4.

Thomas, K. (2000). 'Lessons of Mondragon's employee-owned network', Owners at Work, 12(1): 5–9.

Thordarson, B. (1999) 'Cooperative legislation and the cooperative identity statement', Journal of Cooperative Studies, 32(2): 87–93.

United for a Fair Economy (2006a) 'Closing the racial wealth divide', presentation, Boston, September.

———(2006b) 'New data: the wealth divide widens', Press Release, United for a Fair Economy, February 23. Online. Available http://www.faireconomy.org/press/2006/wealth_divide_widens.html#top (accessed 24 August 2006).

United States Department of Agriculture (1995) What Are Cooperatives? Cooperative Information Report 10. Washington, DC: USDA Rural Business and Cooperative Development Service.

US Department of Health and Human Services, Administration for Children and Families, Office of Community Services (1994) Micro-Business and Self-Employment Monograph Series 200–90, Demonstration Partnership Programme Projects, Summary of Final Evaluation Findings from FY 1990, Washington, DC: US Department of Health and Human Services.

Weiss, C. and Clamp, C. (1992) 'Women's cooperatives: part of the answer to poverty?', in L. Krimerman and F. Lindenfeld (eds) When Workers Decide: Workplace democracy takes root in North America, Philadelphia: New Society.

Williams, R. E. (2000) 'Business ownership patterns among Black, Latina, and Asian women in Massachusetts', Trotter Review: 5–14.

Worker Ownership Fund, Northcountry Cooperative Development Fund (n.d.). Online. Available http://ncdf.coop/WorkerOwnershipFund.html (16 August 2009).

15 Alternative Forms of Enterprise

Peter North

INTRODUCTION

The concept of entrepreneurialism is usually associated with those 'movers and shakers', those heroes who set up new businesses that create the wealth we need to redistribute, and who employ those not so gifted or motivated. As they are so lauded by the political right, entrepreneurs usually engender scepticism from the political left. Yet given that, post-1989, the alternative to an economy based in some way on entrepreneurialism—state planning—has few advocates, is it time to think more deeply about entrepreneurialism and reclaim it for the left? The author poses a number of pertinent questions including: What is the difference between political organising and entrepreneurialism, which use similar skills? Should the focus be on the outcomes of entrepreneurialism, rather than the process? How much profit is 'too much' and how do we use profit? And what other forms of economic life, valued by the left, can make use of entrepreneurialism?

This chapter aims to recapture the concepts of entrepreneurialism and enterprise for the left, away from business. It will discuss whether, by reclaiming entrepreneurism for the left, we are reconciling ourselves to markets, forgetting older left values like production for need rather than for profit, and ignoring the role of planning. It asks what the difference is between an entrepreneur, an activist, an organiser and a leader? When is someone creating value and to be applauded; when are they a ruthless exploiter of value created by someone else (Hart 2001)? Do we need a left conception of enterprise, counterposed to passivity and dependence? Or would it make more sense to leave enterprise and entrepreneurialism as more narrowly defined concepts associated with wealth creation in market economies? While the focus of this book is on enterprise in deprived communities, the aim for this chapter is to widen the discussion to what forms of entrepreneurialism and enterprising behaviour are engaged with by subaltern communities, who may be located in inner cities, rather than inner cities per se. This is a different project from those who argue either that inner cities suffer from market failure or that they form important sites for market activity, with its own specific advantage (Porter 1996). Rather, it seeks to widen our conceptions of what 'entrepreneurial' activity is, to reclaim it from a narrow focus on business or the business 'movers and shakers' that Thatcher saw as the saviours of the inner city (Peck 1995).

The argument will unfold as follows. First, conceptions of enterprise and entrepreneurialism are examined. What is the role of the business person acting as an entrepreneur? How are the factors of production put together in new ways and surplus generated and distributed? The Marxist critique of this picture of the economic process is then examined: that it is the worker, not the entrepreneur, who is the source of value, and that the annexing of that percentage of the wealth generated by the worker beyond that necessary to pay his wages is by definition exploitative. Further, capitalism is characterised not by entrepreneurial energy but by boom and bust, monopoly and takeover in which the small entrepreneur herself often loses out to organised capital. Third, the chapter reviews critiques of this perhaps teleological view of capitalism associated with the writings of J. K. Gibson-Graham (Gibson-Graham 2006a, 2006b). Gibson-Graham argue for a more diverse understanding of rationales for the engagement in economic activity than just profit maximisation, for an appreciation of the diverse ways in which economic life is organised (into cooperatives, between families, through local money networks) and of the many ways in which surpluses can be generated and distributed. Then other forms of enterprise are examined: the social entrepreneur who brings 'business' values to solving social problems; the Latin American solidarity economy in which social values are bought to the problem of creating and sharing wealth; and the trade unionist as entrepreneur. Through this we hope to uncover a much wider landscape of entrepreneurialism and of enterprising behaviour, from other agents than just business people.

THINKING ABOUT ENTERPRISE
AND ENTREPRENEURIALISM

If we are to understand how entrepreneurialism can be understood as having value for subaltern groups, as well as for business people, we need to rethink it conceptually, to understand its etymology. The conventional view of the entrepreneur was neatly captured by Peter Jones, from TV's 'Dragons' Den'. In an article entitled 'Entrepreneurialism: the new rock 'n' roll', Jones said: '[F]or a year or so now I've been telling anyone who cares to listen that business is the new rock 'n roll. Got a great idea? Then get a business plan, some funding, make millions and buy some fast cars and a mansion with a guitar-shaped swimming pool.' [1] Entrepreneurs organise, operate and assume the risk for a business venture.

Richard Cantillon's *Essay on the Nature of Commerce in General*, written in French around 1734, was the economic theorisation that identified the importance of entrepreneurialism in the wealth creation process. He saw it as a form of arbitrage, whereby entrepreneurs buy low, at currently known prices, in the expectation of selling higher, as yet unknown future prices (Murphy 1986). Entrepreneurs, unlike landlords and labourers, looked into the future, weighed up the likelihood of certain events occurring or new needs emerging and acted accordingly, in order to meet these new needs or handle new events. They relished uncertainty and took on the risk of engaging with it on others' behalf. They connected producers and buyers, taking a percentage in business costs and in the hope of profit above that. For Cantillon, entrepreneurs are the key economic actors as their arbitrage enables markets to reach equilibrium, as supply and demand are met through the transfers of goods facilitated by entrepreneurs. Cantillon had a democratic view of entrepreneurialism: everyone who produces and sells is in some way acting entrepreneurially but those who focus on connecting buyers and sellers and accepting the risk that prices might fall rather than rise are key (Hébert 1985).

Adam Smith (Smith 1776/1981) conceptualised the economy as a network of entrepreneurs working according to humanity's innate tendency to barter, truck and trade. Leaving individuals alone to decide their best interests would ensure that the baker fed people in his own self-interest, guided by the famous invisible hand. Schumpeter identified entrepreneurs as the generators of economic development, as they identify and implement new combinations of land, labour, machinery and capital in new production processes that add new value (Schumpeter 1949). Without this process of innovation, development would stall. Consequently, even business crises can be opportunities for 'creative destruction' in that they release factors of production that are no longer profitable so they can be recombined in new, innovative and more profitable ways. Note that, for Schumpeter, not all business owners are entrepreneurs. They may be conservative, sticking to the tried and tested, eventually succumbing to the next business crisis. 'Serial entrepreneurs' enjoy this process of indentifying new ways to combine the factors of production: founder of the Easy-Group of companies, Stelios Haji-Ioannou, showed no interest in running the company once he had established the low cost airline as a new innovation (Martinson 2006).

But the word 'entrepreneur' is a loan word from the old French, *entreprendre*, 'to undertake'. It means no more than that; many other people undertake actions. The worth of the entrepreneur comes from the skill in identifying and organising these new combinations, accepting the risk that they might fail, overcoming barriers and, when they succeed, providing new products, services, innovations and employment for those less innovative and willing to accept risk. They may perceive that they are among the few to recognize or be able to solve a problem. The stakes are high, but the buccaneer entrepreneur can win or lose majorly. They are not safety minded, cautious or conservative; they are, in many ways, the radicals. Entrepreneurialism focuses on opportunity, not on problems or on the impossibility of action. Entrepreneurs stress agency, not structural barriers.

THE LEFT CRITIQUE

The left critique of entrepreneurialism is well known and is based on core Marxist conceptions. Cantillon, Smith and Schumpeter praised entrepreneurs as the driving force of the economy, and Marx agreed that this new force, capitalism, melted 'all that is solid into air' in front of it (Marx and Engels 1848/1980). Capitalism was sublime, breaking up all pre-existing local dominations and petty prejudices before the all-important altar of profit. As seen, Cantillon argued that the entrepreneur was entitled to the profit between buying at known low prices and selling them in the future for as yet unknown higher prices and for accepting the risk that future prices will be higher, 'otherwise he would not do it'. Marx countered that what entrepreneurs actually do is buy labour power at currently known prices from those who have no other option and extract profit by paying the worker less than the also known value of all he has produced. Thus Marx critiques the need to reward risk-taking behaviour.

Taking shoemaking as an example of Marx's concerns, if it takes a labourer six hours to create the value of his or her wages in shoes, the value of the shoes created in the rest of the working day is expropriated by the entrepreneur. This, Marx argued, is inherently exploitative as the source of all value is labour. The labourer produced the shoe, not the entrepreneur, who contributed nothing. Of course this can be debated; the labourer did produce the shoe but with hides bought in advance by the entrepreneur, made on machines provided by the entrepreneur and probably sold in shops provided by other entrepreneurs. For Cantillon, the value would be that shoes produced now at a known price could be sold at a future unknown price, that the design of shoes meets future preferences and as a reward for transporting the shoes from the factory to the market. Schumpeter would see rewards for the entrepreneur who identified ways to make shoes as quickly as possible, to as high a standard as possible, driving down shoe prices and thereby providing labourers producing shoes and other goods with cheap footwear. An artisan shoemaker, for Smith and Cantillon, could be labourer and entrepreneur.

The second leftist critique is that Smith paints a picture of an economy constructed of free producers providing goods and services at the best price out of their own self-interest. He says little about the relationship between the entrepreneur and the labourer who produces that which the entrepreneur sells, assuming it was freely entered into. Karl Polanyi, of course, points in *The Great Transformation* (Polanyi 1944/1980) to the violence of enclosure, in forced emigration to the cities, to the criminalization of trade unions and the violence of the Black Acts (which massively increased the number of capital offences in early capitalist Britain), as examples of the way that state violence was used to create the modern relationship between entrepreneur and worker. Free peasants were forced off the land into the factories as the working class was constructed (Thompson 1981). Workers did not freely choose these relationships, and those with no capital except their labour to sell are similarly in a disadvantageous relationship today.

The third objection would be that uncritical or hagiographic conceptions of the role of the entrepreneur are utopian. Smith himself noted that 'people of the same trade seldom meet together, even for merriment and diversion, but the conversation ends in a conspiracy against the public, or in some contrivance to raise prices' (Smith 1776/1981: 232). He recognised, and Marx emphasised, that capitalism has a tendency to monopoly as larger, more efficient forms buy out Smith's small entrepreneurs until wealth is concentrated in fewer and fewer hands. This is mitigated through inheritance taxes, through periodic bouts of creative destruction and by changes in markets that larger firms fail to adapt to. Entrepreneur, Bill Gates, establishes small firm, Microsoft, which emerges to displace omnipotent IBM, then Google challenges Microsoft. But we also see entrepreneurs selling to large companies: Green and Blacks chocolate by Cadbury, Yahoo by Microsoft. We see violent, corrupt gangster and crony capitalisms. Kovel (Kovel 2007) and Wall (Wall 2005) have little time for what they call a naïve neo-Smithian valorisation of the entrepreneur, arguing that markets have an in-built tendency for growth and monopoly that, in the present environment, inevitably leads to increased carbon emissions and dangerous climate change. For Kovel, capitalism, with its inevitable tendencies towards growth and monopoly, is the 'enemy of the planet'. Frankel (1987) argues that small firms set up for ethical or lifestyle reasons must grow or they lose their competitive edge when a less ethical competitor challenges them on price.

The final objection, from a structuralist perspective, would be that too much emphasis is put on the role of the entrepreneur as the hero who creates value and generates development. Marx argued that people do make history, do have the opportunity to create their world, but they are not completely free to do so; the effects of past decisions hang over them. Some have greater recourses than others. Some are constrained by forces bigger than them. The ability of the entrepreneur to create new value is very small in a globalised economy where money and finance move around the world at the touch of a button and huge global flows can make what was once profitable now unprofitable (Strange 1986; Leyshon and Thrift 1997; Stiglitz 2002). Wages and prices are set through decisions of millions of consumers with individual consumption choices and preferences, entrepreneurs taking or not taking decisions and investing or not investing, banks advancing credit or refusing to, trade unionists fighting for higher pay, and state regulations. The entrepreneur is not free to do as he or she sees fit. Of course, the libertarian right would argue that this is the problem; entrepreneurs should be free to work their magic (Hayek 1944). Polanyi, though, showed that this leads to the destruction of society. We do not therefore have free markets; we have constructed markets that the entrepreneur must work through.

DIVERSE ECONOMIES: THE POST-STRUCTURALIST CRITIQUE

Recent analyses have taken a different tack. The analysis above, they would argue, is totalising and teleological and does not pay enough attention to the diversity of forms of enterprise that characterise the real economy. It seems happier with structural constraints than with possibilities for more interesting forms of economic life. Central to this work is that of J. K. Gibson-Graham (2006a, 2006b). They object that arguing that businesses are inevitably exploitative, profit-orientated or will inevitably be taken over is like assuming that, because women can have children, all women are maternal or child-orientated. Some businesses do focus on profit maximisation but there is a much greater diversity in economic forms, which they called 'diverse economies'.

Gibson-Graham argued that an all encompassing meta-narrative of 'capitalism' occludes the diversity of relations that construct an economy and, in particular, ignores the diversity of actually existing non-capitalist practices and liberatory economic projects that can be identified in the here and now. They argued that it is 'the way that capitalism has been "thought" that makes it so difficult for people to imagine its supersession' (2006a: 3) and that to move forwards we need an idea of the 'economic' that is not so subject to closure, more open-ended and diverse. They argued for a conceptualisation of the economy as 'heterospace' of capitalist and non-capitalist economic forms which includes not only production for profit but mutual aid, household economies, production for need, production for self-consumption, care giving, maintaining the planet's ecology, loving or purchases made for political, ideological or affective (rather than strictly economic) reasons. Other authors have questioned the extent that capitalist values of profit and loss are as all encompassing as structuralist Marxists suggest (Williams 2005), and explored diverse forms of economic activity created by new forms of money (North 2007), through alternative forms of finance (Leyshon et al. 2003) and in markets and cooperatives. Others have pointed to the non-capitalist forms of economy, worker-owned enterprises and cooperatives, found in Latin America's 'solidarity economies' (de Sousa Santos 2006). These perspectives suggest that there might be other forms of entrepreneurial economic activity than that of business operating within a capitalist economy to maximise value and profit.

They have not gone unchallenged. Perhaps the harshest criticism was that of the post-structuralist nature of Gibson-Graham's project. Critics argued that an attempt, in effect, trying to 'think capitalism away' by seeing economic practices in a different light was making what Castree (Castree 1999), following Bhaskar, called the 'epistemological fallacy', which conflates knowledge and the world. For Castree, the economy is a concrete, real-world phenomenon based on real commodities, prices and profitability levels, not a performance or representation. It exists independently of people's ability to call it into reality through practices and has a logic of accumulation that operates outside individual perception. Castree argued that the essential characteristics and logics of capitalism can be theoretically identified, even if they are hard to find in their pure state in the real world, conditioned as they are by other social phenomena.

The second major criticism was that, without any attempt to reconstruct theoretically what alternatives to capitalism might look like, empirical analysis of actually existing alternative economic practices is likely to degenerate into a 'flabby pluralism or explanatory 'everythingism', in which examples of non-capitalist rationality or interesting experiments are uncritically championed (Castree 1999: 145). In a similar vein, Samers (2005) argued that Gibson-Graham and others have a tendency to celebrate 'alternatives' without investigating to what extent they genuinely *are* examples of freer, more unconstrained and liberated forms of economic activity for those who engage in them. Are they better than capitalism or are they coping mechanisms for those excluded from labour for capitalist firms? Samers argued that exploitation (and by implication, what is freely chosen economic activity) is not theorised, while small-scale, local economic activity is privileged with no investigation of its internal power relations, which might be very exploitative. Alternative economic practices might be possible only in spaces cut off from the power centres of capitalism where competition or high property prices might crowd out more marginal alternatives. Large-scale capitalist firms are ascribed an exploitative status and there is no consideration of the extent that the 'local' might be a xenophobic, inward looking system of dominations based on class, caste, gender and kinship. Are non-market relations intrinsically 'good' while capitalism can never promote development (Curry 2005)? Are they also more connected to globalised economic relations than is made explicit, less than 'alternative' (Lawson 2005)? Is Gibson-Graham throwing the wealth-creating baby out with the capitalist bathwater, limiting opportunities (Curry 2005: 129)? Similarly, Aguilar (2005) asked who decides what forms of economic life are 'ethical'? What happens when alternative experiments fail? What about those who are 'reluctant subjects', not convinced of the desirability of the community economy, still attracted to what some call 'excess', others 'wealth'? Cavanagh and Mander (2004) agree that small, locally owned community-focused businesses *can* be exploitative. But, they also argued, this cannot be assumed.

Other critics chastened them for being insufficiently post-structuralist, insisting that 'capitalism' and 'class' themselves were Western concepts that could not so easily be transcribed into Southern economies (Aguilar 2005). At the other end of the spectrum, others saw capitalism as so all-embracing that they had trouble envisioning anything escaping it. Sceptics saw capitalist commodification as so extensive that many economic activities claimed as 'alternative', for example the production of soya milk, could be seen as just the latest commodity generated by a constantly evolving capitalism. Businesses selling 'alternative' goods were just responding to the latest market signals. Sympathetic critics called for a more critical assessment of their potential; what were their limits? Were economic alternatives just a 'palliative to a deeper malaise' (Kelly 2005)? Hostile critics like Watts (2003): 28) were concerned that this was at worst populist myopia, at best vain hope that an attention to diversity can uncover new success stories while ignoring 'the terrible realities of unprecedented global inequality and the crude violence of twenty-first century empire.' Many of the forms of economic diversity uncovered were 'familiar' and nothing that threads of Marxism that paid attention to diversity had not concerned themselves with.

In the second edition of *The End of Capitalism as We Knew It* and elsewhere, Gibson-Graham engaged with the critics (2005). The response was to recognise many of the very valid objections raised but to prefer to see them less as fundamental limits to what can be done through alternative economic projects than as 'challenges, problems, barriers, difficulties—in other words, as things to be struggled with, things that present themselves as more or less tractable obstacles in any political project' (Gibson-Graham 2006a: xxv). Answers would come through engagement. They wanted to examine the conditions rather than the fundamental limits of possibility and stressed being hopeful rather than uncritically optimistic. They saw themselves as 'dancing, participating in creating a reality in which we are implicated and involved', disrupting 'the great clanking gears of capital' (Gibson-Graham 2003: 35). They abandoned the project of mapping and thereby participating in the construction of capitalist dominance. They stressed that they focus on the possible, not the probable: on the 'not yet', not the 'never'. They de-emphasised understanding the barriers in favour of working out ways to overcome them. Their post-capitalist politics is built on: the centrality of subjects and the ethical practices of self-cultivation; the role of place as the site of becoming, and therefore as a ground of a global politics of transformations; the uneven spatiality and negotiability of power, which is always available to be skirted, marshalled or redirected through ethical practices of freedom; and the everyday temporality of change and the vision of transformation as continual struggle to change subjects, places and conditions of life under inherited circumstances of difficulty and uncertainty. They reject 'a simplistic assertion that we can think ourselves out of the materiality of capitalism'. They understand the forces that militate against that which 'may work to undermine, constrain, destroy or sideline our attempts to reshape economic futures' (p. xxx1). They argue that these forces are not dominant with a 'fundamental, structural or universal reality' but are 'contingent outcomes of ethical decisions, political projects and sedimented localised practices, continually pushed and pulled by other determinations.'

They re-read experiences for contingency, not necessity: for difference and diversity, not for dominance. They argue that we need to plant, tend and nurture economic alternatives and harvest the fruit. This is a politics of hope tinged with realism, not with a complacent structuralist smugness that 'nothing can be done', except bewail our fate and rage against those changing the planet for the worse. Surely it is right, academically, to be open, hopeful and looking for connection rather than unnecessarily cautious, privileging analysis, explanation and critique over changing things for the better?

It is in this context that some wider, more diverse examples of entrepreneurial behaviour are now examined: the social entrepreneur who brings 'business' values to solving social problems, the Latin American solidarity economy in which social values are bought to the problem of creating and sharing wealth; and the trade unionist as entrepreneur. Building on Gibson-Graham's work, the next section looks at how 'enterprise' and entrepreneurialism' could be conceptualised in perhaps more progressive ways? What do we need to produce and how can needs be met? What do we want to consume, who should consume what, what should be invested, consumed or redistributed? What can we make over what we need? How shall we distribute surplus? How can we build feelings of community, commonality and conviviality through economic actions?

ALTERNATIVE FORMS OF ENTERPRISE

The Social Entrepreneur

We will start with social entrepreneurialism. The 'social entrepreneur' is conceptualised as undertaking the classic entrepreneurial role but to create social or environmental value rather than for monetary gain. This may be through creating and running voluntary or community organisations to address social problems in entrepreneurial ways (Leadbetter 1997). It might be through developing new social innovations (Mulgan et al. 2007). Examples here might be Robert Owen (utopian communities, alternative currencies), Otavia Hill (housing) or Michael Young (pioneered innovations that led to NHS Direct, after school clubs). Social entrepreneurs run social enterprises that use business skills to develop businesses that do not distribute profit to shareholders or owners, have a democratic structure and generally a triple bottom line paradigm which makes sure that social and environmental as well as economic issues are addressed. Social enterprises fulfil a social purpose as well as seek financial sustainability through trading. They adopt 'financially sustainable strategies to address social aims, and address a wide range of social problems such as unemployment, inequalities in access to health and social care services, low quality housing, high incidences of crime, deprivation and social exclusion' (Haugh 2005: 1).

The social enterprise network argues that:

> Social entrepreneurs are exceptional people. They have a great idea for making their community better places for those who live in them.

They have the vision, drive, commitment and determination to change their local communities through practical local action. They are skilled at spotting and re-using underused and abandoned resources such as buildings, equipment and open spaces. . . . While entrepreneurs in the business sector identify untapped commercial markets, and gather together the resources to break into those markets for profit, social entrepreneurs use the same skills to different effect. For social entrepreneurs, untapped markets are people or communities in need, who haven't been reached by other initiatives. But while they may read from a different bottom line, social and business entrepreneurs have a lot in common. They build something out of nothing. They are ambitious to achieve. They marshal resources—sometimes from the unlikeliest places—to meet their needs. They are constantly creative. And they are not afraid to make mistakes. . . . The most successful embody a curious mixture of idealism and pragmatism—high-mindedness wedded to hard-headedness. . . . Social entrepreneurs never say 'it can't be done'. (http://www.sse.org.uk/programme.php?sub=ABOUT, accessed 25 March 2010)

Social entrepreneurs are entrepreneurial as they generate social value specifically by recognising and creating opportunities to create this value, innovating, tolerating risk and refusing to accept current resource constraints (Paredo and McLean 2006). But we need to dig deeper to examine the real, lived economies of the fruits of social entrepreneurship, asking the questions raised by Gibson-Graham. What does 'financially sustainable' mean, when traded against social and environmental values? How much exploitation is 'acceptable'? How much risk do they accept, compared with other actors: workers going on strike, for example? Secondly, Leadbetter (1997) argues that social entrepreneurs are leaders, storytellers, people managers, visionary opportunists and alliance builders. But again is this an over-individualist conception of social change; isn't the change bought about by those who work for the social enterprises or voluntary organisations established by entrepreneurs? Does the wider structure, an implicit valorisation of entrepreneurship as a specific way of organising the creation of value above others (organising, protesting) matter? Amin, Hudson and Cameron (Amin, Cameron, and Hudson 2002), for example, point strongly to the importance of a supportive local state and dense infrastructure of like-minded social entrepreneurs in explaining the success of the social economy. Thirdly, what if the client or recipient cannot pay the economic cost? Here 'social' means providing the service anyway and levering in subsidies, grants, donations and voluntary work. But should some needs be met anyway, irrespective of the ability of the market to meet them through trading? Valorising the 'social entrepreneur' implicitly assumes that business skills are the best way to address social issues, rather than starting from the conception that cooperation, freedom and the provision of unexploited nice work is the best way to create meaningful value and provide livelihoods. Why not turn this on its head and, rather than take wealth creating values to solving social problems, take social values to the problem of creating wealth? This is the conception of the solidarity economy in Latin America, where 'another production is possible' (de Sousa Santos 2006).

The Solidarity Economy: Bringing Social Values to the Problem of Creating Wealth

Social entrepreneurship applies business skills to social and environmental problems. If we move to Latin America, we see in the conception of the solidarity economy as very different way of looking at this, applying social values to the problem of wealth creation. In December 2001 Argentina's economy fell apart in a classic currency crisis accompanied by a bank run (Halevi 2002, Rock 2002, North 2007a and b). The economy collapsed to the extent that GDP sank by 16.3 per cent in the first three months of 2002, whilst manufacturing output was down by 20 per cent. Fifty-two per cent of the population, 19 million people, lived in poverty. Twenty per cent of Argentines were reported as living in 'severe' poverty, which meant they could not meet basic daily nutritional needs. Twenty per cent were unemployed, while 23 per cent were underemployed (Rock 2002). The crisis dragged on into 2002 until it began to revive on the backs of the newly competitive peso. Argentines responded to this crisis with what can only be described as an explosion of entrepreneurial behaviour. Neighbours formed assemblies to enable them to support each other through the crisis and to develop projects to improve their situation, sacked workers occupied their enterprises and ran them themselves, unemployed people set up schools, kitchens, organic gardens and micro-enterprises, and millions supported themselves through micro-businesses using alternative forms of currency (North and Huber 2004).

In the months after the December events, neighbourhood assemblies emerged across Argentina as '[neighbours] met on street corners, maybe the open air, to discuss things, interchange ideas, find . . . solutions to the problems they were facing. One of the big problems . . . was the increase in bills of utilities that had been privatised, so a lot of these meetings were about . . . how to change things.' (*Asambleísta*, Buenos Aires). Other assemblies developed projects to meet local needs, for example projects for the *cartoneros* who collected paper to recycle each night, collective kitchens, projects for children, food cooperatives and organic farms (Dinerstein 2003). Assembly members did not just protest; they entrepreneurially created alternatives.

Other workers who lost their jobs did more than protest. As the crisis hit and business after business went bankrupt, 130 bankrupt enterprises, employing approximately 10,000 workers, were occupied by their former employees who then carried on production under workers' self-management

(*The Economist* 2002). When former owners tried to recover their property, Argentine judges often sided with the workers to protect jobs. By 2003, the national network of *empresas recuperadas* (recovered enterprises) claimed 147 members (Dinerstein 2007). Some elected a manager, others wanted to be municipalised, some were cooperatives, while others were run through workers' self-management. Some wanted to make a small profit; others focused on need not profit, outside the market, within a solidarity economy, irrespective of the extent or otherwise of capitalist demand (Aufheben 2003). Other reclaimed enterprises acted as a focus for community-based activities. For example, the long-established IMPA cooperative in Buenos Aires wanted to demonstrate its support to and from the wider community, so gave space to the local barter network, a theatre, small ceramics micro-producers and artists. Neighbours using the premises, it was felt, would demonstrate that the value of the company was being spread widely and provide support networks, and the presence of large numbers of people would work as a deterrent to the police. This was not just done out of necessity but was seen as a wider process of social change through the construction of a 'solidarity economy', described thus:

> Most of the organisations that are struggling for the solidarity economy now are not just doing it out of necessity, but also out of a greater plan, an idealism. What they want to do is construct a counter force to the capitalist system, and they have different values. Instead of competition, it's co-operation. People should not be exploited, but working together, producing with responsibility. . . Certainly there is an intention to create a better society, in lots of ways. Some believe in it less than others, but other elements of this better society is to look more after the environment. There is a whole movement against GM soya, there are those who say that people deserve more than just cheap food, but it should be good quality.' (Solidarity Economy Co-ordinator, Buenos Aires City Council, May 2004, Author's fieldnotes)

The pickets were organisations composed of long-term unemployed people (Dinerstein 2001). Some of them focused on blocking roads to win demands from the state but others were more entrepreneurial. They focused on trying to build the economy they wanted in the here and now, not waiting for future salvation to be delivered from on high. For example, the *MTD Aníbal Verón* stressed the development of micro-enterprises and community self-provision, to support themselves and to demonstrate that alternative forms of production were possible, based not on control but on autonomy (Chatterton 2005). They conceptualised what they were doing thus:

> In practice, we organise in the neighbourhood for social change. . . .
> We give time in the neighbourhood for ideas and ideology to ripen,

before we put them into place. An example is the organic farms where people discuss it and wonder what to do. All the *campañeros* know exactly what is going on, where they want to go, what they are doing, what they are heading for. . . . There are always urgent things to do that we concentrate on any one time, so at the moment there is the problem of hunger so we are concentrating on communal feeding; there is the problem of unemployment so we are fighting for subsidies: but at the same time our more long term goal is to build a new logic of living, so its broader than an alternative economy—that's part of it, but when we think about production, to eat and to sell, but also production of a new logic of thinking and how to change the whole way of living. (Member, *MTD Solano* (*part of MTD Aníbal Verón*) (North and Huber 2004: 976–77)

As much as any entrepreneur, the members of *MTD Solano* were putting together the means of production they had to hand to create wealth but in solidaristic ways. They were not passive, waiting for the state, and they did more than resist. They were creative.

Outside the ranks of those organised by the pickets, the 'new poor' had to rely on informal work or, increasingly, on *trueque*, the barter markets that sprung up from 1997 across Argentina. The *trueque* was a network of markets in disused factories, car parks, vacant lots and the like where people set up stalls trading goods that they had made or no longer need using alternative forms of money printed and circulated by community organisations and NGOs. The barter networks worked through a chaordic (truss-like) structure made up of 'nodes' where traders (called *prosumidores*—'prosumers'—after Alvin Tofler's consumers and producers) exchanged goods, such as honey, empanadas, pancakes, pizzas, green vegetables and fruit, jams, wine, vinegar, breads, biscuits, shoes, shampoos, jumpers, nightgowns, haircuts and manicures. By 2002, barter markets had spread all over Argentina; organisers claimed 4,500 markets were used by half a million people spending 600 million credits (Norman 2002). The real figure is unknowable. The value system of the networks was solidarity, not the self-interested invisible hand. A leaflet distributed at nodes explained the values:

- *Don't buy credits.* All this does is fatten the pockets of the unscrupulous people who are selling them.
- *Produce with solidarity.* Take what you can produce and what you know others will need to the node.
- *Distribute with solidarity.* Don't trade all of your products with one prosumer. Let many prosumers obtain your products.
- *Consume with solidarity.* Only consume what is necessary, and give other prosumers the opportunity to consume the same as you. (North 2007a: 155)

The organisers claimed a market based not on competition, but community, cooperation and ecology, a market that works by different values:

> Our main stand is that barter networks are able to reinvent the market and not only reinclude people that have been excluded by globalisation, but—even beyond—can include people never included before. We believe that we need not oppose this new market to the formal market, but we need rather to develop our ability to join (it), in different rhythms and forms, if we choose to do it . . . to build democratic life with equity and solidarity instead of competition and exclusion. Finally we believe that barter networks are able to re-shuffle cards to build a new social game. (Primavera, De Sanzo and Covas 1998)

Through the barter networks, the organisers—entrepreneurs—organised and ran a complex support system which enabled millions of Argentines an alternative source of survival. Fernando Sampayo, a former entrepreneur in Buenos Aires, had run a number of successful businesses. Now the crisis had hit, he used his business skills to run a well-organised and extremely efficient network of markets, through which vegetables and grain were imported from the countryside. In inner-city Buenos Aires, trueque organiser Charli saw it as a way of helping those who had had the stuffing knocked out of them by the crisis to get back on their feet:

> It's a matter of changing people's way of thinking . . . from that of an employee to that of a businessperson who runs a micro enterprise, a producer. All this means changing people's ways of thinking. . . . They say: 'There are no jobs.' I respond: 'There is no employment, but there is work.' (. . .) 'And there is work, because there are needs to be met; and some of these we can cover with work, no? (North 2007a: 162)

John Holloway (Holloway 2002) has argued that the liberatory project needs to be refocused away from resisting that to which we object—the state, the power of capitalism to control out lives—to developing our power to create the sort of world we want. It's not good enough to shout 'no!' just to oppose. Holloway would not use the word but he is arguing for a new creative politics of possibility, of dignity and of autonomy, that is actually entrepreneurial, while refusing desiccated capitalist conceptions of entrepreneurialism, based on selling high after buying low. This is what the Argentines did.

The Trade Unionist as Entrepreneur— Communities Surviving the Miners' Strike

In the mid 1990s, I was involved in a research project examining business leadership in three Northern English towns not well known for business mobilisation (Wood, Valler, and North 1998; Valler, Wood, and North 2000; North et al. 2001). I was struck by one response when exploring the values of the private sector in that stronghold of municipal labourism, Barnsley:

> I believe that there was more entrepreneurs during the miners' strike in. . . . a square mile in this area than I have ever seen in my life . . . People made a living and I'll tell you something, they had more good ideas . . .—fantastic. Entrepreneurs are people who've found something, found they can do something, found a service, all these sort of things, that is a little bit unique and gives them a start—I believe we have got loads of them . . . (TEC Director). (North, Valler and Wood 2001: 840)

In neo-liberal discourses, the miners were 'the enemy within', organised labour dedicated to obstruct the manager's right to manage within a feather-bedded, subsidised nationalised industry. When their pits became uneconomic, they tried to keep them open through 'mob rule', neo-liberals argued. The defeat of the miners epitomised the replacement of labourite Britain with entrepreneurial Britain. Even sections of the left saw miners' villages as the epitome of socially small 'c' conservative, white male, manual working class values (Massey and Wainwright 1985). Yet within the pit villages themselves, Women Against Pit Closures (WAPT) groups were set up to support the strike collectively. Families of striking miners were not left to sink or swim; they were collectively supported. Food would be cooked collectively, Christmas parties organised (Loach 1985). The Barnsley WAPT group organised a kitchen within five weeks of the strike starting. Offered £50 by the union, they insisted on it being a loan to ensure that they controlled it. While it can easily be objected that the women were corralled into a supportive position, providing nurturing work traditionally ascribed to women, their contribution did not stop there—they went picketing with their men: 'Out of the material need to provide food their energy has been released and they have drawn strength from the powerful role they play' (Loach 1985: 174). Twenty years later, WAPT members felt:

> We all speak with one voice when we say that the strike absolutely changed our lives in understanding the power of collective action as women. We were unique in the twentieth century as an organisation of working-class women coming together as women. Collective strength was the result. After that, the women who were involved were never isolated at home again. (Gillan 2004)

The strike happened in isolated, homogenous one-industry villages, away from where most of 'us' live. Yet it was supported by an upwelling of entrepreneurial activity as supporters across the country set up a complex support system that raised money, food and other forms of support and transmitted it to the pit villages, keeping them going for a year. Deprived of state benefits, this support fed and watered the strikers so they were not starved back to work. For Massey and Wainwright:

> With trade union leadership at sixes and sevens, their creaking structures, and their lack of credibility unable to lead any response, and with party political leadership embarrassed by the whole affair . . . there has sprung up a completely different way of organising support, indeed an expansion of what the concept of support means. 'The grass roots', people of all sorts, previously politically active and not, have just 'got on with it'. Often in the most unexpected ways and places, support networks have been organised, fundraising events launched, and distribution systems established. (Massey and Wainwright 1985:150–51)

Merseyside, a city at the time in desperate poverty, raised a million pounds in 1984–85. The Garston group door-knocked for food contributions, collected donations in the pubs and organised raffles and jumble sales. A Christmas party was organised for 150 kids in Bolsover. Ford Halewood generated about £1,000 a fortnight. Unemployed people staffed and ran the unemployed resource centre. A concert was organised and local bands played for free to 3,000 people. The PAs were donated at cheap prices by local companies. Prosperous Cambridge had gigs, ceilidhs, house meetings, college collections, an art sale and street collections, and sent £600 a week. Holidays and presents were organised for miners' families.

Is this solidarity or entrepreneurialism? It is both. Some places did have deep-seated, local cultures of solidarity but that was not the case in other areas, especially in the prosperous south. The support networks needed to be constructed, opportunities identified and capitalised on, and resources produced—money, food and solidarity for the miners. While the pit villages were in many ways centres of old style solidarity, in many other places a new, vibrant, creative urban left put the factors of production together in new ways to create value. As a comment from Liverpool put it:

> There is a constant flow of information about the strike . . . people feel really involved in the strike . . . it doesn't feel like charity. When miners arrive they are immediately put to work. They feel involved in the organisation, part of the same movement, rather than the recipients of charity. (Massey and Wainwright 1985: 157)

The entrepreneurial skills required included explaining to potential supporters why they should feel common cause with the miners, working out what they had to offer, working out how to get what where, making sure that resources continued to flow from supporters to the miners, and communicating back to supporters what was happening to money raised and donations, to ensure that resources would continue to flow. This was a creative feat of organisation, coordination and production, making sure that resources were produced and directed to where they were needed most. South Wales developed a sophisticated multi-level coordination system to manage the hundreds of pounds that flowed into the miners' villages, making sure that support went where it was needed. Individuals bought and sold BT shares to raise money, others visited temples and mosques, shook buckets in town centres. Peace women marched from nuclear power stations to pits, explaining the issues on the way. Millions of pounds was generated, managed and distributed according to need.

The organisation that went into the miners' support networks later generated a more conventional form of entrepreneurship: the Worker's Beer Company that waters Glastonbury and other pop concerts runs the Bread and Roses public house in south London and runs Ethical Threads, a supplier of T-shirts made by workers paid a living wage (Benjamin 2003). In 2003, the company had a turnover of £8 million. Supplying Europe's largest music festival is a mammoth logistical undertaking; employees and casual staff—all former miners—run 19 bars around the 800-acre site, with names ranging from Bread and Roses to District 6 (in Johannesburg) and Red Flag. More than 40 tankers containing beer, cider and stout are attached to cooling machines and dispensing equipment in bars serving 5,000 pints an hour. The ex-miners are joined by 800 servers, 300 managers and 200 technicians. Each volunteer server is paid £5.60 an hour to donate to a cause of their choice. Profits from the Workers Beer Company are used to fund union and Labour Party campaigns and, for example, to fly a Colombian trade unionist to the UK.

When British Coal said that Tower Colliery in South Wales had no future, 239 workers pooled their £8,000 redundancy cheques and bought it. They ran it as a cooperative until January 2008. The mine kept 239 men in work and a community alive for 15 years. As Tyrone O'Sullivan, former NUM lodge secretary and, later, chairman put it: 'We took on the people who said we couldn't do this and we beat them' (Morris 2008). Tower's experience shows that working people can be entrepreneurial in developing indigenous responses to long-term structural problems of the economy, such as manufacturing decline. Such indigenous responses might work better than subsidies for inward investors will little commitment to place (Scott Cato 2004).

CONCLUSION

The left usually object that entrepreneurs appropriate too much of the produce that is produced, as, in the Marxist schema, wealth is created not by putting the factors of production together in new ways (as in discourses of entrepreneurialism) but through applying labour to what are before that dead factors of production. Even if they are nice people who pay their workers a living wage, for the left they are still technically exploiters, since they appropriate for themselves the profit created by working people. The skills of entrepreneurialism are restricted to business by both left *and* right. Social entrepreneurs use business skills to solve social problems. Outside the Latin American conception of the solidarity economy, we focus less on applying social skills and community resources to the problem of creating livelihoods. Perhaps we should. While the left labels processes of putting things together to create new organisations, which is what entrepreneurs do in the field of enterprise, as 'organising' or 'activism', many organisers and activists are exceptionally entrepreneurial. Why should we give up the concept to those who often do little more than run large monopolies badly, gaining huge bonuses even when they fail? Following Gibson-Graham, do we need to rethink entrepreneurialism to widen the way we think about the problem of generating and redistributing wealth away from binary think-ing about either capitalist markets on one hand or state planning on the other? Do we need to focus more on what John Holloway (Holloway 2002) calls our power 'to', to be creative, to not accepting limits, to widening pos-sibilities rather than stressing either resistance or waiting for the state to deliver? I believe that we do.

NOTES

1. http://news.bbc.co.uk/1/hi/business/4542280.stm.

BIBLIOGRAPHY

Aguilar Jr, F. V. (2005) 'Excess possibilities? Ethics, populism and community economy. A commentary on J. K. Gibson-Graham's "Surplus possibilities: post-development and community economies"', Singapore Journal of Tropical Geog-raphy, 26(1): 27–31.

Amin, A., Cameron, A. and Hudson, R. (2002) Placing the Social Economy, Lon-don: Routledge.

Aufheben (2003) 'Picket and pot-banger together: class recomposition in Argen-tina?', Aufheben, (11): 1–23.

Benjamin, A. (2003) 'Good Intent: the Worker's Beer Company', The Guardian, 25 June.

Castree, N. (1999) 'Envisioning capitalism: geography and the renewal of Marxian polit-ical economy', Transactions of the Institute of British Geographers, 24(1): 137–58.

Cavanagh, J. and Mander, J. (2004) Alternatives to Economic Globalization, San Francisco: Berrett-Koehler.

Chatterton, P. (2005) 'Making autonomous geographies: Argentina's popular uprising and the "Movimiento de Trabajadores Desocupados (Unemployed Workers Movement)"', Geoforum, 36: 545–61.

Curry, G. N. (2005) 'Reluctant subjects or passive resistance? A commentary on J. K. Gibson-Graham's "Surplus possibilities: post-development and community economies"', Singapore Journal of Tropical Geography, 26(2): 127–31.

de Sousa Santos, B. (ed.) (2006) Another Production Is Possible: Beyond the capitalist canon, London: Verso.

Dinerstein, A. (2001) 'Roadblocks in Argentina: against the violence of stability', Capital and Class, 74: 1–7.

———(2003) 'Que se Vayan Todos! Popular insurrection and the *Asambleas Barriales* in Argentina', Bulletin of Latin American Research, 22(2): 187–200.

———(2007) 'Workers' factory takeovers and new state policies in Argentina: towards an "institutionalisation" of non-governmental public action?', Policy and Politics, 35: 529.

The Economist (2002), 'Under workers' control', The Economist.

Frankel, B. (1987) The Post-Industrial Utopians, Cambridge: Polity.

Gibson-Graham, J. (2003) 'The Impatience of familiarity: a commentary on Michael Watts' Development and Governmentality', Singapore Journal of Tropical Geography, 24(1): 35–37.

———(2005) 'Traversing the fantasy of sufficiency: a response to Aguilar, Kelly, Laurie and Lawson', Singapore Journal of Tropical Geography, 26(2): 119–26.

———(2006a) The End of Capitalism (as We Knew It): A feminist critique of political economy, Minneapolis: University of Minnesota Press.

———(2006b) A Post Capitalist Politics, Minneapolis: University of Minnesota Press.

Gillan, A. (2004) 'I always thought I was thick: the Miner's strike taught me I wasn't', The Guardian, 10 May 2004.

Halevi, J. (2002) 'The Argentine crisis', Monthly Review, 53(11): 15–23.

Hart, K. (2001) Money in an Unequal World, London: Texere.

Haugh, H. (2005) 'A research agenda for social entrepreneurship', Social Enterprise Journal, 1(1): 1–12.

Hayek, F. (1944) The Road to Serfdom, London: Routledge.

Hébert, R. (1985) 'Was Richard Cantillon an Austrian economist?', Journal of Libertarian Studies, 7(2): 269–79.

Holloway, J. (2002) Change the World without Taking Power: The meaning of revolution today, London: Pluto.

Kelly, P. (2005) 'Scale, power and the limits to possibilities. A commentary on J. K. Gibson-Graham's "Surplus possibilities: post-development and community economies"', Singapore Journal of Tropical Geography, 26(1): 39–43.

Kovel, J. (2007) The Enemy of Nature, London: Zed Books.

Lawson, V. (2005) 'Hopeful geographies: imagining ethical alternatives. A commentary on J. K. Gibson-Graham's "Surplus Possibilities: post-development and community economies"', Singapore Journal of Tropical Geography, 26(1): 36–38.

Leadbetter, C. (1997) The Role of the Social Entrepreneur, London: Demos.

Leyshon, A., Lee, R. and Williams, C. C. (eds) (2003) Alternative Economic Spaces, London: Sage.

Leyshon, A. and Thrift, N. (1997) Money Space: Geographies of monetary transformation, London: Routledge.

Loach, L. (1985) 'We'll be here right to the end and after. Women in the Miners' Strike' in H. Benyon (ed.) Digging Deeper: Issues in the Miner's Strike, London: Verso.

Martinson, J. (2006) 'The Big Easy enters choppy waters', The Guardian, 15 May 2006.

Marx, K. and Engels, F. (1848/1980) The Communist Manifesto, Harmondsworth: Penguin.

Massey, D. and Wainwright, H. (1985) 'Beyond the coalfields: the work of the miners' support groups' in H. Benyon (ed.) Digging Deeper: Issues in the miners' strike, London: Verso.

Morris, S. (2008) 'When the coal finally ran out', The Guardian, 26 January 2008.

Mulgan, G. et al. (2007) Social Innovation: What it is, why it matters and how it can be accelerated, Oxford: Skoll Centre for Social Entrepreneurship.

Murphy, A. (1986) Richard Cantillon: Entrepreneur and economist, Oxford: Oxford University Press.

North, P. (2007a) Money and Liberation: The micropolitics of alternative currency movements, Minneapolis: University of Minnesota Press.

———(2007b) 'Neoliberalizing Argentina?', in K. England and K. Ward (eds) Neoliberalization: States, networks, peoples, Oxford: Blackwell.

North, P. and Huber, U. (2004) 'Alternative spaces of the "Argentinazo"', Antipode, 36(5): 963–84.

North, P., Valler, D. and Wood, A. (2001) 'Talking business: an actor centred analysis of business agendas for local economic development', International Journal of Urban and Regional Research, 25(4): 830–46.

Paredo, A. and McLean, M. (2006) 'Social entrepreneurship: a critical review of the concept', Journal of World Business, 41: 56–65.

Peck, J. (1995) 'Moving and shaking: business elites, state localism and urban privatism', Progress in Human Geography, 19: 16–46.

Polanyi, K. (1944/1980) The Great Transformation, New York: Octagon.

Porter, M. (1996) 'The competitive advantage of the inner city', in R. LeGates and F. Stout (eds) The City Reader, London: Routledge.

Primavera, H., De Sanzo, C. and Covas, H. (1998) Reshuffling for a New Social Order: The experience of the global barter network in Argentina, workshop Enhancing people's space in a globalising economy, Espoo, Finland.

Rock, D. (2002) 'Racking Argentina', New Left Review, 2(17): 55–86.

Samers, M. (2005) 'The Myopia of "Diverse Economies": or a critique of the informal economy', Antipode, 37(5): 875–86.

Schumpeter, J. (1949) The Theory of Economic Development: An inquiry into profits, capital, credit, interest and the business cycle, Cambridge, MA: Harvard University Press.

Scott Cato, M. (2004) The Pit and the Pendulum: A cooperative future for work in the Welsh Valleys, Cardiff: University of Wales Press.

Smith, A. (1776/1981) The Wealth of Nations, London: Pelican.

Stiglitz, J. (2002) Globalisation and Its Discontents, London: Allen Lane.

Strange, S. (1986) Casino Capitalism, Oxford: Blackwell.

Thompson, E. (1981) The Making of the English Working Class, London: Penguin.

Valler, D., Wood, A. and North, P. (2000) 'Local governance and local business interests: a critical review', Progress in Human Geography, 24(3): 409–28.

Wall, D. (2005) Babylon and Beyond: The economics of the anti-capitalist, anti-globalist and radical green movements, London: Pluto.

Watts, M. (2003) 'Development and governmentality', Singapore Journal of Tropical Geography, 24(1): 6–34.

Williams, C. C. (2005) A Commodified World? Mapping the limits of capitalism, London: Zed Books.

Wood, A., Valler, D. and North, P. (1998) 'Local business representation and the private sector role in local economic policy in Britain', Local Economy, 13(1): 10–27.

16 Conclusion
The Role of Enterprise in Addressing Social and Economic Inequalities

Alan Southern and Caroline Parkinson

INTRODUCTION

There can be little doubt that to position enterprise as the panacea to deprivation is misguided. The tendency to promote enterprise as a policy solution to the social and economic ills of target groups or areas has already come under wide attack (for example, MacDonald and Coffield 1991, Leitner and Garner 1993, Blackburn and Ram 2006), and a brief reading of the social exclusion literature would suggest that the multifaceted, inextricable causes and effects of deprivation (see Levitas 1998, 2006, Hills and Stewart 2005) are unlikely to be addressed by enterprise strategies alone. Many of the chapters in this collection have reminded us of the continuing investment in enterprise in targeted areas, based on assumptions that enterprise is inclusive and will fix all where other strategies and markets fail. As expected, reservations about the cause and effect relationship are reiterated here.

It is easy to understand how promoting enterprise has become an idealised means of addressing economic and social inequalities and creating opportunity. The temptation to generalise and idealise has been compelling in light of entrepreneurial success stories (see Lionais' chapter 11 on Silicon Valley for example) and a modern culture of enterprise that buys wholesale into a reified concept (Ogbor 2000, Nicholson and Anderson 2005, Howorth et al. chapter 12). It is, though, the blind faith in the neo-liberal underpinnings of enterprise (Jennings, Perren and Carter 2005) and market-based solutions to social and economic disadvantage, discussed among others by Bates and Robb (chapter 3) in reference to Porter's inner-city thesis, that cuts to the heart of the project of this book.

As the introduction set out, we are concerned with the propinquity of enterprise and deprivation as caught in the polemical argument between market-led solutions, at one end, and political interventionist strategies at the other, in which profitability and competition are pitted against paternalism and dependency, economic against social orders. In the process, the suggestion is that discussions of tackling poverty and inequality have been marginalised in favour of deprivation and social exclusion, of which enterprise has become an inextricable facet.

The ubiquitous challenges to Porter's theories, referred to throughout, alert us to the conceptual pitfalls of a free-market approach built on 'economic self interest and genuine competitive advantage' (Porter 1995: 304). Other long-standing critiques have pointed to the same end: of urban policy reliance on private sector approaches to regeneration (Gripaios 2002, Acs and Armington 2004, Blackburn and Ram 2006); of claims linking entrepreneurship and deprivation levels (Lloyd and Mason 1984, Begg 2002; Haywood and Nicholls 2004); and of the evidence used to argue that disadvantaged people will benefit from area-based (enterprise) initiatives (Atkinson and Kintrea 2003, Kearns and Parkes 2003, Blackburn and Ram 2006), for example.

Many chapters remind us of what is at stake here; the dangers of a flawed approach are most significant for people and communities, some of whom are already among the most marginalised in society. The risks of area-based approaches for those communities targeted have been well highlighted in the regeneration and social exclusion literatures (see for example Chatterton and Bradley 2000, Amin 2005, Hills and Stewart 2005). In turn, the sometimes hard reality of enterprise, as documented in various chapters, can mean worsening exploitation, financial hardship and isolation, a far cry from the upbeat notions laden in the enterprise discourse to which Western societies famously subscribe.

Fired by these concerns, the collective project here has been to question the conceptual link made between enterprise and deprivation and discuss a new framework for considering the relationship that would allow us to consider a more systemic process, of which complex structures and institutions are a part. After Myrdal (see the discussion in the introduction to this book), it would presume that no deprivation or enterprise effect could be attributed to any one cause but rather to the accumulation of various interwoven factors, both economic and non-economic, over time.

In pursuit of this alternative conceptual basis, the collection has tried to look across a range of perspectives through different political lenses. It places centre-stage factors such as race and class (Bates and Robb chapter 3, Jones and Ram chapter 4, Dawkins chapter 5, Gordon Nembhard chapter 14, Rubin chapter 6), while exploring questions around lock-in effects, structural inequalities and reasons for associating enterprise in deprived areas with particular attributes and populations.

This concluding section offers some reflections on those questions and the book's broader quest to throw light on the conceptual link between enterprise and deprivation. It is hoped this will help reflect on the ultimate, overarching question: how can we understand the role enterprise really has in helping turn around conditions in some of our societies' worst affected communities and neighbourhoods?

DISCUSSION

One of the concerns of this book has been to what extent and why certain lock-in effects occur and, moreover, whether these effects ameliorate or exacerbate structural inequalities. Empirical studies reported here have indicated strongly that communities and enterprise can become locked into deprivation in spite of, or perhaps because of, the enterprise investment and institutional intervention in addressing deprivation. The chapters focusing on race and ethnic minority business offer key insights into this.

Race of course has been recognised as a serious barrier to take-up, partly down to inequitable access to resources across majority and minority groups (see Dawkins chapter 5, Rubin chapter 6 and Gordon Nembhard chapter 14). That and the evidence that EMBs are linked to higher attrition rates pose a fundamental challenge to the premise behind approaches that focus on minority businesses in deprived areas. Bates and Robb have highlighted the high risk of failure for neighbourhood businesses targeting minority clientele, which as a niche are linked to increased rates of firm closure. They argue that inner-city areas with minority communities are not lower risk zones of opportunity, as policy has presumed, and self-employment will not alone address the social and economic ills affecting them. Jones and Ram too (chapter 4) have questioned why a revolution should be expected from EMBs in deprived communities when the reality is that they occupy precarious market niches, pursuing often desperate survival strategies. Despite evidence of the positive benefits of micro-enterprise programmes generally for subaltern populations in the US, Gordon Nembhard does point to the risks for these groups, particularly African Americans for example, who despite long involvement with cooperative ownership are nevertheless constrained by economic and racial discrimination. The homogeneous treatment of minority groups with a raft of other groups and businesses associated with low income neighbourhoods, as a market, as Rubin attests in reference to the EDM concept, is not only built on fallacies but can lead tangibly to further disinvestment in underserved communities.

Important for the question of lock-in is the observation that EMBs endure social and economic exploitation in which they are often complicit—and in which class is as much a contributing factor as ethnicity itself to their success or marginalisation (Jones and Ram). In some ways, EMB entrepreneurs could be seen as perpetual victims of social exclusion, and forms of segregation are visible that are driven by complex structures of race and class and lived out in, and reinforced by, enterprise (generating little improvement to those populations' situations and negatively conditioning enterprise realities).

The dynamics into and out of self-employment are clearly complex then, for a raft of reasons extraneous to the individual or community. Not only will self-employment in itself not necessarily equate to changes in social circumstance, for either individuals or areas, as noted by Dawkins, Baines et al., Gordon Nembhard and Jones and Ram, but the dynamics within which communities and individuals are already trapped can have very real and self-perpetuating consequences that seal their social exclusion. We may well be witnessing systemic path dependency in our communities.

Thus at the root of these lock-in effects is a series of structural influences, race, class, peripherality and so on. Lionais (chapter 11), Pemberton (chapter 9) and others argue that the macro factors that create inequalities as well as opportunities, including institutional infrastructure, are often overlooked. At the extreme, processes of disinvestment experienced in some deprived communities are argued to affect their capacity to sustain local enterprise. Illustrating perhaps elements of history and path dependency referred to earlier, Lionais suggests that economic exclusion over time means the community becomes less capable of developing its own capacity for growth; areas lacking the institutional infrastructure to support any growth certainly cannot expect other forms of enterprise, including social enterprise, to succeed. Bates and Robb question whether deprived communities have been sent beyond the point of no return. Failure may indeed be the inevitable outcome for such depleted areas and is entirely consistent with the warnings made by Polanyi decades ago.

As part of the cumulative causation proposition that could be applied here, a policy rationalisation process is in play that frames the effects of exclusion (or deprivation) economically, using narrow definitions such as worklessness according to Pemberton, rather than as the result of structural factors for which welfare responses may be at least part of the solution. Economic strategies are then pursued that fail to link workless neighbourhoods to regional economic opportunities or develop the institutional infrastructures lacking within marginalised areas. Instead, as Chatterton and Bradley (2000) claim, the onus is placed on local factors rather than wider structural forces (see also Geddes and Newman 1999). Whether or not the solution lies in linking areas and communities to the right quality of opportunity, appropriate to their specific human capital as is suggested here, the operation of more severe structures that prevent access and take-up, as Rubin argues, remains critical.

This rationalisation then is seen as part of the problem. Contrary to theories that locate the management and development of local areas within a political and social order, rather than just an economic one (see for example Wacquant 1999, Moulaert et al. 2007), evidence here is that two separate orders are indeed evident and we might therefore reiterate Polanyi's theory of economic and social/political orders as discussed in the introduction. The economic focus distracts attention from structural factors driving deprivation and, as Amin (2005) describes in reference to the new localism, 'reinforcing the effects of macroeconomic policies biased towards growth regions' (Amin 2005: 613–14).

This rationality can have a pragmatic resource consequence. In his review of UK CDFIs, Dayson (chapter 7) has argued that the transfer of CDFI responsibility and budgets to the English RDAs was the result of an economically framed decision that ultimately has lead to significant disinvestment, watering down the social impact of increasing access to finance by the most deprived groups targeted by CDFIs. This demonstrates how the economic rationality has the argumentative effect of subjugating the non-economic, with very real impacts.

Fuelling this rationalisation, some authors suggest, are the methods of measurement and evidence gathering relied on in policy formulation that are not capable of capturing the specific dynamics of depleted communities and lead instead to generalisation. In arguing for a new metric that separates out changes in business and owner's prosperity, Frankish et al. (chapter 2) have challenged the data dependency of claims about enterprise levels in deprived vs prosperous areas, while others have called for more qualitative data on social issues at play, to complement quantitative and statistical evidence.

The importance of understanding the social order as more than simply the separate other of the economic order is strongly represented in this book. As Lionais has demonstrated with his examples of place-based businesses, most have at least local motivations rooted in place that have social benefits for the incumbents of that place, if not social motivations per se. Integral to the notion of embeddedness is the importance of social capital and networks (Johannisson 1986, Anderson and Jack 2002), picked up by various contributors here, including Whittam and Birch (chapter 13) in their critical review of social enterprise policy, and Baines et al., who highlight the importance of family relationships and gendered practices in the rural business context. Gordon Nembhard's chapter demonstrates how micro-businesses have much to learn from the recognition given to collaborative and peer-to-peer aspects of enterprise in the cooperative movement, providing examples of how this works in socially embedded enterprise practices in less affluent communities around the world. These perspectives together call for more intelligent readings that recognise the social order in which the enterprise-deprivation link is mediated, plays out and determines economic possibilities.

The authors in this book have offered views on how the discursive constructions of enterprise, perpetuated in policy as well as other media, can serve to lock in and out certain parts of the population from enterprising options by reconstructing and reinforcing power relations. North (chapter 15) has called for us to challenge the binaries created by the hegemony of the modern enterprise culture, 'exclusive and blinding as they are'. The battle between discourse hegemony and resistance, in itself an enterprising facet of community, is portrayed by Howorth et al. (chapter 12). Jones and Ram (chapter 4) talk of the hegemony of the enterprise discourse working against the socially mediated nature of policy and Bates and Robb (chapter 3) of the hegemony of the free-market concept as pervasive in US policy.

These processes defining power relations are not simply a matter of rhetoric or semantics but of very real impacts. As well as the risk of increasing certain people's or communities' exclusion through targeting others that is noted by Whittam and Birch (chapter 13, 'too much inclusion'), some contributors (Baines et al. chapter 8, Pemberton chapter 9, Whittam and Birch, chapter 13) argue that policy encouraging enterprise could mean worse conditions if failure is the outcome. This matters to those for whom entrepreneurship is already a desperate measure, those operating at the margins of survival in the rural context (Baines et al.), a gruelling and desperate survival strategy where nothing else is on offer (Gordon Nembhard, Jones and Ram).

This is all part of a picture in which it is suggested communities are blamed for their own demise, the result of a culture of lack of enterprise (Pemberton), rather than structural issues such as race and financial exclusion. The proponents of discourse and rhetoric approaches in this book reinforce the danger of pinning the blame on communities themselves. Like Amin (2005), who is critical of the dualism created by New Labour's Third Way bestowing deprived ('hard-pressed') and more advantaged ('prosperous') areas with different (ontological) principles and practices that cast blame on them for their own decline, and Chatterton and Bradley (2000) who note how targeted areas become stigmatised and held ultimately responsible for their own failure, this book warns of the implications of asking enterprising solutions from those with the least resources and strongest barriers.

Undoubtedly, this is partly carried out through our (that is, researchers' as well as policy makers') tendency to associate enterprise solutions in deprived areas with certain attributes and populations, as alluded to in the introduction, that reinforce the sense of marginality. EMBs, social enterprise, the informal economy and rural business are examples often associated with deprived areas but persistently treated as marginal contexts of enterprise. Not only are marginality theses now being contested, as Williams (chapter 10) asserts in reference to the informal economy literature, but the contributions in this book collectively challenge the implicit agenda of mainstreaming the margins that underlies much discussion of how to 'fix' deprived areas. The consequences of strategies to support 'marginal' forms of enterprise, conventionally associated with deprived areas or neighbourhoods, are shown here to be negative in various ways.

To focus briefly on the example of the informal economy, research and policy have traditionally embraced the neo-liberal perspective at the heart of the capitalist market economy, portraying the informal economy as a criminal and exploitative alternative to the formal market (Williams 2006) rather than as a more positive, coherent force that has power to regenerate and drive change. Considering the facets of the informal economy, as Williams has presented in chapter 10, deterrence and lais-sez-faire approaches to addressing the informal economy could be seen as inappropriate and further reinforcing the marginalisation of informal economic activity.

The opposite could be argued of social enterprise, in the sense that it is the 'mainstreaming' of the sector, using a structured ideal of enterprise as a vehicle, that is seen here to be disarming the radical, social and redistribu-tive nature of community and social sector. Whittam and Birch have argued that the positioning of 'trading' as a route to sustainability becomes fraught with problems that undermine the very social purpose of social enterprises. In arguing for alternative forms, such as the Latin American solidarity economy, North points out how our conceptualisation of social entrepre-neurship has been restricted to business skills, instead of social values that could in turn be applied to the problem of creating wealth. The studies dis-cussed in Howorth et al.'s chapter also suggest that by policy locking into a narrow and structured view of enterprise, that privileges certain (usually economic players) over say communities, the social regenerative potential from social or local enterprise may be lost. On the closely connected theme of community development finance, Dayson questions the ideology behind this discursive move from social purpose (in this case financial inclusion, getting micro-credit out to those most in need) versus an increasingly eco-nomically rationalised emphasis on institutional sustainability.

It could be argued from these discussions that the polemic view of enter-prise and deprived areas (laissez-faire economics vs social protectionism) is intensified and perpetuated in our collective conceptual and ideological treatment of the concepts. Considered together, these examples illustrate how our treatment potentially becomes both part of the cumulative causa-tion problematic and the embodiment of it.

CONCLUDING REMARKS

A clear note of caution resonates throughout the book: using enterprise as a tool for addressing deprivation, without critical understanding of spe-cific contextual and structural factors or the enmeshed nature of causa-tion, is likely to be ineffective in changing the circumstances for people in those communities. None of the chapters seeks for one moment to sug-gest approaches are inherently flawed but, on the contrary, that for policies and interventions supporting enterprise in the right areas to be continued, their underpinnings and potential impact—and our collective treatment of them—should be critically reviewed if they are to benefit those suffering social and economic inequality without further destabilizing conditions.

That is certainly not to deny that enterprise has a significant role to play for some and can create benefits for the many. Nor is it to dispute the notion that enterprise is or should be accessible to all, a mundane and ubiquitous process (Steyaert and Katz 2004), lest we should re-enter the heroic type trap. It is perhaps, in North's words and those of Gibson-Graham before him, a call to recapture enterprise, 'to rethink entrepreneurialism to widen the way we think about the problem of generating and redistributing wealth away from binary thinking about either capitalist markets on one hand or state planning on the other' (page 294 of this volume) to avoid the narrow business focus that is instilled in 'exclusive and blinding' binaries and that in Howorth et al.'s terms 'locks in' and also 'locks out'.

Conceptually, this collection has proposed an alternative modus for examining the enterprise-deprivation connection. It suggests that the individual and institutional elements at play could well be converging in a process of 'dynamic social causation' that materialises in an apparent link between vicious cycles of deprivation and low levels of enterprise. The systemic character of this process and the interconnected resources we use to talk about them certainly warrant further study. The thinking in this book contributes to that endeavour.

Finally, the hegemonic influences of the enterprise culture and the free market, mediated through policy, practice and research, are attracting increasingly critical attention and, appropriately, are accorded significant space in this book. The danger of reinforcing inequalities and structures that sustain inequality, and of creating potentially negative impacts on already disadvantaged communities are raised. This discursive but nonetheless political perspective exposes our collective role in the causation process and how, by unquestioningly adopting the enterprise and social exclusion binary, policy and research could indeed play a role in reinforcing disadvantage.

BIBLIOGRAPHY

Acs, Z. J. and Armington, C. (2004) 'Employment growth and entrepreneurial activity in cities', Regional Studies, 38: 911–27.

Amin, A. (2005) 'Local community on trial', Economy and Society, 34: 612–33.

Anderson, A. R. and Jack, S. L. (2002) 'The articulation of social capital in entrepreneurial networks: a glue or a lubricant?', Entrepreneurship and Regional Development, 14(3): 193–210.

Atkinson, R. and Kintrea, K. (2002) 'Area effects: what do they mean for British housing and regeneration policy?', European Journal of Housing Policy 2: 147–66.

Begg, I. (ed.) (2002) Urban Competitiveness: Policies for dynamic cities, Bristol: The Policy Press.

Blackburn, R. and Ram, M. (2006) 'Fix or fixation? The contributions and limitations of entrepreneurship and small firms to combating social exclusion', Entrepreneurship and Regional Development, 18(1): 73–89.

Chatterton, P. and Bradley, D. (2000) 'Bringing Britain together? The limitations of area-based regeneration policies in addressing deprivation', Local Economy, 15: 98–111.

Geddes, M. and Newman, I. (1999) 'Evolution and conflict in local economic development', Local Economy, 14: 12–27.

Gripaios, P. (2002) 'The failure of regeneration policy in Britain', Regional Studies, 36: 568–77.

Hanley, M. and O'Gorman, B. (2004) 'Local interpretation of national micro-enterprise policy', International Journal of Entrepreneurial Behaviour and Research, 10: 305–24.

Haywood, G. and Nicholls, J. (2004) 'Enterprise dynamics in the 20% most deprived wards in England', report, Betamodel Limited.

Hills, J. and Stewart, K. (2005) A More Equal Society? New Labour, poverty, inequality and exclusion, Bristol: The Policy Press.

Jennings, P. L., Perren, L. and Carter, S. (2005) 'Guest editors' introduction: alternative perspectives on entrepreneurship research', Entrepreneurship Theory and Practice, 29(2): 145–52.

Johannisson, B. (1986) 'Network strategies: management technology for entrepreneurship and change', International Small Business Journal, 5: 19–30.

Kearns, A. and Parkes, A. (2003) 'Living in and leaving poor neighbourhood conditions in England', Housing Studies, 18: 827–40.

Leitner, H. and Garner, M. (1993) 'The limits of local initiatives: A reassessment of urban entrepreneurialism for urban development', Urban Geography, 14: 57–77.

Levitas, R. (1998) The Inclusive Society: Social exclusion and New Labour, Basingstoke: Macmillan.

——(2006) 'The concept and measurement of social exclusion', in C. Pantazis, D. Gordon and R. Levitas (eds) Poverty and Social Exclusion in Britain, Bristol: The Policy Press.

Lloyd, P. and Mason, C. (1984) 'Spatial variations in new firm formation in the United Kingdom: comparative evidence from Merseyside, Greater Manchester and South Hampshire', Regional Studies, 18(3): 207–20.

MacDonald, R. and Coffield, F. (1991) Risky Business? Youth and the enterprise culture, London: Falmer Press.

Moulaert, F., Martinelli, F., Gonzalez, S. and Swyngedouw, E. (2007) 'Introduction: social innovation and governance in European cities: urban development between path dependency and radical innovation', European Urban and Regional Studies, 14(3): 195–209.

Nicholson, L. and Anderson A. R. (2005) 'News and nuances of the entrepreneurial myth and metaphor: linguistic games in entrepreneurial sense-making and sense-giving', Entrepreneurship Theory and Practice, 29(2):153–72.

Ogbor, J. O. (2000) 'Mythicizing and reification in entrepreneurial discourse: ideology-critique of entrepreneurial studies', Journal of Management Studies, 37(5): 605–35.

Potter, J. (2005) 'Entrepreneurship policy at local level: rationale, design and delivery', Local Economy, 20: 104–10.

Steyaert, C. and Katz, J. (2004) 'Reclaiming the space of entrepreneurship in society: geographical, discursive and social dimensions', Entrepreneurship and Regional Development (3):179–96.

Wacquant, L. (1999) 'Urban marginality in the coming millennium', Urban Studies, 36: 1639–47.

Williams, C. C. (2006) The Hidden Enterprise Culture: Entrepreneurship in the underground economy, Cheltenham: Edward Elgar.

Contributors

Susan Baines is Reader in Social Policy at the Research Institute for Health and Social Change, Manchester Metropolitan University. Her research interests include self-employment and atypical work, in particular how vulnerable livelihoods depend on changing inputs from the household, the market and the state.

Timothy Bates is Distinguished Professor of Economics, Wayne State University, and co-director of the Minority Entrepreneurship Research Center at the University of North Carolina, Chapel Hill. His research interests include the role of minority entrepreneurship in urban revitalisation, small business viability and growth, and the nature of the minority-oriented venture capital industry.

Kean Birch is a Lecturer in Human Geography at the University of Strathclyde where he teaches courses on globalisation and neo-liberalism. His current research is focused on varieties of neoliberal restructuring and adjustment across Europe as well as post-petroleum and geographies of open science.

Casey J. Dawkins is Director of the Metropolitan Institute and an Associate Professor of Urban Affairs and Planning at Virginia Tech. He is widely published on the topics of metropolitan housing market dynamics; the causes, consequences, and measurement of residential segregation; and the link between land use regulations and housing affordability.

Karl Dayson FRSA is the Director of Sociology at Salford University and the co-founder of Community Finance Solutions. His research interests include micro-finance in Europe, community ownership of assets, British building societies and theoretical understanding of economic sociology.

Julian Frankish is a Senior Economist in the SME Market Analysis Team of Barclays Bank plc.

Jessica Gordon Nembhard is a political economist and Associate Professor of Community Justice and Social Economic Development in the Department of African American Studies at John Jay College for Criminal Justice, City University of New York. She also has affiliations with Howard University and University of Saskatchewan, Canada.

Carole Howorth is Professor of Entrepreneurship and Family Business at Lancaster University Management School. Her research combines quantitative and qualitative methods and centres on the juxtaposition of business and social values within entrepreneurship.

Trevor Jones is Visiting Professor at the Centre for Research in Ethnic Minority Entrepreneurship (CREME) at De Montfort University. He is one of the UK's leading researchers on ethnic minority enterprise and was responsible for the first major study of the topic in Britain. Trevor has published in a wide range of journals on the subject of ethnic minority business

Doug Lionais is Assistant Professor in the MBA Community Economic Development program at Cape Breton University, Shannon School of Business. His research involves three inter-related themes: uneven development and depleted communities; entrepreneurship and business development; and social enterprise and place-based business.

Matthew MacDonald has been a Senior Lecturer in Social Enterprise at the University of Cumbria. He is currently undertaking ESRC funded PhD research at Lancaster University Management School and is a Director of Shared Futures C.I.C., a social enterprise.

Peter North teaches geography at the University of Liverpool, UK. He has a long-standing interest in alternative currencies, community businesses and social enterprises and local economic development policy. His current research focuses on local economic development in the context of climate change and resource depletion.

Elizabeth Oughton is a Principal Research Associate at the Centre for Rural Economy, Newcastle University. Her research on the rural household in different settings has developed around the question, 'How do people in their domestic relations create their lives and livelihoods, and what constraints and opportunities does the natural environment offer?'

Caroline Parkinson is an ESRC funded PhD student at the Institute for Entrepreneurship and Enterprise Development, Lancaster University Management School. Her research interest is in relationships between deprived communities and enterprise. She has also published in the area of social entrepreneurship.

Simon Pemberton is Senior Lecturer within the School of Public Policy and Professional Practice at the University of Keele, UK. His research interests are focused around the governance of regeneration and social exclusion and he has published widely on such issues.

Monder Ram is Professor of Small Business and Director of CREME at De Montfort University. He has published widely on ethnic minority enterprise and small firms. Monder also holds the positions of Visiting Fellow at the Industrial Relations Research Unit at Warwick University, and the Herbert Felix Visiting Professor at Lund University in Sweden.

Alicia Robb is a senior fellow with the Kauffman Foundation and a senior economist with Beacon Economics. Her latest book, *Race and Entrepreneurial Success: Black-, Asian-, and White-Owned Businesses in the United States*, co-authored with Rob Fairlie, was published by MIT Press in 2008. Dr. Robb's research focuses upon minority entrepreneurship, firm dynamics and entrepreneurial finance.

Richard Roberts is the SME Market Analysis Director and Head of the SME Market Analysis Team for Barclays Bank plc. He is also an Associate Fellow at the Centre for Small and Medium-sized Enterprises, Warwick Business School.

Julia Sass Rubin is an Assistant Professor of Public Policy at the Edward J. Bloustein School of Planning and Public Policy at Rutgers University. Her research interests are in the fields of community economic development and community development finance.

Alan Southern is at the University of Liverpool. His research interests lie in enterprise and regeneration.

David Storey is Professor in the Department of Business Management and Economics at the University of Sussex. His research interest is in Enterprise Policy.

Jane Wheelock is Emeritus Professor of Socio Economics at Newcastle University. She has researched and published extensively on household provisioning, unpaid work, the political economy of insecurity, rural economy and the environment, and regional socio-economic change.

Geoff Whittam is a Reader in entrepreneurship in the Business School at the University of the West of Scotland. He is Director of the Paisley Enterprise Research Centre. He has recently published in the areas of social entrepreneurship, the informal investment market and minority ethnic businesses.

Colin C. Williams is Professor of Public Policy and Director of the Centre for Regional Economic and Enterprise Development (CREED) in the Management School at the University of Sheffield. His research interests are in developing theory and policy towards the informal economy.

Index

context, 247. *See also* social
capital; embeddedness.
solidarity, 214, 262, 266–267, 292,
294; economy, 278, 282, 285,
287–290, 303; ethnic, 67.
spatiality, 60, 124, 137, 173, 201–202,
284; spatial variance, 4, 6,
185–186.
state, the: and private sector, 242;
relationship between state and
market, 7–8, 158, 304; violence,
280.
subaltern populations, 262, 270,
277–278, 299.
survival: of start-ups by the unemployed, 172; rates among cooperatives, 259, 261; rates among
minority clientele firms, 78; rates
in urban areas, 46–52; strategies,
59, 61, 299, 302.
symbolic violence, 232, 234.

T

Third sector, 199–200, 229. *See also*
social economy.
Third Way, the, 12, 127, 130, 302.

U

UK policy: City Growth Strategy, 3,
167; Community Investment
Tax Relief, 128–129, 135; Inner
City 100, 3; LABGI, 167–170;
LEGI, 3, 167–171; neighbour-
hood renewal, NSNR, 159, 161;
Working Neighbourhoods Fund,
170–171; Scottish regeneration

policy, 242; SEU/Policy Action
Teams, 127–129, 159, 161, 225;
National Minimum Wage, the,
61, 69, 161.
unemployment: and ethnic minorities, 163; impact on individuals, 166; rural, 142. *See also*
worklessness.
uneven development, 6, 201–202, 212,
215, 218, 245.
US policy 74, 101: micro-enterprise
programmes 39–41; micro-
finance, 125- 127; SBA lending,
82–83, 93.

V

Venture capital, 100, 106–107, 110;
and people of colour, 108; and
women-led firms, 107–8; problems of the information failure
explanation, 108–109. *See also*
community development venture
capital.

W

Weber, Max, 62.
welfare, 61, 170, 200, 211–212, 218,
224; welfare-to-work, 74,
159–160.
welfare state, the, 130, 159, 200, 210,
218; dependency, 39, 172; and
social enterprise, 224.
worklessness: as cultural way of life,
171; characteristics of, 163;
concentrations of, 161, 163. *See
also* unemployment.